KITCHENER'S WAR

Also by George H. Cassar

Asquith as War Leader

Beyond Courage: The Canadians at the Second Battle of Ypres

Kitchener: Architect of Victory

The Forgotten Front: Britain and the Italian Campaign, 1917–1918

The French and the Dardanelles: A Study of Failure in the Conduct of War

The Tragedy of Sir John French

KITCHENER'S WAR

BRITISH STRATEGY FROM 1914 TO 1916

GEORGE H. CASSAR

Potomac Books
An imprint of the University of Nebraska Press

Copyright © 2004 by Potomac Books, Inc.

Published in the United States by Potomac Books, Inc. (formerly Brassey's, Inc.). All rights reserved. No part of this book may be reproduced in any manner whatsoever without written permission from the publisher, except in the case of brief quotations embodied in critical articles and reviews.

Library of Congress Cataloging-in-Publication Data

Library of Congress CIP Data is available under
LCCN : 2004008338

Hardcover ISBN 1-57488-708-4 (alk. paper)
Softcover ISBN 1-57488-709-2

Printed on acid-free paper that meets the
American National Standards Institute Z39-48 Standard.

First Edition

To Carole and Sylvie

Contents

Maps

Figures

Abbreviations

ADC	Aide de Camp
BEF	British Expeditionary Force
CGS	Chief of the General Staff
CID	Committee of Imperial Defence
CIGS	Chief of the Imperial General Staff
C-in-C	Commander in Chief
CIR	*Commission Internationale de Ravitaillement*
DMO	Director of Military Operations
FO	Foreign Office
GHQ	General Headquarters, British Army
GOC	General Officer Commanding
GQG	*Grand Quartier-Général*, French Army Headquarters
HMSO	His Majesty's Stationary Office
K	Kitchener
KAR	King's African Rifles
MEF	Mediterranean Expeditionary Force
MGO	Master-General of the Ordnance
OHL	German Army Headquarters
RGC	Russian Government Committee
RPC	Russian Purchasing Committee
WO	War Office

Preface

THIS is my second study on Kitchener, a subject that has fascinated me for the greater part of my professional career. Although my first book, *Kitchener: Architect of Victory* (1977), focused on his role as secretary for war, I did not feel at the time that I had fully developed his grand strategy and its implications. Quite apart from space constraints, I realized that this was a complex subject, deserving its own treatment and interpretation.

Several factors make this an appropriate time to undertake such a project. Although Kitchener died in 1916, his reputation continues to arouse as much controversy as ever. A wealth of unpublished sources in the United Kingdom, not available in the 1970s, is accessible today. Moreover, since my earlier volume appeared, a number of scholars, notably Keith Neilson and David French, have dealt with elements of Kitchener's strategy, making the task more manageable.

Kitchener's long experience as an administrator and soldier abroad gave him a much wider frame of reference for viewing the Great War than that of any other leading British official. From the outset he appreciated the complexities and demands of the global conflict, recognizing that it would last at least three years and require the deployment of a mass army. His war aims included strengthening British security against allies and enemies alike, and preserving Britain's independence and status as a great power by preventing its subjugation at the hands of the Central Powers.

Kitchener's stay in Egypt and the Sudan made him very much aware of the significance of the Ottoman caliphate and Empire to British interests in the East. As soon as Turkey joined the Central Powers, Kitchener sought to instigate an Arab revolt with the object of setting up a separate caliphate in Arabia under British auspices. As the only member of the Cabinet with knowledge of the East, Kitchener also played a dominant role in the decision leading to the projected partition of the Ottoman Em-

pire among the Allies. He was no less determined to protect Britain's interests against its allies, suspecting that once the common enemy had been
defeated, there was a strong possibility that old rivalries would resume.
That being the case, he wanted to ensure that neither Russia nor France
made significant gains at Germany's expense.

Kitchener used various expedients to fulfill Britain's commitment to
the Empire because most of the nation's resources were required to fight
the main German armies on the western front. Another of Kitchener's
concerns was the state of the Russian Army, as he considered the western
and eastern fronts to be indivisible. He believed that if the Russians were
knocked out of the war, the combined British and French forces would be
unable to hold the line in the west. Russia had an inexhaustible supply of
manpower, but it was grievously deficient in all types of armaments.
Kitchener devoted considerable attention to purchasing ammunition, rifles, and artillery for Russia, so that its forces could remain viable in the
field, at least until 1917. By then the New Armies would have reached
maximum strength and, with all the belligerents exhausted, be in a position to intervene decisively on land, crush the German armies, and enable
the British government to dictate the peace settlement.

No study of Kitchener, in my view, would be complete without an
investigation of other significant and heatedly debated aspects of his wartime leadership, in particular his role in the origins of the Dardanelles
campaign and in the munitions crisis. Otherwise, I tried hard to avoid
repeating myself, preferring to venture into areas of Kitchener's activities,
hitherto neglected or insufficiently explored by his biographers.

My research reinforced the favorable view of Kitchener that I had previously held. While this book does not gloss over the shortcomings, or
whitewash the misjudgments, of its subject, it is unapologetically pro-
Kitchener. Ever since Lloyd George's poisonous and skewed memoirs
were published in the 1930s, Kitchener has been misrepresented, misunderstood, and excessively criticized in numerous books. In recent years
scholarly opinion has moved, albeit slowly, towards a more sympathetic
interpretation of Kitchener's achievements, derived from newly accessible
documentary sources and an array of specialist studies. It is hoped that
this volume will encourage that trend and reach those skeptics and critics
who are open to reasoned analysis based on a wide range of archival and
printed sources.

George H. Cassar
Ypsilanti, Michigan

Acknowledgments

THE longer I pursue scholarly inquiries, the more conscious I am of what I owe to colleagues, friends, archivists, and my own institution. Over the years that this book has been in the making, I have incurred large debts of gratitude. On two occasions, Eastern Michigan University made it possible for me to do research in Britain and, in addition, provided much of the funding. Under the supervision of Dr. Robert Ward, Chris Norman graciously gave of his time to prepare most of the maps for this volume—a few were drawn from my previous books. My department head, Dr. Gersham Nelson, who has consistently supported my research, kindly arranged my teaching schedule so as to provide me with large blocks of writing time. Miss Nancy Snyder, the departmental secretary, was extremely patient in attending to my many requests, some of which went beyond the call of duty.

It is small repayment, but at least I can mention professional colleagues and friends who helped along the way. Dr. Keith Neilson, Dr. Janice Terry, Dr. Richard Goff, and Dr. Michael Neiberg set aside their own research and read the manuscript in whole or in part. Keith, whose knowledge of Anglo-Russian relations during World War I is unrivalled, made valuable comments that saved me from snares of my own creation. Similarly, Janice gave me the benefit of her expertise on British-Arab diplomacy for the same period, allowing me to understand a complicated subject more thoroughly than otherwise would have been the case. Dick went through every sentence of the manuscript with meticulous care and made many editorial suggestions for its improvement. Michael's insights were also very important, particularly in ironing out the fine details. Others who provided me with relevant information, gave me the benefit of their own scholarship, or acted as a sounding board for my ideas include Dr. Robert Citino, Prof. Riyadh Bahkali, Dr. Walter Moss, Rev. John

Pollock, Dr. Ron Delph, Mr. George Contis, Prof. Joseph Engwenyu, Dr. David Geherin, Mr. Bruce Liebowitz, Dr. Peter Liddle, Dr. Margot Dudley, and Dr. Michael Schroeder. To each, I offer my heartfelt thanks. Responsibility for any remaining errors of fact and interpretation is mine alone.

My project owes much to the personnel of the British archives, in which I carried on my research. Key individuals, deserving more than an anonymous vote of thanks, include Dr. John Fisher and William Spence, reader advisers at the Public Office; R. W. A. Suddaby, the keeper of the Department of Documents at the Imperial War Museum; Patricia Methven, archivist at the Liddell Hart Centre for Military Archives; Colin Harris, principal assistant at the Bodleian Library; and Pamela Clark, deputy registrar at the Royal Archives.

Earl Kitchener showed me great kindness, and in London it was a pleasure to receive the friendship and hospitality of his niece, Emma Kitchener, and her husband, Julian Fellowes.

The following have graciously given me permission to quote from material to which they own the copyright: Earl Kitchener; Viscount Esher; the British Library; the Trustees of the Imperial War Museum; the Master, Fellows and Scholars of Churchill College; the University of Durham; and Trustees of the National Library of Scotland. Crown copyright material has been reproduced by permission of Her Majesty's Stationary Office. My sincere apologies are due to the holder of any copyright I may have infringed upon inadvertently.

My greatest debt is to my wife, Mary, who edited the manuscript and brought her keen eyes to the reading of the proofs. What I owe her as the bearer of the real burdens created by my scholarly activities, I cannot begin to acknowledge adequately.

1

THE MAKING OF A WARLORD

WHEN Kitchener was appointed Secretary of State for War on Britain's entry into the European conflict in August 1914, he was undoubtedly the most acclaimed soldier in the land. Yet when he was starting out as a young subaltern in the royal engineers, there was little to suggest that he would achieve great success and fame. He did not have the advantage of birth, wealth, or social influence. He did not possess outstanding intellectual gifts. He never formally studied the science of war or showed ability as a tactician. He never passed through the staff college. He paid scant attention to the habits and customs of the British Army. He never formed part of an influential clique or a recognized school of military thought. Tall, with broad shoulders and a long bushy moustache, his appearance was forbidding and his manner unsympathetic. How then was Kitchener able to beat the odds and rise to such eminence in the Army?

Horatio Herbert Kitchener was born on June 24, 1850, near Listowel in County Kerry, Ireland, the second son of Lt. Col. Henry Horatio Kitchener, a retired Army officer, and his first wife, Frances Anne, daughter of the Rev. John Chevallier of Aspall Hall in Suffolk.[1] The first of his given names was borrowed from his father (who was born two days before the Battle of Trafalgar and named after Nelson), although his family always called him Herbert. The colonel had no use for public schools and until the age of thirteen, Herbert's education was haphazard, dependent as it was on a succession of transient governesses and tutors. As the damp Irish weather did not suit Frances Anne's ailing lungs, the colonel moved his family to Switzerland, where he hoped the pure mountain air would improve her health. Unfortunately, her condition continued to deteriorate and towards the end of 1864, to the great grief of her family, she died in Montreux.[2] Having decided to remain in Switzerland, the colonel sent Herbert and two of his brothers to a boarding school at Rennaz at the eastern end of Lake Geneva. There, under the general supervision of the chaplain of the English congregation in Montreux, they remedied some of their educational deficiencies. Herbert became fluent in French and acquired a rudimentary knowledge of German, in addition to discovering a latent aptitude in mathematics. He had his heart set on obtaining an Army commission and, mindful of gaps in his knowledge, worked hard to prepare himself for the entrance to the Royal Military Academy at Woolwich. During the final phase he was coached by a crammer in London and succeeded in entering the academy in 1868.

Called "the shop," the academy was a training center for officers commissioned into the artillery and engineers. It was an institution known for its strict discipline and high standards of learning. Kitchener found the work grueling and struggled to keep up with his classmates. Already grown to his full height of six foot two and slim, he missed an entire term during his second year because he had overtaxed his strength. He left behind an undistinguished academic career when he passed out of Woolwich in December 1870.

Kitchener was gazetted into the royal engineers on January 4, 1871, while he was spending the Christmas holidays with his father, who had remarried and was living in Dinan, Brittany. It was not a festive time in France, which was approaching the end of a disastrous war with Prussia. Encouraged by his father to experience the war first hand, Kitchener joined an ambulance unit of the French Second Army of the Loire—composed largely of reservists and conscripts lacking spirit and discipline—under Gen. Chanzy. At Le Mans he witnessed the horror of war when the Second Army was badly mauled in a three-day battle. Shortly after the engagement, Kitchener ascended in a balloon with a French officer and, as he was lightly clad, caught a chill that turned into pneumonia and pleurisy. Lying in critical condition in a cold and unsanitary billet, he was rescued by his father and brought back to Dinan.[3] As soon as he was fit enough to travel, Kitchener returned to England.

After several years of uncongenial routine service at home, Kitchener was lent to the Palestine Exploration Fund, which had been founded to conduct scientific research in the Holy Land, then part of the Ottoman

Empire. The fund's current project, under the supervision of Kitchener's friend and former classmate Claude Conder, was the survey of the west bank of the Jordan. It was at Conder's urging that Kitchener applied and was accepted to replace a member of the party who had died of fever.[4]

Kitchener had never been happier. He gathered information about the country, took innumerable photographs, made notes and sketches of ancient sites, and acquired archeological techniques. In his spare time he studied Arabic (which he would master before long) and Turkish. Early in 1877 Kitchener was put in charge of the survey party when Conder's health no longer permitted him to work in the field.

For Kitchener, the experience of his first command was invaluable in helping increase his knowledge of Ottoman affairs, develop his leadership qualities, and shape his work habits. He learned firsthand of the corruption and inefficiency of Ottoman rule, of the threat its collapse would pose to Britain's trade route through the Suez Canal, and of Arab aspirations. He gained an insight into diplomacy by negotiating arrangements with local authorities. He was introduced into the art of administration, managing men, and operating within strict economic guidelines. Moreover, he kept the party's spirits up, for the work was difficult and at times dangerous. The countryside was hilly, and hauling heavy surveying instruments under the blazing sun was exhausting. From time to time members of the party, including Kitchener himself, had to cope with bad bouts of fever.

Turkey was at war with Russia and had withdrawn its troops from the countryside so that no policing authority was available to protect the survey party against hostile tribesmen. Kitchener was certain that he could handle any potential dangers and rejected any suggestions by fund officials in London that he and his team should return home. Still there was a need to conclude the survey as quickly as possible without sacrificing the quality of the work. Accordingly, Kitchener set a backbreaking schedule that called for his men to work twelve hours a day, seven days a week. They responded so wonderfully that by the end of September 1877 the survey of western Palestine was completed on time, a major feat under such trying conditions. Kitchener and his party had surveyed and triangulated over three thousand square miles, corrected errors of previous mapmakers, investigated all known archeological sites, photographed points of interest, and written reports describing every village and its state of water supply.

Fund officials praised Kitchener for his leadership, zeal, thoroughness, and scrupulous attention to economy—the survey was conducted for a sum less than had been allocated in the budget.[5] All in all, as Professor Samuel Daiches, a noted Palestinian scholar observed in a public lecture in 1915, Kitchener displayed initiative, sound judgment, mastery of details, single-mindedness, intense work habits, a high sense of duty, and an ability to inspire subordinates—characteristics for which he was well known in later life.[6]

Kitchener avoided a return to barracks life when he agreed to carry out a survey of Cyprus, then to serve as military vice consul at Kastamanu in northern Anatolia. In February 1883 his great opportunity came when he was posted to Egypt, recently occupied by the British. Along with two dozen British officers, he was selected to train the new Egyptian Army under Sir Evelyn Wood along European lines. On arriving in Cairo, he joined the only cavalry regiment as second in command to Lt. Col. Taylor. As an engineer, with little knowledge of cavalry tactics, Kitchener had a lot to learn, but he never shied away from hard work and before long had mastered the intricacies of cavalry drill and discipline.[7]

Unconcealed ambition induced Kitchener to forgo social activities and even annual leaves to England in order to improve his professional qualifications. His aloofness and obsessive industry made him unpopular with his fellow officers, but not with his superiors. Lt. Col. Taylor was extremely impressed with Kitchener, describing him as a thorough professional who possessed judgment, tact, and unfailing self-reliance. Kitchener even caught the attention of Wood, who wrote, "This is an excellent officer in every respect—a good Arab linguist—a fine horseman—great determination and courage."[8]

Kitchener remained attached to the cavalry for a year before he found more congenial work as an intelligence officer. Taking advantage of Kitchener's knowledge of Arabic, Wood assigned him to gather information on the Sudan where an uprising against Egyptian rule, inspired by Mohammed Ahmed, who proclaimed himself the Mahdi (the expected one), was growing rapidly. In March 1884, Kitchener volunteered to open communications with Maj. Gen. Charles Gordon when the Mahdi's forces began to invest Khartoum.[9] During the latter part of the summer, Gladstone, bowing to public pressure, authorized a relief force to march southwards from Egypt to lift the siege of Khartoum. Kitchener was assigned as an intelligence officer to this force, which was commanded by Sir Garnet Wolseley.

Riding well ahead of the relief column, Kitchener, accompanied by a few native scouts and disguised as an Arab, acted as Wolseley's eyes and ears, sifting through vast amounts of information to interpret the designs of the Mahdists, testing the loyalty of the tribes, exploring suitable sites for camps, and sending messages back from Gordon, with whom he formed a special bond.

Kitchener reveled in his role, which allowed him to experience the solitude of the desert, the culture of its people, and the excitement of the unknown, as well as the satisfaction of approaching his task in his own fashion. He became more confident and assertive in dealings with native tribesmen. Because of his inflexible devotion to duty and his passionate belief in his mission, no amount of discomfort or risk to his personal safety deterred him from carrying out his assignments. The long, hard excursions in the desert toughened his constitution, and his lean frame filled out and became heavier and more muscular. As the British public's interest in the Sudan increased, leading newspapers in London, through their correspondents, featured stories about Kitchener and praised him lavishly for his courage and enterprise. A case in point was the comment made in the *West Morning News*: "Every war brings its heroes; and when the military operations in the Sudan are over, the name and deeds of Major Kitchener will be remembered."[10] Kitchener was naturally delighted to see his name headlined in newspapers. It was the kind of public recognition that all ambitious soldiers on active duty craved.

All of Kitchener's heroics, however, proved futile. Ordered to return to his base at Korti, Kitchener was not present when the slow-moving relief expedition came within sight of Khartoum on January 28, 1885. It was too late. Two days earlier, the Mahdists had stormed the walls of the city, and in the bloodbath that ensued, Gordon had been killed, his head severed from his body and placed on a pole. Since nothing more could be done, the desert column turned back. Subsequently Wolseley asked Kitchener to prepare a full account of the fall of Khartoum. Bitter and sick at heart over the death of Gordon, Kitchener's report, in which he interviewed such witnesses as were available, is incisive and the only authentic account of the siege of Khartoum.[11]

In the summer of 1885, Kitchener resigned his commission in the Egyptian Army and sailed for Britain, where he spent several months enjoying the fruits of his growing fame. In August he was selected to represent Britain on a joint commission, which also included German and French members, to delimit the territory of the Sultan of Zanzibar—a work made necessary by the European powers' scramble for colonies in

Africa. A year later, his part in the negotiations over, he set off on his journey back to England, but he had reached only as far as Suez when he received a cable telling him that he had been appointed governor-general of eastern Sudan and the Red Sea Littoral. It was a grandiose title, but, as Kitchener discovered when he arrived at his headquarters in Suakin on the Red Sea, his authority inland extended only a few miles beyond the town. Suakin was the last remaining British outpost in the Sudan, and, as such, was constantly menaced by Osman Digna, the local dervish leader. On January 17, 1888, Kitchener, with a mixed force of Regulars and Irregulars, stormed Osman's camp at Handub. As Kitchener was trying to rally his men in the face of an enemy counterattack, he was struck by a bullet that penetrated his jaw and lower neck. Kitchener managed to hang on, but his second in command was left to extricate the force from battle. The raid had really been a failure, but in the press it was hailed a victory with Kitchener as the hero. He had won the day with Egyptian troops, which were not held in high esteem, and he seemed to be the only one doing something to avenge Gordon.[12]

Kitchener spent the summer of 1888 on leave in England, often as the chief attraction at dinners and other fashionable gatherings. The highlight of his social calendar was a stay at Hatfield House, Lord Salisbury's country home, where he was told that he had been appointed adjutant-general of the Egyptian Army. Kitchener arrived in Cairo in September, but before he could settle into his adjutant-general's chair, a new emergency arose. The troublesome Osman Digna had laid siege to Suakin and the new sirdar, or commander, of the Egyptian Army, Sir Francis Grenfell, responded by dispatching two brigades, one of which was commanded by Kitchener, to the area. On December 20, 1888, Kitchener's brigade played a key role in the victory over the dervishes outside the walls of Suakin. Grenfell reported that Kitchener had sustained his high reputation, handling his brigade "with coolness and gallantry."[13]

In January 1889, when pressure on Suakin had eased, Kitchener returned to Cairo and took up his new duties as adjutant-general, but in midsummer he found himself in the field again. In June Wad el Nejumi, a faithful emir of Abdullahi Ibn Mohammed, known as the Khalifa or "the successor,"[14] attempted an invasion of southern Egypt with about thirteen thousand warriors. Kitchener was in charge of the cavalry at Toski (a short distance inside the Egyptian border), on August 3, when Grenfell annihilated the dervish army, putting an end to the Khalifa's expansionist dreams. Kitchener's services in the campaign were acknowledged by Grenfell in his dispatches to the War Office.

Back in Cairo, Kitchener was asked to take on the additional responsibilities of inspector-general of the Egyptian police. To reform the police force, known for its lax discipline, corruption, and brutality was in itself a daunting task. Two previous inspector-generals had already tried and failed to bring the police force in line with British practices. But Kitchener agreed to the move, presumably because he assumed, or Sir Evelyn Baring, the British agent and consul-general in Egypt, hinted that his chances of succeeding Grenfell would be enhanced.[15] Since Kitchener could not effect major changes without seriously disrupting the traditional role of local government, he had to content himself with improving the workings of a run-down system. Still, he eliminated the torture of prisoners, reduced corruption among officials, based promotion on merit rather than bribery, and tried to impress that the purpose of the police was to help the poor, not oppress them. In a little over a year, his reforms reduced crime by 50 percent and doubled the number of criminal convictions.[16]

Grenfell resigned as sirdar in April 1892 and Baring urged London to appoint Kitchener in his place. There were officers with better claim to the office, but Baring was looking ahead to the liberation of the Sudan. The forty-one-year-old Kitchener had spent many months up the river and knew better than any other British officer in Egypt the country, its resources, and the habits and language of its people. He had given ample proof of his mania for strict economy, a vital concern since the cost of the eventual campaign into the Sudan would have to be borne mainly by the Egyptian treasury. As an engineer, Kitchener lacked fighting experience. But he was thorough and painstaking, with a proven reputation for rising above the most difficult challenges, virtues that were deemed more important than tactical flair. Both Grenfell and Salisbury likewise concluded that Kitchener was the best man for the job. In April 1892 Kitchener was appointed sirdar of the Egyptian Army, with the rank of major general, to the surprise and outrage of his military peers. Reflecting on the appointment fifteen years later, Baring (now Lord Cromer) wrote, "A better choice could not have been made."[17]

In a span of ten years, Kitchener had risen from an obscure lieutenant to major general and commander in chief of the Egyptian Army with a solid record of military and administrative accomplishments. He was single-minded, autocratic, and a workaholic, undistracted by social or domestic ties. Kitchener never married. As a young officer he had shown plenty of interest in women, but at a point he became so wrapped up in pushing forward his career that he had not devoted the time to find a suitable mate.[18] His only real romantic relationship occurred shortly after his arrival in Egypt in 1883. Kitchener had become friendly with Sir Samuel Baker, the explorer, and his brother Gen. Valentine Baker. Valentine's eldest daughter, Hermione, then sixteen, fell in love with the thirty-three-year-old Kitchener. By all accounts Kitchener was equally attracted to her, and the Bakers took it for granted that they would eventually marry. Those fond hopes were shattered when Hermione died of typhoid fever in Cairo on January 21, 1885, while Kitchener was with the Gordon relief force in the Sudan. It is said that as a memento of their relationship, Kitchener wore around his neck for many years afterwards a gold locket containing a miniature portrait of Hermione.[19]

Because Kitchener was a perfectionist and in the past had operated in circumstances in which he could only depend on himself, he developed the habit of delegating as little as possible. At this stage, it was perhaps an asset, but later would prove a disadvantage when he was confronted with managing a large-scale enterprise. Kitchener did not care whether people liked him as long as they feared and respected him. He projected the image of a severe and unsympathetic taskmaster, an unemotional and humorless man, intolerant of professional lapses or human weaknesses. However, the few who knew him well judged him less harshly. For example, Reginald Wingate, the Director of Military Intelligence, wrote that, notwithstanding his reputation, Kitchener "had one of the kindest of hearts, and under his cold exterior, there was a fund of real sympathy and even affection."[20]

Foremost in Kitchener's mind was his conviction that he had a mission to avenge Gordon and rid the Sudan of the Khalifa's tyranny. During the next four years, he devoted himself to preparing the Egyptian Army for the day of reckoning. During his annual leave in Britain, he interviewed officers at the Junior Service United Club in London to serve on his administrative staff and to command the troops in the field. By setting exacting standards, Kitchener collected around him a group of talented, energetic, and loyal officers. With their help, he transformed the Egyptian Army, much strengthened by the addition of elite Sudanese battalions, into an effective fighting force.

The day that Kitchener had longed and prepared for came on March 13, 1896, when he was authorized to march on Dongola in northern Sudan

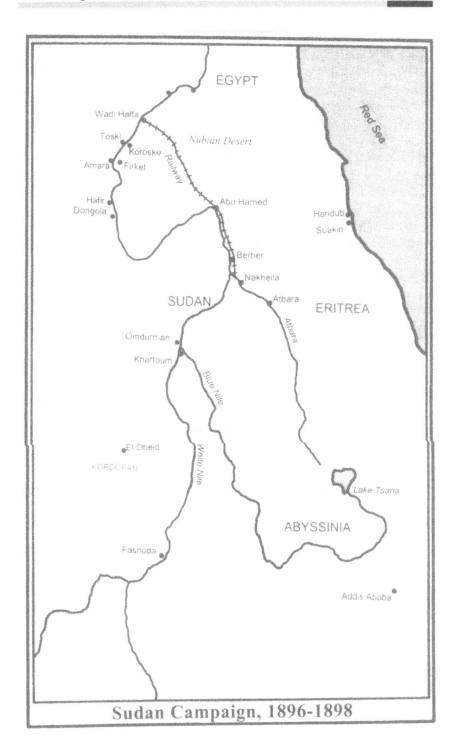

Sudan Campaign, 1896-1898

in order to relieve pressure on the Italians, who had been badly defeated by the Abyssinians at Adowa a fortnight earlier. To ensure his supply requirements, Kitchener refused to rely on camels or the river and, instead, proposed to build a railroad. As a start, he turned to an obsolete railroad that ran some thirty-five miles from his base at Wadi Halfa into the Sudan. Broken down rails and antiquated rolling stock, mostly unsafe even when repaired, were relaid by a motley crew hastily assembled from different areas of Egypt. By makeshift of every kind, the work progressed, although not painlessly.[21] There were instances when some of the men went down with heat apoplexy; stretches of the line were washed away and had to be rebuilt; or a locomotive derailed and primitive solutions were devised to put it back on the tracks. Kitchener was on the scene whenever difficulties arose, offering advice, improvising solutions, inspiring the men to greater efforts, and frequently rolling up his sleeves and working with pick and shovel.

From Wadi Halfa, Kitchener proceeded up the Nile slowly and cautiously, consolidating his conquests and extending the railroad as he advanced. His network of agents kept him informed of the enemy's movements, as well as the features of the terrain and the state of the bridges ahead. In June he executed a surprise attack on the fortified village of Firket, killing eight hundred dervishes and capturing eleven hundred. Kitchener brought up supplies and built up his strength for the next forward move, which was delayed by a severe outbreak of cholera and unseasonable torrential rainstorms. Towards the end of the summer, his twelve-thousand-man army headed towards Dongola and, along the way, disposed of another dervish force outside of Hafir before occupying the town on September 23. For his handling of the first phase of the campaign, Kitchener—who had already been awarded a CMG, CB, and KCMG—received a KCB and was promoted to the rank of major general in the British Army.

In November 1896 Kitchener, having received Baring's pledge that he would allow a further advance into the Sudan, provided the necessary funding was forthcoming, went to Great Britain, and in a lightning campaign convinced the leading political authorities of the merits of his cause. Returning to the Sudan, Kitchener spent the better part of 1897 building a new railroad from Wadi Halfa to Abu Hamed, short-circuiting the great loop in the Nile, including the second, third, and forth cataracts. In so doing Kitchener went against the advice of almost all the experts who felt that the problems of laying tracks across inhospitable and uncharted territory were simply too daunting. Kitchener owed much of the success of the enterprise to the genius of Lt. Percy Girouard, a twenty-nine-year-old French Canadian engineer and surveyor.[22]

With the construction of the railroad advancing rapidly, Kitchener was within striking distance of the projected terminus at Abu Hamed by the end of July. Accordingly, he dispatched a flying column to storm the town, which was easily accomplished on August 7. The capture of the town threw the irresolute dervish commander in Berber into such panic that he pulled back with his forces. On September 5 Kitchener occupied Berber without opposition.[23] Thus far, nature and problems associated with the expedition had proven more formidable than the dervishes, but Kitchener knew that the next phase would involve heavy fighting.

Kitchener received unexpected bad news when Baring refused to allow him to complete the conquest of the Sudan. Baring claimed that the campaign, even with expenditures pared to the bone, had drained the Egyptian treasury, and he would need time to accumulate the necessary funds for a further push. The frustration of being overridden when victory was within his grasp, on top of the anxieties of directing an eighteen-month campaign in enemy territory, drove Kitchener near to the breaking point. Then, in December 1897 intelligence reported that the Khalifa was planning to march on Berber with his entire army.[24] Kitchener warned Baring that his forces would not be able to stem the dervish onslaught without a stiffening of British Regulars. Baring alerted the Salisbury government, which agreed to send Kitchener whatever he required to deal with the imminent threat.

Internal feuds had prevented the Khalifa from leaving his capital at Omdurman. As he could not afford to delay any longer, he sent an army of twenty thousand men, commanded by a young emir called Mahmud, to hurl back the invading column. Mahmud crossed the Atbara, but seeing that Kitchener had anticipated his move, changed direction and formed an entrenched camp with his back to the river. Kitchener pondered for days as to whether he should attack, but when he finally decided to do so at first light on April 8, 1898, the battle was over within an hour. Mahmud himself was captured, along with two thousand of his men, and no fewer than three thousand lay dead in the trenches. Anglo-Egyptian casualties had not been light—583, of whom 125 were British. Riding on a white charger, Kitchener led a triumphal parade into Berber. In a spectacle reminiscent of the Roman Army's triumphant entry into Rome, Mahmud, his hands bound and dragging chains riveted around his ankles, was made to run behind the cavalry as he was pelted with rubbish by a jeering crowd and driven forward by Sudanese guards who lashed him when he stumbled.[25]

Before opening the final phase of the campaign, Kitchener strengthened his army by adding more British troops and extending the railroad to Berber. He took a month's leave in Cairo, while his army slowly concentrated in an entrenched camp north of Atbara in preparation for his final target, the dervish capital of Omdurman. Kitchener's twenty-five-thousand-man army stretched for three miles when it began its march up the west bank of the Nile on August 24. Outside Omdurman the Khalifa had sixty thousand warriors at his disposal. The disparity in numbers was more than offset by Kitchener's advantage in artillery and automatic weapons. On September 1, a British patrol sighted the Khalifa's hordes moving across the plain of Kerreri, seven miles north of Omdurman. Kitchener ordered a halt and took up a defensive position, with his army, its back to the Nile, deployed in a wide arc. The Khalifa's only chance was to attack at night, and when he failed to do so, he sealed his own fate.

The battle of Omdurman, which took place on September 2, was fought in two phases. In the first the dervishes struck after dawn in waves at the center and right flank of the Anglo-Egyptian Army, only to be cut down in swathes by artillery, maxim, and rifle fire. With the surviving dervishes in retreat, the sirdar ordered his men to advance on Omdurman. As Kitchener's force was on the move, the Khalifa's reserves fell on his rear brigade, which was commanded by Maj. Gen. Hector Macdonald. A disaster was averted thanks to the courage and brilliance of Macdonald and the steadfastness of his brigade. This assault being beaten back after the dervishes had sustained enormous losses, organized resistance ceased. Kitchener's spectacular victory had been won at the low cost of 48 killed and 434 wounded. Against this, the count of dead dervishes totaled eleven thousand and an additional sixteen thousand were taken prisoners.[26] The Khalifa managed to escape, but was eventually hunted down and killed in the ensuing skirmish.

Kitchener's success in the Sudan campaign, as later in South Africa, stemmed more from attention to detail and brilliant improvisation than from genuine tactical brilliance. He was not a keen student of war and was not afraid to admit it. Shortly before the battle of Atbara, an aide asked Kitchener how he proposed to attack. Kitchener replied that he had no idea. He had brought his army fifteen hundred miles into the desert, fed it, and now expected his generals to do the rest.[27] Nevertheless, there was no doubt that Kitchener had been the architect of victory. It was his courage and perseverance that had persuaded reluctant political authorities to authorize successive forward movements in the Sudan. Furthermore, by overcoming the difficulties of supply and transportation, he had brought his army to Omdurman, where modern weapons had determined the outcome.

Two days after the battle, Kitchener held a memorial service in Khartoum outside the ruined palace where Gordon had fallen. Both the Union Jack and Egyptian flag were hoisted and saluted. The service was simple and ended with the singing of Gordon's favorite hymn, "Abide with Me." Kitchener, who had a horror of any outward display of emotion, was so overcome that he broke down and wept openly. The strain of the past two years had ended in a magnificent triumph that had avenged Gordon's cruel death and redeemed Britain's honor.[28]

Before returning home, Kitchener was compelled to deal with a political crisis brought on by French action in the upper Nile region. In June 1896 a small expedition, led by Maj. Jean-Baptiste Marchand, had set out from French Equatorial Africa with the object of creating a French east-west corridor across central Africa. After a three-thousand-mile journey, much of it through wild unexplored country, Marchand and his party reached the Nile and planted the tricolor in the town of Fashoda. Alerted to Marchand's presence, Kitchener loaded up five gunboats with soldiers, artillery, and maxim guns on September 10 and steamed up the river. On arriving at Fashoda, Kitchener held a dramatic meeting with Marchand who was adamant that he could not haul down the French flag without instructions from Paris. Kitchener had a superior force and could have forcibly ejected the French, but instead comported himself in a judicious and statesman-like manner. Speaking in French and in a respectful tone, Kitchener understood that Marchand was driven by a high sense of duty just as he was. Patiently, he explained to Marchand that, as he had just defeated the Khalifa's forces, he had come to claim the area of the upper Nile in the name of the Khedive, and he insisted on putting up the Egyptian flag. Marchand indicated that he was in no position to prevent Kitchener from doing so, and the confrontation ended with both men wisely agreeing to refer the matter to their respective governments. Subsequently, there was a brief period of saber rattling on both sides of the channel, but Salisbury stood firm, and finally the French government, having carried its bluff act as far it could, capitulated and recalled Marchand.[29]

In October Kitchener returned to a hero's welcome in Britain. Towns and universities showered him with gifts and honors. The Queen conferred on him a peerage as Baron Kitchener of Khartoum and Aspall. He received the thanks of both houses of Parliament and a grant of £30,000. While in Scotland, Kitchener appealed for £100,000 to establish a college in Khartoum in memory of Gordon. Before the end of the year, he had raised £110,000 for what became Gordon College.

On December 7, 1898, after a two-month round of receptions, banquets, and presentations, Kitchener left Britain to return to the Sudan as governor-general. Kitchener found the work of administrating the Sudan as congenial as anything he had done in the past. Everything from finance to education lay in his hands, and he was not hampered by a system of divided authority.[30] But his tenure in the Sudan lasted only one year. In December 1899 he received a call to serve in South Africa.

The Boer War, which broke out in October 1899, did not initially proceed the way the British had expected. Boer sharpshooters put up a spirited fight and in one week in December inflicted a series of humiliating defeats on the overconfident but ill-prepared British Army, commanded by Sir Redvers Buller. The Salisbury government reacted by replacing Buller with Earl Frederick Roberts, the nation's most able and experienced general, and appointing Kitchener as his chief of staff. Kitchener joined Roberts at Gibraltar on December 27, and together they sailed for Capetown, arriving on January 10, 1900. The two soldiers worked well together, despite vast differences in temperament and experience. Kitchener rarely performed the duties of a chief of staff, and, as he was used in a variety of ways, acted far more as Roberts's second in command.[31]

Roberts devised a plan that was simple, but sound. He would march his army through the Orange Free State and the Transvaal, capture the capital cities, and dispose of any Boer force that tried to bar his way. Kitchener's lone opportunity to command a force in the field occurred at Paardeberg where British columns had trapped a large Boer convoy. Before the convoy surrendered, after enduring a merciless bombardment, Kitchener, with full authority from Roberts, ordered and directed an attack. As he lacked the means to coordinate effectively the movement of British troops scattered over a wide area, his attacks were therefore disconnected and repulsed in succession.

Throughout the spring and summer, Roberts pressed forward in overwhelming strength, sweeping the Boers before him. He entered Bloemfontein on March 13 and on June 5 rode in triumph with Kitchener into Pretoria. By the end of November, the Boer republics were completely occupied, their forces scattered, and their political leaders on the run. Judging that the war was over, except for mopping-up operations, Roberts handed the command to Kitchener and left South Africa on December 11.

The war, however, was far from over. It had merely entered into a new phase. The Boers, no longer capable of facing the British in pitched battles, turned to guerrilla warfare. Aided by a strongly sympathetic population, they ambushed supply wagons and small patrols, raided outposts, and harried communications and supply lines. By prolonging the war, they hoped to exasperate the British or induce one or more of the great powers to support their cause actively.

To meet the novel conditions, Kitchener developed drastic, but effective, tactics. In order to deny the guerrillas supplies and shelter, he adopted a scorched-earth policy, burning farmhouses, destroying crops, and confiscating livestock. This made it necessary to provide for noncombatants, who were herded into so-called concentration camps, where, regrettably, overcrowding, unsanitary conditions, and inadequate medical care produced many unnecessary deaths. Simultaneously, Kitchener constructed a network of blockhouses, manned by military sentinels and joined to each other by barbed wire, thus dividing the country into small districts. Large drives were organized within the fenced areas. British mounted columns were drawn at a convenient starting point and advanced abreast, sometimes trapping small Boer units or driving them like wild animals against the blockhouses. These methods gradually wore down the Boers and forced them to sue for peace.

Kitchener had won another war and, predictably, was showered with countless honors on his return to Britain. He accepted the freedoms of a number of towns and was made a viscount, appointed as one of the original members of the Order of Merit, and promoted to full general. Parliament thanked him and awarded him £50,000.

While considering his next professional move, Kitchener turned down the government's offer to serve in the War Office and play a leading role in reforming the British Army. Instead, he opted to become commander in chief of the Indian Army, which he believed would be a more rewarding assignment. The Viceroy of India, Lord Curzon, was able to lure Kitchener by promising to give him free rein to effect whatever changes he deemed necessary. Kitchener probably would not have gone to India if he had known that Curzon was headstrong, arrogant, and tactless, with a need to control every detail in his administration—like Kitchener in many ways.

Kitchener landed in India on November 28, 1902, and would remain there for the next seven years. Initially, he got along well with Curzon, who did not set any restrictions on what he could do. Kitchener proposed to reorganize the Indian Army, traditionally confined to parochial duties, to answer the larger needs of the Empire. In his view the main function of the

Army was not to maintain internal order and to safeguard against another insurrection, but to defend the frontiers against external aggression. Russia's activities in central Asia had led Kitchener to think that an invasion of India's northwest frontier was likely. In case his worst fears were realized, the Army had to be in a position to stand steady until reinforcements from overseas arrived. Kitchener's reputation allowed him to make far-reaching and radical changes with a minimum of outside interference. Some regiments with poor records were disbanded and reformed with new recruits from tribes known for their martial qualities. The groupings of the garrisons were rearranged. Training was modernized and the machinery for mobilization improved. Kitchener sought to obliterate the memory of the Indian Mutiny and to increase the trust and harmony between Indian and British units. To that end, divisions were reorganized to include both British and Indian brigades. A staff college was established at Quetta, and a process was begun to allow Indians to gain commissions. To increase the efficiency of the Indian Army, its units were provided with artillery and equipped with Lee-Metfords, instead of rifles of an earlier issue.[32]

Kitchener, however, ran afoul of Curzon when he tried to transform the higher administration of the Army, which he believed was hampered by a system of dual control. Kitchener could not operate effectively unless he had, as in Egypt and the Sudan, total control. Lying outside the purview of his office was the Military Department, which was responsible for all noncombatant Army services. The head of the Military Department was always a major general, and as a military member of the Viceroy's council, his duty was to make policy suggestions to his civilian chief, as well as to supervise all Army expenditures. Although inferior in rank, the military member was thus in a position to dictate to, or sabotage the projects of, the commander in chief. Given Kitchener's temperament, it is no wonder that he considered the existing system unworkable and wanted it abolished. On the other hand, Curzon wanted no changes, determined as he was to maintain the supreme authority of the viceroy. The dispute dragged on, with neither side giving ground. Eventually, the matter was referred to London, which ruled in favor of Kitchener. Curzon felt humiliated, and on August 21, 1905, submitted his resignation.[33] Kitchener found his successor, Lord Minto, much more compliant, and there were no further serious disagreements over Army policy.[34] All in all, Kitchener replaced a system that was semiobsolete and on the verge of breaking down with one that was rational and highly effective. It was enough, wrote Philip Mason, author of a book on the Indian Army, "to earn posterity's gratitude."[35] Without a thorough overhauling, the Indian Army could never have served the Empire to the extent that it did during the Great War.

On September 10, 1909, Kitchener relinquished his command in India, and the following day was promoted to field marshal. Given leave to travel at public expense, he set off for the Far East. He had been invited by the Japanese government to observe its army's annual maneuver and, subsequently, to assess the defense capabilities of both Australia and New Zealand. Kitchener headed back home via the United States, where he visited Yosemite Valley in California and the military academy at West Point.[36] His proposed tour of a Civil War battlefield in Virginia was cancelled when he learned from friends in London that Minto's retirement as viceroy of India was imminent. As Kitchener had his heart set on succeeding Minto, he hurriedly left for London to press his claim. Kitchener could count on a number of influential allies, but the ultimate decision rested with the Secretary of State for India, John Morley, who turned thumbs down, having determined that the appointment to such a sensitive post of a soldier regarded as brutal and unfeeling would lead to political unrest in the country. It came as a bitter blow to Kitchener when he was told that he had been bypassed in favor of Sir Charles Hardinge.[37]

In the summer of 1910 Kitchener found himself unemployed for the first time since leaving Woolwich. He still had abundant energy and a desire for a new challenge, but he was approaching sixty years of age, and he had to face the possibility that if no suitable employment came his way, he would be forced to retire. As he had no house of his own, he looked throughout south and southwest England for an appropriate place to settle down. In the autumn he was attracted to a five-hundred-acre estate called Broome Park near Canterbury, which he formally purchased the following April for £14,000. He laid plans to beautify the grounds, reconstruct the interior of the seventeenth-century house, and fill it with treasures he had accumulated from Africa and India. Sadly, he was never able to live in it. The alterations were still unfinished when he died five years later.[38]

Kitchener's comparative leisure was broken by his duties as a member of the Committee of Imperial Defence[39]—to which he had been appointed after his trip to the Far East—and by his visits to Turkey and the Sudan and a tour through British East Africa. In the summer of 1911, the Liberal government looked for someone to replace the current British agent and consul-general in Egypt, Sir Elton Gorst, who was dying of cancer. Kitchener became the obvious choice, as it was felt that a strong man was needed to defuse rising nationalism in Egypt. Kitchener was de-

lighted with the appointment. He spoke Arabic, understood Muslim habits and customs, and considered Egypt, where he had lived for fourteen
years, his spiritual home.

On September 28, 1911, Kitchener's ship docked at Alexandria, where
he was greeted by cheering crowds. During the next three years, Kitchener
devoted his attention to developing the economy, removing unjust laws
that were a legacy of the past, and combating the tide of nationalist agitation. Egypt was an agricultural country, and its economy depended heavily
on the export of cotton. Kitchener took great pains to protect and improve
the condition of the fellaheen (peasants). He passed laws that prohibited
moneylenders from charging more than 3 percent interest; prevented the
small farmer who owned five feddans of land (just over five acres) or less
from losing his property if he fell into debt; gave peasants easier access to
the courts; established rural savings banks; improved the country's irrigation schemes; and set up a mobile corps of midwives to provide services
in remote villages. These measures boosted the morale of the peasants and
gave them a feeling that Kitchener was on their side, making them much
less susceptible to the blandishments of aggressive nationalists.

As an ardent imperialist whose vision of Egypt's future did not include self rule, Kitchener had no intention of preparing the way for the
establishment of democratic institutions, although the Foreign Office had
encouraged him to continue Gorst's gradual program of reform. In what
was supposed to be a concession to Egyptian nationalist sentiment, Kitchener introduced a law that created a legislative assembly with a greater
proportion of elected officials and wider powers than the two councils it
replaced. The new body could delay legislation, interrogate ministers, and
discuss proposals for new taxes. It was not much of a constitutional advance, for it remained, like its predecessors, essentially an advisory body.
As a further safeguard, Kitchener restricted the franchise by substantially
raising property qualifications, ensuring that wealthy conservative landed
interests would control the legislative assembly.[40] By the autumn of 1913
Kitchener had appreciably reduced the influence of the nationalists as a
political force. To a friend, he wrote with satisfaction that at a meeting of
Egyptian nationalists in Geneva, their leader had concluded "that they
could do nothing with the people of Egypt so long as I was there."[41]

On June 17, 1914, the British government, in recognition of Kitchener's services to the Empire, announced that he had been created an earl.
It was an honor that gave him a good deal of personal satisfaction. The
next day he left for England on his annual leave. He never set foot on
Egyptian soil again, for greater events would supervene.

2

WAR PLANS

ITCHENER arrived at Dover on June 23, 1914, and headed straight for Broome Park, ten miles away to inspect the changes that had been made in his absence. The next morning, he motored to London and stayed with his old friend Pandeli Ralli at 17 Belgrave Square, which also served as his social headquarters. On Monday, June 29, while at the home of Lord Desborough, Kitchener learned that Archduke Franz Ferdinand, presumptive heir to the Austrian throne, and his wife had been assassinated by a Bosnian fanatic in Sarajevo.[1] The incident attracted little attention in Britain because the public was focused on the crisis in Ireland, which seemed on the brink of civil war. On July 2, the events in the Balkans were crowded off the front pages of newspapers by the death of Joseph Chamberlain, the former Colonial Secretary. For the next three weeks, the Balkans received only minimal coverage.

During this period, Kitchener paid visits to the country homes of friends, spent weekends at Broome Park supervising work on the house and grounds, and attended the 128th meeting of the Committee of Imperial Defence, where discussion centered on the feasibility of building a channel tunnel—a project that he opposed on security grounds.[2] Then, on July 26 (the Serbian reply was sent to Vienna a day earlier), Kitchener was having breakfast when he learned that the Serbs had refused to accept all the exacting demands made by the Austrian government. His only comment was, "This means war."[3]

Although Britain had no formal commitment to go to war in support of the Entente, Kitchener felt that it was morally obligated to stand by friends when they were in trouble. On July 31 he lunched with H. H. Asquith, the Prime Minister, and Winston Churchill, First Lord of the Admiralty, and impressed them with his perceptive grasp of the international situation. In the course of the discussion, he told them bluntly that if Britain abandoned France, it could never again claim the right to be a world power.[4] Sir Edward Grey, Secretary for Foreign Affairs, would echo Kitchener's sentiments when he addressed the House of Commons on August 3.[5]

As the European world slid closer to the abyss, the Foreign Office ordered all heads of mission on leave abroad to return to their posts at once. Accordingly, Kitchener wrote farewell letters to friends and made plans to begin his journey back to Cairo. On the morning of August 3, he motored to Dover to catch the 12:55 P.M. channel steamer to Calais. Because the additional traffic of the Bank Holiday weekend had disrupted the railroad timetable, the boat train from Victoria was late arriving at Dover. Pacing up and down the deck in a state of nervous anxiety, Kitchener worried that he might miss the train departing from Calais at 2:50 P.M. He sent Col. Oswald FitzGerald, his personal military secretary, and Edward Cecil, his financial adviser in Egypt, to urge the captain to leave immediately. While they were in heated discussion with the captain, a message arrived from the Prime Minister requesting that Kitchener return immediately to London.[6]

Back at 17 Belgrave Square, Kitchener waited impatiently for further instructions from Asquith. He dreaded the prospect of remaining in England in a consultative capacity without defined responsibilities. He had no interest in serving as secretary for war, an appointment the *Times* had urged on the morning of August 3 in place of Asquith, who had been acting as caretaker since the previous March when Jack Seely had resigned in the aftermath of the Curragh Incident.[7] As he saw it, his proper place was to stay in Egypt until 1915, when he hoped to succeed Hardinge as viceroy of India.

Asquith's purpose in recalling Kitchener was not to put him in charge of the War Office, but to have him present at the forthcoming Council of War.[8] It is true that Asquith was looking for a suitable secretary for war because, with hostilities imminent, it was obvious he could not continue to combine both offices. Asquith had given the matter of finding a successor serious thought and, during a private talk with J. A. Pease, a Cabinet minister, on August 2, indicated that he intended to ask Jack Seely to return to his old job.[9] When he approached Seely, presumably on the morning of August 3, he was turned down. Sir George Riddell, a newspaper proprietor, wrote the following in his diary after a talk with Seely on August 6:

> He told me that he had an interview with the Prime Minister who had offered him one of the two vacant seats in the cabinet which he had declined telling the P.M. that he felt it his duty to go to the front.[10] Seely said the interview took place in the P.M.'s motor as he was driving to the House of Commons.[11]

During the afternoon of August 3, Asquith entrusted Richard Haldane, the Lord Chancellor, with the task of deputizing for him at the War Office. Haldane's hope that this would be the prelude to a permanent arrangement was shattered by a press campaign, which accused him of pro-German sympathies.[12] Many newspapers, troubled by Haldane's presence in the War Office, had joined the *Times's* lead in pressing for Kitchener's selection. This was no time, it was stressed, to place an amateur at the head of the nation's military organization, and only a professional soldier of proven worth like Kitchener could furnish the desired technical efficiency and leadership. As a new appointment was needed, Asquith interviewed Kitchener on the evening of August 4. There is no record of the proceedings, and what little we know about the discussion is based on piecemeal information Kitchener subsequently imparted to friends and aides. Apparently, Kitchener told Asquith that he would prefer to return to Egypt, but that he would stay in Britain if assigned a responsible post. No firm decision was taken at the meeting.[13]

Kitchener's awareness of his own limitations made him anxious to avoid joining the government as secretary for war. He could lead and execute a policy, but he was incapable of teamwork.[14] To make matters worse, he was deficient in the arts of oral expression and persuasion, which would be needed in full measure in dealings with Cabinet ministers. For over forty years, he had lived outside Britain, as a result of which he possessed little knowledge of prearranged military plans, British Army organization, and British politics.

Britain found itself at war on the expiration of an ultimatum to Germany at 11:00 P.M. on August 4. By early the next morning, Asquith had made up his mind to send Kitchener to the War Office, a decision aided in part by the flurry of press comments. For twenty-four hours the Prime

Minister had carefully considered Kitchener's qualifications for the post. Asquith's information on Kitchener, whom he knew only superficially, was that he was autocratic, inflexible, and difficult to work with. Nor was he sure whether Kitchener would submit to the constraints of Cabinet rule. His sense of uneasiness, however, was overshadowed by the assets the field marshal would bring to the government. He could provide the ministry with expert military advice and galvanize the War Office into emergency action, and his immense prestige would be invaluable in unifying the nation in a time of danger.[15] His presence in the Cabinet, furthermore, would symbolize the seriousness of purpose of the government, which for years had made defense issues a low priority.

Before making a formal announcement, Asquith had to persuade Grey that Egypt could be left in other hands.[16] That done, Asquith telephoned 17 Belgrave Square and asked to see Kitchener, hinting that he was prepared to meet the field marshal's conditions. During the afternoon, Asquith and Kitchener reached an agreement. Of the meeting Asquith wrote:

> Kitchener was (to do him justice) not at all anxious to come in, but when it was presented to him as a duty he agreed. It is clearly understood that he has no politics, & that his place at Cairo is kept open—so that he can return to it when peace comes back. It is a hazardous experiment, but the best in the circumstances, I think.[17]

Kitchener's experience and his training would serve him well in his new capacity. In the past he had approached war from the point of view of an engineer, not that of a conventional soldier. It was important for him to stand back and look at a problem from different angles, weighing the consequences of each option, rather than to seek short-term solutions. In India he had linked his reforms to the larger issue of imperial defense, just as he would take a long-range and global approach to the problems of the Great War. He had become an exceptionally talented improviser (maybe the best the British Army ever produced), an asset that was indispensable in view of the deficiencies in the British Army in 1914. In planning operations, whether in the Sudan or South Africa, he had understood that war took unpredictable turns and had prepared for every contingency. He believed that victory was the result of careful planning, persistence, attention to detail, and overcoming of obstacles. No one had a better appreciation of the military resources of the Empire as a whole than Kitchener. In recent years he had examined on the spot the military problems of Egypt, India, Australia, New Zealand, and East Africa, and from this knowledge the Empire would reap enormous benefits. In short, when he entered the War Office in August 1914, his vision was large and clear, he had never flinched in the face of serious adversity, and when he had perceived new possibilities, he had shown the courage to act on them.

The public greeted the announcement of Kitchener's appointment with relief and rapturous delight. No Englishman since Wellington had rivaled the popular esteem in which Kitchener was held.[18] It may be argued that Kitchener's reputation owed much to his physical size, to the element of mystery surrounding his character, and that it stood higher than his actual military and administrative accomplishments warranted. Yet, to the ordinary man in the street, Kitchener was a national institution, possessing unusual courage and energy and a character above reproach with a soldier's high conception of duty and service. In their eyes he could do no wrong. He had throughout his long imperial career gone from one success to another, and there was never any doubt that he would again find a way to defeat Britain's enemies. During the immediate prewar years, the country had been wracked by a series of political and social crises. The war pushed domestic problems into the background, but did not remove public mistrust in the political leadership. Kitchener's presence at the helm of the war effort dissipated much of the anxiety that had gripped the nation since the declaration of war on the previous day. Projecting an image of massive strength and selfless devotion to duty, Kitchener became the embodiment of Britain's will to persevere until victory.[19]

There was less enthusiasm for Kitchener's presence in the highest military circles. This was due not so much to his unpopularity, as to a fear that he might disrupt the British Army's plans and detailed arrangements with the French. As an outsider, Kitchener's vision was uncluttered by fatal illusions. One of the major failings of British Army planners had been a tendency to slavishly follow the views of the French high command, no matter how illogical. Kitchener had never been consulted about the secret talks between members of the British and French general staffs, which had committed the British Army to take a position on the left of the French in case of war with Germany.[20] While he was not happy over the informal agreement to subordinate British strategy to French interests, he had no qualms about giving France direct support.[21] Only the French possessed an army capable of preventing the German annexation of Belgium, which was the real reason His Majesty's Government had gone to war. The least that the British could do was to send such forces as were at their disposal.

Kitchener had not yet been named Secretary for War on the morning of August 5 when he attended a meeting of the Council of War, convened by Asquith to decide whether to ratify or overturn the General Staff's Continental arrangements. Others present included the service ministers and the nation's leading soldiers. The majority of members agreed that the British Expeditionary Force (BEF) should be dispatched immediately across the channel. Kitchener, however, objected to the number of divisions detailed to go and, once there, to the staging area. He wanted one of the six Regular Army divisions retained for home defense, and he was dismayed over the choice of Maubeuge as the point of concentration—a choice that had been based on the assumption that the main German maneuver would not take place in Belgium. Kitchener was convinced that the Germans would execute a wide sweep through Belgium, north as well as south of the Meuse, in order to roll up the left flank of the French Army. He reasoned that Germany would not have dragged Britain into the conflict by violating Belgium's neutrality unless Belgium had bulked large in their plans to deliver a rapid knockout blow at France. If his prediction proved correct, he warned that the BEF would be overwhelmed if it deployed around Maubeuge. He recommended Amiens, seventy miles in the rear, as a safe alternative.

It was pointed out to Kitchener that arrangements had already been made to align the BEF in a zone that best harmonized with French strategic designs. The soldiers who spoke doubted that the Germans, faced with a war on two fronts, had the requisite manpower to undertake a powerful flanking movement in northern Belgium such as Kitchener envisaged. They considered that the Germans would advance either through the Ardennes or south of the Meuse. The French counted on the British to move up to Maubeuge to guard their left flank while they launched a massive assault in Lorraine on either side of Metz, with the aim of breaking into the heart of Germany and dislocating any German advance through Belgium. Before the meeting adjourned, it was decided to send all six divisions of the BEF abroad, leaving the staging area to be settled at a later date.[22]

The next day, the Council of War reconvened late in the afternoon with the same personalities in attendance. The only difference now was that Kitchener had assumed the seals of the War Office. Earlier in the morning, the Cabinet had agreed in principle to send the BEF to France but, owing to an invasion scare that brewed up overnight, had opted to hold back two divisions for the time being.[23] In deference to Kitchener's wishes, the ministers further decided on Amiens, rather than Maubeuge, as the place of concentration. This renewed the debate at the second Council of War, which put off a final resolution, pending consultation with the French general staff.[24]

Horrified over the prospect that complicated military plans would be altered at the eleventh hour, the French responded in haste, sending a delegation to London led by Col. Charles Huguet, the former military attaché, now designated to head the military mission to the British Army. Huguet collected Sir John French, the British commander in chief, and several members of his staff before heading for the War Office. The British officers were as upset as their French counterparts, seeing nothing but irresolution and bad faith in going anywhere except the place agreed upon. They could not understand why Kitchener was so adamant, given that he was an engineer and untrained in tactics and had not been privy to the mass of information that they had mastered.

For three hours, various members of the Anglo-French party took turns in pleading with Kitchener to accept the existing arrangements over a concentration further back. Kitchener's military logic and instinct told him that he was correct, but he could not offer conclusive arguments to support his case because he had not studied or been actively involved in the complex problems of Continental planning. Not fully convinced, he went over to 10 Downing Street and put the matter before Asquith, who ruled in favor of Maubeuge, seeing that it would be unwise to overrule the combined opinion of the British and French general staffs.[25] Kitchener's fears would be justified in the opening clash of battle.

Kitchener also possessed a more realistic appraisal of the relative strength of the principal belligerent armies than did the British general staff. As a rule, British military observers overestimated the capability of the French and the Russian armies and believed that their combined strength would be more than a match for the Germans. They anticipated a brief conflict in which the British Army would assist the French in containing the Germans, until the Russian steamroller crushed them from the east.[26]

Kitchener saw things differently. As far as he was concerned, Russia and France lacked the capacity to defeat so formidable and determined an enemy as Germany. A nation with a population of sixty-five million, Germany had a first-rate army, large reserves of manpower, and fine leadership and was thoroughly organized for war. "It should be assumed," Kitchener told Lord Esher, who served as his private factotum, "that before Germany relinquishes the struggle, she will have exhausted every possible supply of men and material."[27]

By contrast, Kitchener held a rather low opinion of the Entente's military capacity. France, with a much smaller population than Germany, had already placed most of its men in the field. Kitchener, moreover, regarded the French Army with something approaching contempt. In 1911 he had predicted that if war broke out, the Germans would scatter the French "like partridges."[28] His doubts about the French Army stemmed not so much from the quality of the rank and file, as from its inept leadership and obsession with a military theory that emphasized spirit over firepower.[29] He was convinced that the French would be unable to stem the German onslaught without British help.

Kitchener's estimate of the Russian Army, based on observation while in India, tended to be more favorable. He shared the General Staff's view that the Russian Army had largely recovered from its debacle at the hands of the Japanese a decade earlier.[30] All the same, he was certain that it would not be a match for the Germans, let alone a decisive weapon. He recognized that, while it had size, its offensive power was "untried and unproved."[31]

Kitchener reserved much of his scorn for the British Army, which he judged wholly inadequate for the type of conflict the country faced. In August 1914, the total strength of British forces, that is the Regular Army, its Reservists and the Territorial Army, amounted to 733,514 officers and men. The Regular Army numbered 235,000 men, nearly half of whom were posted overseas. The six infantry divisions stationed in Britain, which formed the BEF, were earmarked for France on mobilization. The Territorials stood at around 268,000 men of all ranks and were organized into fourteen divisions and an equal number of mounted brigades. These troops were intended for home defense only, and the level of their training was far below that of the Regular Army.

Although during the pre-1914 period, the General Staff had consented to send the BEF to fight in a Continental war, it had not fully understood the implications of its commitment. It did not have a continental-size army to make a difference in a land war or a blueprint to produce mass armies with a corresponding growth in munitions output. Thus, the British general staff lacked the means to carry out its chosen strategy.

It did not take long for Kitchener to recognize the wide chasm between the General Staff's Continental strategy, which he endorsed, and the nation's actual military establishment and future plans. "I am put here to conduct a great war, and I have no army," he lamented on entering the War Office.[32] He was virtually alone in predicting that the war would last at least three years and that Britain would need to raise a huge army to win it—ultimately he set the number at seventy divisions. Conventional wisdom proclaimed that European economies could not sustain a modern conflict for more than a few months. Kitchener's successful campaigns in the Sudan and South Africa had not only been of long duration, they also had been conducted on a shoestring budget. It was his opinion that financial exigency had never stopped a war in progress. He had been a keen student of the American Civil War, in which the South had managed to hang on for four years. He remarked to Lord Esher that there "was no hardship that the South did not undergo before the end came."[33]

Kitchener placed much of the blame on the General Staff and its leadership for the nation's unpreparedness for the type of war in which it found itself. He understood that before 1914 the public's parsimonious mood had encouraged the Liberal government to keep military spending to a bare minimum. Nevertheless, he felt that the chiefs of the General Staff had neglected their duty by failing to alert politicians of all parties of the inadequacy of existing arrangements. Given his attitude, it is not surprising that he placed little confidence in Gen. Sir Charles Douglas, a hard-working, but unimaginative, officer, whom Asquith had appointed a few months earlier. Already in ill-health when hostilities began, Douglas remained in the War Office as chief of staff, at least in a nominal capacity. Kitchener continued to act as his own chief of staff, as he had done in the Sudan and South Africa. He used Douglas in a variety of ways, but never to formulate plans. When the ailing Douglas died in October 1914 from overwork, Kitchener disregarded the claims of several staff officers recommended by acquaintances, including those of Sir William Nicholson, a former chief of staff, and selected instead Gen. Sir James Wolfe-Murray, a pathetic incompetent who trembled in his presence.[34] Sir Herbert Creedy, Kitchener's departmental secretary, later maintained that his chief turned to Wolfe-Murray because he "was practically the only person available [in Britain], he was senior, and he had been a member of the Army Council . . . and he had a knowledge of the War Office and War Office procedure."[35] He added that Kitchener was well aware of Wolfe-Murray's limitations and, for that reason, made his appointment temporary, until someone "with a first-hand knowledge of warfare" could be found.[36] The unavailability of a competent administrator reinforced Kitchener's instinctive desire to be his own chief of staff. It made little difference in the short run, but as the war spread and problems multiplied, Kitchener would not have the time to do the work properly.

In the past Kitchener had made everything he touched a one-man show. His independent commands abroad had fostered in him a sense of despotism and an intolerance of interference and opposition. By instinct and practice, he was a centralizer, with a habit of disregarding normal procedures and delegating as little responsibility as possible. His style of administration had served him well in Africa and India, as evidenced by his glittering career. But he was now sixty-four years old, and the problems of modern warfare far transcended previous human experience. To make matters worse, the government entered the war without a blueprint for industrial mobilization or any clear idea of the resources that might be required. For that reason, Asquith and the Cabinet placed an inordinate burden on Kitchener's shoulders. Apart from the routine work of his department, Kitchener continued to manage the internal affairs of Egypt and provide for its defense; undertook to greatly expand the output of munitions; supervised operations on the western front and in certain areas of the Empire; procured war supplies for Russia; and raised, trained and equipped an army of unprecedented size (which was in itself a mammoth task). Kitchener never complained, but it is hard to imagine how any one person could have borne such Herculean responsibilities. The sad part is that none of his colleagues had a clear idea of the amount of work he was doing. The Prime Minister, rather than provide him with assistance, kept assigning him more tasks, too often inconsequential ones. In fact, he did not seem to think that Kitchener was all that overworked. When confronted in 1917 by a member of a commission who felt that Kitchener had been expected to do the job of four men at the War Office, Asquith replied, "There is no doubt that Lord Kitchener was doing two men's work . . . But he was a very industrious man, and he was a quick worker; he had excellent health, and the best nerve I should think ever a man was endowed with. . . . [H]e never complained of being over-driven."[37]

In any case, Kitchener himself could have lightened his immense burden if he had made greater use of the machinery at hand. Unfortunately, he was incapable or unwilling to adjust his ways to conform to the new circumstances. It did not help that the most talented officers on the General Staff, save for Sir John Cowans, the Quartermaster-General, had left to accompany the BEF to France.[38] Their places were taken by their deputies, officers recalled from Egypt, and "dugouts"—an uncharitable name given to retired officers recalled to duty—who were expected to learn on the job. These men were petrified of Kitchener, and while they stood ready to carry out his orders to the best of their ability, none ventured to argue questions with him on a man-to-man basis. Kitchener was reluctant to take into his confidence, or to solicit advice on military planning from, officers who had not proven themselves. He only worked well with men he knew and trusted.[39] For Kitchener, the ideal solution would have been to avail himself of the services of members of his old team who were familiar with his methods and idiosyncrasies. But they were scattered around Egypt and India, and reassembling them at this critical period would have been impracticable, if not impossible.

Kitchener evidently recognized after the first few months of the war that he was having great difficulty keeping up with the work, but he did not trust War Office personnel, and, according to his personal private secretary, Sir George Arthur, did not wish to handicap Sir John French by recalling experienced staff officers from France.[40] Arthur's assertion is not overstated. French, far from being able to spare staff officers, kept asking Kitchener for more—particularly after the Army began to grow. As might be expected, Kitchener did his best to accommodate him. To Gen. Sir Beauchamp Duff, Commander in Chief in India, he sent the following wire in September: "Sir John French sends urgent request for more well trained officers and it is very difficult for me to find them in England. Can you help me in this?"[41] Kitchener also contacted Lt. Gen. Sir John Maxwell, Commander in Chief in Egypt, with an identical request. Maxwell, whose headquarters staff had already been raided by the War Office, sent his regrets, but Duff agreed to send eight officers from each infantry battalion.[42]

Unwilling to bring back top-level administrators from French's command, Kitchener should have at least tried to rebuild the General Staff from available material in Britain. Had he made an effort to do so, he would have been surprised to find out, as he belatedly did, that some of the supposedly tired old men, such as Maj. Gen. Sir C. E. Callwell, the Director of Military Operations, were very reliable and competent and, if given an opportunity, could have relieved him of a mountain of trivial matters. By reducing the General Staff to the status of clerks, Kitchener was compelled to do practically everything himself. It was a load that no single individual, even of his great capacity, could sustain for long. Equally important, without the reasoned arguments of an active general staff to buttress his case in the Cabinet, where invariably he had difficulty in expressing himself, he opened the way for the ideas of amateur strategists to gain ascendancy over professional judgment.

Kitchener assumed a special status in the Cabinet, symbolized by the fact that he sat next to the Prime Minister at meetings.[43] The Asquith Cabinet consisted of an exceptionally talented group of personalities. Since 1908 Asquith had not only accomplished a good deal in terms of social reform, he had also guided his government though exceptionally troubled political waters with calm, magisterial skill. Although he was respected for his savvy as a parliamentarian and for his rare intellectual gifts, it would soon become evident that his personality and leisurely methods were not suited to the task of directing the war. Kitchener nevertheless admired and trusted Asquith, with whom he formed a special relationship, once describing him as the "only honest politician in the gang."[44] Besides Asquith, the other dominant politicians in the Cabinet were Winston Churchill, First Lord of the Admiralty, and David Lloyd George, the Chancellor of the Exchequer.

Only forty years old, brilliant, possessing a formidable vocabulary, impulsive, and with a mania for self-advertisement, Churchill had risen in politics as rapidly as he had accumulated foes and detractors. Kitchener worked hand-in-hand with the Admiralty in the early months of the war, impressed as he was by Churchill's obvious intelligence, resolution, energy, and buoyant personality. As the war dragged on, however, Kitchener's opinion of Churchill changed, and he came to view him as erratic and meddlesome and the source of many of his troubles.

One of the most electrifying platform speakers, Lloyd George was essentially an opportunist with no fixed principles except a burning desire to succeed Asquith some day. Genial on the surface, but cunning, vengeful, and mean-spirited, his nimble mind and verbal dexterity masked a lack of culture, formal education, and general knowledge. As Kitchener was to find out, to his discomfort and eventual ruin, Lloyd George had no compunction about employing gutter tactics against men who opposed him or stood in his way.

Initially, Kitchener's colleagues stood in awe of his legendary reputation and regularly deferred to his opinion, often too intimidated to raise questions or seek further explanations. "A word from him was decisive," Lloyd George recalled, "and no one dared challenge it at a Cabinet meeting."[45] This suited Kitchener perfectly. He knew that he was out of his depth among such experienced and resourceful politicians and that he could not match them in the cut and thrust of verbal discussion. Added to his inherent distrust of politicians was a suspicion that his colleagues leaked state secrets. Consequently, he refused to divulge classified information to his fellow ministers or to admit them freely into his confidence. He made an exception of Asquith, being somewhat more forthcoming with him during their private talks held at fairly regular intervals. His practice at the council table was to tell the politicians only as much he thought they ought to know and then to get back to the War Office as quickly as possible. Accustomed to exercising absolute power, Kitchener did not fit easily in a highly structured system of collective responsibility.

Kitchener put his colleagues on notice at his first Cabinet meeting in August that the war would be neither brief nor won by sea power. Germany's defeat, he insisted, would come, not after a few land battles, but only when its manpower had been exhausted by a slow process of attrition. Britain's contribution could not be limited to its miniature army, but rather must be on a scale in proportion to its prestige and strength. "We must be prepared to put millions of men in the field and maintain them for several years."[46] Basing his calculations on a war lasting three years, he proposed, as a start, to raise a million men.

Kitchener's declaration was a blunt repudiation of the traditional manner in which Britain had fought its wars over the past two centuries. The Liberal government's prewar doctrine had emphasized the role of the Navy, rather than the Army, in a conflict against Germany. Britain would provide munitions and money to its allies, France and Russia, who would bear the main burden of the land war. Britain would send a token force to the Continent and use the Royal Navy to impose a blockade of Germany and ensure its economic collapse.[47] Implicit in this policy of limited liability was the British government's willingness to risk an Entente defeat.[48]

The Cabinet was stunned by Kitchener's announcement. Grey later noted that Kitchener's prediction of a three-year war "seemed to most of us unlikely, if not incredible."[49] The general feeling among the ministers was that war would be over before the million-man army could be trained and equipped. That being the case, it seemed to them a frightful waste of effort and treasure. Yet the ministers accepted Kitchener's advice meekly and, even more astonishingly, without discussion.[50] Lord Beaverbrook observed that no one but Kitchener could have induced the civil authorities "to act on his conclusions."[51] By permitting Kitchener to transform Britain into a nation of arms, the Cabinet acknowledged the supersession of its concept of a war of limited liability. It was undoubtedly the most far-reaching policy decision of the entire war.

If the politicians had misgivings about the proposal to create new armies, the generals were even less enthusiastic. To train the recruits, Kitchener had withheld a number of officers and NCOs from the BEF—in addition to using retired officers and NCOs and some nine hundred Indian Army officers who had been on leave in Britain on the declaration of war. Lacking Kitchener's broad vision, Sir John French and his staff were persuaded that the decisive battles would occur at once and, so, felt it was criminal to weaken the BEF in any way. They could do nothing to stop Kitchener, but that did not inhibit them from castigating him behind his back. A case in point was the attitude of Henry Wilson, Deputy Chief of Staff of the BEF. He considered Kitchener half-mad and as much of a menace to the Allied cause as von Moltke or von Falkenhayn. Wilson expressed his anti-Kitchener bias freely to his political contacts, including his friend Andrew Bonar Law, the leader of the Unionist Party. He insisted that the war would not last long enough for the recruits to be trained and put in the field and was scathingly critical of Kitchener for starving the BEF for the sake of his "ridiculous and preposterous army," which was "the laughing stock of every soldier in Europe."[52]

On the same day that Kitchener assumed his duties, the government authorized an increase to the Army of five hundred thousand men. Britain alone among the European powers did not possess compulsory military service in 1914. Churchill and others have claimed that Kitchener's prestige was so great that the public would have accepted compulsion passively if he had insisted upon it. They argued that conscription would have allowed both skilled workers in essential industries to remain where they were and the state to call up men as they were needed, avoiding many of the problems in indiscriminate recruiting. These same critics, however, overlook vital facts. The majority of the public might or might not have acquiesced to Kitchener's request for compulsion, but it would have made no sense for him to risk entering a great conflict with a divided nation. In any case, the introduction of compulsion at the start of the war was impossible. The country had no administrative machinery for registration and compulsory enlistment, and if Kitchener had waited until such a system was in place to create a mass army, the consequences might well have been fatal. The determining factor for Kitchener was that he had been out of the country for so long that he had no way to measure the political implications of introducing national military service. Wisely deferring to Asquith's judgment that conscription would endanger the unity of the country, he relied on voluntary enlistment to raise his new formations.

Recruiting posters were placarded all over the country. None was more effective than the one Alfred Leete designed, depicting Kitchener's imposing face, with bristling mustache and piercing eyes glaring directly at the onlooker above the legend "Your Country Needs You." By lending his name to the drive for Army recruits, Kitchener cast an aura of respectability on a profession hitherto regarded by the general public as the last refuge of the riff-raff and the unemployed. Young men from all social classes and occupations responded immediately to his call. So great was the surge of patriotic enthusiasm that long queues, some one mile in length, formed outside virtually every recruiting center in the country.

The peace-time recruiting apparatus was not designed to cope with the flood of men who came forward. It soon broke down, compelling the War Office to enlist the services of municipal authorities, additional clerks and doctors, and to occupy premises of all types—police stations, city halls, factories, and theaters. In one day alone in August, thirty-five thousand men volunteered, more than normally enrolled during an entire year.[53] Between August 1914 and December 1915, 2,466,719 men enlisted, forming the largest volunteer army in the history of any country.[54] These numbers produced wide-ranging problems on an unprecedented scale for the War Office. There were no boots, blankets, equipment, and rifles for many of the recruits. Men trained in civilian clothes and used brooms or sticks instead of rifles. Accommodation was lacking. Army huts contained two or three times the normal number of recruits. Even that proved insufficient and so tents were provided and schools, churches, and halls commandeered. Through improvisation, trial and error, and the hard work and ingenuity of Kitchener and his team, all major obstacles were surmounted in time.[55] It was an incredible achievement.

Kitchener ignored advice from different quarters that he use the framework of the Territorial Army as a basis for his planned massive expansion. His attitude in this regard has been the subject of much debate.[56] There is probably a good deal of truth to the charge that his previous experience—as a young volunteer in Chazy's army in 1871 and later in South Africa with irregular forces—colored his judgment against citizen armies. It is on record that he described the Territorials as a "Town Clerk's Army"[57] and that he preferred "men who know nothing to those who have been taught a smattering of the wrong thing."[58] Still, Kitchener's decision to bypass the Territorial machinery rested on more concrete factors than mere ignorance and prejudice.

Prior to 1914, the Territorial Force was well below establishment. Modern equipment was in short supply, many troops were unfit for service, and only five complete formations had indicated a willingness to serve overseas if required.[59] The Territorial system was not designed for rapid expansion, and it is unlikely that it would have been able to handle the influx of recruits that poured in at the beginning of the war. Since the Territorials were intended to provide for the security of Britain only, Kitchener was reluctant to pressure them to change the terms of their enlistment midstream. A week or two later, when the call went out for the Territorials to undertake foreign service, the response was less than universal. Parents wrote letters to newspapers complaining about the government's request, underlining that their sons had joined Territorial formations to defend their country, not to volunteer for active service abroad.[60] On the other hand, Lloyd George derided Kitchener in his *War Memoirs* for disdaining to make greater use of the Territorials, implying that the young men in these units would have willingly served overseas.[61] It is interesting to note that his attitude was different in 1914 when it involved his own son, Gwilym, then serving in a Welsh Territorial unit. In a letter to his wife, he wrote, "They are pressing the Territorials to volunteer for war . . . You must write Wil telling him on no account to be bullied into volunteering abroad."[62] Such sentiment was common enough to provoke Kitchener into issuing a statement, which was published on August 15, 1914. In it Kitchener observed that while he welcomed those who volunteered to serve abroad, he fully understood that many had good reasons for wishing to stay at home, and he urged them to resist pressure and remain in their Territorial units.[63]

Another point Kitchener considered was the need to maintain a viable home defense force. As he worried about the possibility of an invasion, he had no wish to upset predetermined security arrangements. Looking back, we realize that his fears were exaggerated, but in 1914 there were many others in the country, including naval leaders, who believed that a German invasion could not be ruled out. Finally, and most importantly, the Territorials were held in low esteem by the British public in 1914, and Kitchener did not feel they would attract as many recruits as armies stamped in his own mould. This was abundantly clear after the first few weeks of the war when the New Armies proved a far superior magnet than the Territorials. In Kitchener's eyes it was infinitely better to build an army on fresh foundations, enlist men for the duration of the war, train them according to the demands of that war, and then be able to send them wherever necessary.[64]

Kitchener may not have lavished on the Territorial Force the same care and attention as he did on the New Armies, but it is wrong to assert, as many contemporary and modern writers have done, that he ignored it.[65] Not long after the opening days of the war, he recognized that, until the New Armies were fully trained, there were instances when he would be forced to rely on the Territorial Army. On August 13 he told Esher that he would be willing to use Territorial units who volunteered to go abroad.[66] A fortnight later, Kitchener announced that in response to his request, seventy Territorial units had already given pledges to serve over-seas. Before the close of 1914 the Territorials had contributed twenty-three battalions to bolster the line on the western front, while four divisions had gone either to India or Egypt to release Regular troops on garrison duty. In all, 318 Territorial battalions served abroad between 1914 and 1918. Their contribution to the war effort was immense. When all the facts are con-sidered, Kitchener's decision to keep the Territorials in a subsidiary role was justified by events. As Peter Simpkins has correctly stated:

> Kitchener . . . was able to weld the [Territorial] Force into the national army without dislocating it or totally destroying its original character. His policy permitted it to retain its place in the home defence structure but also to reinforce the BEF at a critical juncture in 1914–1915, even if considerable waste and duplication of effort resulted from allowing two organizations to exist side by side.[67]

Kitchener's strategy from the moment he entered the War Office was guided by three principles: to husband Britain's resources so that its army could deliver the coup de grâce at the appropriate moment; to enhance the security of Britain and its Empire against both allies and enemies; and to defeat Germany, sweep away Prussian militarism, and preserve Brit-ain's status as a great power.

Kitchener planned to place just enough men in the field to prevent Britain's allies from collapsing under the weight of the German onslaught. He expected the British Army to reach its maximum strength early in 1917, by which time the major belligerents on the Continent would have fought each other to a standstill. Britain, with the strongest army in the field, would be able to deliver the final blow against Germany and dictate the peace settlement.[68]

The conflict was only a few months old when Kitchener's attention was drawn to the Middle East where British political and strategic interests were threatened by Turkish belligerency. Kitchener reacted by encouraging the Arabs to throw off the Turkish yoke, hoping to weaken the Ottoman Empire and eventually transfer the caliphate to an independent Arabia, which would remain under British influence. While talks with Arab leaders were going on, Kitchener, as the lone expert in the Cabinet on Middle Eastern affairs, took the lead in pressing British claims in the future disposal of Ottoman territory.

Before the first clash of battle, Kitchener was already looking ahead to the postwar period. Kitchener had no quarrel with the German people, only with the ruling Prussian military caste. He wanted Germany to remain strong enough in central Europe to serve as a counterbalance to Britain's potential enemies in the future. He was convinced that the existing groupings of powers would not last and that later Russia and France might present more of a threat to Britain than Germany. It must be remembered that he belonged to the generation that had witnessed France and Russia as Britain's most bitter imperial rivals. The alliance with France and Russia had been forged to contain Germany, and Kitchener did not expect it to survive beyond the conclusion of hostilities. For that reason he sought to ensure that neither France nor Russia enhanced its power significantly at the expense of a defeated Germany to emerge as a new danger to British security. The New Armies were intended to ensure that Britain did not lose the peace after winning the war. Kitchener told Lt. Col. Charles à Court Repington, the *Times* correspondent, in an interview early in August that there must be "no question of peace except on our own terms."[69]

Although a keen imperialist, Kitchener did not carry the war to Germany's overseas colonies simply to add more territory to the Empire. In fact, he thought that Britain's retention of Germany's territories in Africa would be a mistake, creating a barrier to the resumption of normal relations between the two countries after the war. Still, he understood that there were good reasons why they should be occupied. They could be used as bargaining chips at the peace conference. Moreover, it was necessary to deny German commerce raiders bases and intelligence-gathering sources. Because Kitchener did not consider the war in Africa as having significant bearing in the overall picture, he relied on local resources, strengthened when circumstances dictated by Empire forces.

Kitchener's chief focus was to bring about the defeat of the main German Army. His approach was based on a clear understanding of the nature of a two-front war and of a realistic appraisal of the resources available to both sides. While he never deviated from the notion that the war would be won on the western front, he realized in 1914 that Britain and France were still several years away from that objective. Until the New Armies were ready, it was imperative that the Russians exert strong pressure from the east to hold down a sizeable segment of the German Army. If Russia went out of the war early, and the French followed suit, a German invasion of Britain was likely. In Kitchener's eyes, the Russian Army, with its huge framework and immense reserves of manpower, was the centerpiece of his plans, vital to the defeat of Germany and to forestalling an invasion of Britain. Treating the war on the eastern and western fronts as inseparable, Kitchener's strategy during the first year of the war rested to an unusual degree on events in Russia and on the fluctuating fortunes of its army.[70]

3

IMPERIAL ISSUES AND PERIPHERAL THEATERS

WITHIN forty-eight hours of joining France and Russia, Britain elected to extend the war beyond Europe. On August 6, the Cabinet approved a recommendation by a subcommittee of the CID to mount military operations against German colonies to protect British overseas possessions and to deny enemy warships bases from which to attack Allied shipping.[1] While the British authorities had no interest in annexing conquered territories, they hoped to use them as bargaining chips at the peace conference.

The direction of the war outside of Europe was divided among a number of state departments and did not rest exclusively with the War Office. Under longstanding arrangements, the India Office, the Colonial Office, and the Foreign Office managed separate armies and had been allowed to wage little wars of their own, relying on the War Office to provided them with advice, key personnel, and such war matériel as they were unable to provide for themselves.[2] Each army was administered and supplied differently, and each had its own customs and way of doing things.[3] Whatever benefit, if any, such a system of divided authority offered in peacetime, it was wholly unsuitable for the purposes of war. The most obvious disadvantage was that the chain of command was greatly lengthened by the number of authorities who had to be consulted. Confusion and frustration were also inevitable when British, Indian, or native troops were called upon to work together.

For the War Office, there were other drawbacks. It did not know from day to day what demands the government might make upon it, how to assess their urgency as compared with the needs of other theatres, what help it could expect from other quarters for its own operations, and, on occasion, whether a given problem lay within its purview or that of one of the other state departments. Kitchener had to play the hand that he was dealt, even though it was obvious to him than a coherent imperial strategy could not be crafted and executed unless the various operations undertaken were dealt with as a whole and all instructions issued through one channel.

Kitchener and the War Office were not involved at the operational level in any of the secondary theaters during the first three months of the war. The first German colony to fall in Africa was the tiny territory of Togoland (now divided between Ghana and Togo), sandwiched between the British Gold Coast (now Ghana) and the French colony of Dahomey (now Benin). On August 7, the Colonial Office ordered a unit of West African Rifles from the Gold Coast to invade Togoland, while French Senegalese troops struck from the west. Their target was a recently completed wireless station at Kamina, so powerful that it could communicate directly with Germany. The campaign in Togoland lasted three weeks. Anglo-French forces drove back and penned in the heavily outnumbered defenders, who surrendered on August 26 after destroying the wireless facilities.[4]

It took longer to subdue the Cameroons, Germany's other colony on the west coast, located just above the equator. It was an inhospitable territory larger than France and Germany combined and enclosed on three sides by British and French possessions. The initial invasion by British-led native troops from Nigeria to the northwest encountered heavy resistance and was turned back with heavy losses. French forces from Equatorial Africa to the east and a Belgian contingent brought up from the Congo to the southeast joined the next British attempt, by sea, which resulted on September 27 in the capture of Duala, the chief port and capital, although most of the German garrison, after destroying the wireless station, escaped into the interior. The Allies pursued the Germans southeast to nearby Edéa, which they occupied on October 26. After failing to recapture the town, the main German forces fell back to Yaunde, a hundred miles to the east, where a new seat of government and munitions facilities were located. The Allies resumed their advance, which was hampered by enemy ambushes, intense heat, tropical diseases, and an almost

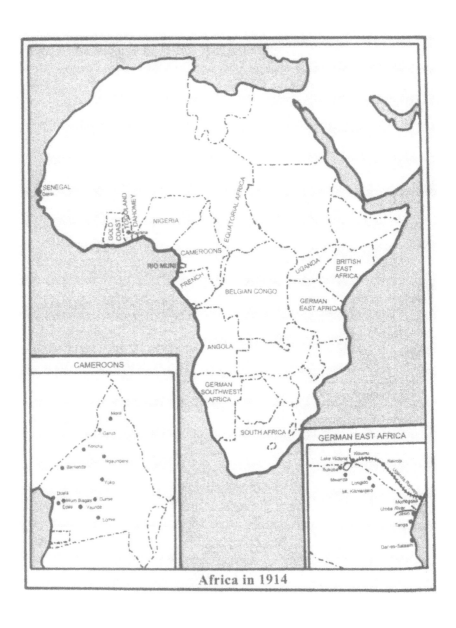

Africa in 1914

impassable terrain. Any expectation that this would be a brief campaign faded.[5]

On the opposite side of the continent, along the Indian Ocean, lay German East Africa (today Tanzania), the largest and richest of Germany's overseas possessions. The struggle for German East Africa proved to be the lengthiest and most difficult of any of the operations in Africa. The German colony bordered Uganda and British East Africa (today Kenya) to the north, the Belgian Congo (today the Democratic Republic of the Congo) to the west, and British Nyasaland (today Malawai) to the southwest. British forces in the adjacent colonies were almost negligible at the start of the war and required reinforcement. The British enlisted whatever natives they could, but, more importantly, transported two brigades of British and Indian troops from India, bringing the strength of their forces to about eleven thousand men. The troops had no experience in bush warfare, and a good number of their senior officers were apathetic old fossils. It did not help that the brigade commanders did not know their regimental officers and that the latter had not seen their troops before embarkation. The commander, acting Maj. Gen. Arthur Aitken, was not a gifted leader, lacking experience, drive, and character. On top of this, he committed the sin of underestimating his foe, expressing open contempt for German officers and their native troops and predicting that he would wind things up by Christmas.[6] He was wrong. His opposite number, Lt. Col. Paul Lettow-Vorbeck was an experienced campaigner, crafty, determined, and thoroughly professional.[7] Isolated and cut off from any hope of reinforcement, he commanded a small contingent of German officers and NCOs and about three thousand natives, the Askaris, who were excellent fighters, familiar with the country, and inured to local disease.

Once the war started, Lettow-Vorbeck sent raiding parties into Uganda and British East Africa. The British responded with similar forays into German territory. After the arrival of the troops from India, the British invaded German East Africa with a two-pronged assault against the vital port of Tanga and the town of Longido, just across the frontier. There was nothing wrong with the strategy, but Aitken ignored local advice and made no effort to learn what he could about the enemy and the terrain where he proposed to advance.[8] The neglect of details in an enterprise is usually a prescription for failure. The British thrust at Longido early in November, intended as a diversion, was known about in advance and easily broken up. In the meantime, an eight-thousand-man force under Aitken landed on the coast and moved against Tanga, which was defended by a force of about one thousand men. Aitken not only suffered heavy losses in an unsuccessful attack, but also left behind most of his supplies and ammunition when he ordered his men back to the ships.[9]

The British reverses at Longido and at Tanga came at an especially bad time. In Flanders, the outcome in the desperate fighting around Ypres was still uncertain; Austria, again invading Serbia, had captured Belgrade; and in a naval encounter off Coronel near the Chilean coast, a German squadron commanded by Adm. Graf von Spee sent two British cruisers to the bottom, leaving not a single survivor. The government had no wish to dishearten the public with more such news, and it was not until several months later that it allowed a censored version of the affair at Tanga to be published. In a move that was hardly surprising, it transferred control of all subsequent operations in East Africa to the War Office.

Aitken was unable to offer a plausible explanation for his thrashing at the hands of a force one-eighth the size of his own. He did not help himself when he gave an inflated estimate of the number of defenders at Tanga, which was found to be inaccurate. Kitchener, already bitter over what the official historian calls "one of the most notable failures in British military history," ordered Aitken to hand over command to his subordinate, Brig. Gen. Richard Wapshare, and return home.[10] Kitchener refused to grant Aitken an interview when he arrived in London. Aitken's career was finished. He was reduced to the substantive rank of colonel and forced to retire on half pay.[11]

It is questionable whether the new British commander was any improvement over the old one. Wapshare is described by Capt. Richard Meinertzhagen, the perceptive British intelligence officer, as a "dear fatherly, old gentleman, kind and considerate," but "he has little military instinct and is nervous of responsibility, mainly because he is hopelessly ignorant on all subjects connected with his profession."[12] Actually, Wapshare had inherited his post by default. Good commanders were at a premium and, at this stage, reserved for the western front. Kitchener does not appear to have had much confidence in Wapshare for he closely supervised his activities. Kitchener's first meaningful directive was to warn Wapshare to postpone any extensive operations until he could be reinforced. As every man was required for more vital theaters, Kitchener could not tell when he would be able to make arrangements to send him more men. For the time being, he instructed Wapshare to maintain his existing position and to improve it by initiating such minor enterprises as might be found practicable.[13]

The Germans, following their twin victories at Longido and Tanga, made incursions into British East Africa, along the coast below the Uganda Railway—which ran from Mombassa to Lake Victoria. In December, Wapshare sent a force of eighteen hundred men to reclaim the region from the enemy. The operation exceeded expectations: the British not only swept the frontier clean, but crossed the Umba River and seized Jasin, a fishing village two miles inside German territory. Not to be outdone, Lettow-Vorbeck struck back, and on January 19, 1915, recaptured the stoutly defended town.[14] Wapshare, who did not possess the strongest nerve, took an exaggerated view of the loss and confided to close associates that he expected to be recalled.[15] Instead, Kitchener sent him a strongly worded telegram, questioning the wisdom of having gone into Jasin at all:

> I think that you ought to . . . give up risky expeditions that may lead to a serious situation being created in East Africa where we cannot reinforce you sufficiently to be sure of success. You are entirely mistaken in supposing that offensive operations are necessary: the experience of Jasin shows that you are not well informed of the strength of the enemy, and this casual scattered fighting is liable to bring about a dangerous situation.[16]

A relieved Wapshare indicated that he would give up the attempt to cling to the border region and would withdraw before the start of the rainy season. He hinted that he would like to resume the offensive as soon as he obtained reinforcements.[17] Kitchener replied immediately, restricting Wapshare to the defensive and ruling out any hope that active operations would be resumed in the foreseeable future.[18]

British operations in Africa had been conducted with local or adjacent resources supplemented when necessary by troops from India. Kitchener used the Indian Army as a sort of "imperial fire brigade."[19] The Commander in Chief of the Indian Army, Sir Beauchamp Duff, worried that the withdrawal of too many of his troops for overseas duty would encourage another mutiny or attacks by Afghans along the northwest frontier. When he complained that his army was being stretched dangerously thin, he received a curt reply from Kitchener:

> I do think you quite realize in India what the war is going to be. If we lose it, it will be worse for India than any success of internal revolution,

of frontier attacks, for there will be no one to reconquer India when it is over, so it will be better for India to see that we win.[20]

Britain's contribution to the imperial war in Africa was confined to paying part of the bill and providing officers and some NCOs to lead the native and Indian rank and file. The War Office was not keen on diverting its limited resources to secondary theaters, although it made somewhat of an exception in the case of Egypt, which controlled the strategically important Suez Canal, the principal route to India and to Britain's possessions in the Far East. It was also, it must be said, Kitchener's spiritual home and the place where he proposed to return should he fail to succeed to the viceroyalty of India at the end of the war.

The Foreign Office did not immediately seek to find a replacement for Kitchener in Cairo and left Milne Cheetham in temporary charge of the British Agency. Kitchener controlled the internal affairs of Egypt, directly through the British Agency until January 1915 and then indirectly after his successor was named. Grey, who should have made the decisions, regularly deferred to Kitchener because he knew very little about Egypt and the Middle East. On one telegram Cairo sent to the Foreign Office, Grey minuted, "Does Lord Kitchener agree? If so I approve."[21] He could have penned the same refrain practically each time a Middle East policy decision had to be taken. Still, Kitchener was careful to elicit Grey's approval of any directive sent to the British Agency.

Just before Kitchener joined the administration, Churchill commandeered two dreadnoughts that the Turkish government had contracted with British shipyards to build in 1911 and paid for by popular subscription. The incident exacerbated the tension that already existed between Britain and Turkey. By the end of August 1914, Kitchener was convinced, as were most of his colleagues, that war with Turkey was highly probable. If it came to war, Kitchener did not see Turkey as much of a military or naval factor. Its army, which was no longer highly regarded, would have to fight on several fronts—in the north against the Russians and in the south against Britain. What concerned him most was the prospect of a concerted effort by the Turks to subvert the loyalty of tens of millions of Britain's Muslim subjects, from Egypt to India. In particular, he worried about the effect it would have on the masses of Muslim soldiers in the British Army. The bulk of the Indian Army was Muslim; the armies of both Egypt and the Sudan were all Muslim.

Kitchener was certain that an attack on the Suez Canal would be among Turkey's first aggressive moves. To do so, the Turks would have to cross the Sinai Desert, which stretched 130 miles east of the canal. No railway or roads fit for wheeled traffic crossed the desert, and, of the possible routes, none normally provided enough water to sustain a large force.[22] A number of military experts in Egypt doubted that the Turks would even try to cross the Sinai, but Kitchener thought otherwise. The most serious problem facing the Turkish crossing would be the water supply, but, as the wells were overflowing owing to the unusually heavy rainfall in the autumn of 1914, there was good reason to think that the desert could sustain much larger numbers than were supposed.

Backed by a mere five thousand troops, British rule in Egypt rested on the collaboration or passive acquiescence of the population. Kitchener feared that if Turkey joined the Central Powers, Egyptian Muslims would find themselves in a dilemma, forced to choose between their British masters and the Ottomans, whose sultan was also the Caliph, that is, the spiritual head of their faith. Kitchener was not at all confident that Egyptians would remain quiet. Reports from Egypt were mixed. Native opinion in urban centers was generally pro-German, and this attitude was almost certain to spread and deepen if Turkey joined the Central Powers.[23] There was also the risk of trouble in the western desert from the Senussi, who had sided with Turkey in the Italian campaign of 1911–1912 in Cyrenaica. However, the countryside appeared relatively content, not out of "sentiment or gratitude," but because agriculturists realized that their only hope of disposing of their cotton crop, Egypt's main export, rested with the British.[24] But even that element of good will began to dissipate in the weeks immediately after the conflict broke out.

The war drastically shrank the cotton market, and the fellaheen's inability to sell their just-harvested crop had serious consequences, not only for the individual growers, but also for the government. The mainstay of the budget was the land tax. If collection fell short of expectation, the budget could not be balanced. In early autumn, there were signs that the fellaheen would default on their tax obligations, placing the state in a dilemma. If the financial authorities postponed the collection of the tax, they could not effectively operate the government. On the other hand, if in the face of default they seized the debtor's cattle and crops, they would cause his ruin. With revenue falling from other sources, the financial department resorted to strong-arm methods to collect the taxes due. This caused dismay among high-ranking British administrators in the government, and Ronald Graham (adviser to the Ministry of Interior), among others, tried in vain to persuade Edward Cecil (financial adviser) "to make some compromise . . . between sound finance and political suicide."[25] In desperation he and others turned to Kitchener. Typical was this letter Graham sent to Kitchener:

> The really excellent feeling towards us which prevails throughout the Provinces has practically vanished and has been replaced by suspicion and mistrust—it has taken about ten days to work the change and the financial situation is almost entirely responsible for it. What has happened is that the Finance [Department] has had to use great pressure . . . to bring in the taxes. The people . . . might have stood the pressure all right only that it coincides with the discovery that they can't sell their cotton at any price and that the Government apparently does not intend to do anything at all to help them. The situation has been pounced upon by the German, Turkish and nationalist agitators who are all over the country—they tell the people that Germany and Austria were only too anxious to buy the whole Egyptian [crop] at a good price but that we will not allow it because we want to beat down prices as low as possible for the benefit of the Lancashire spinners.[26]

Graham went on to explain that he had just seen Hussein Rushdi Pasha (the pro-British prime minister), who was horrified at the adoption of the stringent financial measures. Graham reported:

> [H]e declared that we must be mad, that in a week we had destroyed the work of thirty years, that the fellaheen, our best and only friends, considered themselves betrayed and that, if the Turks attacked us, whereas we had the whole country behind us, we might now have risings anywhere.

Graham observed that he had tried to discuss the problem with a high official in the finance department, but that he "is completely unsympathetic, pooh-poohs the whole agitation and will not realize its serious nature." Graham begged Kitchener to step in and set matters right before it was too late.

Kitchener worked in close collaboration with Grey to resolve this potentially explosive issue.[27] As usual, all his correspondence with Egyptian officials was cleared with Grey in advance. To Cheetham, Kitchener wrote on October 23, "Can you take any measures or suggest anything we can do to help. I am prepared to ask the Treasury to reconsider any decisions taken hitherto that paramount political reasons render necessary. A liberal manner of dealing with the situation seems advisable."[28] Ten days later, Kitchener sent a personal note to Cecil. It ran as follows:

> The present . . . situation in Egypt is one in which everything should be done to ensure that all the sympathies of the various classes of the people are with us. I hope you are taking measures to render our administration as popular as possible by remission of taxation where the people are hard up and by relaxing any stringent financial regulation. . . . You can look upon this as an authority to you to risk considerable deficits in the future in order to conciliate all Egyptians during this period of crisis. It is also most essential that . . . all British officials should work most cordially in their effort to keep the Egyptians with us. I am sorry to hear that lately there has been a distinct change for the worst in the feeling of the people toward us, that this is due to severe action having been taken by the Financial Department in the collection of taxes. I should like to be assured by telegram from you that in this time of stress all is going well with you all in Egypt.[29]

Beginning his career as a soldier, Cecil was the son of Lord Salisbury, whom Kitchener warmly admired. With practically no experience in finance, Cecil had been appointed to his post by Kitchener, principally because he could be counted on to follow orders to the letter. Devoted to Kitchener, Cecil replied that "he would act as directed."[30] Kitchener then wrote to Graham, "I wired Cecil. All things all right now—Most essential that sympathetic attitude should be adopted by all British officials."[31] Measures were taken for the Egyptian government to purchase the cotton on the open market on behalf of the British government and for the finance department to postpone collecting the last installment of the land tax.

The improvement in public feeling was immediate and dramatic. Graham wrote to Kitchener on November 8, thanking him for his intervention, which, along with "the help given by His Majesty's Government, saved the situation here" at a time when "we were rapidly drifting into the position of war against Turkey with the whole population hostile."[32] Cheetham expressed himself similarly, saying, "Results good and public feeling distinctly improved."[33]

Until practically the end, Kitchener retained a slim hope that war with

Turkey might be averted or, failing that, put off as long as possible. He could not spare any troops from France to defend the Suez Canal, and some time must elapse before Empire contingents could reach Egypt. Every week's delay in keeping Turkey out of the conflict meant a corresponding increase in Britain's strength. Furthermore, to avoid inflaming passions among Muslims in the British Empire, Kitchener considered it essential that, if the worst happened, the conflict must be seen as having been caused by the unprovoked action of Turkey.[34] For these reasons, he urged that the Cabinet avoid taking any measure against Turkey that might be construed as provocative. In following such a policy, the British government repeatedly overlooked Turkey's flagrant breeches of neutrality.

On August 31, 1914, Kitchener and Churchill met to consider a Greek offer to place its entire military and naval resources at the disposal of the Entente. Churchill, still smarting from the escape of the *Goeben* and *Breslau*,[35] was very enthusiastic about an immediate strike against Turkey, setting his sights, in particular, on the Gallipoli Peninsula. Such an operation, in his view, would not only lead to the defeat of Turkey, but induce the neutral Balkan states to join the Allies as a united block. Kitchener agreed with Churchill's suggestion that two staff officers from the War Office and two from the Admiralty should examine and work out a plan to capture the Gallipoli Peninsula "by means of a Greek Army of adequate strength, with a view to admitting a British fleet to the sea of Marmora."[36] The idea, as far as Kitchener was concerned, was to make a preliminary investigation, not to start a conflict with Turkey. Still, if Turkey could not be persuaded to remain neutral, there were distinct military advantages to being ready to strike first. If a successful landing on the Peninsula could be effected, Turkey might capitulate, removing the threat to Egypt and the Suez Canal.

Three days later Maj. Gen. Callwell, the DMO, handed Kitchener a report in which he concluded that capturing the Gallipoli Peninsula would be extremely difficult and should not be undertaken with fewer than sixty thousand men.[37] On September 4, Churchill instructed the chief of the British naval mission to Greece to open discussion with the Greek authorities. Constantine, the Greek king, made it clear that he would intervene only if the Bulgarian Army simultaneously attacked Turkey. Soon afterwards, he placed another condition, namely that he would not commit his country to war unless it was first attacked by Turkey.[38]

The project collapsed, and Kitchener turned his attention to other matters.

With Turkey apparently slipping deeper into German hands, Kitchener considered it vital that Egypt should have sufficient troops on hand for its defense and security. After deciding to replace the British Regulars with a Territorial division, Kitchener arranged to send an Indian (Sirhind) brigade to Egypt. If the situation worsened in the meantime, orders would be issued to retain part of the original garrison.[39] Simultaneously, he recalled Maj. Gen. Julian Byng, Commander in Chief of the Egyptian Army, whose services were needed in a more important theater of operations, and appointed in his place Lt. Gen. Sir John Maxwell.[40] It was a wise move, and not because Maxwell was a "Kitchener man." Maxwell did not enjoy Byng's reputation as a field general, but he was a first-class administrator. He had an abundance of common sense, careful determination, and a cheery disposition, and, most importantly, he was thoroughly acquainted with the complex political, religious, and military problems of Egypt, where he had spent the greater part of his career.[41]

In October, the drain on Britain's reserves caused by the desperate struggle on the western front compelled Kitchener to request the dispatch of the Sirhind Brigade, currently on the canal and the only fully trained troops in Egypt. Maxwell was concerned about Turkish activities across the Egyptian frontier. Intelligence reported that in Syria and Palestine roads were being repaired and watering places constructed, strengthening the possibility that the Turks would attempt a massive assault against the canal the moment war was declared. There were also reports that a party of Germans, disguised as Arabs and carrying explosives, had crossed into Egypt and were heading towards the canal at Qantara. Kitchener quieted Maxwell's fears with assurances that steps were under way to send eight battalions and a camel corps from India for the defense of Egypt. The Sirhind Brigade was to remain in place until the first of the Indian reinforcements (the Lucknow Brigade) arrived in Egypt.[42]

Maxwell's forces were confined mainly to guarding the Suez Canal. He had no quick way of knowing when and where Turks would cross the frontier, in the event that they did so, as most of his Arab agents east of the Sinai Peninsula had been arrested.[43] Consequently, he wanted to send out British-led patrols into the Sinai to monitor the movement of Turkish troops.[44] Kitchener, however, prohibited such a move, lest it upset the Turks, but directed Maxwell to destroy the wells in the Sinai. He suggested that Maxwell rely on Bedouin frontier guards to inform him when the Turks crossed into Egyptian territory.[45]

When the severance of relations with Constantinople appeared unavoidable, Sir Edmund Barrow, military secretary to the India Office, submitted a memorandum to the British government in which he urged the landing of Indian troops on Abadan Island, at the head of the Persian Gulf, so as to safeguard the oil works and pipeline and to raise the Arab population of Mesopotamia against the Turks.[46] Kitchener supported the suggestion—with the proviso that no action be initiated as long as Turkey remained neutral—and the British Cabinet gave its approval during the first week in October. Assembling at Bahrain, the Indian forces waited for a formal declaration of war with Turkey (which occurred on November 5) before occupying Abadan.[47] From there, they moved inland, seizing the port of Basra, and by early December, advancing as far north as Qurna, situated at the confluence of the Tigris and Euphrates.[48] The fifty-five miles covered by Indian forces had been accomplished with such ease that some of the British planners looked longingly at the rest of Mesopotamia.[49] The India Office wanted to know what Kitchener thought of an advance to Baghdad? He had firsthand knowledge of the area, and he had undertaken a similar campaign when moving up the Nile to Khartoum. Kitchener replied in the following terms:

> I think we must wait events: a great deal depends on the attitude of the Arab tribesmen. Following the bends of the Tigris river it is about 500 miles from Basrah to Bagdad. We have advanced about 50 miles to Kurnah. . . . Bagdad is an open city of 150,000 inhabitants—The garrison consists of a weak division of probably bad troops—The lines of communication would be important factor in a military expedition to Bagdad but if the Arabs are on our side this problem would be greatly facilitated.[50]

Kitchener, mindful that Baghdad was still far distant and the future uncertain, worried about the possibility of retirement in the face of superior Turkish forces. If Arab help was forthcoming, an advance to Baghdad, in his view, was eminently feasible. But, for the time being, there seemed to be no reason to extend the operation beyond its original limits. The oil installations on Abadan Island were safe, and no worthwhile military objectives lay immediately ahead. The India Office agreed with

Kitchener, at least initially, and came down against the idea of forging ahead.

Since the War Office was periodically called upon to supply assistance, Kitchener was kept informed of the progress of the operations in Mesopotamia. But, except for offering advice when requested, Kitchener made no effort to influence the India Office's policy in Mesopotamia. He had more than enough on his plate without involving himself in matters outside his jurisdiction.

During this period, Kitchener's attention was distracted by events in Egypt. One question that needed to be addressed, after the imposition of martial law on November 2, was the future status of Egypt, since it was nominally still part of the Ottoman Empire.[51] The choices were either to incorporate Egypt into the British Empire or to declare it a protectorate, with Britain replacing Turkey as suzerain. Kitchener and the British Agency were divided over the issue. Kitchener felt that direct control was the safest and most effective course. The officials at the Agency, led by Cheetham, held that a veiled British authority over Egypt would cause the least objections from its people.[52] The one thing both sides agreed on was that the current Khedive, Abbas II, who was clearly antagonistic to the British, should be removed in favor of a more compliant ruler.[53]

Grey, influenced by the dispatches from Cheetham, proposed to recommend the establishment of a protectorate.[54] The matter does not appear to have been debated in London until after the formal declaration of war between Britain and the Ottoman Empire. Kitchener pressed for annexation, and his views prevailed in the Cabinet on November 13.[55] Kitchener informed Maxwell of the Cabinet's decision the following day and ended by saying, "I hope you will agree that this course is the right one."[56] As it happened, Maxwell did not.

After conferring with Cheetham, Graham, and Cecil, Maxwell made a last-minute appeal to his chief. He informed Kitchener that he, along with the authorities at the Agency, were unanimous in their opinion that a protectorate was the most practical solution for Egypt. He pointed out that unless Egypt was promised a measure of self-control, Prince Hussein Kamel, (Abbas's uncle and designated successor) would not accept the throne. Maxwell went on to say that Britain was ill equipped to deal with some of the complex administrative, religious, and judicial difficulties that annexation would raise. Probably his most telling point was that annexation would alienate public opinion and, in view of the state of war with Turkey, oblige Britain to take drastic precautionary measures.[57]

The prediction of dire consequences had a sobering effect on Kitchener, who yielded to the advice of the men whose judgment he trusted. On hearing that Kitchener had reversed his position, Grey sent Cheetham the following message on November 18:

> I understand from a telegram from GOC to Lord Kitchener that you and he and others are all of opinion that the best course is to proclaim a protectorate. . . . I am prepared to authorize this course if you have a decided opinion that it is preferable from the point of view of the internal situation to annexation.[58]

Cheetham's reply, in which he marshaled his previous arguments, confirmed his opposition to annexation.[59] The matter was reintroduced in the Cabinet, and it was decided to defer to the opinion of the men on the spot.[60] A protectorate was formally proclaimed on December 18. On the same day, Cairo announced the deposition of Abbas, who was on holiday in Turkey, and the accession of Hussein with the new title of sultan.

Turkey's entry into the war was accompanied shortly thereafter by the Sultan's proclamation of a jihad, which aimed at igniting revolts among Muslims in Entente territories. For the British, haunted by the Indian Mutiny and more recently by the Mahdist revolt in the Sudan, both of which had been incited by religion, the prospect of a Muslim holy war against Britain was a never-ending nightmare. The challenge was to find a way to convince Muslim subjects within the British Empire that war with Turkey, whose ruler was the spiritual leader of Islam, was not inconsistent with continued loyalty to their masters.

It was a dilemma that caused Kitchener a good deal of anguish. Indeed, even before Turkey formally announced its decision for war, Kitchener was contemplating options to counter the perceived threat to Egypt and India. One way to neutralize, or at least lessen, the effect of the Sultan's call to arms was to enlist the support of other prominent Islamic religious leaders.

While in Egypt, Kitchener had become acquainted with a number of prominent Arab nationalists, including Emir Abdullah, the second son of Sharif Hussein, custodian of the holy cities of Mecca and Medina in the Hejaz district. They had great respect for him, not only because of his reputation, but also because of his known sympathy for Arab causes—as evidenced when, as British agent, he had involved himself in the successful effort to free the Egyptian-born Aziz Ali al-Masri who had been sen-

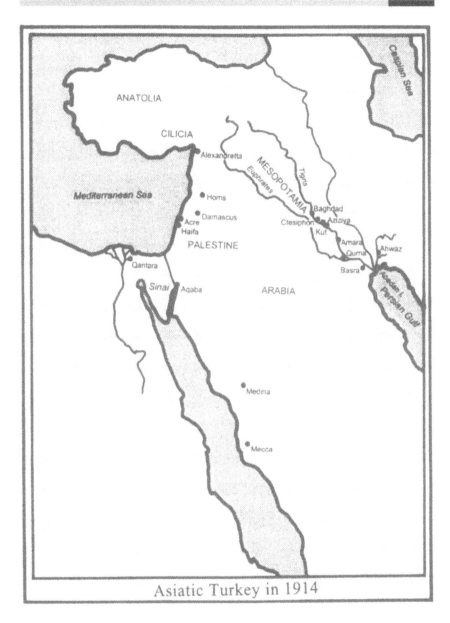

Asiatic Turkey in 1914

tenced to death by the Ottoman government.[61] From them, he learned of
their discontent with the Young Turk regime and their hope of someday
establishing an independent Arab caliphate.[62]

In February 1914, Abdullah had approached Kitchener with the object
of determining his attitude towards Arab aspirations as well as of solicit-
ing British support in the event that the Ottoman authorities tried to
depose his father.[63] Privately, Kitchener cherished the idea of an independent Arab state patronized and controlled by Britain. He had long concluded that the collapse of the Ottoman Empire was imminent[64] and that,
once this became evident, the Arabs would shake themselves free of the
Sultan's grip. In these circumstances, Britain's interest mandated that it
acquire indirect, if not direct, control over Arab lands critical to its position in India and Egypt. All the same, Kitchener gave Abdullah no encouragement, careful as he was not to further strain Anglo-Turkish
relations.[65]

On his way back from Constantinople in April 1914, Abdullah
stopped in Cairo and once again called at the British Agency. Since the
Turks had made it known earlier that they disapproved of such meetings,
Kitchener referred Abdullah to Ronald Storrs, his Oriental secretary.[66]
Angry at the cold reception he had received in the Ottoman capital, Abdullah pressed hard for British support, claiming that rival chiefs in the
Arabian Peninsula would unite behind his father in opposing the Sultan.
He suggested a future relationship between Britain and Arabia similar to
that between the Amir of Afghanistan and the Indian government—in
which the former exercised internal self-rule, but allowed the latter to
control its foreign policy. Storrs, under instructions, told Abdullah that
he could expect no help from the British government.[67]

Kitchener had given the matter no more thought until September 1914
when his memory was jogged by a private letter from Storrs, suggesting
possible cooperation with Sharif Hussein.[68] Kitchener recognized at once
the immense political and military benefits Hussein would bring to
whichever side enlisted his support. His prestige among Arabs was
unique, not only because of his guardianship of the holy places, but also
because he claimed direct descent from the Prophet. He could raise a considerable force with which to isolate Turkish forces in the Arabian Peninsula. There was also the possibility that other parts of the Arab world
would join in the rebellion. Here was a potential for a large uprising that
might seriously strain the Turks without placing much of a drain on
Britain.

Kitchener understood that, once in the war, the Turks would make every effort to rally the Sharif to their side. With the latter's backing, the Turks could use the Arab tribes to attack Egypt and restrict access to the holy cities for the pilgrimage, which every Muslim was commanded to make at least once in a lifetime. Muslims in Egypt and India might not react against Britain for waging war against an Islamic power, but it was less certain that they would acquiesce in the disruption of the pilgrimage that played so important a role in their lives.

Kitchener wasted no time in authorizing Storrs to send a trusted messenger to Mecca to ask Abdullah whether "his father and the Arabs of the Hejaz would be with us or against us" should Turkey be drawn into the conflict.[69] Before receiving a reply, Kitchener was caught up in a broader British initiative in the Arab-speaking region of the Ottoman Empire.

On October 17, the British Agency in Cairo reported to the Foreign Office that intelligence, derived from two influential and reliable Syrian Muslims, confirmed Ottoman military preparations in Syria and the general perception of an imminent attack on Egypt. Cheetham pointed out that German and Ottoman agents were attempting to arouse Muslim feelings in Egypt and suggested that the British government seek out and extend expressions of good will to the ruling chiefs in Arabia to counteract enemy pressure and because their overt support "would have great effect on Egyptian and Senussi Arabs."[70]

Grey showed the telegram to Kitchener and asked him to draft a reply, which was sent the following day:

> You should inform the Arabs that England has always supported the Arabs, and will continue to do so. Great Britain has no quarrel with the Arabs, and even if Turkish Government, forced by Germany, commits acts of aggression against us which necessitate acts of war, England will not consider that the Arabs are involved in this war, unless they by overt acts take part in assisting German-Turkish forces which we have the utmost confidence they will not do even under coercion.[71]

Alerted to what his superiors wanted, Cheetham became actively involved in secret diplomacy to make the Arabs change camps. A few days later, he notified London that prominent members of the Pan Arab movement living in Cairo had approached him about Britain's attitude towards Arab aspirations for self-government should Turkey bring matters to a head. His reply had conveyed the sense of Grey's telegram (as already noted, it was Kitchener who had composed it) of October 18. As a consequence, they had sent agents to communicate the message verbally to Arab chiefs in Arabia, Syria, and Palestine. Cheetham indicated that he had turned over a considerable sum of money to the promoters of the movement, who were also encouraging local Arabs to send letters to their influential friends in these areas, "urging them to do their best to dissuade the Arabs from joining Turkey against their own interests."[72]

A fortnight later, Cheetham notified London that he had it on good authority that the Syrians were anxious to throw off the Turkish yoke. To that end, they would gladly side with the British if they could be guaranteed that France would not occupy Syria.[73] Since the time of the Crusades, the French had established close economic, cultural, and religious ties in the Levant, particularly in the coastal area of Lebanon. The British government was well aware of France's long-standing interest in the region. In fact, in 1913 Grey had acknowledged that Syria was within the French sphere of influence.[74]

Kitchener, unlike the Foreign Office, was not prepared to cede Syria to France, but he had to tread warily for the time being. His reaction to Cheetham's telegram was guarded and contained in a note he sent to the Foreign Office:

> Given the whole, I think, we should leave this alone for the present, and await developments. It will be difficult even to hint to the French any limitations of activity in Syria, while if Bin Saud[75] and the big sheiks move against the Turks, the Syrian Arabs will probably be swept in. It is only if we find Bin Saud and other important people hanging back for the reason here given that I think we should approach the French.[76]

From a different Arab region came good news. On October 30, Storrs's messenger returned to Cairo with Abdullah's answer. The note was guarded, but friendly and favorable. Abdullah hinted that his father would accept a close union with Britain on condition that it agreed in writing to protect the "rights of our country and the rights of the person of His Highness our present Emir and the rights of his Emirate and its independence," as well as promised effective support against any foreign aggression.[77] The following day, Cheetham forwarded the gist of the telegram to London with a request for immediate instructions.

Kitchener drafted the reply, which was transmitted to Abdullah on November 16 through the British Agency in Cairo. The note opened with the announcement that war had broken out between Britain and Turkey. In return for Arab cooperation against Turkey, it promised that Britain would not intervene in the internal affairs of Arabia and would give all possible support against external aggression. It further held out that the Sharif could count on Britain's recognition if he were proclaimed caliph.[78] In translating the message into Arabic, Storrs attempted to clarify some of Kitchener's ambiguous points. In so doing, he gave them a more far-reaching meaning. In particular, he committed Britain to guaranteeing the "independence, rights and privileges" of the Sharif against all external aggression, as well as to unqualified support for an Arab movement and a Mecca-led Arab caliphate.[79] The last point practically arrogated to the British the power to determine the new spiritual leader of Islam. Still, it is unlikely that Storrs went beyond what Kitchener had intended. In a private letter to Grey on November 11, 1914, Kitchener wrote, "Supposing that the Arabs took up arms against the Turks. I think it would be our policy to recognize a new Khalif at Mecca or Medina of the proper race; and guarantee the Holy Places from foreign aggression as well as from all internal interference."[80]

Kitchener saw that Arabia could serve British interests not only during the war, but afterwards. Bringing the caliphate back to Arabia, with Britain as its protector, was part of Kitchener's wider strategy to prepare for the rivalry with Russia and France that he was certain would resume once the war ended. He does not appear to have understood, however, that it was politically unwise for a Christian state to dictate a successor to the Sultan of Turkey. Although Kitchener's professional ability and knowledge of the East was unquestioned at home, in reality, he was no expert on Islam. Both he and his advisers in Egypt thought it was possible for the Caliph to be the spiritual leader only, without understanding that in Islam, all aspects of life, including government, fell within the purview of Mohammed's successor. They missed another important point when they failed to appreciate the extent of Islamic disunity. Finally, they gave exaggerated importance to the stature of the Caliph, who was merely the temporal protector of the Islamic faith and its laws. They saw him as a sort of Muslim pope, more or less capable of uniting the community of Muslim believers under the green flag of Islam. Thus, according to their thinking, the country that controlled the caliphate would enjoy preponderant influence in the Muslim world.

Kitchener clung to the notion that Russia still harbored designs on India. With Russia likely to take possession of Constantinople and other vital areas of the Ottoman Empire at the end of the war, its control of the Caliph would pose a mortal threat to Britain's position in India. Kitchener's defense against such a contingency was for Britain to place its own nominee as caliph at the end of the war. Since the Prophet had been a native of Arabia, it seemed fitting that his successor should come from that region. This would allow the Royal Navy to patrol the Arabian coastline, insulating the Caliph from Britain's European rivals.[81]

Kitchener's note, as modified by Storrs, was carried to Mecca. Abdullah was delighted with its contents, particularly the unexpected and gratuitous reference to the caliphate—a subject he had not broached on his earlier visits to Cairo. He interpreted it as an offer to make his father the ruler of a vast kingdom, such as any caliph would have enjoyed. Any suspicions he may have entertained about Britain's willingness to hold to promises made were allayed by the fact that the note was sent in the name of Kitchener, whose fame in the Middle East, as George Antonius[82] put it, "was then greater than that of any living Englishmen and whose word was accepted without question."[83] Abdullah's answer, which reached Cairo early in December, confirmed that his father would cast his lot with the British. The rupture with Turkey could not take place immediately, however, and he requested time to await a convenient pretext.[84]

For the time being, Kitchener could therefore not count on Arab forces to undertake operations against the Ottomans or to help in the defense of Egypt. In mid-November some of the Indian troops who had recently arrived in Egypt were moved to the Suez Canal, relieving the Sirhind Brigade, which set sail for France on November 23 to join its division. Kitchener, moreover, informed Maxwell that he was diverting the Australian and New Zealand contingents (subsequently known as the Anzacs) to Egypt to complete their training. They were on their way to Salisbury Plain, but the already unmanageable congestion there prompted a last-minute change in plans.[85] Eventually, Kitchener intended to transfer them to France, but in the meantime they would serve as reserves and to impress public opinion.[86] They landed early in December.

There was no contact with Ottoman forces during the last two months of 1914, save for a minor clash near Qantara on November 20. Here, some two hundred Bedouins, approaching under a white flag, fell upon a British patrol, which somehow managed to extricate itself, although not without heavy casualties.[87] The absence of serious fighting enabled Maxwell to deploy his forces properly and to strengthen his defenses. The most recent intelligence reports indicated that a large Turkish Army was moving south through Palestine and would soon be in a position to advance on the Suez Canal.

In London, there was discussion about the possibility of taking action against the Turks as the best way to preempt an attack on Egypt. On November 25, Churchill tried to resurrect the idea of a joint naval and military attack on the Gallipoli Peninsula, which he asserted would ensure British control over the Dardanelles and effectively eliminate Turkey from the war. Kitchener considered the enterprise unfeasible because he lacked the requisite land force to accompany the fleet. Countering with a less ambitious scheme, Churchill proposed a feint at Gallipoli, with the main thrust occurring on another part of the Turkish coast, such as Haifa. Kitchener recognized the value of interrupting Turkish communications, but held that the moment to act had not yet arrived.[88]

It was evident from Kitchener's discussion on November 25 that he felt less anxiety than before about the security of Egypt. Maxwell was preparing to defend Egypt along the line of the Suez Canal, confident that the Turks would be unable to send large forces across the Sinai Desert. He was further encouraged by the Senussis' apparent disinclination to take up arms against the British.[89] The Sultan's call for a jihad against the Entente had failed miserably. The Egyptian people took their transfer from Muslim to Christian suzerainty with remarkable calm, as did the Army. Yet, Kitchener was never really at ease about Egypt or, for that matter, India. His fear of a universal rising among Muslims within the Empire would persist, deeply affecting British Middle East policy throughout 1915.

4

STUMBLING COLOSSUS

KITCHENER would have been more than human if in the past he had not harbored deep suspicions about Russia, but his will to win conditioned his war relations with its military and civil authorities. As a member of a coalition, Britain was obliged to fight alongside of, and in cooperation with, its allies. When devising war policy, Kitchener had to pay particular attention to the needs and wishes of France and Russia. In so doing he worried less about the French than he did about the Russians. Although Britain and France were not bound by a military convention prior to August 1914, staff talks regarding military planning had been going on since 1905. After the war began, Anglo-French armies shared a common front with a commitment to defeat Germany and to reconquer captured French and Belgian territory. While the western Allies frequently argued over practical matters, some of which strained their relationship, their need to stand together ensured the survival of their partnership.

In contrast, Britain had not conducted prewar talks with Russia and had no clear idea of its intentions or strategic plans. The link with Russia was tenuous, held together only by a common foe. Forced to fight alone on two, and later three, fronts, Russia might eventually choose to achieve some of its war aims through a negotiated settlement. That option was not open to either Britain, determined to prevent Germany's hegemony of Europe, or to France, eager to reclaim territory previously lost. Their prospects hinged on keeping Russia in the war.[1]

Kitchener had acquired a newfound respect, albeit a modest one, for the Russian Army. It was reported that a new national spirit and pride in Russia's military had erased the memories of its humiliation at the hands of Japan in 1904–1905. As a result of recent Army reforms and reorganization, Russian military leaders were confident that they could meet the challenge ahead. British and French Army planners had created the myth of a "Russian steamroller," whereby hastily mobilized troops, by sheer weight of numbers, would be able to sweep through any adversary in central Europe. Mindful of the enemy's strength, Kitchener was reluctant to subscribe to such a rosy scenario when all he knew for sure about the Russian Army was that it had access to an almost unlimited supply of manpower. Prior to 1914, Russian leaders had been secretive about their military affairs. Even the French, with whom they had forged an alliance dating back twenty years, were kept largely in the dark.[2]

Fulfilling a commitment to the French, the Russians took to the field within fifteen days after mobilization. As they advanced into East Prussia, they relieved pressure on the Anglo-French armies in the west at a critical juncture. Kitchener was heartened by the early success of the invading Russian armies. What he did not realize was that they suffered from overhasty preparation, grave defects in logistical support, and a lack of coordination at the command level. Nor did he suspect that the Russian Army as a whole would soon be crippled by shortages of munitions and weapons of all types.

The general perception that the war would be brief had led the Russian authorities to spend their money stockpiling guns and shells, rather than adding to their capacity to produce such supplies. Defense had absorbed a disproportionate part of the state's annual revenue in prewar years, and the policy of purchasing war matériel from foreign manufacturers, instead of building up their own armament factories, which in peacetime would lie idle, was a money-saving device.[3]

News emanating from Russia was piecemeal and often misleading. The head of the British military mission at the *Stavka* (Russian high command) was Lt. Gen. Sir John Hanbury Williams, who until recently had served on the War Office staff. He had left London in such haste that the War Office had neglected to provide him with a personal cipher, which meant that his memos and telegrams went through diplomatic channels.[4] It was not a satisfactory arrangement for the security-conscious Kitchener, who desired direct communication with his men on the spot. As it was, messages were liable to be intercepted. Kitchener was less concerned about communications falling into the hands of Russian officials than about the damage done if classified information became public knowledge. The Germans had built up an efficient intelligence service in Petrograd, and they could count on the support of large numbers of influential Russian sympathizers.

The fifty-five-year-old Hanbury Williams owed his appointment essentially to an accident of birth—he came from a prominent family and was a direct descendent of a popular British ambassador to Catherine the Great's court.[5] He was charming and hardworking, perceptive enough to know when things were going wrong, and able to point them out to his hosts without causing irritation or offense.[6] However, his knowledge of eastern Europe was shaky and, more seriously, he spoke no Russian, with the result that he was dependent on such information as his hosts were willing to impart. Grand Duke Nicholas Nicholaievich, Commander in Chief of the Russian Army, objected to allowing secret plans to be telegraphed even in code, to say nothing of his distrust of the discretion of politicians. Consequently, both he and the French-speaking members of his staff provided Hanbury Williams with only vague and general information about their military affairs. To make matters worse, Hanbury Williams received little help from his French counterpart, Gen. de Laguiche, and none at all from the knowledgeable British military attaché, Lt. Col. Alfred Knox, who came to Russia in 1911. Knox was professionally jealous of Hanbury Williams and had as little to do with him as possible. As he had established useful military connections, spoke Russian fluently, and knew the country and its army well, he felt that he should have been given Hanbury Williams's appointment. Capt. James Blair, the outstanding assistant military attaché, was temperamentally different from Knox, but, like him, was conversant in Russian and on excellent terms with Russian military authorities. While Knox was at the front reporting on the activities of the Russian Army, Blair spent most of his time in Petrograd, acting as liaison between the Russian War Ministry and the British Embassy.[7]

Rumors that the Russian Army was experiencing munitions shortages were heard initially in September 1914, but the Russian War Ministry and its artillery department dismissed complaints from field generals as without serious merit.[8] If there were shortages, in their view, it was because the infantry was wasteful or did not know how to use the guns—artillery experts were attached to infantry, but their responsibility was to ensure that the guns were in good working order, not to command them. Thus, it was not surprising that Hanbury Williams and his colleagues were practically silent on the subject in their dispatches to the War Office. If Kitchener's attention had been drawn to the few passing references to the want of munitions, he probably would have attributed it to the improper use of shells or to logistical failure.

Strangely enough, it was from the Japanese, who were providing their former foe with aid, that the War Office received the first direct hint of munitions problems in the Russian Army. The message, arriving in early October 1914, made no mention of rifles or artillery, only that the Russians were likely to run out of ammunition soon.[9] Kitchener was puzzled. As far as he knew, the Russian authorities had not alluded to serious ammunition or equipment needs. It was difficult for him to see how Russia could be running out of ammunition within two months of the outbreak of war. Presumably Russia, like the rest of the Continental powers, had a huge stockpile of munitions. After all, intelligence data seemed to indicate that military spending in Russia in recent years had been higher than in either Germany or France.[10]

Of more immediate concern to Kitchener was finding a way to induce the *Stavka* to reveal its intentions. As he considered the two fronts interdependent, full and constant communication between the two allies was needed. This became more urgent when reports began to come in that Russian forces in East Prussia had met with calamitous defeats.

At the beginning of September, Sir George Buchanan, British Ambassador in Petrograd, telegraphed the Foreign Office that the Russians had received a "severe check" in East Prussia.[11] After fighting that lasted five days (August 26–30), the battle of Tannenberg had ended with the destruction of the Second Russian Army under Gen. A. V. Samsonov. More bad news followed a fortnight later, when Gen. P. K. Rennenkampf's First Army was badly mauled at the Masurian Lakes (September 6–15). The Russians lost nearly five Army corps in these two battles, although the scale of these defeats was not known in London for some time. It was a different matter in Galicia, where the Russians had sent Austrian forces reeling back with staggering losses, uncovering the German flank, from East Prussia to Silesia.[12]

The Russian victory did much to dissipate the gloom caused by Tannenberg, inspiring the *Stavka* to consider an invasion of Silesia through Cracow. Much would depend on future Allied plans in the west. On September 19, Grand Duke Nicholas inquired whether the goal of the Anglo-French armies was simply to expel the Germans from France or to drive into the heart of Germany "in order to dictate peace." If the British and the French agreed on the latter course, he was prepared to disregard the

The Eastern Front, 1914–1915

recent events in East Prussia and, once matters had been settled with Austria, march on Berlin with all the troops that would then be available, even at the risk of leaving open to the enemy the road to Petrograd and Moscow.[13] Kitchener made it clear that the Allies intended to prosecute the war with the utmost vigor and advance as far as possible into Germany. He endorsed the grand duke's plan, observing that it was a bold move, but that with the Russians enjoying a vast numerical superiority, the prospects of success were good.[14]

The German military commander in the east, Gen. Paul von Hindenburg and his brilliant chief of staff, Gen. Erich Ludendorff, recognized the threat to the rich mining and industrial area of Silesia, as well as the need to come to the rescue of their faltering ally to the south. They scraped together a new army (the Ninth) and, using their excellent railroad network, rapidly shifted it to the lower Vistula. On September 24 the Russian minister for foreign affairs, Sergei Sazonov, told Buchanan that the Germans were concentrating in force north of Cracow. Buchanan inquired whether the Russian armies would delay their advance until they could scatter the Germans or, instead, bypass them by advancing south of Breslau. Sazonov replied that the Russians could not march on Berlin without defeating the opposing enemy armies; otherwise, they would expose their flank to an attack. The French, however, urged the grand duke to adhere to his plan, presumably to tie down more German troops in the east.[15] When Kitchener's attention was drawn to the French plea, he assumed that they did not fully understand the military situation on the eastern front. It was evident to him that the grand duke had only one option. While he had enough men to hold back the German field armies in East Prussia, he had to deal with those in front of him before advancing on Berlin.[16] But, divided counsels within the Russian military hierarchy were as much of an obstacle to the invasion of Silesia as the presence of German troops.[17]

As it happened, the proposed Russian thrust never materialized. Toward the end of September, the Germans struck, seizing crossings on the lower Vistula and making rapid progress. By October 12 they were within twelve miles of Warsaw. The city not only had important defensive value, but by capturing it the Germans would be denying the Russians an excellent base from which to launch an invasion of Silesia. The grand duke redeployed his forces, giving top priority to defeating the Germans before taking further action against the Austrians.

Kitchener had little knowledge of what was happening on the eastern front.[18] Hanbury Williams admitted to his chief in a dispatch that he was unable to draw much essential information from the Russian general staff:

> One makes an inquiry for some information and is answered most courteously and promised all possible assistance, so as to leave one under the impression that one is to get anyhow part of what one wants but when it comes to the rock of business the reply is worth practically nothing. I went so far as to suggest that they might cable a message to their own embassy in London for delivery to Lord Kitchener but they did not accept the suggestion which I merely made to prove that I was not asking questions "on my own."[19]

Kitchener's anxiety about the progress of Russian operations was compounded by intelligence reports of German intentions to launch an invasion of Britain from the channel ports.[20] He needed answers quickly. If the Russians were driven back or adopted a defensive posture, he would need to take measures against a possible German invasion of Britain. Alternately, if they intended to go on the offensive, he would feel secure enough to send troops to France. His action was therefore contingent on what the Russians proposed to do. With the approval of the Foreign Office, Kitchener contacted Sir George Buchanan:

> It is most important that we should be kept accurately and continuously informed as to real progress of the fighting on the Eastern frontier of Germany in the next few weeks. Upon this will depend the critical decisions that we shall have to take as regards sending troops abroad or keeping them at home. If the Russians defeat or continue to push back the Germans we can with safety send fresh troops abroad to help French and Belgians. But if there is a deadlock between Russian and German forces and the Germans are able to maintain a defensive line, we must be prepared for an attempt to land German troops in England and if we are misled as to real intention that develops between Russian and Germans and denude this country of regular troops in the winter we may suddenly be confronted with a situation at home that would not only be critical but fatal.[21]

Buchanan spoke to Sazonov and assured him that all military data "received will be treated in the strictest confidence." Sazonov promised to relay Kitchener's concern to the *Stavka*.[22] It had no effect. The Russian chief of staff, Gen. N. N. Ianushkevich, bluntly told Hanbury Williams that the grand duke was giving the British as much information as he could, but that there were certain details he would not disclose. Hanbury Williams resented being treated like a "military attaché of a foreign army," rather than the representative "of an Allied army." He was convinced that the Russians, notwithstanding assertions to the contrary, were more forthcoming with the French. This was, he felt, partly because their military attaché, Gen. de Laguiche, was the doyen of attachés and a close personal friend of the grand duke, and partly because Gen. Joseph Joffre was seen in Russia as the commander of the joint Anglo-French armies in the West.[23]

Kitchener then approached the French government through Sir Francis Bertie, the British Ambassador in Paris.[24] The French government, Bertie replied, was unable to offer any insight into Russia's future military plans.[25] Russia's refusal to cooperate with its allies was handicapping the war effort. Rather than synchronizing their offensives, the Entente partners were acting independently on their own fronts, permitting the Germans to shift their reserves to where they were most needed. Kitchener reflected his irritation with the Russians at a Cabinet meeting on October 14 and a week later, returning to the same theme, stressed that "the movements in both theatres of war are, in fact inter-dependent; and the success of the joint campaign is involved in the concert of plans and cooperation in actions."[26]

In desperation, Kitchener considered sending Gen. Sir Arthur Paget to act as his personal conduit to the *Stavka*, in effect superseding Hanbury Williams. He wrote to Grey:

> I do not like the look of things in Russia and our representatives there, Gen. Hanbury Williams and Colonel Knox, do not apparently inform us of what they ought to be able to see for themselves. It has occurred to me to send Paget who is persona grata with the Emperor.[27]

After interviewing Paget, Kitchener sent a second note to Grey. It ran as follows:

> Would you send something like this to Petrograd [i.e., to Buchanan]. The War Office proposes to send General Sir A. Paget to be attached to the Russian army and take up the duty of keeping us informed through

Hanbury Williams, and Colonel Knox would act under his orders. Sir A. Paget is well known to the Imperial family and would therefore probably be a *persona grata* and obtain the information we require. Please wire if there are any objections to this.[28]

Buchanan sounded out Sazonov, only to be told that Hanbury Williams was well liked by both the grand duke and the Tsar and that the "latter was particularly pleased to have a great grandson of a former British ambassador to the Empress Catherine." Sazonov intimated that the British government was obviously free to replace Hanbury Williams if it was dissatisfied with him, but he doubted that his successor would gain access to more military information. Buchanan reported his interview with Sazonov and ended by saying:

> It is clear from what Minister of Foreign affairs told me . . . that Grand Duke is annoyed with us for pressing for more information than he is prepared to give and I am afraid that if Paget takes General [Hanbury] Williams' place His Imperial Highness may regard it as an attempt to force his hand and that he may be even less communicative than before. . . . My . . . fear is that we may offend Grand Duke who is our only source of information.[29]

On the strength of this note, Kitchener abandoned the idea of sending Paget to Russia. He was pleased to hear that Hanbury Williams enjoyed cordial relations with the grand duke and that he was not the cause of Russia's secretiveness. Kitchener's initiative had at least produced one positive result. The grand duke promised, presumably at the urging of Sazonov, to communicate directly with Kitchener and Joffre, giving them a report of the disposition of his forces and current operations.[30]

Kitchener found, at least for a while, that the *Stavka* was less restrictive in disseminating military information. It may have been because its armies were doing well. Heavy pressure had built up against the Germans before Warsaw. To elude envelopment, the Germans broke off the fighting and struggled back to their starting point.[31] The German offensive had not resulted in any territorial gains, but it had upset Russian plans.

The Russian victory was followed by the entry of Turkey into the conflict. For the Russians this meant another front and a greater strain on their resources. Far from being disturbed, however, Sazonov told Buchanan that his government welcomed the war against Turkey as a golden opportunity to settle the straits question once and for all.[32] Kitchener and his colleagues worried that the *Stavka* would shift much of its military effort to the southwestern and Caucasian fronts, canceling or weakening the drive against Germany at a time when there was desperate fighting around Ypres. The challenge now was to keep the attention of the Russians focused primarily on fighting the Germans.[33] To do so, Grey had to reassure them that their interests could best be served by remaining within the Entente. With the Cabinet's approval, Grey notified Sazonov that, after the defeat of Germany, the matter of Constantinople and the straits would be resolved in accordance with Russia's wishes.[34]

The promised concessions to Russia came at a propitious moment, just when there was a radical shift in German strategy—in effect a reversal of the Schlieffen Plan. During the first part of November, the German high command slackened its attacks against the Anglo-French line as it began transferring large bodies of troops eastwards in an effort to dispose of the Russians. Wielding a club in one hand, the Germans held an olive branch in the other. Through various intermediaries, they approached Russia with offers of a separate peace.[35] Buchanan reported the activities in Petrograd of antiwar groups who were working for a speedy negotiated settlement, but gave assurances that their views were not representative of the Russian government.

The reports of Buchanan, Hanbury Williams, and Knox, however, gave the policy makers in London some reason to worry about the eastern front. On November 11, the Germans attacked the First and Second Russian Armies, which had begun their advance towards Silesia. Driving a wedge between the opposing armies, the Germans nearly annihilated the First Army, and only hard fighting and the timely arrival of the Fifth Army allowed the Second Army to escape a similar fate. Both Russian armies fell back on their supply base at Lódz, with the Germans in hot pursuit.[36] From a variety of sources, Buchanan gathered that the Russians had been "severely handled" before retiring, but he predicted that, as in the past, the German offensive would stall. In his view, the ongoing process of advance and retreat was likely to be repeated in the future, and, while he had no doubts that the Russians would eventually break into Germany, "we must be prepared for their taking some time to do so."[37] Knox and Hanbury Williams echoed Buchanan's observations.[38]

On December 4, Kitchener received a personal appeal from the grand duke, who gave a less than reassuring picture. The Russian commander observed that if the Germans continued to move troops from the west to the east, he would be obliged to abandon his offensive strategy and dig in. To assist his beleaguered men, he requested that the British and French armies resume the offensive, stressing that "in common interest of Allies, order to advance may not long be delayed." In transmitting the message to the Foreign Office, Buchanan complained that the Russian authorities were "so reticent that it was difficult to form opinion as to actual state of affairs." He added that there was a growing feeling among the general public that both Britain and France were not pulling their weight and had allowed Russia to carry the burden of the war.[39]

The news from the eastern front was bad enough, but adding insult to injury was the inference that the Anglo-French authorities had left the Russians in the lurch. To set the record straight, Kitchener asked Grey to transmit the following note to Buchanan:

> In our front a certain number of German troops have been withdrawn but they have been replaced by others and from the latest reports the numbers in our front are still superior to our men. . . . Answers about future operations will no doubt be given by French Government after consultation with Joffre. With reference to your penultimate paragraph surely it is realized in Russia that we have been doing our utmost by sending to France all the regular forces that could possibly be spared and that since the outbreak of the war we have been making the utmost preparation for training and equipping very large forces to be sent abroad as soon as ready. In fact what we are doing is on a scale unprecedented in this century.[40]

The next day, Kitchener sent a telegram to Hanbury Williams, asking him to give his views on the military situation on the eastern front. The head of the British military mission replied immediately. He pointed out that the Germans' excellent railway system enabled them to bring up large masses of troops from France at short notice. While he had no hard evidence, it was his impression that the Germans were withdrawing some of their better-trained divisions in France to fight the Russians and replacing them with inferior troops, since trench warfare did not call for men highly skilled in maneuvering. If that assumption proved correct, it followed that the Germans had given up hope of making further progress in the west and were leaving a containing force there "to set their teeth and tackle the Russians in great force."

Hanbury Williams remarked that, although the Russian soldiers were not equal to the Germans in training and discipline, they were keen and numerous and "could afford to play a waiting game . . . instead of pushing on." If in the near future they were forced to evacuate Warsaw, or even Petrograd, they would only be drawing the Germans into a country with bad communications and a harsh winter, producing a logistical nightmare for them. He reported a recent conversation that he had with Ianushkev-ich, who had expressed himself as quite satisfied with the operations that were winding down. Summing up, Hanbury Williams told Kitchener, "I see no reason to consider the [Russian] position anything but good."[41]

On the surface, Hanbury Williams had reason to feel optimistic. Ini-tially, the Germans had advanced rapidly through the Russian lines, but it was evident that they lacked the numbers to maintain their momentum for long. The fighting before Lódz was confused and ferocious, with nei-ther side appearing to have an advantage. As the battle was drawing to a close, it was reported that the grand duke, after pausing to bring up sup-plies and replacements, had contemplated resuming his offensive into Si-lesia.[42] If he had, he evidently changed his mind, for on December 6 he evacuated Lódz and retired behind the Russian frontier. The Germans followed, but their advanced petered out some thirty miles southwest of Warsaw.

Kitchener remained hopeful that after a respite the Russians would be able to resume the offensive. All such thoughts ended when the Russian War Ministry's artillery department belatedly acknowledged that the Army faced a growing munitions shortage. Kitchener learned of the crisis bit by bit, as the Russians only grudgingly opened up to the British. On December 10, Knox informed the War Office that he suspected that the Russian operations were hampered by a shortage of guns and ammuni-tion.[43] The news from Hanbury Williams was more ominous. In a sudden burst of candor, Ianushkevich had admitted to him that Russia's muni-tions reserves were exhausted. Hanbury Williams's report continued, "Russian factories, though working at full pressure, could not supply deficit. Attempts were being made to obtain these elsewhere, but requisite amount could not be obtained before July." Under the circumstances, Hanbury Williams was told that the grand duke did not want to run the risk of advancing into Silesia until his stock of ammunition and stores had been replenished.[44]

Over the next few days, Russian intelligence noted that the Germans were concentrating fresh troops in the neighborhood of Cracow. Since there was a scarcity of guns and munitions, masses of Russian recruits could not be sent to the front. Accordingly, the grand duke indicated to his allies that he would have to fall back to a stronger defensive position.[45]

On December 20 Kitchener received a personal letter from Hanbury Williams, who was at liberty to express himself more freely than in official correspondence:

> It is a pity that he [Ianushkevich] never spoke out so freely before—however its no use crying over spilled milk and all one can do now is to hope that they will keep us more in their confidence—instead of evidently telling one of trouble after having led one to believe that all was going well. . . . None of us Allies know what they have lost here actually in personnel or material but . . . the Russians will have to remain more or less on the defensive till their wants can be supplied. The C. G. S. in Petrograd had cabled Russian military attaché in London setting forth quite clearly what their actual and pressing requirements were. I am afraid that even if you could help them it would mean some long delay—and then the difficulties of communication with this country now the winter has set in. . . . The Q. M. G. has said this morning to me they had 800,000 men quite ready to go into the ranks, but that they were all hung up thro[ugh] lack of ammunition. . . . The annoying part of it is that I cannot help feeling they must have foreseen this difficulty and did not act quickly enough.[46]

The next day Knox submitted to Kitchener a lengthy memo dealing with the state of Russia's ammunition supply. He complained about the lack of candor on the part of certain high-ranking Russian officials, including the Minister of War, Gen. V. A. Sukhomlinov. In particular, he alluded to an incident in September when Joffre had sent a telegram to the *Stavka*, inquiring whether the resources of the Russian government permitted "the indefinite continuance of the war at the then rate of expenditure of ammunition," and, if it did not, "up to what date did the supply suffice." The Russian high command had replied that "the rate of expenditure of ammunition gave no cause for anxiety."

As best as Knox could determine, the output of factories in Russia amounted to thirty-five thousand shells a day, about ten thousand fewer than the Army's expenditures at the front. He believed that the stockpile of ammunition on mobilization was half of what had been reported and that, in September, the Russians had only two more months' supply. Whether out of blind optimism or an unwillingness to represent things as they were to avoid incurring the wrath of his superiors, Sukhomlinov had failed to make up the shortfall by placing orders abroad.[47]

Kitchener felt certain that that the output of shells in Russia was even lower than the Russian officials claimed. It seemed to him that they failed to take unforeseen difficulties into consideration, not the least of which was the likelihood of strikes.[48] His hunch proved correct. The maximum output of shells from Russia's factories, according to a reliable Russian source, was at most thirteen thousand.[49]

The revelation of Russia's munitions shortages, just when the Russian Army seemed on the verge of turning things around, was disheartening to Kitchener. Much as he wanted to, he could not provide the Russians with quick deliveries of war supplies. All the ammunition and guns that he could purchase, at home and abroad, were more than absorbed by the rapidly growing British Army. Under the current circumstances, Kitchener estimated that the Russians would be, as Callwell put it, "practically hung up for four or five months."[50]

That being the case, Kitchener worried that the Germans would transfer a considerable number of their divisions west for a major assault.[51] If he was to gain some idea of the conditions he would have to face in the west in the coming months, it was essential that the Russians be more forthcoming in their dealings with their allies. Kitchener required to know, first, when and how far Russian forces would be pulling back; second, whether the *Stavka* could estimate how many German divisions on its front would be sent west during the period its armies were on the defensive; and lastly, if the Russians had any clear idea of the severity of German losses during the recent battles in Poland. Grey acknowledged in his telegram to Buchanan that these were delicate questions to ask, but that Hanbury Williams might assure the grand duke that "the secret information" was "for Lord Kitchener personally."[52]

As requested, Hanbury Williams approached the Russian military authorities with Kitchener's questions in hand. Ianushkevich gave brief and sometimes vague answers to the points raised. The Russian Army hoped to withdraw to the Bzoura-Ravka line, but no further than the Vistula. He claimed that before the operations each German company had had between two hundred fifty and three hundred men. German prisoners interviewed stated that their companies had been reduced to between sixty and eighty men. Finally, it was pointed out that the Germans had between twenty and twenty-three corps in the east. The *Stavka* would report any transfer of German troops back to the western front.[53]

Kitchener discussed the latest developments in Russia with Sir John French, who had crossed over from France to explain his future plans to the Cabinet.[54] The conference occurred at Walmer Castle, the Prime Minister's weekend retreat near Deal in Kent. Kitchener expressed his fear that the Russian Army's shortage of war matériel would almost certainly compel it to evacuate the enemy territory it had won and might even necessitate a retirement behind the Vistula, if not the Bug, with the loss of Warsaw and other important strongholds. Once the Germans consolidated their position, they would turn their attention to the western front. Kitchener was not sure that the Anglo-French line could withstand the shock of an all-out enemy assault.

French disagreed with Kitchener's pessimistic outlook. He was convinced that the Germans had lost their best troops and officers and that, even if they were able to drive the Russians beyond the Vistula, which he did not for a moment think possible, no amount of troops they could bring back from the east would enable them to penetrate the Allied front.[55] Witnessing the field marshals' heated exchanges, Asquith chuckled privately over the benefits of having an optimist at the front, balanced by a pessimist in the rear.

At the Cabinet meeting on December 22, the talks, not surprisingly, centered on Russia. Kitchener did not conceal his anxiety. He indicated that he needed more clarification about the real state of the Russian Army and its munitions supply. One Cabinet minister recorded the following in his diary:

> K. told us he could get no news from Russia, but that he believed that Russian resistance was collapsing for want of ammunition, and he had heard the Russian troops had both in attack and defence to rely on the bayonet. . . . Whereas our orders for ammunition placed already provided 20 rounds for every gun, and the French were the same, the Russians only ordered 3 1/2 officially, and unofficially it was only two.[56]

Sir John French, who was in attendance, was invited to give his views. In contrast to Kitchener, he was certain that the Russians would be able to hold their own, and he felt it was more likely that the Germans would become frustrated at their inability to achieve decisive results and would divert troops to the west for a massive assault in the spring against the Anglo-French line. In these circumstances, French proposed launching an offensive along the Belgian coast, while the Germans were still preoccupied in the east. Kitchener had initially shown an interest in the scheme, but, as will be seen later, he changed his mind on learning of Sir John's exorbitant demands for additional men and munitions, which were not yet available. The Cabinet was not impressed either and instructed French to solicit Joffre's opinion on the effect Russia's munitions shortages would have on Allied plans.[57]

On December 27, several days after returning to France, Sir John met Joffre at Chantilly to discuss the state of affairs in Russia. The French commander doubted that the Russian munitions shortage was as serious as Kitchener seemed to think. He pointed out that French manufacturers, as well as the French government, had made arrangements to supply the Russians with considerable quantities of munitions, but that it would take some time for this stock to reach them. The shortages were therefore temporary, and for the next six weeks the Russians would have to remain on the defensive. In the interim, the best way to help the Russians would be to attack in the west so as to prevent the Germans from sending further forces eastward.[58] Joffre showed a lack of concern about Russia's predicament, despite the fact that the French were receiving the same gloomy reports from their representatives in Russia as the British. On the previous day, the French military attaché at the *Stavka* was told, in the presence of Knox, that "a real offensive could not be undertaken till the end of July if Russia had to depend on her own resources."[59] This confirmed what Maurice Paléologue, French Ambassador to Russia, had reported a week earlier.[60] It is probable that Joffre deliberately downplayed Russia's plight out of a desire to wrest as many troops as he could from Kitchener in order to continue his offensive strategy in the west.

It appears that by the time Kitchener received an account of the interview, his own views had changed somewhat. He now began to suspect that the Russians were to a certain extent bluffing. The dispatches from Buchanan, Knox, and Hanbury Williams were no longer filled with gloom and showed that the Russians were doing well in their operations. Questions he had put to the Russian authorities, which would have helped clarify matters, went unanswered. Kitchener learned, moreover, that the Russian military attaché in London, although kept in the dark by his own government, presumed that the Russian Army had a sizeable stock of reserve ammunition. It may be, Kitchener felt, that Russian authorities were exaggerating their munitions problems because they were trying to obtain a loan of £40 million from the British government. "Anyway," Kitchener told French, "their action in the field does not look as if they were as badly off as they make out."[61]

Even if things were not as ominous as they first appeared to be, Kitchener understood that Britain faced the prospect of having to provide both funds and arms to Russia to enable it to remain an effective member of the coalition. As 1914 came to a close, it was apparent that the Russian steamroller was not the trump card that many had predicted it would be. Nevertheless, Kitchener continued to cling to the belief that the Russian Army, notwithstanding serious weaknesses, was essential to victory. For as long as Russia remained a viable partner, it guaranteed the Entente a superiority of manpower and, equally importantly, obliged the Central Powers to divide their forces between two fronts.[62]

5

THE EARLY TEST OF LEADERSHIP

MOST members of the British Cabinet remained under the impression that the dispatch of the BEF to northern France did not imply the beginning of a major land commitment. They assumed that if the French were routed in the initial encounters, the BEF could retreat to the coast and sail back home.[1] Kitchener, however, recognized that such a course would shatter the solidarity of the Entente and lead to defeat. He was determined to keep the British Army in France until the Germans were "completely crushed."[2]

Although small, the BEF, according to Brig. Gen. James Edmonds (the official historian), was the best-trained, -equipped, and -organized army Britain had ever sent abroad.[3] With all due respect to Gen. Edmonds, his statement, which omits any assessment of the higher commands, would be true only if the BEF had been called upon to play a limited role in a conventional war. To be sure, the rank and file of the BEF were highly disciplined Regulars with rigorous training in rifle marksmanship, and its regimental officers were generally reliable. On the other hand, its preparations were insular, almost parochial, without arrangements made to provide the means to carry out its Continental commitments.[4] As the British Army was in the process of transition, from colonial to European warfare, it had not developed a doctrine of its own before 1914, simply fastening onto that of the French—the offensive under all circumstances. Moreover, its staff officers and many of its field generals were inadequately prepared for the conditions of 1914.[5]

It is perhaps an exaggeration to say that the Chief of the General Staff, Lt. Gen. Sir Archibald Murray, was a nonentity, as he was described by some of his contemporaries,[6] but he was not the right man for the job. He was cultured and intelligent, but his health was frail, as he had never fully recovered from a serious wound in South Africa. Nor did he possess strength of character. If he disagreed with his superior, rather than admit it, he would weakly acquiesce in order to avoid a confrontation. Lacking the requisite physical and mental toughness, he was apt to faint in a crisis (as he would on two occasions during the great retreat in August 1914).

Murray's superior, Field Marshal Sir John French, was hopelessly out of his depth as commander in chief of the BEF. A short, stocky cavalryman, French owed his rise to eminence to his exploits in the Boer War, particularly to his spectacular charge, which had cleared the road to Kimberley. He was unquestionably a brave man, and he enjoyed a good rapport with the rank and file, inspiring respect and affection. On the debit side was his inexperience in staff work and handling large bodies of troops, lack of mental acuity, massive insecurity, disdain for the study of military strategy and tactics, and mercurial temperament. Added to his liabilities was his inability to speak or understand French, despite his surname. When he tried to read a speech in French after witnessing French Army maneuvers in 1910, the audience began to call out to its military attaché, *Huguet traduissez, traduissez.* The field marshal had so mangled the language that the French thought he was speaking English.[7]

There were few senior British officers who liked or respected French, although he was popular with the public. He owed his appointment essentially to political and personal considerations. His resignation in the wake of the Curragh incident had raised his stock in the eyes of Asquith, who had been appalled at the behavior of the mutineers.[8] At the time Asquith had promised French that, should Britain be involved in a Continental war in the near future, he would be appointed to lead the BEF.[9] On July 30, 1914, the appointment was officially confirmed.[10]

Kitchener played no part whatsoever in French's selection, which had occurred a week before he entered the War Office. If the decision had been left up to Kitchener, it is safe to say that French would have been given a lesser command, if he had been given one at all. Fifteen years earlier, Kitchener had been French's commanding officer in South Africa. By the time the Boers capitulated, Kitchener had become disillusioned with French. In command of the cavalry, French had shown energy, resourcefulness, and resolve during the first half of the war. Kitchener could not have been more pleased with French's work and said so in his communications with London.[11] Indeed, when Kitchener found out that French's next assignment would be the Aldershot command, he wrote to the Secretary for War, warmly commending him on his choice.[12] French was one of the few field commanders whom Kitchener left alone, trusting him to do the job on his own. Kitchener's opinion would change after he transferred French to Cape Colony in the summer of 1901 to hunt down the last Boer commandos in that territory. Perhaps because of the tedious nature of his assignment, French's movements during this period lacked the characteristics of his earlier operations. Kitchener tried to urge French on, only to be put off each time with a healthy dose of "soothing syrup." Kitchener complained to Roberts in January 1902, "French has not done much lately in the colony. I cannot make out why, the country is no doubt difficult but I certainly expected more."[13] According to Edmonds, then an intelligence officer on Kitchener's staff, "Kitchener would gladly have sent him home, but did not feel himself quite strong enough with the British public—which had made a popular hero of French after his ride to Kimberley—to do so."[14] After the South African War, the two soldiers went their separate ways and their professional paths did not cross again until August 1914.

It is interesting to speculate as to whom Kitchener would have selected to command the BEF, if he had occupied the War Office when the decision was made. In my view, he would have picked his loyal and trusted protégé, Gen. Sir Ian Hamilton. At sixty-two and approaching retirement, Hamilton's experience was longer and broader than that of any serving officer in the British Army. He spoke French, which was a valuable asset in dealings with Joffre, the French commander in chief. He was courageous, imaginative, resilient, and a capable tactician. A genuine intellectual and gifted writer, he was, moreover, a decent, charming and kindly individual. Hamilton hero-worshipped Kitchener, under whom he had served in South Africa, and there existed a close, if unacknowledged, bond between the two.[15] Hamilton's appointment would have permitted Kitchener to work hand in hand with the BEF's commanding officer and to play an active role in planning operations in the west. As it was, Kitchener was saddled with a soldier he did not think was fit to hold the highest command in wartime.

Although the BEF was subsumed into French strategic planning, Kitchener was opposed to placing it formally under Joffre's orders, even though it is a well-known axiom in the Army that unified military direction is immeasurably preferable to divided leadership. In fact, Kitchener's long-range goal was to establish a single command (possibly with himself as the directing authority) as soon as Britain's Army had grown large enough to dominate the western coalition. In August 1914, however, he was willing to allow France, by virtue of its predominant army, to have the leading voice in shaping the alliance's strategy.

Kitchener's instructions to French reflected his concern about the need to preserve the BEF as a nucleus for the future.[16] But, as John Terraine has pointed out, in view of the novelty of the situation and the unforeseen imponderables, "their wording was in places necessarily vague and even contradictory," sowing the seeds of "controversies that would bedevil the British Command throughout the war."[17] Kitchener stressed that since the numerical strength of the British force and "its contingent reinforcement" was strictly limited, it was vital to exercise "the greatest care towards a minimum of loss and wastage." Sir John was warned not to run risks or expose his army to a superior enemy force without first consulting the War Office. He was told that, while he was to cooperate with General Joffre, his command was to be "entirely independent."[18]

Things got off to a bad start. Gen. Sir James Grierson, the capable, but overweight, commander of the Second Corps, died suddenly of a heart attack in a train on the way to the concentration area.[19] French at once wired Kitchener, asking that Grierson be replaced by Gen. Sir Herbert Plumer, head of the of Northern Command.[20] Kitchener ignored Sir John's request and instead sent out Gen. Sir Horace Smith-Dorrien. It was a controversial choice, and not because Smith-Dorrien was unequal to the task. Quite apart from the fact that a commander was normally given a subordinate of his choice if at all possible, it was common knowledge in the Army that Smith-Dorrien and French disliked one another intensely.[21] Kitchener never offered French an explanation, other than to say that Plumer could not be spared at the moment,[22] a statement challenged by Callwell.[23] According to Sir George Arthur, his chief selected Smith-Dorrien because he feared that Plumer, for all his professional ability, was not sufficiently independent minded. Given Kitchener's belief that the BEF's position on the left of the French exposed it to serious danger, he wanted a corps commander with sound professional judgment and robust moral courage "to resist an order which, if implicitly obeyed, might spell disaster."[24]

Kitchener had good reason to be extra cautious. By August 14 information from Belgian sources pointed increasingly to the concentration of German strength in northern Belgium. Tailoring facts to fit his preconceptions, Joffre dismissed these reports as exaggerations. His only response was to allow Gen. Charles Lanrezac to shift his Fifth Army west of the Ardennes, into the triangle formed by the juncture of the Meuse and Sambre Rivers. He had no intention of abandoning his offensive in Lorraine and the Ardennes, confident that the German sweep in Belgium was limited in scope and could be held up by the rivers and by the forces of that country with minimal Anglo-French help.[25] If the German right wing turned out to be more powerful than had been supposed, Joffre proposed to check it by sending Lanrezac's army along with the BEF. Without reference to the British, Joffre had fundamentally modified the BEF's role, from supporting the French offensive in Belgium and Luxembourg to possibly participating in a risky counteroffensive against enveloping enemy forces of undetermined strength.[26]

French accepted the change of plans without demur when he met Joffre for the first time on August 16. The next day, Sir John reported enthusiastically to Kitchener that he was very impressed by the French general staff and that he had arrived at a "complete understanding" with Joffre, but he gave no details of their arrangement.[27] Although French had been directed to keep the War Office informed of all important developments as they occurred, he withheld that vital piece of information until the eve of the battle—when it was too late for Kitchener to object.

Lacking sound judgment, Sir John showed himself to be as myopic as his French counterpart. Inspired by Joffre's robust confidence and subjected to a daily dose of Francophile infallibility by Maj. Gen. Henry Wilson, his Svengali and deputy chief of staff, Sir John saw no reason to doubt GQG's estimates, even though it meant turning a blind eye to his own aerial reconnaissance, which reported the presence of long columns of German troops marching southwards from Brussels, bearing down outside of Lanrezac's army.

Kitchener, with only the Belgian reports to digest, lay awake at night, powerless to stop what he feared was an impending disaster. On August 19, he gave the Cabinet a military appreciation, which the Prime Minister disclosed in brief terms to his attractive confidante, Venetia Stanley: "He [Kitchener] thinks that the Germans are coming round in a big enveloping movement, & will try to break through into France over the frontier between Maubeuge and Lille."[28] Everything would then hinge on the resistance of Namur, which Kitchener assumed would hold out for some days, possibly as long as a fortnight.[29] While the fortress did so, there existed the possibility of dislocating the German right wing by striking its inner flank.

On the same day (August 19), Kitchener reminded French of his prediction: "The movement of the German right flank through Belgium, north of the Meuse, which if you remember I mentioned as likely to happen, seems to be definitely developing."[30] Within twenty-four hours Kitchener sent French another wire, saying that he was sending him a fifth division and adding:

> I hope you will let me have . . . an idea of how your own and the neighbouring French forces are disposed. I think the French ought to reinforce all they can so as not to allow penetration between Maubeuge and Lille without considerable resistance. If held there and you are on their flank, they ought to be in an awkward position. All depends on the French holding on to the south of Namur: this is vital.[31]

French's only response to the two notes was a brief message to the effect that he had a fair grasp of the military situation, and, as far as he could tell, "I regard it as quite favorable to us."[32] Hardly reassured, Kitchener persisted in trying to elicit additional information from French:

> You know everything about the formidable German force advancing through Belgium and I trust the French have massed sufficient troops to resist it. . . . I very much hope that the messenger this evening will bring something from you about the situation on our side to meet the German onslaught. The absolute secrecy maintained does not enable me to judge for assistance whether certain risk should be run and the 6th Division sent off or not—and I feel my responsibility rather acutely. Pray relieve me if you can by letting me know what forces (and some idea of how disposed) the French may have ready to resist the northern attack. Remember except what you told me in your last [letter] I know nothing. If you cannot give me details something in general terms that you are satisfied with the situation would relieve me of some anxiety. Anything you send me I will keep absolutely secret.[33]

On August 22, French forwarded a long message to the War Office, crammed with military news and data. After a rundown of the disposition of the Allied forces, French discussed the relative strength of the opposing armies on his part of the front. The German turning movement in Belgium was estimated at six Army corps, three cavalry divisions, and two or three reserve divisions. Arrayed against this force was Lanrezac's Fifth Army, composed of five Army corps, three cavalry divisions, and two reserve divisions, as well as the two corps of the BEF. After leaving contingents to cover Antwerp and Namur, French believed that the Germans could bring only five and a half corps and three cavalry divisions against the Allies, whose forces totaled seven Army corps and four cavalry divisions. That being the case, the Allies enjoyed a comfortable numerical superiority, not to mention that behind their frontline forces stood the heavily defended fortress of Maubeuge and a strong garrison of French Reserve and Territorial troops protecting Valenciennes.

French outlined Joffre's plan, and for the first time disclosed the changed role of the BEF. He noted that Joffre's thrust in the Ardennes was already underway and that the French Fifth Army and the BEF would soon be advancing against the German flank marching through Belgium. Early reports showed that the Germans were not pressing their attacks on the Sambre between Namur and Charleroi. French ended by saying that the concentration of the BEF had been completed and that his men were in the highest of spirits.[34]

Kitchener breathed a sigh of relief when he read the note, which reached him at 8:00 P.M. on Sunday, August 23. His big fear that the Germans would strike while the BEF was in the process of assembling had been removed. There was also encouraging news in other areas of his concern. The Allies appeared to be numerically superior to the Germans on the left flank, and the absence of strong enemy pressure between Charleroi and Namur suggested that the French would be able to retain control of their pivotal position to the south. Much comforted, Kitchener concluded that perhaps his fears had been groundless after all. As he was about to retire for the night, he turned to a friend and said, "Nothing is certain, but I think we may have really good news in the morning."[35]

Kitchener's optimism was short-lived. The German armies north of the Meuse totaled thirteen corps, instead of the six or so corps estimated by GQG. The BEF itself faced not one or possibly two corps, as was supposed, but three, with another close behind. Plunging into the unknown, the BEF ran into the German First Army, which was advancing in a southwesterly direction in order to swing around and envelop the French. The British took up a position on the Mons Canal, an extension of the line of the Sambre, on Lanrezac's left. British riflemen laid down such a

Western Front at the Close of 1914

swift and murderous hail of fire that the Germans, believing they were
facing a mass of machine guns—actually the BEF, like the German
Army, had two machine guns per battalion—broke off their assault. On
the afternoon of August 23, Sir John learned that the supposedly impregnable bastion of Namur, its forts smashed by heavy howitzers, had fallen,
and that the French Fifth Army had been roughed up. Sir John meant to
stand on the same line the next day, but in the evening he discovered,
through a British liaison officer, that Lanrezac, without bothering to inform him, was preparing to retire.[36] Although Lanrezac's move was inevitable in view of the state of the Fifth Army and its precarious position,
his callous disregard of his ally was inexcusable. French, with one of his
flanks already exposed, was in danger of finding his other unprotected as
well. Clearly, he had no alternative but to withdraw.[37]

Sir John's anger with Lanrezac, fuelled by the complete debacle of

Joffre's offensive on the frontiers, turned into hostility towards the entire French Army. Sir John's main concern was to save his army from annihilation, even if it meant acting independently of his unreliable French ally. In the early hours of August 24, Sir John informed Kitchener of the action at Mons and of the tenacious resistance by his men. However, he pointed out that, as Namur had fallen and Lanrezac's army had been driven back, he was ordering a general retreat. "I think," he concluded, "that immediate attention should be directed to defence of Havre [British base at Le Havre]."[38] What Sir John proposed to do after he reached the coast was not clear.

Kitchener was startled by the announcement, which confirmed his fears about GQG's plan of campaign and the quality of the French Army. Nevertheless, he remained imperturbable[39] at a time when some of his colleagues were in a state of panic. At a session of the Cabinet on August 24, Charles Hobhouse, the Postmaster-General, entered the following comment in his diary: "LlG [Lloyd George] was for 'taking the people into our confidence,' in other words scaring them out of their senses. If things go wrong he will try to cut us adrift of our allies, and make terms at any price."[40] Kitchener disregarded this irrational outburst, but indicated that it might become necessary for Sir John French to retreat to a fortified position across the Cherbourg Peninsula. He unveiled a scheme which, with the inclusion of Territorial and colonial troops, plus overseas garrisons, would enable him to put between six and seven hundred thousand men in the field by the spring of 1915. For the time being, he would wait on events and hold back the Sixth Division in case the French had to be extricated.[41]

On August 25 Kitchener wired Sir John, congratulating him on his men's steadiness and achievements and allowing him discretion to conduct the BEF's line of retreat. Kitchener requested that Sir John keep him advised of Joffre's new plans.[42] Sir John's telegram that same day, which indicated that the retreat had begun and was proceeding in good order, discussed the spirit of his men, who, in his words, were behaving "quite magnificently," but revealed nothing about Joffre's future strategy.[43] This prompted Kitchener to repeat his request, but with a greater sense of urgency:

> It is vital that at the earliest possible moment we should have some reliable information as to General Joffre's intentions. The constant retirements that are taking place and the failure to stand in position or take

the offensive appear to show that there is something seriously wrong
with our allies, and, as far as I can see, if these tactics continue, they will
shortly put the Germans in a position of such superiority that the campaign in France will in effect be lost, and our present form of cooperation will then cease to be effective. Please give me at once your candid
opinion on the future resistance that may be expected from the French
Army. Are they broken or what has happened to them?[44]

Late in the morning on August 26, French held a meeting with Joffre
at general headquarters (GHQ) in St. Quentin in an atmosphere that was
markedly less cordial than that of their first encounter. If Joffre's new plan
of campaign was to work, he needed British cooperation. What he had in
mind was a rearguard action by the Fourth and Fifth Armies, as well as
the BEF, in order to gain time while he organized a new army, the Sixth,
on the Somme, with which to launch a counteroffensive against the enemy's right flank.[45] Sir John, however, refused to take part in any maneuver
that would put his army at risk and insisted on continuing the retreat. His
men were weary, and he did not want to place himself in a position that
would preclude an escape to the coast in case of a French collapse. The
meeting broke up with feelings running high on both sides.[46]

On August 27, Kitchener received word that on the previous day
Smith-Dorrien, claiming that his men were too exhausted to continue the
retreat, had turned and fought at Le Cateau. The Second Corps had repulsed all enemy attacks, and, in the early hours of the morning of August
27, had withdrawn from the battlefield, having shaken off the German
pursuit.[47] It was not known at the time that the Second Corps, by its gal-
lant stand at Le Cateau, may well have saved the BEF from destruction.
Kitchener's faith in Smith-Dorrien's ability to react sensibly in a crisis had
paid greater dividends than anyone could have imagined.[48]

French reported only a few minor skirmishes on August 28, and on
August 29 indicated that the BEF had halted and rested all day.[49] Ever
since Mons, Sir John had constantly complained that the French had left
him to withstand the enemy's hammer blows without providing any
meaningful help. Kitchener accordingly dispatched a strongly worded letter to Joffre on August 29, hinting at the want of French cooperation and
urging him to make a determined stand.[50]

Joffre did not need to be reminded that his only salvation lay in a
successful counteroffensive, but he exercised no jurisdiction over the BEF,
which formed a necessary component of his plan. He was even more trou-

bled on reading Huguet's pessimistic reports, which questioned the viability of the BEF, in light of the action at Le Cateau, and revealed the possibility that it might retire to Le Havre.[51] To relieve pressure on the British, Joffre gave orders for the Fifth Army to pivot west and attack the flank of the German First Army. French rejected Lanrezac's request to mount a diversionary attack in order to hold the German First Army in place. Distrustful of Lanrezac, Sir John would not take the chance of being left in a dangerous forward position a second time if the Fifth Army were to retreat again. Besides, French believed that his men were extremely fatigued and should take advantage of the respite the operation was designed to give them.[52] On August 29, Lanrezac turned about and struck the pursuing Germans hard (in what came to be known as the Battle of Guise), then cleverly disengaged his army and slipped away.[53]

French's telegram to Kitchener on August 30, describing Lanrezac's successful counterattack near Guise, came as more good news. Kitchener could see that the BEF was slowly inching beyond the reach of the pursuing Germans. British losses turned out to be less severe than he had anticipated, and reinforcements, already sent from home, were more than enough to replace them. The two French armies were in close contact, with the Fifth Army on the right of the BEF and the rapidly gathering Sixth Army on the left. The Allies now appeared to be working together cordially, having surmounted the difficulties and strain inherent in an enforced retirement.[54] All in all, Kitchener was encouraged to think that the stage was set for the Allies to turn things around, that sooner or later circumstances would permit them to resume the offensive. He was not ready for what occurred later in the day.

Joffre had received reliable intelligence that thirty-two trains loaded with German troops were on their way to the eastern front. Concluding that German pressure on the Anglo-French force would inevitably diminish, he ordered his commanders not to yield any ground unless absolutely necessary. The Fifth and Sixth Armies could not carry out their mandates if a gap existed between them. Accordingly, Joffre urged French on August 29 to slow his retreat so that the French armies on either side of him could catch up.[55] But, with the return of the German First Army to the vicinity of the BEF, Sir John was reluctant to keep in line with the flanking French formations, given that he considered the one on his left untested and the other on his right unreliable.[56] The intense strain of the past ten days had taken its toll on French, plunging him into deep despondency. He could think only of saving his army and cutting himself adrift from the French. He told Joffre, but not Kitchener, that his men were in no condition to fill the gap between the two French armies and that he intended to retreat southwest behind the Seine River in order to allow them to rest and refit.[57] "Much dismayed . . . we must go to Havre and home," wrote Maj. Sidney Clive, French's liaison with GQG, in his diary.[58]

On August 30, through Maj. Gen. F. S. Robb, the BEF's inspector-general of communications, Kitchener learned of French's designs.[59] Kitchener was stunned as Sir John's last message, only a few hours earlier, had been quite hopeful. Kitchener queried French about the meaning of Robb's telegram.[60] French confirmed that he proposed to quit the battle line to give his weary men much-needed rest. He attributed this decision to his disenchantment over the continued French retirement. He then proceeded to blast Joffre's policy: "I should have liked to have assumed a more vigorous offensive at once, and this has been represented to him, but he pleads in reply the present inability of the British Army to go forward as reasons for retirement and delay." He concluded, "I have no idea of making any prolonged and definite retreat."[61] Sir John followed up this letter with a second in which he adopted a similar tone:

> My confidence in the ability of the leaders of the French Army to carry this campaign to a successful conclusion is fast waning, and this is my real reason for the decision I have taken to move the British Forces so far back. . . . I feel most strongly the absolute necessity for retaining in my hands complete independence of action and power to retire on my base when circumstances render it necessary. . . . I have been pressed very hard to remain, even in my shattered condition, in the fighting line; but I have absolutely refused to do so, and I hope you will approve of the action I have taken. Not only is it in accordance with the spirit and letter of your instructions, but it is dictated by common sense.[62]

Sir John was wrong on both counts. In the first place, it was not consistent with Kitchener's instructions. Giving priority to the safety of his own force over rendering support to a beaten ally was one thing, but leaving the French in the lurch in their most desperate hour was quite another. On the last point, moreover, the idea that somehow he could slip out of the line and return at his convenience days later shows that he did not understand the real nature of the conflict. The British Army could not afford to replay the Boer War, where defeat in battle or loss of a stronghold was relatively insignificant in the overall picture. Retreating towards the coast would have left the Fifth Army's left exposed to the German First Army's wheeling movement from the north and almost certainly would have spelled defeat for the French.

Kitchener may be forgiven if he questioned the state of Sir John's mind after analyzing the two telegrams. They were badly worded, confusing and, at times, contradictory. If, for example, the Army was too weak to remain in the front line to fight defensively, how could it be ready to mount a vigorous offensive? Equally disturbing was the inference that a breach had occurred between French and Joffre. Although alarmed, Kitchener sent French a delicately worded telegram:

> I am surprised at your decision to retire behind the Seine. Please let me know, if you can, all your reasons for this move. What will be the effect of this course upon your relations with the French Army and on the general military situation? Will your retirement leave a gap in the French line or cause them discouragement, of which the Germans might take advantage to carry out their first programme of first crushing the French and then being free to attack Russia?[63]

That done, Kitchener hurried off to a Cabinet meeting, which Asquith had summoned at his request. After reading French's telegrams, he stressed the serious political and military implications that would flow from the BEF's departure from the battle line. It would threaten the cohesion of the alliance and almost certainly bring about France's defeat. If France were compelled to capitulate, Britain would also lose the war. In short, Britain could not escape from its obligations to France, even though it meant imposing restrictions on the BEF's freedom of action. Kitchener characteristically appears to have been at some pains in explaining his case. There followed a heated debate.[64] The Cabinet had assumed at the outset that, if the war took a turn for the worse, the BEF would be pulled out of France. Much sympathy was expressed for both Sir John's difficulties and his motives for his proposed move. Grey was among several ministers who felt that perhaps French ought to be given a free hand. But Asquith understood, if they did not, that pragmatic reasons precluded a rupture with the French. In the end, the Cabinet, by a near unanimous vote, authorized Kitchener to instruct Sir John to adhere to his original instructions.[65] Kitchener returned to the War Office where he wrote out a second message to French:

The Government are exceedingly anxious lest your force, at this stage of
the campaign in particular, should, owing to your proposed retirement
so far from the line, not be able to co-operate closely with our Allies and
render them continual support. They expect that you will, as far as possible, conform to the plans of General Joffre for the conduct of the campaign.[66]

Kitchener waited on tenterhooks all evening for Sir John's reply. It
arrived shortly before midnight, and Kitchener ordered that it be read to
him word for word as deciphered. "If the French go on with their present
tactics," Sir John wrote, "which are practically to fall back right and left of
me, usually without notice, and to abandon all idea of offensive operations, of course then the gap in the French line will remain and the consequences must be borne by them." The Second Corps was "shattered," as
a result of which the BEF was in no condition to withstand an attack by
even one German corps, let alone two or three. He went on to say that an
offensive movement lay open to the French, which probably would enable
them to close the gap by uniting their inner flanks. But he doubted that
they would take advantage of such an opportunity and thought it was unfair to ask him to run the risk of "absolute disaster" in order to save them
a second time. His only concession was a pledge to limit his withdrawal
north of a line running east-west through Nanteuil, as long as the French
held their current position. "I think you had better trust me to watch the
situation, and act according to circumstances," French concluded.[67]

Sir John had sought to justify his action by misrepresenting the
facts—a pattern he would often repeat throughout his tenure as commander in chief of the BEF. The French were far from beaten, and Joffre,
contrary to allegations that he had no plans other than to withdraw, was
actually trying to organize a counterattack to hurl back the invaders. Ironically, it was Sir John's refusal to cooperate that had militated, at least in
part, against Joffre's resumption of the offensive. Moreover, even someone
as imperceptive as Sir John ought to have foreseen that Joffre would have
courted military disaster if he had tried to close the gap in the line by
bringing together the inner flanks of the Fifth and Sixth Armies.

Kitchener's anxiety was not relieved by French's note, which reiterated, in a petulant tone, his reasons for an independent movement. In
Kitchener's view, a retreat to the coast was out of the question. While he
had abhorred Joffre's prewar battle plan, he understood that, for good or
for ill, the protection of British interests and the security of the BEF were

inextricably tied to the fortunes of the French Army. In the first days of
the war, he had told Abby Hunter, the sister-in-law of Gen. Archibald
Hunter, a close friend and former subordinate, that it was the "duty of
civilization to crush the overbearing Prussians" and relieve the world of
their constant menace. "And we shall do it or die in the attempt."[68]

No longer able to rely on Sir John's judgment and military instinct,
Kitchener made up his mind to go over to France and see for himself how
matters stood. As time was of the essence, Kitchener did not want to wait
until daybreak for the Cabinet's authorization. Hurrying to 10 Downing
Street, he conferred with Asquith and such ministers as could be assem-
bled at short notice. Approval for his trip was quickly granted, and
Churchill, who was present, arranged for a fast cruiser to take him to Le
Havre.[69]

For the exhausted Secretary for War, the long, trying day was still not
over. He went home to collect his things, then wired French to expect
him the following morning.[70] Around 2:00 A.M. he roused Grey from
sleep, gave him a copy of French's telegram, and informed him of his mission. Grey was probably not in the state of mind to say much but, after
Kitchener had left, he sat down at his desk and penned his thoughts.
French's offer to retreat to the Nanteuil line and see how things developed
was, in his opinion, a fair compromise. Grey labeled Joffre's request that
Sir John halt until the French armies on his flank caught up as "mon-
strous," since it would leave the BEF "exposed in the same way as before."
It only seemed reasonable, given the condition of the BEF, that Sir John
"be allowed to retire before the other forces do." Summing up, he expressed the view that if "the French armies do not keep their present position then I think the British force should not remain in the Nanteuil line
but should continue to retire as French proposed."[71] Grey ought to have
known better than to take a position on matters about which he knew
practically nothing. Even if Grey's letter had reached Kitchener before he
departed for France, he would not have given it a second thought.

Kitchener left Charing Cross by special train, boarded the waiting
cruiser at Dover, and reached Paris before luncheon. The meeting between Kitchener and French took place at the British Embassy on the
afternoon of September 1. Besides Sir Francis Bertie, representatives of
the French government—who had begged London to order Sir John to
remain in the line—were also present. The interview was acrimonious
from the start. Huguet, who witnessed the encounter, noted that while

Kitchener was "calm, balanced, reflective," Sir John was "sour, impetuous with congested face, sullen and ill-tempered in expression."[72]

Sir John lost his composure as soon as he caught sight of Kitchener in a field marshal's uniform. Quick to perceive slights where none were intended, French took it as a personal affront, believing that, in effect, Kitchener was trying to pull rank on him and undercut his authority with the French. But, Kitchener was still a serving soldier, and he habitually wore his field marshal's uniform at the War Office. He had no idea that French would take offence.

French was further inflamed when Kitchener announced that he wanted to inspect the troops in the field. Sir John protested that such a move would call his leadership into question and damage his relationship with the Army. His real reason, as John Terraine has perceptively argued, was to prevent Kitchener from talking with the corps commanders and from seeing the BEF as it really was: Although it was weary and had suffered heavy casualties, it was far from shattered, as Sir John had claimed.[73] Bertie sided with French, and Kitchener later dropped the idea.

The debate became more heated as the two field marshals deadlocked over the key strategic question. Kitchener, both embarrassed and irritated that French's Irish temper was out of control, suggested that they retire to an adjoining room to continue the discussion in private. Kitchener would certainly have been justified in sacking French in light of his panicked withdrawal and subsequent contentious and insubordinate behavior during the interview. If he had done so, he would have spared himself and the country a good deal of grief.

There is, unfortunately, no impartial account of what occurred behind those closed doors. French's record of the interview has been proven unreliable and should not be used as a source.[74] The only thing for certain are the results which Kitchener revealed in a telegram to the Cabinet shortly after the meeting: "French's troops are now engaged in the fighting line where he will remain conforming to the movements of the French Army though at the same time acting with caution to avoid being in any way unsupported on his flanks." Kitchener sent French a copy, adding that he felt sure that the conclusion represented the agreement they had come to, but, in any event, "please consider it an instruction."[75]

Kitchener had emerged triumphant in the contest of wills and averted a likely military catastrophe. The affair, however, caused a breach with French that never healed and, in fact, widened as the war progressed. The two soldiers remained outwardly cordial in their relationship and on occasion would reminisce about the good times they had shared in South Africa, but beneath the surface there was mutual distrust and, particularly on French's part, deep resentment.

While Kitchener tried hard during his visit to Paris to foster a new rapprochement between GHQ and GQG, he only partially succeeded in removing Sir John's deep-rooted doubts about the reliability and competence of Joffre and the French. The BEF's retreat continued unhindered during the next four days with French interpreting Kitchener's orders very literally. By September 4, Joffre realized, in light of information that the First German Army was changing direction and swinging southeast in front of Paris, that the moment for his counterattack was fast approaching.[76]

French was weary of Joffre's communiqués expressing vague intentions of resuming the offensive that, for one reason or another, were never carried out. Anticipating that Joffre's new battle plan would be, like the others, either poorly prepared or unrealistic, French begged Kitchener to spare his men the ordeal of participating in it.[77] Kitchener chided French for keeping him in the dark about Joffre's future battle plan and reminded him that if "we can keep the French Army in being we shall one day have a big force."[78] In fairness to Sir John, while in recent days he had neglected to keep Kitchener abreast of events on his front, he did not know the details or time of Joffre's planned counteroffensive until the night of September 4–5.[79]

Joffre's scheme depended upon the participation of the BEF, and this, notwithstanding Kitchener's intervention several days before, was by no means certain. Unwilling to take any chances, the general sent a message to Kitchener (through the French government), urging him to impress upon Sir John the necessity of his wholehearted cooperation.[80] Kitchener immediately wired GHQ on September 5:

> I am informed by the Ambassador that General Joffre now considers the strategical situation to be excellent, and has decided to employ all his troops on [sic] a most vigorous offensive. General Joffre considers it very essential that you should fully realize that it is most important that you should cooperate most vigorously with him.[81]

By the time the telegram arrived, Sir John had already consented to take part in Joffre's forward movement planned for the following day.[82] The so-called First Battle of the Marne, in which the small BEF played a vital role, lasted four days. To meet the Allied advance, the commander of the German First Army shifted his forces south. In so doing he created a gap between his forces and those of his colleague on the left, allowing the BEF to interpose itself between the two armies. Fearing that the First Army would be caught in a pincer, the Germans withdrew on September 9 to more defensible positions north of the Aisne River.[83] The battle of the Marne was an immense strategic victory for the Allies, wrecking Germany's bid for a swift victory over France and forcing it into a protracted two-front war.

The news was a great relief to Kitchener after days of intense strain and anxiety. He paid generous, but undeserved, tribute to French in the House of Lords on September 17 for his "skilled leadership" and "calm courage."[84] In truth it was Kitchener who deserved the praise. It was his farsighted military appreciation, swift action, and courage to take on the heavy responsibility of overruling the commander on the spot that had averted a disaster and made it possible for Joffre to deliver his bold stroke at the Marne.

Kitchener, who hated to have his picture taken, is caught wearing civilian clothes in the early days of the war and, even more unusual, actually smiling *(U.S. Army Military History Institute)*.

Asquith around 1914. He would age dramatically after his eldest son was killed on the Somme *(Imperial War Museum)*.

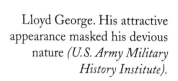

Lloyd George. His attractive appearance masked his devious nature *(U.S. Army Military History Institute)*.

Alfred Leete's original artwork was the most effective
recruiting poster of the war *(Imperial War Museum)*.

Recruits for Kitchener's army, headed by a band, in London, September 1914
(Imperial War Museum).

Sir John French. The old cavalryman did not possess the experience,
temperament, or intellectual qualities for so taxing a command as the BEF
(U.S. Army Military History Institute).

6

From Antwerp to the Close of 1914

THE Allies, following up their success at the Marne, made ill-advised frontal attacks against the strongly entrenched German Army along the Aisne. When battering-ram tactics proved unsuccessful, Joffre attempted an envelopment movement on his left. The Germans stymied this maneuver by extending their right, then mounted an equally unsuccessful flank attack of their own. A series of bloody engagements followed in late September and early October in which each side, in succession, made futile bids to turn the other's flank. The result of these operations, commonly called the Race to the Sea, was to extend the front further and further north.

As the battles in France moved towards the coast, the OHL (German high command) planned to settle unfinished business by reducing the fortress of Antwerp, which posed a threat to its army's right wing. Early in September, the Belgian authorities, detecting an increase in German troops south of Antwerp, prepared for the worst. Their sixty-five-thousand-man army was inadequate both to defend Antwerp and to keep open communications with the Allied forces along the coast to allow a withdrawal if necessary. Since King Albert of Belgium considered that the primary task of the field army was to garrison the city, his government asked London for thirty thousand troops to hold open the road between Antwerp and Ostend.

Kitchener had much sympathy and admiration for the Belgians, who had mounted attacks to draw off German troops during the British retirement and again prior to the battle of the Marne. Besides, Britain had treaty obligations to defend Belgium. In the opening days of the conflict, the BEF had quickly been driven from Belgian soil and Antwerp represented Britain's first real opportunity to honor its pledge.

Kitchener's wish to help the Belgians, however, was circumscribed by insufficient means. All of Britain's trained forces, save the Seventh Division, recently formed with regular units withdrawn from overseas duty, were committed to support the French. Not only did the Seventh Division fall far short of the estimated number of men required for the dangerous task, but the Cabinet, a little nervous about the possibility of an invasion, was reluctant to allow it to leave the country. There were plenty of Territorials on hand, but they could not be used. They were armed with antiquated rifles, for which only a limited reserve of ammunition was available. Moreover, the Territorial force was not fully trained, and Kitchener was unwilling to employ it in any active operations abroad requiring great mobility and skilled leadership in all ranks.[1] What made it easier for him to turn down the Belgian appeal was his belief that the danger to Antwerp was not immediate.

The first realization that he had been wrong came on September 28 when heavy Austrian Skoda howitzers began pounding Antwerp's outer defenses with projectiles weighing over a ton.[2] As each shell struck its target, whole section of walls crumbled to their foundation. Morale in the city slumped. Without outside help, the Belgian Army would be forced to leave the city to the mercy of the Germans.

Kitchener fully understood the effect the loss of Antwerp would have on Britain's maritime security. The fortress protected the whole line of channel ports from Ostend to Boulogne. In the event that the Germans gained control of the channel ports, they would be able not only to sever the supply lines to the BEF, but also to attack Allied shipping—and even launch an invasion of Britain.

On September 30, Sir Francis Villiers, British Ambassador in Antwerp, telegraphed London that the Belgian government, emphasizing the one-sidedness of the battle, had formally requested military assistance. Villiers added that, in the opinion of his military attaché, even the presence of a small British unit would greatly raise morale in the city.[3] Kitchener at once sent Col. Alister Dallas to survey the scene and to act as his liaison with the Belgian authorities. If things appeared bleak, Dallas was to urge the Belgians to disregard their forts and to entrench themselves in the intervening spaces and "challenge the Germans to come on."[4] Kitchener evidently did not realize then that deep entrenchments were impossible in that waterlogged land.

From the Admiralty, Kitchener borrowed the services of Vice Adm. Sir Henry Oliver, Director of the Naval Intelligence Division. Kitchener told Oliver that numerous German merchant ships had anchored in the Scheldt and instructed him to sink them so that they could not be used to carry troops to invade Britain. Oliver performed his mission admirably. For five days he worked practically around the clock. Assisted by only six Belgians—a single officer, four privates, and a boy scout—he inserted explosive charges between the cylinders of thirty-eight large vessels, rendering them inoperative. As a result, none was fit to go out to sea during the remainder of the war.[5]

On the same day that Villiers cabled London (September 30), Bertie signaled the Foreign Office that the French government was willing to send a division to aid the Belgians, providing the British would do the same.[6] The French did not specify the quality of the troops, arousing suspicion in the British Cabinet that they were Territorials. At Kitchener's urging, the Cabinet relented and consented to send the Seventh Division to Antwerp on condition that the French government furnish Regular troops. It was further agreed to send some heavy artillery and gunners to strengthen the city's defenses.[7]

Kitchener hoped that, if the immediate help proved insufficient to raise the siege of Antwerp, it would at least prolong resistance for several weeks. This would permit French to complete the redeployment of the BEF,[8] whereupon he would be available to undertake relief operations—unless of course Joffre's plan to envelop the German right flank was successful and relieved the pressure on the defenders at Antwerp.

On October 1, Dallas began his communications with the War Office, both by telephone and telegraph.[9] Dallas personally inspected the scene and had a discussion with the Belgian prime minister, Comte de Broqueville, who considered the situation "very critical." De Broqueville doubted that "resistance to the German attack" could be maintained solely "by defensive measures . . . within the fortress." In his opinion, the "only way to save Antwerp from falling is by a diversion from outside on the German left flank."[10]

Kitchener's apprehension was not relieved by news that Joffre was unwilling to allow any French relief effort to compromise his outflanking

maneuver. Under duress from his own government, Joffre agreed to release a Territorial division and possibly a marine brigade in ten days,
which, at best, would have served only as token support to the Belgians.
Joffre considered any operations outside his own of secondary value. His
solution called for the Belgian Army to evacuate Antwerp and to link up
with the Allied force engaged in the flanking movement.[11]

Kitchener told the Cabinet on October 2 that, in view of the tepid
French response, the chances of saving Antwerp appeared slim. Asquith's
note to Venetia Stanley explained Kitchener's dilemma:

> The . . . only relieving that the French offer is a mass of territorials and
> the like, who would be of no use for hard fighting and are quite unfit to
> co-operate with a trained division of ours like the 7th. On the other
> hand to send the 7th alone is to court almost certain disaster. . . . He
> [Dallas] says . . . that "any definite statement of assistance that could be
> given to Belgian Government would have immediate and excellent ef-
> fect." But it is no good to lure them with false hopes.[12]

Kitchener sent Sir Percy Girouard, an old comrade from the Sudan
campaign, to Antwerp to impress upon Dallas the need to do everything
he could to stiffen the Belgian resolve. Although Kitchener feared that
the relief operation he was organizing would fall short of requirements,
he was not in a position to promise a greater effort. Joffre's inadequate
offer of troops prompted Kitchener to warn Dallas not to raise Belgian
hopes by suggesting that Anglo-French support would soon be arriving.[13]

All the same, Kitchener was not ready to throw in the towel. At his
instigation, Grey contacted the French government to say that Joffre's
offer of Territorial units, even in combination with what the British proposed to send, was judged inadequate by War Office military authorities
to compel the Germans to raise the siege of Antwerp. The British were
prepared to put first-line troops in the field, but they would not do so
without the support of a regular division from France. Unless more could
be done, it would be better to abandon the dispatch of an Allied contingent, rather than risk it against a superior German force. The effects of
the loss of Antwerp on the campaign was emphasized, and the French
government was urged to persuade Joffre to send Regular troops to the
region of Dunkirk, from whence they could operate in conjunction with
British reinforcements (Seventh Division).[14]

Haste was no less crucial than a requisite force. Heavy German howit-

zers were smashing the forts at Antwerp one by one, just as they had done
at Namur and other Belgian strongholds on the Meuse. The main stum-
bling block to meeting the Belgians' needs was Joffre's obstinacy. This was
again confirmed by Bertie, who reported on the afternoon of October 2
the gist of his conversation with Théophile Delcassé, the French minister
of foreign affairs:

> Minister for Foreign Affairs stated that from a telephonic conversation
> with General Joffre he gathered that the general could not spare any
> troops from his armies . . . for relief of Antwerp, and such being the
> general's view, it would be a grave matter for French government to
> press him to alter it.[15]

The general impression of the French authorities was that the situation in
Antwerp was serious, but not critical, and that the place would be able to
hold out until the effect of Joffre's main battle brought relief. Delcassé
told Bertie that the Belgian government appeared more alarmed than circumstances warranted. He read a letter from the French Ambassador in
Antwerp, who asserted that the 160,000-man garrison (an inflated figure
even counting Irregulars)[16] was more than adequate for the defense of the
fortress and that part of it might even be spared for field operations.[17]

The differences with the French remained unresolved when the
course of events forced Kitchener's hand. On the evening of October 2,
Villiers wired the Foreign Office that the Belgian government planned to
leave for Ostend the following day, while the King and the Army withdrew to Ghent to protect the coastline and later to cooperate with the
main Allied armies. The decision to abandon Antwerp had been made to
ensure that the King and the government did not fall into German hands.
It was claimed that the fortress would continue to hold out for an additional five or six days, but Villiers doubted that resistance would last that
long once the court and the government were gone.[18]

Since Asquith was in Cardiff to make a recruiting speech, Grey
rushed over to Kitchener's home in Carleton Gardens. Roused from sleep,
the field marshal was shown Villiers's telegram.[19] As he read it carefully,
he could scarcely believe its contents. The last message from Dallas, received early in the afternoon, indicated that the Belgians were standing
firm and had gained such confidence from thwarting German progress
that they were about to undertake a counteroffensive.[20] What could have
occurred in the last few hours to cause the Belgians to give up hope?

Kitchener and Grey agreed that they needed to consult Churchill, who was on his way to Dunkirk by special train, before taking any emergency action. Intercepted about twenty miles outside of London, Churchill was knocking at Kitchener's door shortly before midnight.

In anxious conclave, the ministers were confronted with the choice of either doing nothing and letting Antwerp fall or taking a far-reaching decision in haste and without full knowledge of the local conditions. All three were united that Antwerp should not be cast away without a struggle. Churchill suddenly proposed to cancel his trip to Dunkirk and instead head for Antwerp to see what could be done. The First Lord was being disingenuous when he later asserted that it was Kitchener who "expressed a decided wish that I should go."[21] It should be pointed out that Churchill was trying to justify his self-imposed assignment, for which, on his return, he was assailed mercilessly by the press and by many of his colleagues as a madcap errand for glory and adventure. Grey, who had no axe to grind, stated categorically that the idea came from Churchill himself and that initially he had voiced strong objections. Kitchener, like Grey, recognized that the First Lord ran the risk of being shut up in the city. But, he reserved his judgment until he heard what Churchill had to say.[22]

According to Churchill, the Germans lacked the strength to mount a full-scale attack on Antwerp. He attributed all the destruction and mayhem to one large gun. If the Allies could spare two divisions, he was confident that the German force could be driven off and the city saved. Kitchener said that he could provide a division, but he was not sure that the French would match it with one of their own. Since much was at stake, he would again approach the French. Churchill insisted that he could not wait for the exchanges with the French, that he must go now or not at all. It was then that Kitchener gave his consent, as did Grey, albeit somewhat reluctantly.[23]

That done, the ministers had to improvise a plan, a heavy responsibility in view of the Prime Minister's absence. At length they came to the following decisions: that on arrival Churchill should take what steps he deemed necessary to ensure that Antwerp held out until relief came; that Grey was to ask King Albert and his government to postpone their departure and to continue to resist, if only for a few days; and that a brigade of Royal Marines in Dunkirk should be sent at once to the beleaguered city.

In the early hours of October 3, Grey motored to the Foreign Office, where he sent Villiers a telegram with a message for the Belgian government.[24] As he was about to leave, Grey received a wire from Bertie, saying that he had been informed that the French government proposed to send to Antwerp without delay two Territorial divisions, with a full complement of cavalry and artillery. Bertie had then gone to the Quai d'Orsay (French Foreign Office) to discuss the matter with Delcassé. The French government, Delcassé asserted, would not go back on its decision to use Territorials, and he stressed that it proposed to send two divisions instead of one. He claimed that they were good troops, better in some respects than certain Regulars. He added that, as a matter of urgency, Joffre intended to launch a major offensive in Lille, which would have the effect of inducing German troops in the neighborhood of Antwerp to abandon the siege. Delcassé showed Bertie the latest report from the French military attaché at Antwerp, estimating (inaccurately) the attacking German force at no more than two corps and describing the military situation as "not good" but not "really bad" either.[25]

Much as he resented it, Kitchener had no choice but to settle for what the French were offering. At 9:40 A.M. on October 3, he asked Alexandre Millerand, the French minister of war, (through Bertie) to make all preparations to send the proposed two divisions, along with the cavalry and artillery, as soon as possible and to let him know when they would be ready to depart.[26] During the course of the day, telegrams were exchanged between the War Office and the French authorities regarding the size and composition of the proposed relief forces.[27] Amidst the messages, Kitchener signaled Dallas, asking his opinion of the size of the force required to help the Belgian field army lift the siege of Antwerp. He continued:

> The French Government say they will send two divisions . . . but I do not yet know when they will be available. If a corps of our troops under Sir John French, together with the VIIth Division and a Cavalry Division from here, concentrated at Lille in order to attack the right flank of the main German Army and drive it back, would this action, if accomplished in about four or five days, in your opinion relieve the situation at Antwerp quickly enough to prevent the fall of the place or must any troops employed to relieve Antwerp be sent there . . . and if so can you give me approximately the longest time we can have to get the troops there, so that I can inform French Government?[28]

At 5:50 P.M. Dallas's reply was sent by Churchill, who had arrived at Antwerp in the middle of the afternoon. Dallas believed that the aforementioned forces would be formidable if applied directly to the Antwerp besiegers, but that action from Lille against the German right flank would not materially lessen the pressure on the city.[29] Presumably, Dallas was unable to answer the remaining questions posed by Kitchener.

An hour later, Churchill forwarded a message of his own to the War Office. The Belgian authorities, he was happy to report, had agreed to prolong the defense of the fortress for at least ten days. The British government was to state unequivocally within three days whether or not it could send a relief force. If no assurance was given, the Belgian Army would be free to abandon the city, should it see fit. In such an event, the Belgians wanted the British to help their army escape by sending troops to cover the line of retreat. If the Belgian proposals were accepted, Churchill requested that two naval brigades be sent via Dunkirk to Antwerp.[30] These brigades were still in the elementary stage of training, and some of the men had never fired a rifle, even in practice. They were quite unfit to take the field. Unlike Kitchener, who would not send raw recruits into heavy action under any circumstances, Churchill evidently believed that the stakes justified the risk.

Kitchener was filled with admiration for what Churchill had been able to accomplish in just a few hours. There was now hope that the relief force he was in the process of putting together would gain sufficient time for the BEF to provide more substantial reinforcements. Kitchener counted mostly on British unilateral action to save the city. Although he had no wish to do anything that would impair the effectiveness of Joffre's envelopment movement, he was not overly optimistic that it would raise the siege of Antwerp.

At 10:30 A.M. on October 4, Prince Louis of Battenberg, the First Sea Lord (who was temporarily in charge of the Admiralty), indicated that the two naval brigades requested by Churchill would embark at Dover in the afternoon and should reach Dunkirk between 7:00 and 8:00 P.M.[31] During the early part of the afternoon, the French government notified the War Office of the dates on which its relief forces would be ready to move: The Territorial division would depart from Le Havre on October 5 and reach Ostend, the point of disembarkation, between October 6 and 8; the brigade of marines, which had been substituted for the other Territorial division, would leave Paris on October 7 and arrive at Ostend on October 8, at the latest.[32]

The next morning, the Cabinet gave its blessing to the arrangements Kitchener had made. The Seventh Division and the Third Cavalry Division were to form part of the relief expedition. The Cabinet was reassured that these units would return to Britain after their mission was completed and not join the BEF. It was understood that the Seventh Division would eventually replace both the marine brigade, already in the trenches at Antwerp, and the naval brigades, which at the moment were still in the country. Lt. Gen. Sir Henry Rawlinson, who had been released from temporary command of the Fourth Division on the Aisne, was to take charge of the Antwerp relief force—although Churchill had hoped to have the job himself.[33] Kitchener announced that the Anglo-French force earmarked for Antwerp totaled some fifty-three thousand men. Together with the Belgian garrison—sixty-five thousand Regulars plus thirty thousand or so Irregulars—it would face an investing force estimated to be between fifty and sixty thousand second-line troops. If Kitchener's numbers were correct, one could not fault Hobhouse's optimistic entry that evening that "we ought easily to relieve the city."[34]

Rawlinson arrived at Antwerp on October 6. His instructions were to support the Belgian Army defending Antwerp and, in conjunction with the French contingent, to endeavor to attack the left flank of German investing forces.[35] Rawlinson's orders were vague and reflected the confusion and uncertainty within the Anglo-French camp. The crux of the problem was that no mechanism existed to coordinate British interests with French strategy.

From the start Joffre and Kitchener "had been working at cross purposes."[36] Kitchener wanted to use part of the BEF to save Antwerp, but he had no authority over the men in the field. On October 2, Kitchener suggested to French that, as he was disengaging from the line, he should reinforce the Seventh Division with as many troops as were necessary to relieve the fortress, while the remainder of his force moved into new positions.[37] Sir John, realizing that the loss of Antwerp would imperil the security of the channel ports, was initially sympathetic to Kitchener's proposal. He would hasten to concentrate all available troops in the vicinity of Lille, he replied to Kitchener, either to strike the right flank of the main German Army or to raise the siege of Antwerp.[38]

For personal reasons, however, Sir John's enthusiasm cooled over the next few days. The fact that everything had been decided and prepared behind his back and that he had not been kept fully informed of British plans aroused his suspicion that Kitchener was trying to create a new army outside of his authority.[39] This impression was strengthened when Rawlinson, whom he distrusted, was given an independent command at Antwerp.[40] By October 5, he was beginning to question the wisdom of

Kitchener's rescue expedition. In that state of mind, it did not require much persuasion on the part of Joffre to win him over.

Joffre rarely, if ever, considered British interests when formulating plans. Currently, his main concern was to turn the right flank of the German Army, and he had no wish to see Allied strength dissipated on secondary objectives. Behind Kitchener's back, he worked to undermine the relief operation. On October 5, he extracted a promise from Sir John that he would aggressively engage the German flank, as the BEF arrived north, corps by corps. Sir John accepted the principle that the main operations should not be jeopardized for the sake of defending Antwerp. Next Joffre sent a special envoy to Antwerp to urge King Albert to withdraw with his army and to join up with the Allied left wing. Finally, Joffre was determined to block the French government's decision to send a relief contingent to Ostend, when, in his opinion, its true place was in the battle in Flanders.[41]

Joffre's underhanded activities coincided with the worsening conditions at Antwerp. In the early hours of October 6, the Belgians mounted an attack with the object of driving the Germans back across the Nethe. The assault failed, and the Belgians, in the face of a strong German counterattack, retired shaken and dispirited. For the defenders, the only good news was the arrival of the two British naval brigades. But these six thousand inexperienced troops by themselves could do little. Concurrently, the Seventh Division and the Third Cavalry Division were disembarking at Dunkirk and Ostend, but could not possibly reach the city that day. The Allies had not met the minimum conditions arranged with the Belgians. As the ground gained by the Germans that morning would soon enable them to bring their heavy howitzers to bear on the city itself, the Belgian Supreme Council, no longer convinced that fresh Allied troops, even in large numbers, could bring relief, decided to withdraw the Army across the Schelde. Here, the Belgian Army would avoid the risk of being trapped and yet be in a position to cooperate with any relief movement by Allied forces.[42]

Before leaving the city, Churchill notified Kitchener of the unexpected turn of events.[43] Kitchener, thereupon, wired Rawlinson who had returned to Bruges to organize the relief effort:

> I greatly fear . . . you will be unable, with the troops at your disposal, to deal with German investing force. . . . If you rely on Sir John French for reinforcements it will be some considerable time before they can arrive,

and their withdrawal from left of French line, which is none too strong, may create a serious position there. . . . I am urgently asking France for more troops to be sent to Ostend at once. . . . Let me know your views on this fully and privately.[44]

Rawlinson replied that, in view of the demoralization of the Belgian Army and the questionable value of the French Territorial division, which had not yet arrived, attempting offensive operations with what forces he had on hand was extremely risky. Since he considered the Seventh Division and Third Cavalry Division to be his only reliable troops, he was not strong enough to protect his line of communications and at the same time relieve Antwerp.[45]

With the cupboard bare at home, Kitchener looked to Sir John and Joffre to strengthen Rawlinson's force. When sounded out, Sir John stated emphatically that "the success of the principal and general operations would certainly be imperiled at the present critical moment if the British forces were withdrawn from the role which had been assigned to them."[46]

Kitchener had no better luck with the French. Far from providing him with an additional division, as he had requested, they failed to live up to their commitments. The Territorial division was diverted to Poperinghe, and the marine brigade was sent towards Antwerp, both with orders to cover the withdrawal of the Belgian Army and facilitate "its junction with the Anglo-French forces."[47] This was presented as a fait accompli and without prior consultation with Kitchener.[48] As Kitchener had to pass through the French Ministry of War to communicate with Joffre, interminable delays occurred in the exchange of messages. It did not help that Joffre took his time answering Kitchener's inquiries, possibly as a deliberate move. By October 8, Kitchener realized that the race to save Antwerp was over. Antwerp surrendered to the Germans on October 10, twenty-four hours after the departure of the last elements of the Belgian field army. Thereupon, Kitchener, with the reluctant approval of the Cabinet, directed Rawlinson to place himself under Sir John's orders.

Determining whether the city could have been relieved with Joffre's speedy cooperation is problematical. It may be that there simply was not enough time. But Joffre's behavior during the crisis was inexcusable, dooming any chance to succor the fortress. Kitchener, who since the start of the war had done his best to accommodate Joffre, felt betrayed and justifiably so. In a letter to Sir John on October 11, he flailed Joffre sharply, holding him in large measure responsible for the fall of Antwerp and observing that the French general needed to be put on notice that the British government reserved the right to exercise strategic independence.[49] Kitchener had laid down a principle that he must have known, even in anger, could not be applied, at least to operations in France.

After the curtain fell on Antwerp, there was an outcry against Churchill in the press,[50] and some of his own colleagues, including the Prime Minister,[51] spoke derisively of his conduct behind his back. On the other hand, Kitchener had warm words of praise for Churchill, whose mission, he felt, had been justified, even if unsuccessful. Thus far, the two men had enjoyed a smooth and cordial working relationship. The transport of troops in August and September had gone off without a hitch, prompting Churchill to tell Kitchener, "It is a great pleasure to work with you and the two Departments pull well together."[52] Not one to stand on formalities, the Secretary for War asked Churchill to dispense with his title and simply address him as Kitchener. In September, Churchill sounded Kitchener out about the possibility of finding a job for his cousin, the Duke of Marlborough. Kitchener did so immediately, assigning the duke to the War Office as a special messenger.[53]

Kitchener's first serious disagreement with Churchill was over the vital question of home defense. As seen in a previous chapter, the concentration of German troops in the vicinity of Cracow towards the end of September had derailed the grand duke's planned advance on Berlin. To mask the transfer of troops from west to east, the Germans had spread false rumors that they meant to invade Britain from the channel ports.[54] Kitchener took the intelligence reports seriously and brought the matter up at a meeting of the CID on October 7, the day Churchill returned from Antwerp. Kitchener pointed out that a deadlock on the eastern front would liberate sufficient German troops to permit an invasion of between one hundred fifty and two hundred thousand men. If there were a general fleet action in progress away from the channel, German transport vessels would be able to make the crossing.

Churchill was certain that the Royal Navy could destroy any fleet and transports before they could land a significant force. In fact, he was willing to assume the responsibility for preventing an invasion if the War Office would guarantee the defeat of any raid (that is up to seventy thousand men). Kitchener was not prepared to make such a commitment, saying that he had too few trained troops at home and that withdrawing men from the Continent at the present juncture would be most inadvisable. He hoped to have enough trained troops by the middle of January 1915 to thwart any attempt at an invasion. Churchill assured Kitchener that, if the danger of an invasion became extreme, he would not exclude laying mines along the coast.[55] At this point the meeting broke up.

The fall of Antwerp, followed by the loss of Ostend a week later, kept alive Kitchener's invasion jitters. At Cabinet meetings he demanded that the Admiralty should take more specific precautions against a possible German landing. Touchy from nervous exhaustion—the First Lord was being hammered daily in the press and in political circles for naval set-backs and for his conduct of Admiralty affairs—Churchill took umbrage at what he sensed was an inference that he was shirking his responsibility. He felt that Kitchener was ignoring three CID investigations (between 1903 and 1914), which had concluded that only a limited German strike of no more than seventy thousand troops was feasible.[56] But the CID had investigated the chances of an invasion in force from Germany itself. Kitchener was worried about a prolonged Russian pause, which might allow the Germans to seize the channel ports, or worse, compel France to surrender. As Maurice Hankey noted, "I had many conversations with Kitchener on the subject and can bear out that he was anxious, not about the immediate present, but about the position if things went seriously wrong in France."[57]

On October 19, Churchill wrote a sharp letter to Kitchener, suggesting that before action was taken he should set up a committee of military experts to analyze in detail the possibility of a cross-channel invasion.[58] Paying no heed to the contents of Churchill's letter, Kitchener drew up a memorandum in which he laid out the same old arguments, ending with a jab at Admiralty policy: "The one deterrent that they [the Germans] have always felt would have made an invasion impossible—our fleet—has now been removed to such a distance by their action that the opportunity is probably now considered by them a favorable one."[59]

The note was circulated to the Cabinet on October 21, and there ensued a long and wearing discussion. Asquith gave Venetia Stanley a summary of what happened:

> His [Kitchener's] view is that the Army is doing all it can both at home and abroad, and that some of the big ships ought to be brought into the home ports. Winston made a very good defence of his policy, which is . . . that the function of the Great Fleet is not to prevent the landing of an invading force (which is the business of the torpedo flotillas & submarines) but to strike at and destroy the enemy's covering fleet.[60]

Churchill may have been skeptical, but many of the leading officials at the Admiralty shared Kitchener's concern about the dangers of an invasion. Consequently, the First Lord allowed himself "to succumb to the suppressed excitement" and joined the War Office in making defensive preparations.[61] The Admiralty arranged to bring part of the fleet to home waters, as well as to lay mines and sink block ships in the mouths of undefended harbors. Military preparations included the deployment of Territorial forces along the east coast, constant surveillance of possible landing places, and trains kept in readiness to bring a striking force to any threatened area. But when nothing happened, particularly on days favorable to nocturnal landings, the invasion issue receded into the background, only to be revived from time to time.

In retrospect it is obvious that it would have been suicidal for the Germans to attempt to cross the channel when they did not possess general command of the seas. But, before Kitchener is derided too sharply for his seemingly irrational fears, it should be pointed out that in 1940, after the fall of France, there were many Britons, including Churchill, who considered an attempted invasion quite possible.

More real and persistent dangers existed in France in the autumn of 1914, as the final action in the Race to the Sea centered on the town of Ypres. Aiming for a strategic victory, the Germans had initially struck on a broad front, but, as the assault continued, it became concentrated increasingly on the British-held sector of the line. As a stream of German reinforcements were brought up from quiescent parts of the front, the British found themselves outnumbered by a margin of four to one and in places as high as seven to one.

At the height of the desperate fighting, Kitchener traveled to Dunkirk on November 1 to hold talks with French leaders—President Poincaré, Millerand, and generals Joffre and Foch—on a range of subjects. First and foremost was Kitchener's desire to obtain French help for Sir John's beleaguered forces. "I am afraid," he said to his hosts, "that the British army, which is still far too small, will bend under such an onslaught. We count on you to assist us." Gen. Foch, who had been charged by Joffre to coordinate the movement of the Allied armies in the battle, promised to send all the reinforcements he could spare, but added, "do send us your new divisions as soon as possible." Kitchener promised that one million men would be on French soil within eighteen months, but before he could finish, Foch interjected to say that he would prefer fewer men arriving a little sooner. Joffre wanted an immediate British commitment, so that he could continue to pound away at the Germans. He was unconcerned about a long-range strategic reserve because he anticipated that the war would be over in a few months. Kitchener, however, was adamant, saying that there would be no substantial reinforcements before the spring. While the New Armies were being trained, the French would have to be content with the better Territorial battalions and the remnants of the Regular Army.[62] Besides the Seventh, Kitchener had created four more regular divisions, numbered the Eighth (already earmarked for France), Twenty-seventh, Twenty-eighth, and Twenty-ninth, by recalling imperial garrisons. Implicit in Kitchener's remarks was the promise that the remaining regular divisions would join the BEF in due time, as would the New Armies when ready. Kitchener had no idea then that the western front would be deadlocked before the year was over.

Kitchener considered Joffre inflexible and formed a higher impression of Foch, but he was dismayed by the undue optimism of both generals.[63] The French, according to Kitchener, "were quite assured that the Germans could not sustain their attack, would go back quite quickly, and under pressure from Russia would make peace on fair terms at an early date."[64]

At some point in the discussion, Joffre indirectly criticized Sir John French by claiming that the BEF did not appear thoroughly committed to the defeat of the common enemy. Kitchener sensed that Joffre had run out of patience with French—something he could identify with. Since he could not allow a breach to occur, he offered to replace French with Ian Hamilton. Quite apart from Hamilton's proven qualifications, his appointment would enable Kitchener to exercise close supervision over operations in France, which hitherto he had been unable to do.

Joffre would have welcomed Henry Wilson, who was known to be very sympathetic to GQG's policies, but he was not willing to gamble on an unknown quantity, lest he lose what influence he exercised over the BEF. He declined Kitchener's proposal, supposedly on the grounds that he worked "well and cordially" with French and that a change in command at such a stage in the campaign would undermine the morale of the BEF.[65] Kitchener said no more on the subject. Several days later, Foch indiscreetly reported Kitchener's offer to Wilson and suggested that Sir John ought to be informed.[66] On hearing the news, French exploded in anger, denouncing what he regarded as Kitchener's unspeakable treachery. Never again would he feel secure in his position, and his hatred and distrust of Kitchener would approach paranoia.

In the weeks after Kitchener met the French at Dunkirk, there was considerable pressure on him to send more British troops to the western front. The savage fighting at Ypres tapered off in mid-November, principally because OHL reinforced Hindenburg with troops from the west to enable him to frustrate Russia's planned invasion of Silesia. As already noted, the grand duke sent an alarmist telegram to Kitchener on December 4, calling for a resumption of the offensive against the Germans on the western front so as to relieve the pressure on his forces in Poland. It so happened that Churchill had developed a plan with French for a combined operation along the Belgian coast to recapture the ports of Ostend and Zeebrugge. As has been already seen, Kitchener had given his provisional approval to the proposal, known as the Zeebrugge plan, thinking that it could be carried out at minimal costs.[67] He agreed with Churchill that it was important to win back the channel ports before the Germans could turn them into submarine bases. He promised to send Sir John a Regular division, the Twenty-seventh, which promptly left Britain and disembarked in France on December 23.[68]

The Zeebrugge plan, however, was bedeviled from the start. French had been persuaded to participate in the coastal venture after he had promised to extend his own line and support Joffre's offensive around Arras—supposedly in response to the Russian appeal. Predictably, Joffre was cool to the idea of an independent British operation, which threatened to compromise his arrangements with Sir John French. As he never understood the importance the British attached to gaining the naval bases, he coerced French into falling in line with his plan.[69] Sir John, in an attempt to carry out both the Zeebrugge operation and his understanding with Joffre, requested that Kitchener send over fifty Territorial or New Army battalions, sufficient artillery, and fifty rounds per gun per day, on top of what he had already been promised—the last two Regular divisions, the Twenty-eighth and Twenty-ninth, and the First Canadian Division.[70]

A close study of the area would have revealed the inherent weakness of the plan. The terrain over which Sir John contemplated making his main thrust was soggy and flat with practically no cover, being intersected and divided by drainage canals and wet ditches. Because German coastal defenses were still at a rudimentary stage, a landing from the sea near the ports in good weather was eminently feasible, but apparently it was never discussed.[71]

Kitchener withdrew his support when he realized that the advance along the Belgian coast would be no easy task and would require far more men and munitions than he could provide. The New Armies were not ready to take the field, and he was not about to dispose of much of the Territorial force and endanger the security of the country.[72] Besides, French's prodigious demand for artillery shells could not be met when the current output was about thirteen rounds per gun per day. To make matters worse, Kitchener felt compelled to ship some munitions to Russia from his meager supply in order to avert a Russian collapse.[73] Thus on December 17, Kitchener notified French that he was fed up with what he described as Churchill's "wild cat" scheme.

The testy tone of Kitchener's letter to French was in part due to his resentment over Churchill's frequent visits to GHQ. Churchill, who saw himself cast in the Napoleonic mold, did not feel that the Admiralty offered enough scope for his talent as a strategist. Whenever he could, he escaped to the front, where he was cordially entertained by French, with whom he discussed plans and the latest military developments. As a matter of course, Churchill always requested Kitchener's permission before leaving and received it. But his cross-channel junkets at the slightest pretext began to irritate Kitchener, who suspected that Churchill was meddling in military affairs behind his back.

Another sore point with Kitchener concerned the Admiralty-controlled naval units operating on land. Kitchener believed that these formations, which were packed with political appointees and Churchill's friends, caused discontent and trouble out of all proportion to their utility. If the purpose of the irregular naval formations was to allow certain officers and gentlemen without military experience to take part in the war, and, more importantly, if they were to be retained, Kitchener wrote sarcastically to Churchill, they ought to form part of the Army and not be identified as separate entities under the Admiralty's direction.[74]

Matters came to a head on December 17, when Churchill again proposed to visit France. Kitchener complained to Asquith that, while Churchill was at liberty to go over and look into naval matters at Dunkirk, he should not attempt to see French. Kitchener felt that Churchill's excursions to GHQ were adding to the friction between himself and French.[75] The First Lord was livid that Kitchener had troubled the Prime Minister over a question he could easily have resolved and accused the warlord of making misleading statements. Churchill considered that his meetings with French were quite harmless, but the fact that Kitchener resented them should have been reason enough for him to stay away from GHQ. Even his own wife was uneasy about his trips to France and wondered why he could not be satisfied "with the unique position you have reached thro' years of ceaseless industry and foresight."[76] How would he have liked it, one ought ask, if Kitchener had corresponded and discussed joint planning with Adm. John Jellicoe (the Naval Supreme Commander)? But, seeing the other side's point of view was never Churchill's most notable quality.

The dispute between Kitchener and Churchill escalated, requiring Asquith's mediation. In the face of Kitchener's strong objections and threat of resignation, Asquith forbade Churchill from making any more trips to GHQ.[77] The incident left its mark on both men, dissipating much of the mutual good will and trust of the early months of the war.

Such clashes between Kitchener and Churchill sometimes resulted from temperamental and policy differences, but often they occurred because there was no clear-cut system for running the war. By informal delegation from the Cabinet, war policy had been entrusted to the heads of the two service departments, acting in consultation with the Prime Minister. Consequently, there was no mechanism in existence to coordinate the work of the service departments, to prepare contingency plans, or to provide clear direction and rapid decisions on a multitude of diverse issues that arose as the war progressed. Recognizing at last that the structure of supreme command required modification, Asquith set up a War Council (without abolishing the CID which continued to exist on paper) towards the end of November 1914. Membership was at first limited to Asquith, the service chiefs and their advisers, Richard Haldane, Sir Edward Grey, David Lloyd George, and Arthur Balfour, who was chosen because of his prewar experience on the CID and not as an official representative of the Conservative or Unionist Party. The indispensable and perceptive Maurice Hankey acted as secretary and informal adviser.

Far from bringing about the expected improvements, the War Council displayed fatal weaknesses. The original membership would swell to thirteen within a few months, so that any advantage inherent in a small directing authority was lost. Asquith, in keeping with peacetime constitutional practices, insisted that conclusions of the War Council be referred for approval to the full Cabinet, where a second debate took place, causing endless delays and hampering secrecy. In contrast to the CID, where the professional experts were genuine members with the freedom to express their views frankly, those brought into the War Council had second-class status in the sense that they were advisers to their own departmental chiefs and spoke only when asked. Finally, the War Council was not designed to supervise the day-to-day fluctuations of the war, but met only when Asquith deemed it necessary, usually to deal with an emergency or to discuss larger questions of policy.[78]

For Kitchener, who took no pleasure in attending Cabinet meetings to engage in verbal jousting during or after a hard day's work, his required presence at the War Council was akin to taking a double dose of castor oil. He often questioned the value of the War Council since the same ground was again covered in the Cabinet and distracted him from his real work. He further resented having to exert himself to obtain the consent of men who were not qualified to pass judgment on his proposals. Then, too, it meant that he would be under greater pressure to reveal military secrets. In the Cabinet, Asquith had not pressed Kitchener for details or encouraged others to do so. In the War Council, he would not be able to conceal information on which the members would need to base their decisions.

Kitchener had good reason to worry about his loquacious colleagues. Lloyd George regularly shared classified information with press barons.[79] Churchill disclosed a confidential matter to Violet Asquith, the Prime Minister's daughter, and gave her permission to divulge it to several of her friends. Asquith withheld nothing from Venetia Stanley, as his letters to her attest. Proposed military operations were openly discussed at dinner parties, much like a sporting event. A member of Parliament (MP) in the House requested information on the new machines called "tanks"—a weapon as yet unknown to the enemy that had come to his attention[80]—as if the subject were a new housing project about to be unveiled. In short, Cabinet ministers responsible for the nation's security and for the lives of the men in the field showed appalling lapses in judgment, all but ignoring the skill with which enemy agents could extract and piece together information overheard or unwittingly disclosed to them. Kitchener was aware of the gossip, which was rampant in certain London circles, and it reinforced his tendency towards secretiveness.

The awesome burden of directing the nation's war effort was beginning to tell on Kitchener. Although remarkably fit for a man of his age, he was living a hectic and pressure-filled life with comparatively little sleep or rest. Between Monday and Friday he arrived at the War Office at 9:00 A.M. and, without bothering to go out for lunch, remained at his desk until 6:00 or 7:00 P.M. Often, he would bring work home or would return to the War Office late at night to deal with urgent matters. On weekends, he occasionally drove down to Broome Park, leaving Saturday morning and returning to London the following evening. Otherwise, he took no time off. Because there was never any let up in the volume of work, he evidently felt that he could not justify even a brief leave. But, it would have served him better in the long run if he had spent more time away from the War Office so as to renew his energy and maintain his focus. Before the year was over, he was already showing the effects of toiling for inhumanly long hours. "[Sir Reginald] Brade says that K. is showing signs of age," Sir George Riddell, a newspaper proprietor, noted in his diary after a discussion with the Secretary of the War Office. "He is not the man he was when the war started. The strain has told on him."[81]

Although Kitchener could never shake the nagging feeling that he could do more,[82] he had no reason to be unhappy over what had occurred thus far. His program to create mass volunteer armies was taking shape, and he had arranged to supply and arm them; the battle of the Marne, made possible by his prompt intervention to keep the British in the line, had halted the German juggernaut, and, time being an ally of the Entente, practically assured that the war would last long; the Russian Army had shown signs of weaknesses, but it remained a potent factor, compelling the Germans to divide their forces and guaranteeing that the Allies would continue to possess a superiority in manpower; the Empire was secure and the imperial war was going well. All in all Kitchener had every reason to be satisfied with what had been accomplished in the opening months of the conflict.

The key to Kitchener's success was the Cabinet's willingness to allow him to do as he saw fit. He had not been compelled to defend his policies, or coerced into adopting a course of action against his better judgment. All this would change in 1915 with unfortunate consequences. The deadlock in the west would give rise to many problems that were unprecedented and not easily resolved. Exacerbating the difficulties were the politicians who, impatient over the lack of progress on the western front, decided they could do a better job of managing the war than Kitchener.

7

DRAWN INTO THE
DARDANELLES VORTEX

FTER the fighting around Ypres died down during the
third week in November, the western front became stationary along a line of twisted trenches that stretched
from Switzerland to Nieuport on the North Sea. The flanks around which
decisive results had been traditionally achieved by maneuver had disappeared. The men who led the opposing armies had been schooled in a
different era and were quite unprepared to cope with trench warfare.
Their solution was to mount mass frontal assaults, preceded by artillery
barrages, with the object of piercing the enemy's front and restoring the
war of mobility and maneuver. Such an approach, apart from its futility,
exacted a deadly toll in lives. None appreciated that conventional weapons, particularly the machine gun, made nineteenth-century offensive tactics obsolete. Kitchener was as perplexed as the generals by the novel
conditions of warfare. "I don't know what is to be done," he frankly admitted, "this isn't war."[1]

It was apparent to Kitchener that, with both sides commanding immense courage and skill and roughly equal resources, the advantage lay
with the defense. After the failure of Joffre's offensive in December, he
became convinced that the Allies could not break the German line without a greater superiority in manpower and an increased supply of munitions.[2] As the year was drawing to a close, he paused to take stock and

weigh his options. On account of his growing estrangement from Sir John French, Kitchener had been deprived of intelligence from GHQ. Consequently, he had relied on other sources—notably Lt. Gen. Henry Rawlinson, his ADC in South Africa and now commander of the Fourth Army in Flanders, and Col. H. Yarde-Buller, his liaison officer at GQG—to keep him abreast of events on the western front. At the end of December 1914, he received a report from Rawlinson detailing the military prospects in the existing theaters. Rawlinson thought that the Germans would adopt a defensive policy in the west, while concentrating their main efforts against the Russians. He attributed the failure of recent Allied offensives against the Germans to a lack of munitions and insufficient reserves with which to exploit break-ins. He did not expect the Allies to make any significant progress in driving the Germans from occupied Belgium and France until these deficiencies had been made good.[3] Rawlinsons's appreciation served to reinforced the conclusions Kitchener had already reached about the futility of hammering away at the German line.

At this point, the members of the War Council, emerging from Kitchener's shadow, began to take an active role in shaping strategic policy. Like Kitchener, they were dismayed by the prospect of an interminable war of attrition in the west and by the policies being forced upon them by Sir John and Joffre. It was their contention that, if the British were to succeed anywhere in the near future, it would have to be outside of France.

Kitchener himself was sympathetic to a minor diversion that would boost morale at home, avoid frittering away the New Armies on hopeless offensives in Flanders, and produce some political and strategic benefits. He became increasingly interested in a plan that was the brainchild of Maxwell for a landing at Alexandretta (in the Gulf of Iskanderun), a short distance from the Baghdad railway. The Turkish garrison in the area was known to be small, and it could not be reinforced at short notice because the railway tunnels through the mountain ranges east and west of the gulf were still unfinished. Kitchener was sure that a comparatively small force would have no difficulty establishing itself on Turkish soil, especially since intelligence reports indicated that the invaders would almost certainly be welcomed and assisted by elements of the local population. Kitchener saw that the operation would have the effect of severing Turkey from Syria, removing the threat to the Suez Canal, and helping the Russians, who were experiencing difficulties in Armenia.[4]

There were three other projects under consideration by the War Council at the start of 1915. The authors—Churchill, Hankey, and Lloyd

George—were agreed on one major point, namely that the war in the west could not be won by frontal attacks. Churchill advocated the seizure of the island of Borkum as a preliminary step to the invasion of Schleswig-Holstein. The resulting control of the Baltic would not only make a German invasion or raid of Britain impossible, it would also enable a Russian Army to land near Berlin.[5] Hankey, in his paper, dismissed the notion of a direct strike against Germany. Schleswig-Holstein could be reached only through Denmark or Holland and, in his opinion, neither country was likely to enter the war voluntarily. Instead, Hankey urged a land campaign against Turkey, the weakest of Germany's allies. He thought that if three corps of the New Armies were available and, if Greece and Bulgaria could be persuaded to cooperate, it should be possible to capture Constantinople.[6] Lloyd George, for his part, suggested that the British Army ought to be removed from France, except for a reserve force to assist in case of an emergency, and that it should be employed in an attack upon Austria via Salonica or some port such as Ragusa on the Dalmatian coast. He was confident that Serbia, Romania, and Greece would be willing to cooperate "if they knew that a great English force would be there to support them."[7]

Before the War Council could entertain embarking on a new initiative, Kitchener considered it vital to establish a policy for the western front. On January 2, 1915, he wrote to French that the feeling was gaining ground among his colleagues that, owing to the stalemate in the west, troops, above and beyond what was necessary to hold the line there, would better be employed elsewhere. He requested the opinions of Sir John and his staff.[8] Kitchener might have received reasoned and impartial advice from a rebuilt General Staff at the War Office, but certainly not from GHQ, which opposed diverting any reinforcements from the western front.

Kitchener's note stunned French, who was unaware "of the shift of strategic opinion in London."[9] It had never occurred to him that the British government would ever consider lessening its commitment to offensive operations in the west. He interpreted Kitchener's move as an attempt to undermine his authority by reducing the importance of the western theater. For French, it was the last straw. His personal relations with Kitchener, under increasing strain since the early weeks of the war, broke down completely.

As French saw it, the only way to maintain the primacy of the western front and his own position was to ensure that the New Armies were sent out to France. In two memos to Kitchener, French insisted that given enough men and munitions, the German front could be broken by direct assault. He subjected other possible theaters to searching criticism, but went on to say that if the government was bent on opening a new front, he hoped it would sanction his Zeebrugge offensive. He considered it necessary to maintain the utmost pressure on the Germans; otherwise, they were likely to concentrate their resources on the eastern front. He warned that if the Germans defeated the Russians and brought back their forces west, he would not be able to resist the onslaught without substantial reinforcements. Either way, he would require every available soldier in Britain. Summing up, French claimed that "there are no theatres, other than those in progress, in which decisive results can be attained."[10]

French's views were incompatible with opinion in the War Council. The battle line was now drawn for a fight over the future direction of strategy. The traditional labels "easterners" and "westerners" are somewhat misleading, since both sides recognized the importance of the western front in defeating Germany. Their differences lay in the way they approached their common objective. Those who favored an indirect or peripheral strategy were mostly British politicians. They felt that it would oblige the Germans to disperse their strength to meet the new threat, opening the way for the Allies to drive them out of France and Belgium. The counterargument, supported by Sir John and the French high command, was that all available Allied troops, save those required to defend imperial interests, should be concentrated in the west, either to achieve a breakthrough or to immobilize the greater part of the German Army, which would facilitate a decisive Russian victory on the eastern front.[11]

On the same day that Kitchener wrote to French, the Foreign Office received a telegram from Grand Duke Nicholas, asking whether the British could arrange to make a military or naval demonstration to draw Turkish forces away from the Caucasus.[12] It is not certain that the plight of the Russians was as serious as the grand duke intimated, but Kitchener took the appeal at face value, worried that any further erosion in Russia's military strength might prompt the Tsarist government to opt out of the war. Nevertheless, he was unable to organize a military demonstration, as the only Regular division on hand, the Twenty-ninth, was needed in case the Germans attacked once more in the west, as he believed they would.

Kitchener's next recourse was to go over to the Admiralty and see if the First Lord could offer naval assistance. He discussed the matter with Churchill, and both agreed that a purely naval demonstration at the Dardanelles might be feasible, particularly if at the same time rumors could be spread that Constantinople was to be attacked.[13] No decision was taken, but on the evening of January 2, Kitchener wired Petrograd, assuring the grand duke that steps would be taken to make a demonstration against the Turks. He feared, however, that any action "we can devise and carry out will be unlikely to seriously affect numbers of enemy in the Caucasus, or affect their withdrawal."[14]

On January 4, the Russians foiled the Turkish envelopment movement in the midst of a violent blizzard, inflicting huge losses on the invaders and capturing most of the survivors.[15] Kitchener learned of the Russian victory on January 5,[16] and the momentous event was announced in several London newspapers that evening. As the raison d'être for a demonstration had disappeared, Kitchener gave the matter no further thought.

The War Council met on January 7 to consider Sir John French's scheme for an advance towards Zeebrugge in conjunction with the fleet. The members were no more attracted to the idea than when it had been broached informally the previous month. Kitchener eliminated any further talk when he insisted that he could not supply the men and munitions that Sir John had requested for the operation. The upshot was that the plan was voted down on the ground that the advantages would not be commensurate with the losses involved.[17]

The next day, the War Council focused on other possible war zones. Kitchener read Sir John's letter, which pleaded against committing large forces to any theater other than France. The Prime Minister expressed the view that French's case was strong, but he was clearly in the minority. There was much more interest in exploring options elsewhere. Lloyd George argued, with passion and conviction, about the merits of his Balkan proposal. Kitchener pointed out that his staff had made a preliminary examination and found it to be impracticable. He went on to say that a direct attack on Austria by way of Ragusa, or any other adequate port on the Adriatic, was out of the question owing to the risk of Austrian submarines, a difficult hinterland, and insufficient roads inland. Salonica was a good port, but it could be used only if Greece became an ally. And the single rail leading to Serbia could not sustain a large army.

Kitchener thought that the Dardanelles was a more suitable objective, as an attack there could be supported by the fleet. If successful, it would eliminate the Ottoman threat to vital areas of the Empire, open a southern sea route to Russia, and draw into the conflict Greece and perhaps other neutral Balkan states. He estimated that one hundred fifty thousand men would suffice for the task, but reserved final judgment pending a closer study.

Kitchener also suggested a landing at Alexandretta as a lesser, but useful, operation, requiring between thirty and fifty thousand men. The matter was still in the exploratory stage and would require further inquiry. But, in his closing remarks, he underlined that he could spare no troops for any subsidiary operation until the result of the next German attack in the west were known. If it failed, then he would favor proceeding with one of the plans suggested. The War Council adopted his recommendations.[18]

On January 9, Kitchener informed Sir John French that the War Council had rejected his Zeebrugge proposal, but continued to regard France as the primary theater for British operations. He gave French the green light to cooperate, as much as his resources permitted, with any offensive movement contemplated by Joffre. But, he warned that if, in the next few months, it was shown that the western front was deadlocked, he would consider it desirable to find another theater where operations against the enemy might not only encounter less resistance, but also have more productive results.[19]

In trying to decide where Britain might best employ its meager military reserves (which, in effect, would determine future strategy), Kitchener was caught between the conflicting demands of the War Council and the Anglo-French high command.[20] While he shared his colleagues' conviction that further offensives on the main front would be ineffective, he could not ignore Britain's obligation to the alliance. An anonymous War Office memorandum prepared at the time clearly shows the acute dilemma confronting Kitchener. The paper underlined the need to maintain the military commitment to the western front: To do otherwise would endanger the alliance with France and possibly allow the Germans to reach the channel ports. Its author favored a passive stance in Flanders, instead of the current policy of vigorous offensives, but recognized that the former option posed perhaps insurmountable political obstacles. As a compromise, the paper suggested an active defense, that is, local attacks, not so much to gain ground as to inflict damage on the Germans and to disrupt their plans.[21] Such a policy appealed to Kitchener, but he held little hope that it would be acceptable to the French and the Russians.

While Kitchener pondered his next move, Churchill came forward with a scheme that seemed to offer him a way out of his difficulties. The First Lord was looking for a way to recoup the prestige he had lost owing to personal missteps and the relatively feeble showing of the Navy. In search of a plan that did not require any troops, as none could be spared, he fastened on the idea of converting a mere demonstration, as requested by the grand duke, into an all-out attempt to force the Dardanelles by ships alone. Churchill had been in touch with the commander of the British squadron in the Aegean, Vice Adm. Sackville Carden, who thought that while the Dardanelles could not be rushed, they might be forced by an extended and methodical operation.[22] Churchill interpreted this guarded appraisal as meaning that the undertaking was feasible.

On January 11, Carden, in response to Churchill's request, submitted a plan which proposed to reduce the forts one by one, beginning at the entrance of the Dardanelles and then proceeding forward to the Narrows, where the minefields would be swept, thus opening the way for the fleet to advance into the Sea of Marmara.[23] The Admiralty War Staff Group[24] was initially enthusiastic about the plan, to the extent that Sir John Fisher, Battenberg's successor as first sea lord,[25] announced his intention to include in the naval force the latest and most powerful dreadnought, the *Queen Elizabeth*, so that it could test its guns against the Turkish forts. Churchill and his naval advisers had been so impressed at the ease with which the high-angle fire of the German heavy howitzers had smashed the powerful fortresses of Liège and Namur in August 1914 that they were misled into believing that the antiquated Turkish forts, with their short-range artillery, would not be able to withstand the 12-inch and 15-inch guns of the British ships.[26]

The First Lord had one more hurdle to overcome if he hoped to sell his plan to the War Council: to win over Kitchener who, only several days earlier, had estimated that one hundred fifty thousand men would be needed to capture Constantinople. Churchill later told the Dardanelles Commission[27] that he had circulated copies of Carden's telegram and plan to Kitchener before the War Council met on January 13.[28] His statement, however, omitted a vital piece of information. Churchill had too much at stake to rely on a few telegrams and technical documents to bring Kitchener around to his way of thinking. He knew that he could not succeed without a face-to-face encounter where he and his advisers could expound on the naval plan and answer any questions.

Accordingly, Churchill contacted Kitchener and arranged a hurried meeting, which was presumably held on January 12. Kitchener identified Fisher and Sir Arthur Wilson (Adm. of the Fleet) as also present. As far as I know, no other scholar of the period has alluded to this critical meeting. It was here that the decision was taken to launch a purely naval attack on the Dardanelles. What occurred at the War Council the next day, that is, on January 13, was a mere formality.

Kitchener, it must be remembered, did not have an opportunity to give his side of the story to the Dardanelles Commission, which was set up after his death. But he did tell a number of his aides—Arthur, Creedy, Cowans, and Maj. Gen. Sir Stanley von Donop (MGO)—that he had attended a conference with Churchill and some of his naval experts, at which time he had consented to support the naval attack on the Dardanelles. Testifying before the Commission in late 1916 and in 1917, none could remember the exact date on which the meeting had taken place, although Arthur thought it was around the middle of January 1915. All told a similar story of what had occurred, particularly the impact the *Queen Elizabeth* had made on their chief. According to them, Kitchener had strongly opposed the First Lord's idea when it was first broached, fortified by the knowledge that none of the previous investigations had ever contemplated unsupported naval action against the Turkish forts. Churchill countered by claiming that Carden's novel approached rendered obsolete Nelson's dictum that ships could not stand up to forts. The Navy, he went on to say, did not intend to rush the straits, but to attack the forts methodically and destroy them one by one. He painted a graphic picture of the Turkish forts crumbling "like the walls of Jericho" under the blistering firepower of the *Queen Elizabeth*.[29]

Although Kitchener appreciated that the super dreadnoughts could outrange the fortress guns, he had no way of knowing how effectively they would fire from an unstable platform at a distance of nine or ten miles. But, as far as he was concerned, this was an Admiralty plan. If the naval experts thought it was feasible, it was not his place to stand in the way. This was apparent in the evidence given by several of Kitchener's former subordinates. Von Donop recalled that he and Kitchener had discussed the naval plan on February 17, 1915: "My impression is that he had been told by the Admiralty that it was a possible thing to do, that he was very doubtful about it, but he was not prepared to give his opinion on a naval matter against the experience at the Admiralty."[30] Creedy said the same thing when asked if Kitchener had consulted military experts about the effect of the *Queen Elizabeth*'s guns against the Turkish forts. "This is a Naval matter," Kitchener had told him. "I must take it from the Naval experts."[31] Any nagging doubts Kitchener may have had were removed by the understanding that if the operation proved too difficult, or too costly, it could be treated as a demonstration and abandoned.

At another sitting, the Dardanelles Commission asked Churchill about the alleged private talks with Kitchener. Churchill, who was endeavoring to shift the blame to Kitchener for the failure at the Dardanelles (there is no better scapegoat than a dead one), denied that such an encounter had ever taken place. He claimed that it could not have happened before, on, or after January 13. Let us test the validity of Churchill's declaration. The transcript of the meeting on January 13 did not reveal the supposed exchanges between the two men, and the *Queen Elizabeth* was mentioned only in passing, as being available to take part in the action. Logic dictated that Churchill would have had no purpose in seeking Kitchener's endorsement after the meeting of January 13, when the War Council sanctioned the naval attack.

Churchill was on much less firm ground when he insisted that he could not possibly have met Kitchener before January 13, because the decision to use the *Queen Elizabeth* had not yet been made. A commissioner reminded him that it "was on the 12th that you sent a wire to Adm. Carden saying you should consider the effect of utilizing the 15-inch guns of the *Queen Elizabeth*." To which Churchill replied, somewhat sheepishly, "I had forgotten about that." Churchill's recollection of events was again wrong when he stated, "I cannot identify any conference of this character nor any protest of this character being made by Lord Kitchener, either when we were alone together, or in the presence of any other person at any time. My memory is very strong on this point."[32] This time Churchill's "memory lapse" escaped the attention of the commissioners, who, we are told, had been "furnished with all the materials necessary to form a correct and deliberate judgment."[33] On May 14, 1915, after the failures of the naval attack and the first military landing, Kitchener read a statement in the War Council. It should be emphasized that Churchill, who was in attendance, did not challenge any part of it. Kitchener essentially repeated what he had told Arthur and the others in January and February 1915:

> When the Admiralty proposed to force the passage of the Dardanelles by means of the fleet alone, I doubted whether the attempt would succeed, but was led to believe it possible by the First Lord's statements of the power of the *Queen Elizabeth*, and the Admiralty staff paper showing how the operations were to be conducted. The First Sea Lord and

Sir A. Wilson raised no objections at this Council or on the Staff Paper issued by the Admiralty, and apparently agreed in the feasibility of carrying out the projects of the Admiral on the spot. I considered that, though there was undoubtedly risk, the political advantages to be gained by forcing the Dardanelles were commensurate with that risk. . . . I regret I was led to agree in the enterprise by the statements made, particularly as to the power of the *Queen Elizabeth*, of which I had no means of judging.[34]

There is no reason to doubt Kitchener's version of what occurred. He discussed it with subordinates before the naval attack, when he was not actively involved in the operation. He repeated it in the presence of Churchill on May 14 in the War Council. Another point to consider was Kitchener's relative passivity at the War Council on January 13 after Churchill unveiled his scheme.

It was introduced just as the War Council was about to adjourn. Churchill presented the outline of Carden's plan with clarity and skill.[35] Although tired, the members were energized by the prospect that, once the ships broke through the Narrows, a revolution would sweep away the unpopular Young Turk regime and bring to power a pro-Entente government eager to negotiate a settlement. The effects would be electrifying: All dangers to Egypt would be removed; assistance could reach the Russians through the Dardanelles; and the Balkan states would be weaned from their neutrality. Kitchener said that the naval operation was worth trying, observing that the bombardment could be broken off if it did not prove effective. His unequivocal support of the naval plan muted any skepticism or dissent. The few members who spoke out shared Kitchener's optimism. Curiously enough, no one inquired why troops, deemed indispensable a few days earlier, were no longer necessary, or what had caused Kitchener to change his mind. The War Council concluded its meeting by authorizing the Admiralty to proceed along the lines Carden had outlined.[36] Apart from offering endless strategic possibilities in return for minimal risks, the operation would silence domestic political clamor for British offensive action outside of the western front and allow Kitchener breathing space, so that he could preserve his options and "avoid showing his hand until . . . German intentions were clear and the Armies were ready."[37]

As Churchill began naval preparations, he suggested to Kitchener that a landing at Alexandretta should take place concurrently with the attack on the Dardanelles. In case the naval attempt miscarried, it would be represented as a mere feint to cover the landing at Alexandretta. Churchill expected the naval operations to commence around February 15. Kitchener replied that he would be unable to assemble the requisite troops by that date.[38] The Anzacs, on whom he had counted for the Alexandretta project, were not fully trained and, moreover, were needed to meet the expected Turkish attack on the Suez Canal.

The War Council's decision in favor of a Dardanelles naval expedition did not prejudice continued debate on strategy. The central issue remained the same, namely where to deploy the New Armies. Interest refocused on Lloyd George's Balkan option after ominous reports reached London of an imminent Austro-German invasion of Serbia.[39] At a Cabinet meeting on January 20, Asquith agreed with Lloyd George that the fall of Serbia would be a serious military setback, in addition to crippling Entente efforts to win over the Balkan states. Kitchener took no position and simply said that he would "examine the situation carefully from a military point of view."[40]

Kitchener might have shown more enthusiasm if he could have been as certain as his two colleagues that the Balkan states would rally behind the Entente the moment they discovered that British troops were disembarking in the region. He did not understand the complex nature of Balkan politics, but he knew that all the states hated or distrusted one another. He had to take into account the possibility that, even with an Allied contingent in the Balkans, they might not enter the war. Most importantly of all, troops sent east, at least a corps in his estimation, would have to be drawn from units destined for, or already in, France.[41] Kitchener proposed to discuss the matter with Millerand, who was expected in London on the following day.

Fluent in French, Kitchener was able to converse with Millerand in his native tongue when he met him on January 22. He was favorably impressed by his French counterpart's rhetorical skills, bearing, and good sense, but there were clear differences between the two men. The French sought maximum British commitment to Continental operations to help them drive the Germans out of France. The British believed that, as their military support of the western front was far greater than they had promised before the war, they should be allowed to exercise strategic independence elsewhere.

Millerand argued that additional British troops were needed in France to take over a greater portion of the line, freeing French forces for Joffre's projected offensive. He knew perfectly well that any diversion of British troops for operations in a secondary theater would reduce Britain's commitment to France. While Millerand was equivocal about the idea of a Balkan expedition, he made it clear that any such move should not be considered until after the offensive Joffre was planning in the west had been carried out. Kitchener observed that it might be too late by then, since the Germans appeared poised to strike against Serbia. If they succeeded the "chance of closing the door to the south would be lost." Diplomacy having failed to bring in the Balkans, the only other option that might work was the sight of khaki. But Millerand remained adamant, insisting that all trained British forces should be fighting in France.[42] Kitchener told Millerand that he had arranged to send Sir John French two Territorial divisions, but made no promise that the New Armies would follow.

At dinner at the French Embassy on January 23, Kitchener and Millerand continued their discussion about the proposed Balkan plan. Kitchener had made it a cardinal principle from the moment he entered the War Office to maintain harmonious relations with the French. The last thing he wanted to do was to provoke a dispute over an issue about which he was somewhat ambivalent. Thus, he assured Millerand that he "would not press the Serbian scheme just now."[43] His arrangement with Millerand placed him at odds with his colleagues.

The War Council met twice on January 28. Churchill opened the morning session by declaring that preparations were well under way to commence the naval operation about the middle of February. There were cheery forecasts of what a naval victory would mean. Kitchener compared its effect to a successful campaign by the New Armies. Balfour was of the opinion that it would cut the Turkish Army in two, place Constantinople under Allied control, and permit Russia to resume its exports. Grey thought that it would finally settle the attitude of Bulgaria and the Balkans.[44] The others indulged in similar rosy predictions, except for Fisher who sat brooding in silence.

Since the meeting on January 13, Fisher had developed serious misgivings about the idea of a purely naval attack on the Dardanelles and had made his views known to practically everyone on the War Council. Kitchener was told that Fisher's objections were based not on technical grounds, but rather on fears that the naval attack would interfere with his own scheme for a major landing in the Baltic. What Kitchener did not know was that Admiralty opinion in general was inclined more and more to the belief that no real success could be achieved at the Dardanelles without the aid of troops. Still, he and the War Council missed an opportunity to subject Churchill's plan to rigorous scrutiny or to probe into Fisher's known objections. In the afternoon, Churchill called Fisher to his office and the two engaged in a long and tumultuous discussion. Under heavy pressure, the First Sea Lord reluctantly agreed to support the naval attack.[45] The Admiralty was now ready to carry out the task with which it had been charged.

For many years, military historians, sickened by the carnage on the western front and impressed by Churchill's apologia in *The World Crisis*, were practically unanimous in viewing the attack on the Dardanelles as a bold and imaginative concept. However, historical interpretations change, and, nowadays, scholarly opinion is divided, but weighs more towards the conclusion that the enterprise was ill conceived. The critics of the campaign have a good case. Germany triumphed in the east, but the war, which it lost, was decided in the west. It is questionable whether massive resources should have been diverted to a secondary theater. Moreover, there can be little doubt that Kitchener and the other members of the War Council entertained unrealistic expectations about the benefits that would accrue from successful action. There is no proof that Constantinople, or for that matter Turkey, would have surrendered. It is unlikely that it would have united the Balkan states in a great coalition against the Central Powers. A southern sea route to Russia would have been opened, but to what purpose? The western Allies could hardly be expected to supply war matériel to Russia when they could not meet their own needs.

Even among those who continue to believe that a diversion to the eastern Mediterranean was sound strategy, there is a consensus that it was justifiable only if it had been planned as a combined military and naval operation from the start. The Dardanelles Commission, which reached a similar conclusion, was highly critical of the War Council for accepting on faith Kitchener's assertion in January that he could not supply the necessary forces. An investigation, it alleged, would have shown that sufficient troops were available for a joint operation at an earlier date than was supposed. The Commission, however, misses the point. The real issue involved not one or two divisions, but rather the prospect of a heavy and continual drain on British resources that a fresh military campaign might impose. As Gen. Sir William Robertson pointed out, to force the Dardanelles, dominate Constantinople, open up the Bosphorus, and defeat, on their own ground, the large enemy forces likely to be encountered would probably require many divisions.[46] It was only reasonable, therefore, that Kitchener would hesitate to embark on a distant venture at a time when defenses in the west were still in a rudimentary stage and when he was under tremendous pressure from Sir John French and Joffre to reinforce the western front.

Kitchener, who had endorsed an operation for which he would eventually be forced to shoulder the responsibility, was in danger of being driven into yet another questionable commitment. At 4:00 P.M. on January 28, a subcommittee of the War Council, recently set up to explore Britain's military options, gathered under Kitchener's chairmanship at the War Office. Churchill, Lloyd George, Hankey, Balfour, and Callwell were its other members. Word had just arrived from Athens that Eleutherios Venizelos, the Greek prime minister, was ready to cooperate, subject to certain conditions: Bulgaria's entry into the war, or failing that, assurances of its benevolent neutrality; Romania's intervention; and two Allied corps, one French and one British, to assist Greek operations.[47]

Lloyd George felt that everything would fall into place if Kitchener committed troops to the Balkans. He seemed to have forgotten that Britain had no control over the first two stipulations and could only partially meet the third. Kitchener, according to Callwell, was "very guarded."[48] He agreed that helping the Serbs was a paramount British interest, but he was not quite sure that the right moment had arrived. He had no surplus troops at present, and it would be difficult to remove the requisite force from France. Lloyd George asked whether he could set a specific date for the release of an Army corps to the Balkans. Kitchener replied that there was no desperate urgency, as an Austro-German invasion of Serbia could not occur for some time, owing to the accumulation of snow in the area.[49]

Discussion on the subject resumed when the War Council reconvened at 6:30 that evening. Kitchener held firm to the views he had expressed earlier, promising to send troops to aid Serbia as soon as they could be spared. Balfour suggested that a nominal force, such as a brigade, be dispatched to Salonica at once as a token of Britain's earnest intentions to send more men when they were available. Grey was convinced that the appearance of five thousand British troops in Salonica might win over Bulgaria as well as Greece. Kitchener was less certain. He feared that a brigade, unless followed soon by larger forces, would become an object of ridicule.[50]

At Kitchener's suggestion, Churchill crossed over to France to try to pry two divisions from Sir John French. The field marshal showed no enthusiasm for the proposed Balkan venture, but Churchill broke down his resistance bit by bit, and in the end he agreed to place two divisions at the disposal of the government from the middle of March onwards.[51]

One obstacle having been overcome, there remained another. Since Kitchener did not want to renege on his promise to Millerand, he needed to reach an accommodation with the French. While in Paris for a finance conference, Lloyd George learned, to his surprise, that Millerand had said nothing to his colleagues about Britain's desire to send an expeditionary force to the Balkans. Lloyd George corrected the omission and lobbied hard for his scheme among the leading French politicians. His efforts elicited a positive response from everyone, save Millerand, who was Joffre's most fervent supporter in the government. The French were attracted to the enterprise partly because of the perceived political and military benefits and partly because they wanted to extend their already considerable financial interests in the region, which they hoped would assist in the postwar economic recovery of the country.[52] At a special meeting on February 4, the French Cabinet agreed to contribute a force, subject to Joffre's approval, for a joint expedition to the Balkans.[53] Delcassé carried his government's decision to London and, in talks with Kitchener, suggested that France and Britain each send a division to Salonica.[54]

Kitchener was not opposed to the idea. The need to help Serbia was more urgent than ever. The Foreign Office reported on February 7 that Bulgaria had obtained a loan from Germany, making its adhesion to the Central Powers appear imminent.[55] Kitchener thought that the presence of an inter-Allied force might tempt Greece to come to the aid of Serbia. The Allied divisions could be deployed to protect Greece's flank against any possible Bulgarian attack. Kitchener insisted that a Russian contingent be included in any expedition to the Balkans. He was under the misguided notion that the Bulgarians would never fire upon their fellow Slavs. A telegram was sent to the grand duke, who replied that he had no troops to spare and could only offer one thousand Cossacks—more trouble than they were worth since they would have to be transported to Salonica via Archangel.[56]

The pressure on Kitchener to find surplus troops had been somewhat eased in recent days by the removal of the immediate threat to Egypt. In the first week of February, a Turkish force of about twenty-five thousand men, having marched across the Sinai, attacked the central sector of the Suez Canal. The Turks were counting on a mutiny by the Egyptian troops and a rising by the civilian population to facilitate their invasion. When neither happened, they stood no chance against a garrison that was better armed and supplied and approached seventy thousand men. Their feeble assault across the canal was poorly executed and easily driven off. In the ensuing counterattack, the British took four hundred prisoners and sent the Turks retreating back into the desert. Maxwell reported to Kitchener that the invaders were of dubious fighting quality, estimating that 2,000 had been killed, while his own losses had totaled 160 men.[57]

Kitchener announced the good news at the War Council, which gathered again on February 9. Most of the discussion centered on the proposed expedition to the Balkans. Kitchener was adamant that only first-line British troops ought to be used. He was prepared to divert the Twenty-ninth Division, originally earmarked for France, and send in its place the North Midland Division, one of the best Territorial units. He added that if it were necessary to send troops to Turkey after the successful action of the fleet, units of the Twenty-ninth Division would be on hand. Sir John French, who was present, objected to the opening of a new front and to the exchange of troops, but he was overruled on both counts. The War Council authorized the Foreign Office to offer Greece the Twenty-ninth Division, in addition to the French division, if it would join the Entente.[58]

It should have been apparent to Allied diplomacy that the offer of two divisions, without the effects that might have resulted from a successful naval attack on the Dardanelles, was wholly inadequate. Indeed, the proposal of such limited aid was a confession of weakness and not likely to influence the Greeks, still less the Bulgarians. As it happened, Venizelos, although pro Entente, required tangible evidence of Allied power in his region if he hoped to shift the Greek king from his self-imposed neutrality. In these circumstances, he declined to drive Greece into the conflict without the collaboration of Romania. But, Romania was unwilling to intervene, unless it had reason to believe that an Entente victory was imminent. That prospect seemed more remote after the Germans opened a successful offensive in Poland against the Russians on February 7. Thus, the Balkan option receded into the background.[59] The attention of British policy makers was now fixed on the Dardanelles, where the ships assigned for the naval attack were on the spot or approaching it.

Several days before the Navy began the bombardment of the Dardanelles forts, Churchill succumbed to Admiralty pressure and began to lobby Kitchener for a military force.[60] Kitchener had already promised at the War Council on February 9 that troops would be available if the Navy required assistance at a later stage.[61] The repulse of the Turkish attack against the Suez Canal, plus the cancellation of the Balkan project, opened the possibility of sending troops to accompany the naval expedition. On February 16, Asquith hurriedly held an informal session of the War Council, with only six of the ten members present. Before the meeting, Kitchener had summoned Capt. Wyndham Deedes, an intelligence officer at the War Office, to ask him what he thought of the chances of a purely naval attack on the Dardanelles. Deedes, who had once served in the Turkish Army, replied that such an operation was bound to fail. As he proceeded to develop his arguments, Kitchener became angry and cut him off, told him he did not know what he was talking about, and dismissed him with a wave of his hand.[62]

Still, Deedes's warning left an impression on Kitchener, and at the War Council he agreed to the immediate dispatch of the Twenty-ninth Division to the island of Lemnos (lent to Britain by the Greek government as a base of operations), to be reinforced, if necessary, by thirty thousand Australian and New Zealand troops in Egypt.[63] Anxious to protect their claims to certain areas of the Ottoman Empire, the French government, which had already sent a naval squadron to serve under Carden, agreed to provide a division as well.[64]

The nature of the operation was beginning to change, but Kitchener remained confident that the fleet alone would force the Dardanelles.[65] As far as he was concerned, the military would be needed only to complete the destruction of the forts, to deal with concealed howitzers, and later to occupy Constantinople should a revolution occur.

More than ever now, the planning stage of the operation depended on the close and amicable collaboration of Kitchener and Churchill. However, Churchill's inability to resist meddling in military affairs once again strained his relationship with Kitchener. During the second week in February, Churchill and Kitchener locked horns over the purchase of Brazilian rifles, then on the market. Churchill not only gave his unsolicited opinion, but pressed Kitchener to buy them for the British Army before it was too late.[66] Kitchener turned on Churchill for involving himself in matters outside his jurisdiction and about which he knew precious little. There were many adventurers engaged in fraudulent practices without the means or intention to fulfill pledges. Kitchener refused to act precipitously, skeptical as he was of the offer. Churchill "emerged from his fearful row with Kitchener by the skin of his teeth," Margot Asquith recorded in her diary, only "to let himself into another."[67] Asquith described Churchill's second misadventure to Venetia Stanley on February 18:

> I am rather vexed with Winston who has been tactless enough to offer Sir John F. (behind Kitchener's back and without his knowledge) a brigade of his Naval Division, and two squadrons of his famous Armoured Cars which are being hawked about from pillar to post. Kitchener came to me and complained very strongly both of the folly of the offer itself and of its being made without any previous consultation with him. French was evidently very puzzled [about] what to do with these unwelcome gifts—the Naval battalions being still raw and ragged, and the only use he would suggest for the cars being to remove from them their Maxim guns for the use of his troops.[68]

Asquith discussed the latest crisis with his wife the next day: "K is of course furious—and says to me he wonders what Winston would say if he . . . was always writing to Jellicoe offering to do this and that. Of course Winston is intolerable. It is all vanity—he is devoured by vanity."[69]

Churchill was not one to admit that he was wrong whenever he was out of line. Rather, it was characteristic of him to strike back and adopt a defiant attitude. In reply to the Prime Minister, he gave a colored version of what had occurred, implying that it was French who had approached him: "I have no power to offer any troops to Sir John French. All I can do is to hand over to the War Office, when they ask me for them, any Admiralty units which may be thought to be of use to the Army in the field." He was angry that Kitchener, instead of raising the matter directly with him, had gone to the Prime Minister. He concluded by saying, "I do not remember that I have ever claimed your aid against any colleagues otherwise than in Cabinet."[70] That is probably an accurate statement, but then, none of his colleagues made it a habit of interfering in Admiralty business.

Churchill was still smarting from the Prime Minister's rebuke when he wrote to Kitchener on February 19. He reminded Kitchener that he had known for some months of the existence of the armored cars and the naval divisions and "what was the intention with which they were called into being." The First Lord claimed there was never any doubt in his mind that it "has always rested and now rests exclusively with you when and how they shall join the army." He said little about the naval divisions, except to indicate that they were no longer available for employment in France, since the Admiralty had decided to send them to the Dardanelles. As for the armored cars, he placed the blame on French for the manner in which he had worded a phrase: "If his letter [to Kitchener] had begun 'I have heard that there are some armoured cars available which the Admiralty have prepared and etc.' instead of by talking about 'the offer of the First Lord of the Admiralty' this whole wearisome incident would have been avoided."[71] Kitchener discounted Churchill's explanation. He knew that French would not have solicited his help, unless he was feeling the pressure from his old friend to accept something he did not want.

The tension between the two men became even more acute in the days that followed. At the War Council on February 19, Kitchener announced that he was countermanding his order to divert the Twenty-ninth Division to the Dardanelles and, instead, would send the Anzacs from Egypt. He feared that if the Russians suffered a decisive defeat in Poland, where they had lost very heavily in men, the Germans would be in a position to bring back great masses of troops rapidly to France. In the event of the Germans making a renewed attempt on the western front, he wanted to have in hand a mobile reserve to throw in at any threatened point. He calculated that the Anzacs, together with the naval division, should suffice to exploit the success of the naval operation. Kitchener's decision to retain the Twenty-ninth Division was prudent in view of the critical situation on the Russian front. In fact, it would have been an act of folly to have allowed the Twenty-ninth Division to proceed to Lemnos when it might have been more urgently needed on the western front.

Churchill, who had not been forewarned of the change of plans, protested vigorously, saying that the men of Twenty-ninth Division were needed to stiffen the far less experienced second-line troops. He pointed out that, with the vast forces massed on the western front, their absence would not be missed, whereas in the Dardanelles they might well make all the difference. He had hoped to have fifty thousand men available to reach the Dardanelles at three days' notice. After weeks of self-deception, Churchill had at last recognized the limitations of naval power. He admitted for the first time that the Navy alone would be unable to keep the straits open for the merchant ships. "We should never forgive ourselves," he exclaimed, "if this promising operation failed owing to insufficient military support at the critical moment." The general sentiment in the War Council supported Churchill's position. Lloyd George, in one of his frequent whimsical moments, went so far as to urge Kitchener to send twice as many troops east as Churchill wanted, reasoning that it was "worth while to take some risks in order to achieve a decisive operation, which might win the war." But Kitchener's only concession was that he would release the Twenty-ninth Division if its presence were required to ensure the success of the enterprise.[72]

After the meeting broke up, Churchill returned to the Admiralty, and, without the approval of either the Prime Minister or War Council, issued a press communiqué, announcing the success of the opening day's bombardment against the Turkish forts at the entrance of the Straits.[73] Quite apart from the fact that Carden's attack had caused little or no damage, the statement, as Lloyd George subsequently remarked, made it impossible for the War Council to contemplate quietly withdrawing the Navy from the scene if things went awry.[74] Some historians believe that the publicity was intended to influence the wavering neutral states.[75] If so, it went against the wishes of the War Council, which would not have leaked information about the naval operation unless reasonably assured of victory. But I am more inclined to believe that Churchill acted out of his own selfish interest. He expected an eventual victory and was positioning himself to reap the lion's share of the credit. Whatever the reason, it was a terrible blunder. Churchill's indiscretion triggered a tragic sequence of events that would, apart from the damage to his own career, "destroy Kitchener's effectiveness in the cabinet and War Council, bring down the Liberal government, set back British diplomacy in the Balkans, and lead to the vain expenditure of tens of thousands of lives."[76]

The reaction to the First Lord's announcement was evident at the War Council on February 24. None of the members openly rebuked Churchill for his irresponsible statement, although some had grumbled about it privately before the meeting.[77] But now that the cat was out of the bag, speaker after speaker believed that the Army must help if the necessity should arise. Kitchener, in an unguarded moment, made a decision that he would live to regret. He indicated that if the Navy could not force the Straits unaided, the Army should see the business through. He went on to say, "The effect of a defeat in the orient would be very serious. There could be no going back. The publicity of the announcement has committed us."[78] It was uncharacteristic of Kitchener to make a critical decision in haste. He evidently hoped that troops would not be required in any great numbers, but he ought to have known that, in war, wishful thinking is no substitute for methodical, dispassionate reasoning.

Since the start of the year, we have seen that Kitchener, mindful of Britain's military penury, had hesitated to embark on a potential major land campaign. Not only did he now unwittingly commit himself to the sort of thing he had desperately wanted to avoid, he did so on the spur of the moment and without having consulted the General Staff, which alone could have given him a reasoned statement of the risks involved and of the number of troops required to ensure the success of the operation. It would not have obliged him to do anything to have set the General Staff to study the military problems scientifically and to work out plans for various contingencies. Only when a thorough investigation had been done would he have been in a position to count the cost and determine whether he was justified in substituting a strenuous combined effort for the limited original plan. To have done otherwise was to court disaster.

The possibility that the Navy would require the assistance of the Army to get through strengthened feeling in the War Council for sending the Twenty-ninth Division to the eastern Mediterranean. The tug-of-war between Kitchener and Churchill continued for the remainder of the meeting on February 24 and resumed at the next one two days later. Churchill trotted out all of the old arguments, reinforced by new ones, but Kitchener, though standing virtually alone, refused to budge. Kitchener persisted in viewing the Dardanelles operation as essentially a naval concern with the Army acting in an auxiliary capacity. Although he had agreed that the Army must play a major role should the ships fall short of their objective, he was opposed to a preliminary military assault on the Gallipoli Peninsula, which, according to unsubstantiated reports, was heavily fortified and supposedly defended by about forty thousand Turkish soldiers.[79]

Churchill's biggest fear was that, having penetrated the straits, insufficient troops would be there to exploit the Navy's success. He called for large numbers of troops, without any clear idea of how, when, or where they would be used. Kitchener was puzzled by Churchill's seemingly confused state of mind. Suspecting that Churchill intended to use troops in the initial assault, he asked him whether he contemplated a land campaign. Churchill replied that he did not, but that it was conceivable that the ships might be held up by mines. In such an event, a local military operation would be required to knock out the forts so that the minesweepers could proceed with their work. Later he changed his position again. He wanted the troops "to occupy Constantinople and to compel a surrender of all Turkish forces remaining in Europe after the Fleet had obtained command of the Sea of Marmara."

Churchill's glowing enthusiasm and persuasive arguments in initially converting Kitchener to the feasibility of a purely naval attack made it difficult for him to build a case for the importance of having a large army on the spot. Kitchener envisaged that, once the fleet broke into the Sea of Marmara, the Turkish garrison on the peninsula would withdraw or be cut off and forced to surrender. In Constantinople, there would be general panic, followed by a *sauve qui peut* with the Sultan, the government, and elements of the Turkish Army fleeing to Asia. Kitchener was certain there would be enough troops on hand to hold what had been won by the ships and undertake minor operations, so he saw no reason to send out his last Regular division as long as the Russian front remained unstable. Churchill pleaded with the Prime Minister to overrule Kitchener, but to no avail.[80]

For three weeks, Kitchener withstood Churchill's onslaught without giving ground. It was not until March 10, when conditions on the eastern front had improved sufficiently, that he consented to dispatch the Twenty-ninth Division. The long period of haggling in the War Council had been an ordeal for Kitchener. It had taken a good deal of staying power to outlast Churchill, who was much more formidable in debate than he was. No less unsettling was the fact that he had been challenged on a question of military policy for the first time. The War Council had grudgingly deferred to his judgment, but it was clear that his military pronouncements no longer had the ring of divine authority.[81]

Kitchener recognized a little belatedly that the operation he had agreed to on January 12 and 13 was changing in nature, from one using ships alone to one that also included using troops in some capacity on the Gallipoli Peninsula. On March 11, Kitchener informed his colleagues that he had selected Gen. Ian Hamilton to command the seventy thousand British troops now being assembled at Lemnos. Kitchener, it will be remembered, had tried unsuccessfully to substitute Hamilton for French in November 1914. Yet, Hamilton had not been his preferred choice. Kitchener thought highly of Hamilton as a subordinate, but had misgivings about appointing him to an independent command abroad. He knew Hamilton to be impulsive and a bit unsteady in purpose and evidently wanted someone steadfast and strong enough in character to assert his authority. Initially, he had set his sights on an old comrade, Sir Leslie Rundle, then serving in Malta as governor and commander in chief. Rundle had compiled a distinguished record in colonial warfare and was known to be tough, resolute without being reckless, and thorough. But, at the last moment, Asquith intervened and, for reasons that are difficult to fathom, insisted that he appoint Hamilton.[82] Kitchener yielded to the Prime Minister's wishes, no doubt because he did not anticipate extensive military operations on Gallipoli.

On March 12, Kitchener summoned Hamilton to his office and notified him of his new appointment. Kitchener described the forces at Hamilton's disposal and made it clear that the Twenty-ninth Division was only on loan and must be returned as soon as its services could be spared. At this point, Callwell entered the room and, with the aid of a map, gave an outline of a pre-1914 Greek plan to seize the Gallipoli Peninsula. When he explained that the Greeks intended to employ one hundred fifty thousand men, Kitchener interjected to say that half that number would suffice, as the Turks were busy elsewhere. The plain truth was that Kitchener had no more troops available. It might have been enough to reach the Narrows if the Army had participated in the initial assault, but not in a later landing after the enemy had been alerted. Before the interview ended, Kitchener told Hamilton, "I hope you will not have to land at all; if you do have to land, why then the powerful Fleet at your back will be the prime factor in your choice of time and place."[83]

As Kitchener had requested, Hamilton returned to the War Office the next day for his final briefing. Since Kitchener had not yet decided on the scope of the operations, Hamilton's instructions on certain points were vague. The Army was not to engage in major land operations until the fleet had exhausted every effort to get through alone. Before carrying out any serious undertaking, Hamilton was to await the assembly of all his forces to ensure that their full weight could be thrown in. Once the Army was committed to action, there could be no thought of abandoning the enterprise. The operation would require time, patience, and methodical cooperation between the naval and military commanders. The essential object, Kitchener reminded Hamilton, was to avoid a check that would jeopardize the chances of strategical and political success.

Kitchener did not preclude minor operations to clear areas from which mobile guns were impeding the fleet's progress or to complete the destruction of Turkish batteries already silenced. Hamilton should restrict such action to the objective in view and avoid permanent occupation of positions on the Gallipoli Peninsula.[84]

For the most part, Hamilton would be operating in the dark. During the immediate prewar years, British intelligence had neglected to survey and map vital strategic areas of the Ottoman Empire.[85] Thus, Kitchener could not provide Hamilton with such elementary information as a current map of, and the disposition of Turkish troops on, the Gallipoli Peninsula.

It is difficult to know what was passing though Kitchener's mind at this time. A General Staff appreciation at the end of January did not contemplate an attack on the Dardanelles unless it assumed the form of an amphibious operation.[86] Given Kitchener's feelings about the General Staff, it is understandable why he did not give the suggestion much consideration. However, he was getting similar advice from other quarters. Reporting from the scene, his own trusted confidant, Lt. Gen. William Birdwood (commander of the Anzacs), had expressed doubts that the fleet could penetrate the straits unaided.[87] Maxwell warned him that the Navy was too optimistic. While Carden would encounter no insurmountable obstacles in silencing fixed coastal batteries, dealing "with moveable armaments is another question."[88] Yet Kitchener discarded their opinions, choosing instead to believe Churchill, a man whose judgment he considered erratic. Evidently, Kitchener had made up his mind that the naval attack would succeed and not even those in whom he placed a good deal of faith could persuade him that he might be wrong.

The almost casual manner in which Kitchener drifted into, and handled preparations for, the campaign can be understood only in light of his belief that Turkey was a feeble military power and that its unpopular and despotic government would crumble after the ships had unleashed a few salvos.[89] At no point in the opening stage did he bother to consult the General Staff, which could have obtained, if given enough time, intelligence to draw up a preliminary plan of operation as required under field regulations and could have made reasoned recommendations about landing sites and the number of troops required for success. Nor did Kitchener seek to define the relationship between Hamilton and the person with whom he was required to work closely, the naval commander. There existed no central mechanism in Whitehall to coordinate the activities of the two services. Thus, the Army and Navy operated as separate entities, often without reference to one another. The question of who would command a combined operation in the Dardanelles, should one become necessary, was never addressed. Kitchener was relying on the Army commander on the spot to use his discretion to pull things together and to devise a workable plan. For a man who normally took his adversaries seriously, left nothing to chance, and prepared for every contingency, Kitchener violated practically every one of his usual practices, as well as the fundamental principles of amphibious warfare.

That night, Hamilton and his hurriedly assembled staff left London and, boarding a swift vessel at Marseilles, arrived at Lemnos at 3:00 P.M. on March 17. The next day Vice Adm. J. M. de Robeck, who had replaced Carden as naval commander,[90] made a full-scale attack on the forts at the Narrows. The outcome was an unmitigated disaster, with six ships sunk

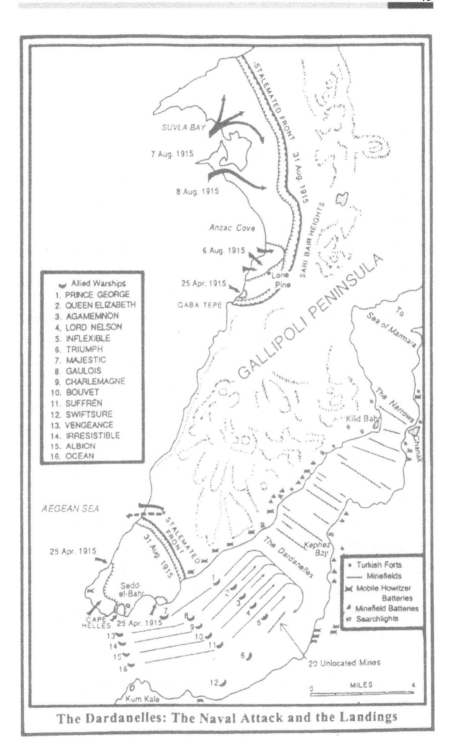

The Dardanelles: The Naval Attack and the Landings

or disabled by Turkish mines.[91] The next day, Hamilton, who had witnessed the naval attack, wired Kitchener that he was reluctantly driven to the conclusion that the straits could not be forced by ships alone. If the Army were to participate, it would take the form not of the subsidiary operation anticipated, but rather of a deliberate advance carried out in force in order to open a passage for the Navy.[92] Kitchener was dismayed by Hamilton's appreciation. Although reluctant to embark on a difficult campaign, he felt he had no choice. He replied at once: "You know my views that the passage of the Dardanelles must be forced, and that if large military operations on the Gallipoli Peninsula by the Army are necessary to clear the way, those operations must be undertaken after careful consideration of the local defences, and must be carried through."[93] On March 23, Hamilton and de Robeck held a conference, at which it was decided to abandon the naval attack in favor of a combined operation. Hamilton reckoned that the Army would not be ready to land before April 14. Unfortunately, neither Hamilton nor de Robeck was trained in amphibious warfare, with the result that the Army, instead of sweeping in after the fleet had engaged the forts, was largely left to its own devices to gain the beachheads in the face of hostile fire.

Looking back, it is clear that an attack on the Dardanelles by ships alone was a dreadful mistake. Churchill maintained in *The World Crisis* that he would never have planned for a purely naval operation had he known that troops would be available shortly.[94] That assertion is certainly not true. Everyone in the War Council was aware that the first divisions of the New Armies would be ready to take the field in April.

It will be remembered that three days before the ships began to bombard the outer forts, altered circumstances had prompted Kitchener to agree to concentrate modest forces in the neighborhood in case they were needed. Despite a vital change in policy, Churchill did not request a revision of his plan, or even a postponement of naval action until military forces, which his own advisers were so sure would be indispensable, could arrive on the spot. He could have hinted that unforeseen difficulties (such as bringing together an efficient minesweeping force capable of operating against a strong current in a narrow channel) made it less likely that the ships alone could silence the forts. This would have opened the way for him to suggest the advisability, now that troops were to be sent, of avoiding the risks of a piecemeal attack and of waiting for a combined operation with all the advantage of surprise. A delay of several months would have substantially increased Kitchener's reserves, and with more flexibility he might well have consented to a joint operation. In the interim, a joint staff committee could have studied the problems of an attack on the Dardanelles and defined the objectives of the operation so that a proper appreciation of the forces needed to attain them could have been made. However, that scenario never materialized because Churchill wanted to act immediately. He saw a chance to change the nature of the war and in the process disarm his critics and revive his flagging career.

Kitchener was drawn into the Dardanelles miasma piecemeal and against his better judgment. Blinded by the First Lord's glowing optimism, he never seriously considered the likelihood of a full-scale military campaign until the naval attack had miscarried. It helps explain, although it does not justify, his failure to make adequate military preparations. But, even if he had taken better precautions, it is doubtful if the outcome would have been significantly different. With the naval operation, the element of surprise had been compromised. The damage could not be repaired. Before the end of February the Turks had slightly less than thirty-five thousand men; by March 18, the date of the naval assault against the forts at the Narrows, the defenders approached the size of Hamilton's army; and, during the five weeks that elapsed between the naval assault and the military landing, their numbers further increased, and their primitive defensive system was placed on a thoroughly sound footing.[95] Hamilton was certainly handicapped by inadequate War Office assistance, but it was the advance publicity that doomed his army before it could land on the beaches.

8

IMPERIAL ISSUES AND
PERIPHERAL THEATERS II

WHEN it became clear to the Foreign Office that Kitchener would not be returning to Egypt in the near future, it decided that a temporary replacement for him was needed. Grey broached the subject to Kitchener, who not only agreed, but indicated that he had someone in mind for the job. With Grey's approval, Kitchener selected Sir Henry McMahon, an old friend from his India days.[1] McMahon was cautious, patient, and likable, but he lacked administrative ability, did not speak or understand Arabic, was unfamiliar with Egyptian politics, and was indecisive and rather dull witted.[2] But he owed his position to Kitchener's favor, and if he lacked qualifications, he could be expected to follow his patron's views and to report to him frequently and fully. McMahon took up his appointment in January 1915 under the new title of High Commissioner. Storrs and his colleagues did not think highly of McMahon and continued to look upon Kitchener as their real chief. Maxwell, who was responsible to the War Office and reported directly to Kitchener, ignored the High Commissioner altogether.

Shortly after McMahon's arrival in Cairo, Russia's drive to achieve its historic ambition opened a new and unanticipated phase of Allied imperialism in the Mediterranean. In February, when the fall of Constantinople and the straits into Anglo-French hands seemed imminent, generalities and vague promises were no longer sufficient for Petrograd. On March 7 Sazonov requested formal recognition of his government's claims to specific Ottoman territories. Anxious to avoid anything in the nature of a breach with the Tsarist government, the western Allies agreed immediately, abandoning their long-standing opposition to Russia's access to the warm waters of the Mediterranean.[3]

Having consented in principle to the partition of the Ottoman Empire, the Asquith government turned next to the matter of formulating its own territorial aims.[4] Months earlier, Kitchener, anticipating the dismemberment of Ottoman territory, had turned to his former staff in Cairo, in particular Storrs and Sir Gilbert Clayton (head of intelligence), to work out the details of his plan for a separate Arab kingdom in the postwar Middle East. At the beginning of March 1915, Storrs wrote to FitzGerald, proposing a North African or Near Eastern viceroyalty that would include Egypt and the Sudan and stretch all the way from Aden to Alexandretta. Such an entity, ruled by Kitchener from Cairo, would "surely compare in interest and complexity, if not in actual size with India itself."[5] What in effect Storrs was suggesting was a confederation of most of the Arab-speaking states under a British protectorate.[6] Storrs did not mention Syria, but in a letter to his parents at about the same time indicated that he would like to see it incorporated into Egypt.[7]

Syria bulked large in Kitchener's imperial vision. He wanted to detach Syria, or part of it, and form a separate entity controlled directly or indirectly by Britain. Here he had no support from the Foreign Office, which considered Syria a French preserve. Kitchener had presented his case to Grey on November 14, 1914, only to be told bluntly, "We cannot act as regards Syria."[8] Kitchener nevertheless persisted, encouraged by reports from various sources that, other than the Maronites, a Christian sect along the Mount Lebanon coast, most Syrians had no more use for the French than for the Ottomans. That being the case, his informants supposed (erroneously it should be added) that the Syrians must be pro-British.[9] They were convinced that the French could be persuaded to give up Syria, except for the Christian areas, which they conceded were probably non-negotiable. Kitchener shared their optimism, reasoning that the French might be willing to confine their claims in Syria in exchange for German colonies in Africa.

British war aims were discussed sporadically in the War Council on March 10 and more fully at the next meeting nine days later. From the outset, it was understood that the nation's territorial claims would be tailored to safeguard the Empire after the war against possible rivals. There was virtual unanimity that Britain's interest lay in destroying German militarism, not Germany.[10] Kitchener and his colleagues blamed the dominance of the Prussian military party for Germany's aggressive policy, which, in their eyes, had led to the war. This perception shaped the notion that the fundamental objective was to inflict a defeat on the German Army of such dimensions as to discredit the Prussian military caste completely and so prevent it from ever gaining control over German policy.

Kitchener believed that a balance of power in a postwar Europe was contingent on a strong, rather than a crippled, Germany. He cautioned against keeping German colonies, as this, more than anything else, would "interfere with the future establishment of goodwill between Germany and ourselves after the war."[11] There was, in Kitchener's view, no need to fear Germany once its leaders were removed, its navy destroyed, and a good portion of its wealth siphoned off to meet huge Allied reparation demands.[12] A chastened Germany, weakened but still powerful, could serve Britain's interests by acting as a counterweight to Russia. Kitchener did not expect the Entente to hold together after Germany's defeat.[13] He considered that, in a postwar world, Russia, and to a lesser extent France, posed a greater threat to Britain than Germany.

If geopolitics induced Kitchener to call for a strong Germany, the same concern led him to quite a different judgment about the future of the Ottoman Empire. Kitchener told his colleagues on March 10 that, with Russia in Constantinople and France in Syria, he worried that in the event Britain found itself at war with either or both of these powers, "our communications with India by the Suez Canal might be seriously endangered and Egypt itself might be placed in considerable jeopardy."[14] For Kitchener, the security of Egypt and the strategic Suez Canal route to India, East Asia, and the newly acquired oil supplies of southern Persia was essential to Britain. In his grand design for a postwar Middle East, Britain would control a swath of territory just beyond the recently annexed island of Cyprus to India, permitting a direct land route that would be safe from interruption by either Russia or France. To that end, he wanted Britain to take possession of Alexandretta, a superb natural port on the Asiatic mainland, Mesopotamia, and part of Syria, with the regions linked by the construction of a long railroad.

Kitchener's views were contained in a memorandum prepared for the War Council meeting on March 19. He omitted any reference to an interest in Syria, which he knew would provoke protests from Grey and the

Prime Minister as bound to involve Britain in a conflict with France. Instead, he confined his case to Alexandretta and Mesopotamia. Kitchener, who on March 10 had stated that the acquisition of Alexandretta was necessary for the defense of Egypt,[15] now had a different explanation:

> The question of a British occupation of Alexandretta entirely depends upon the future of Mesopotamia, for, if there is no intention of acquiring the Euphrates Valley as a result of this war, the occupation of Alexandretta would mean the establishment of a dangerous outpost, and involve us in responsibilities with no commensurate advantage. But if the acquisition of Mesopotamia is contemplated, it at once becomes necessary to hold Alexandretta with a British force.

Kitchener listed a number of reasons why the British should acquire Alexandretta: (1) in case of an emergency, troops dispatched from Great Britain to Mesopotamia would arrive a fortnight sooner if moved by rail from Alexandretta rather than by sea via the Suez Canal; (2) that being the case, Mesopotamia could be garrisoned by a smaller force; (3) the British would be in a better strategic position to counter any Russian threat to Mesopotamia; and (4) it would facilitate British efforts to control the traffic of arms to the Arab tribes of Mesopotamia. Another point, not raised by Kitchener, but surely in his mind, was an observation made by McMahon: "Its possession [Alexandretta] would appear to ensure the settlement of the Syrian question to our advantage in due course of time."[16]

Kitchener went into similar detail when arguing the benefits of incorporating Mesopotamia into the Empire: (1) if the British government passed the opportunity to take Mesopotamia, the Russians would do it sooner or later, thus gaining an outlet to the Persian Gulf and eroding the prestige of Britain, which traditionally dominated those waters, as an Asiatic power; (2) its possession would, along with the Persian Gulf, the Red Sea, and Egypt, enable Britain to secure all the approaches to the Muslim holy places; (3) Mesopotamia, with proper irrigation, could become one of the most fertile and productive agricultural areas of the world and, given its large unsettled areas, provide India with an outlet for its surplus population; and (4) occupation of Mesopotamia would protect British interests in the Persian oil fields, as well as control the land route from the Mediterranean to the Persian Gulf, a future direct lifeline to India. It can be seen that Kitchener's plan was based mainly on strategic considerations.

Kitchener countered some of the objections that he anticipated from his colleagues. While conceding that the territories in question meant an immediate addition to Britain's imperial responsibilities, he predicted that in time they would become self-supporting on account of their great natural wealth. He assumed, too, that the French would lay claim to Alexandretta. If they did, it would not be a legitimate demand, since Alexandretta, in his view, was outside Syria. He felt certain that the French would be content with territory elsewhere as compensation for denial of the port.[17]

Kitchener's memorandum generated more dissent than support in the War Council. Only Churchill and Fisher endorsed it fully. The Admiralty was interested in building a base at Alexandretta and exploiting the rich oil deposits of Mesopotamia. The India Office preferred Haifa or Acre instead of Alexandretta, but was divided over Mesopotamia. The political department coveted it as an ideal field of colonization for the surplus population of India. On the other hand, the military department wanted to preserve the territorial integrity of the Ottoman Empire so as to provide a barrier against a potential Russian threat. Asquith felt that Britain was in possession of as much territory as it was able to hold, but conceded that they would be derelict in their duty if they left other nations to carve up Turkey without taking anything themselves. Grey and Haldane were of a similar mind.[18]

The absence of a consensus in the War Council and the need to remove the issue from the crowded agenda drove Asquith on April 8 to appoint an interdepartmental committee under Sir Maurice de Bunsen, Assistant Undersecretary of State at the Foreign Office, to consider the nature of Britain's desiderata in Asiatic Turkey. Kitchener selected Callwell to represent the War Office, and, in addition, placed Sir Mark Sykes on the committee as his own representative. Sykes, a wealthy young Tory MP, had traveled widely throughout the Middle East and was a recognized authority on Ottoman affairs.[19] Speaking from first-hand knowledge and with the full authority of Kitchener, he dominated the committee's proceedings. Although Sykes rarely saw Kitchener, he reported nightly to FitzGerald and, from him, received his patron's instructions.[20]

The de Bunsen report considered four alternate schemes available to Britain for dealing with the Ottoman Empire in Asia.[21] Its preferred solution was to preserve the Ottoman Empire as an independent state, but one decentralized along federal lines. If that proved impossible, it favored

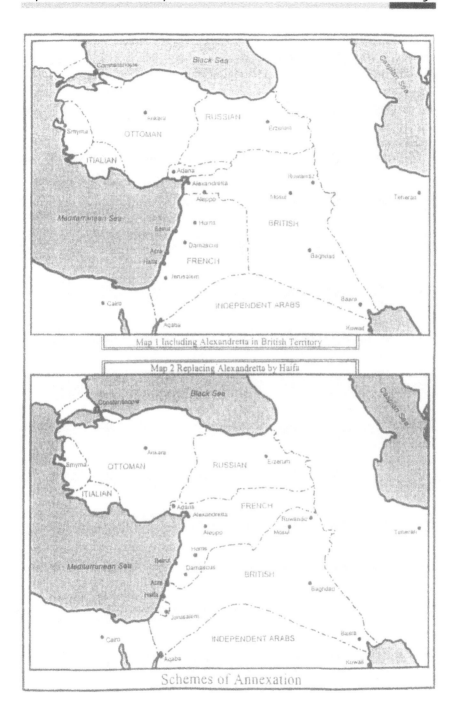

Map 1 Including Alexandretta in British Territory

Map 2 Replacing Alexandretta by Haifa

Schemes of Annexation

the partition of the non-Turkish portions of the Empire, with Britain acquiring a stretch of land between Acre and Amadia in the north and
Aqaba and the Persian Gulf in the south. The report endorsed Kitchener's
views "on the significance of Mesopotamia and of the Mediterranean to
Persian Gulf connection for the British Empire."[22] Similarly, it shared
Kitchener's assessment of Palestine. Lloyd George had pressed for its acquisition at the War Council on March 10, but Kitchener had replied that
"it would be of no value to us whatsoever."[23] The report observed that it
would be unwise to incorporate Palestine, owing to the likelihood of
strong foreign opposition. The same reason would apply to France if it
tried to claim it. The report concluded that the fate of Palestine should be
discussed and settled in concert with other interested powers. Another of
its recommendations emanated directly from Kitchener, who had declared
in his memorandum that "should the partition of Turkey take place, it is
to our interests to see an Arab kingdom installed in Arabia under the auspices of England . . . and containing within it the chief Mahommedan
Holy Places, Mecca, Medina and Kerbela."[24]

Sykes shared many of Kitchener's prejudices and sentiments, and the
two men saw eye-to-eye on every major issue save one. All along, Kitchener had insisted on Alexandretta in order to secure a wholly British line of
communication between the Persian Gulf and the eastern Mediterranean.
Sykes argued against Alexandretta on the following grounds: It would set
Britain on a collision course with France; it was incompatible with Kitchener's preference for a French buffer zone between future British and Russian territories; and the construction of a railway between Alexandretta
and Mesopotamia would be too costly. Instead, Sykes preferred Haifa in
Palestine, which was closer to Egypt and could easily be linked to Mesopotamia by a new railroad. Their differences were hammered out one evening at York House,[25] where according to Sykes Kitchener eventually
became reconciled, "though reluctantly, to Haifa."[26] All in all, the de Bunsen report was a triumph for Kitchener.

The de Bunsen report was composed hurriedly, and its conclusions
were framed in general terms. It was not intended to be a definitive study,
but rather to be a sketch of British desiderata in Asiatic Turkey to guide
the Foreign Office in its upcoming negotiations with the French. While
the Anglo-French discussions were in progress throughout 1915, Kitchener
carried on parallel negotiations with Sharif Hussein through McMahon
at the British Agency.

During the early part of December 1914, the French had startled

Whitehall by proposing joint talks on the future of Arabia. It now became a matter of urgency for the British to establish effective alliances with the most influential tribal chiefs in Arabia. Kitchener planned a new initiative, as his negotiations with Abdullah in the late summer and autumn of 1914 had stalled. The India Office, annoyed that it was not consulted at the time of the correspondence, preferred to pursue other Arab princes instead of Sharif Hussein. It acknowledged that the Sharif's prestige was paramount in certain areas of the Middle East, but doubted that he could rally a large body of supporters in Arabia. On the contrary, Britain's support of Hussein would displease his suspicious neighbors, who could hardly forget that not long ago he had waged war against his enemies, Abd al-Aziz Ibn Sa'ud, Emir of Nejd, and Seyyid Mohammed al-Idrisi, ruler of Asir, on the pretext of asserting the authority of the Ottoman sultan. But the India Office had other reasons for opposing Kitchener's advocacy of an Arab caliphate. It contended that Muslims would not tolerate any religious changes dictated by a Christian power. It also claimed that it would be difficult to fulfill the pledge, if it ever came to a test, of protecting the caliphate against foreign aggression. Lastly, it stressed that a powerful Arab caliphate was not in Britain's interests. Rather, Britain should strive for a weak and disunited Arabia, split up into many small principalities under Britain's suzerainty and forming a buffer against other European powers.[27] The issue was complicated, and Grey was unable or unwilling to mediate the differences between the War Office and the India Office. In the absence of a coordinated Arab policy by the Foreign Office, both departments worked at cross-purposes, improvised as events dictated, and pursued separate avenues to achieve their objectives.

Hussein had been hesitant to move forward on Kitchener's earlier proposal. As 1915 wore on, he found himself playing a difficult balancing act, trying to offer the Sultan proof of his continued loyalty, while assuring the British that he was serious about raising a revolt. Since Hussein had no wish to take on the might of the Ottoman Empire without some Arab cooperation, he needed time to determine the level of real assistance he could expect from Syria and Mesopotamia.[28] He may also have wanted to delay matters because the war was going none too well for the British in the Middle East. The Turks were proving more than a match for the British in the Dardanelles. The Turkish assault on the Suez Canal had been repulsed, but the threat to Egypt remained. The intentions of the powerful Senussi Sheikh, Sayed Ahmed esh Sherif, were unclear, but his close association with Nuri Bey, half brother of Enver Pasha (Turkish minister of war), did not augur well for the British. The Sultan of Darfur in the Sudan was assuming a more intransigent attitude, and it seemed only a matter of time before he responded to the call of the jihad. During the second half of June 1915, Turkish forces invaded the Aden protectorate and advanced on Lahaj, with the apparent intention of attacking the town of Aden.[29]

The only place where the British were not on the defensive was in Mesopotamia, but here too the situation was not entirely reassuring. After the British seized Qurna in December 1914, there was no military action in Mesopotamia for several months. Opposition to the British advance had been negligible, but at the start of 1915, reliable information reached

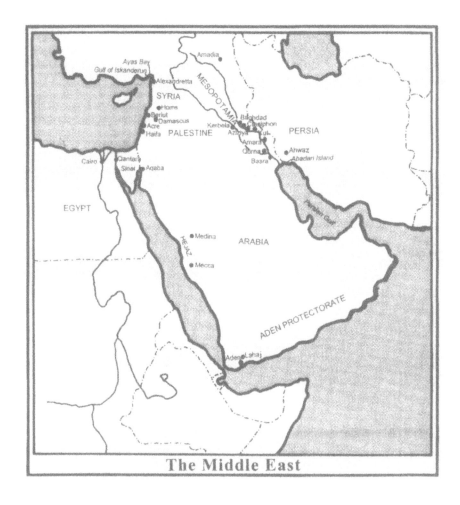

The Middle East

Qurna that the Turks in Mesopotamia were being reinforced and, aided by Arab allies, intended either to mount a counterattack on Basra or march across Persia to threaten the pipelines at Ahwaz. We have seen that in January 1915 Kitchener had wanted to land Birdwood's army at Alexandretta to sever the Baghdad Railway and bleed Mesopotamia white. That plan was delayed because of the threat to Egypt and then cancelled when the Anzacs were diverted to the Dardanelles. The Baghdad railway remained intact, enabling the Turks to send reinforcements down to Mesopotamia.

The possible threat to Ahwaz so alarmed the Asquith government that it induced the reluctant British viceroy in India, Lord Hardinge, to dispatch extra troops to the region. A brigade sent from India proved insufficient. There were signs that Arab tribes in the region were becoming restless, and, to make matters worse, a British unit was severely mauled in a skirmish near Ahwaz in mid-February. There were calls from London for further reinforcements, but the Indian government balked, claiming that its army was already overextended.[30]

Kitchener raised the issue at the War Council on February 24. He pointed out that earlier he had asked the India Office to tell Hardinge that a failure in Mesopotamia would be far more serious than any internal trouble. His intention had been to advise the Viceroy that he should send more troops to Mesopotamia. The message had been passed on to Hardinge, whose reply was read out at the meeting. He quite agreed with Kitchener and hoped that the War Office would arrange to reinforce the garrison there. Kitchener replied that he had no troops to spare. He thought that further pressure ought to be put on the Viceroy.[31] This was the course the Asquith government adopted, although it relieved the Viceroy and the Commander in Chief of the Indian Army of any responsibility for what might subsequently occur in India due to further depletion of their forces.

With the arrival of reinforcements to Basra, the expeditionary force, or Force D as it was called, expanded to two divisions by the beginning of April. Strengthened in the nick of time, the British held off a fierce Turkish-Arab onslaught during two days of almost continuous fighting near Basra, and on the third day routed them in a counterattack. This resounding victory enabled Force D to consolidate its position and averted the almost certain rising of Arab tribes in southern Mesopotamia.[32]

Of more immediate concern to the War Office than events in Mesopotamia was the ongoing conflict in the Cameroons, the management of which it inherited in the spring of 1915. The magnitude of the conflict had exceeded the capacity of the West African colonies to meet its costs and demands for matériel and large reinforcements for replacements. On more than one occasion, the Colonial Office had been forced to turn to the War Office for advice on strategic and tactical matters, and that dependency was bound to increase, particularly in coordinating all the operations by the various Allied forces and in complying with the necessary demands for personnel and matériel. With the British Treasury assuming financial responsibility, conduct of the campaign was transferred to the War Office on March 30.[33]

The British commander in chief in the Cameroons was Quebec-born Lt. Gen. Charles Dobell, a former inspector-general of the West African frontier force. He was well qualified for the post. He had seen active service in different areas of the Empire and was intelligent and resourceful, plus he had the incalculable advantage of being familiar with West Africa and its inhabitants. Notified of the change in the supervision of military operations, Dobell prepared a memorandum for the War Office, which he sent on April 11. In it, he referred to recent communications with the Colonial Office, which gave an assessment of the overall military picture, and he added that unless beneficial results were forthcoming soon from operations east of Edéa, it would be necessary to withdraw the participating troops temporarily, as the rainy season and the transport difficulties would impede further offensive action. Although up until now he had received no specific instructions regarding the military policy to be pursued, he had tried to engage the enemy whenever possible. Finally, he noted that the climatic conditions in the country were taking a heavy toll on his men, and, while there seemed to be no way of replacing the African soldiers, he hoped that the British officers could be gradually relieved.[34]

Kitchener replied on April 14, pledging to make every endeavor to replace the officers who were showing the effects of the local conditions. But, as he could glean only an outline of the existing state of affairs, he asked for further details.[35] Dobell forwarded a long appreciation on April 21 in which he described British and French operations in various parts of the country, pointed out the disposition of Allied forces so far as he knew them, gave an estimate of the forces opposing these columns, and revealed his future plans.[36]

As was his habit with commanders he trusted, Kitchener gave Dobell considerable latitude to frame military policy. Dobell's immediate objective was an advance against Yaunde, a stronghold protected by earthworks and defended by an estimated fifteen hundred men, in conjunction with two French columns, one from the east and the other from the southeast. Dobell attached considerable political and strategic importance to the town, believing that its seizure would practically end all organized German resistance.

All went well until the midway point. Advancing from the north, the British troops linked up with a French column under Colonel Mayer at Wum Biagas. In charge of the united force, Mayer pressed ahead, but ran into obstacles that were much greater than he had anticipated and, with no news about the progress of the other French column, decided to abandon the enterprise. On the way back, Mayer's contingent was roughly handled, losing a quarter of its men, and only the timely arrival of a rescue force sent by Dobell averted a complete debacle.[37]

Dobell apprised the War Office of the grim results of the expedition and requested guidance as to the future policy he should adopt. He drew up a memorandum to assist the War Office in its decision. As the rainy season precluded extensive operations until November, he hoped that the lull would be used to give his exhausted and, in many cases, sick troops leave so that they could rest and recuperate. In discussing his future options, Dobell no longer considered it useful to make another attempt to capture Yaunde, partly because the Germans were said to have moved their capital to Yoko and partly because of the nature of the hurdles likely to be encountered. He proposed instead that the Allies consolidate their hold over captured territory and force a German surrender by interdicting the transit of food and supplies apparently coming through Spanish Rio Muni. He offered a number of suggestions to make the blockade more effective.[38]

Kitchener's telegram on June 15 acknowledged Dobell's difficulties and accepted all of his recommendations. He pointed out, however, that should the combined measures of harrying the Germans and cutting off their supplies fail to bring about their surrender, he hoped that the offensive would be renewed in due course and pressed with vigor. Kitchener went on to say that he would take what measures he could to rotate the British officers and tighten the blockade.[39]

A week later, Dobell sent the War Office a long letter in which he unfolded his forthcoming plans. Adhering to the principle of an active defense in the occupied territory, he intended to direct his main effort to cutting off the enemy's supplies and ammunition reportedly being conveyed through the Spanish colony of Rio Muni. In case the Germans were still holding out by the end of the rainy season, Dobell raised the possibility of another offensive against Yaunde. He conceded that it would be costly in human lives and matériel, and that, even if successful, it would only produce a moral effect. Weighing the costs and the uncertainty of success against the value of the objective, Dobell was unwilling to recommend the idea. His only other solution was to continue the current policy of attacking the Germans' scattered outposts or hunting down their small bands and engaging them during the remainder of the war or until they gave up. Dobell ended by saying that if the War Office disagreed with his views and preferred an offensive, it should let him know by telegraph, as the type of preparations required would take considerable time.[40] The War Office made no reply.

Looking at the war in the Cameroons, Kitchener could at least take comfort in the knowledge that it was running slowly, but decidedly, in Britain's favor. The same thing could not be said about the struggle in German East Africa. Here, the Germans, under the inspired leadership of Lettow-Vorbeck, kept the British off balance and generally held the upper hand. Taking stock after his victory at Jasin, Lettow-Vorbeck judged the costs in men and munitions to have been higher than he could afford, prompting him to forgo set battles in favor of guerrilla tactics.[41] He reckoned that by quick raids across the border, particularly against the Uganda Railway, he could wreak havoc and draw in British troops, who would otherwise be used in other theaters.

As previously noted, Kitchener had discouraged British forces in the region from initiating major incursions into German East Africa by making it plain at the beginning of 1915 that he was unable to send them reinforcements. His advice was that they should remain on the defensive. That presumed that the Germans would remain relatively quiescent. But, the length of the border, together with the inexperience of the British troops, afforded Lettow-Vorbeck ample opportunity to carry out his hit-and-run tactics. In a two-month period, German raiding parties derailed thirty-two trains and blew up nine bridges.[42] Wapshare was at his wit's end. Any countermeasures being contemplated required a substantial increase of troops. But, newly raised units from local sources were the only possible source of reinforcements.

Kitchener had given the matter some consideration, and early in January 1915 he dispatched his older brother, Col. Henry Kitchener, to confer with authorities on the spot "as to the desirability of raising irregular corps for service in East Africa." He notified Wapshare of his brother's mission

and inquired whether he thought "a limited number of officers and selected civilians with East African experience" would be of value.[43] Wapshare's discussions with a number of local authorities and the absence of
response to ongoing formal public appeals led him to conclude that he
could not rely on an appreciable increase in the number of European volunteers. He replied to Kitchener on January 19 that the only solution to
his manpower problem was the expansion of the King's African Rifles
(KAR). He estimated that native recruits would require a minimum of
eight months' training.[44] A week later, he expressed the wish that, if permitted, "he would commence raising two battalions or as many less as I
am directed."[45]

It was known at British headquarters in Nairobi that the Germans,
thanks to a steady flow of African recruits, were able to keep increasing
their forces in the field. There was no reason, it was felt, why the British
could not do the same thing. Wapshare conferred with Col. Kitchener,
who reached Nairobi on February 13, on the whole subject of local forces.
His opinion does not appear to have made much of an impression. In
truth, Col. Kitchener was not the ideal man to conduct the type of survey
with which he was entrusted. His only active experience had been as a
transport officer in campaigns in Manipur and Burma in 1891, and he possessed no knowledge of British East Africa. Although he visited various
parts of the country, he relied too much on the opinions of local civil authorities and particularly the governor, Sir Charles Belfield, who considered it unwise to arm Africans on a large scale. Accustomed to relying on
India for aid, they gave no consideration to the unsuitability of British
and Indian troops for warfare in East Africa or to the possibility of going
beyond traditional sources to meet the demands of the growing conflict.

Col. Kitchener submitted his report to the War Office on March 18.
He considered it impossible to raise more European volunteers in British
East Africa, echoing an observation made earlier by Wapshare. He
thought that, with the help of the Governor of Uganda, he could raise
one thousand good Ugandan soldiers, but doubted that their value would
justify the extra expenditure.[46] The colonel made no mention of the possibility of expanding the KAR. The report convinced Kitchener that no
new units could be produced from local sources.

The first half of 1915, when the British in East Africa lacked the
strength to depart from their defensive policy, provided time for reorganization, preparing plans, and building up supplies for the struggle ahead.
It also gave Kitchener an opportunity to get rid of Wapshare, whom he

considered incompetent. When India was directed to reinforce the expeditionary force in Mesopotamia in March, Gen. Duff asked Kitchener for
the services of Brig. Gen. J. M. Stewart to command a brigade.[47] Kitchener wired back, "If you agree, I would suggest instead . . . that General
Wapshare be sent and General Tighe [be] left in command in East Africa."[48] It was hardly what Duff wanted to hear, but he was not about to
argue with his former chief. Still, he made it clear that he only agreed "in
deference to your wishes," for "Wapshare is not, in my opinion, as good a
brigade commander as Stewart."[49] Thereupon, Kitchener informed Wapshare on April 3 that he was to hand over command to Brig. Gen. Tighe
and proceed at the first favorable opportunity to Basra, where he was
needed to take charge of a brigade.[50] Wapshare was crestfallen at the announcement. He wrote back, "I hope that it is not because you disapprove
of what I have done here that I'm being transferred to the Persian Gulf. I
feel great anxiety about the matter."[51] Kitchener's reply was intended to
pour balm on Wapshare's wounded ego:

> Your transfer to Mesopotamia was not due to any dissatisfaction on my
> part at what you had already done in East Africa, but as active opera-
> tions of some magnitude are taking place near Basra, and Tighe could
> carry on in East Africa where operations must be restricted . . . I thought
> it better that you should be transferred to Mesopotamia.[52]

The new commander, M. J. Tighe, was highly respected and a vast
improvement over his predecessor. He had a thorough grasp of his profession and was tough as nails, with a reputation as a scrapper.[53] As a matter
of course, Kitchener called upon Tighe to give his views on the military
situation.[54] Tighe recommended an offensive in the Kilimanjaro and
Tanga areas, provided he was reinforced with at least one and a half brigades of good troops. As a preliminary move, he would attack Bukoba
and Mwanza, an operation he hoped to coordinate with a Belgian advance
from Ruanda. If successful, it would deprive the Germans of their chief
base of operations against Ruanda, thus relieving pressure on the southern
border of Uganda.[55] Kitchener was as uncompromising now as he had
been in January. Apart from the demands of the western front, the war in
Mesopotamia was imposing an ever-increasing drain on India's material
and human resources. Kitchener advised Tighe not to undertake any serious offensive, as it was impossible to supply him with further reinforcements.[56] Ten days later, Kitchener reiterated his concern even more

forcefully: "It is unwise with the existing forces . . . to embark on projects involving occupation of German territory and you should limit your endeavors to protection of our own possessions."[57]

To do even what Kitchener ordered was becoming more and more difficult. Under the cover of seasonal rains, Lettow-Vorbeck was not only striking often, but also extending the range of his activities. His Askaris, immune to the fever and increasingly gaining war experience, were daring, excellent stalkers and could endure extraordinary hardships in carrying out their assigned objectives. Usually able to slip by British patrols and sentries, they attacked outposts, ambushed small columns, and blew up railway tracks. The lack of success in thwarting Askari raids, the sickness among Indian troops, and having been reduced to a defensive role caused British morale to sink.

Tighe's frustration mounted and mounted until he could no longer stand to remain inactive. Despite Kitchener's orders, he devised a plan to attack Bukoba, one of his earlier proposed targets about twenty-five miles inside German territory on the shores of Lake Victoria. A German administrative center, Bukoba had vast quantities of stores and ammunition, and a powerful wireless station with a two-hundred-foot tower. It had some strategic value, but the main purpose of the campaign was to boost the spirits of the Indian troops. Tighe begged the War Office to remove its veto on offensive operations.[58] Kitchener relented after receiving assurances that nothing would be undertaken that would lead to further complications, as had occurred at Jasin.[59] The affair was over quickly. On June 22 Tighe's men took the town and destroyed the wireless station in a well-prepared assault that cost only a few casualties. Although not far-reaching, the victory was the only ray of light in what had otherwise been an ominously dark sky and, according to the official history, "did much to restore and revive the morale of the British forces."[60] For Kitchener, news of the capture of Bukoba provided some consolation, coming as it did when he was still reeling from the effects of major British defeats on two fronts and serious personal difficulties at home.

9

MOUNTING TROUBLES

I N the spring of 1915, Kitchener was caught between two
competing and mutually exclusive strategies, one advocated
by the War Council and the other by the Anglo-French
high command. His decision would determine whether Britain's limited
resources would be partially deployed in the eastern Mediterranean or
concentrated wholly on the western front. In November 1914, when there
seemed to be no other option, he had committed Britain's total military
resources in support of Joffre's western offensive strategy. But, that understanding occurred before trench warfare had set in. Now he was much
more in sympathy with an eastern, rather than a western, strategy.

Still, political considerations restricted Kitchener's freedom of action.
At stake was the delicate matter of Britain's trustworthiness as an ally.
Kitchener's solution was to try to balance the claims of the soldiers and
the politicians, supplying the French with Territorial units, while keeping
a strategic reserve for operations in the east. As with most compromises,
it satisfied neither side. Kitchener could slip out of his colleagues' periodic
and flaccid arm-twisting attempts, but the French were relentless in their
strident demands for more British troops. Curiously enough, it was not as
if GQG placed great stock in the fighting abilities of British troops. Joffre's assessment, based on what he had seen, was that they lacked the élan
of French soldiers. He felt that they could be usefully employed in holding
a static line and in diversionary movements to draw German reserves,
while French troops got the real job done. Joffre may have held a low
opinion of British troops, but he nevertheless recognized that, without

162

their support, he could not hope to defeat the Germans. For that reason, Joffre and his generals called for a total commitment of British resources. They had received more than they had a right to expect, but in their eyes it was not enough. They were especially unhappy about the retention of the Twenty-ninth Division, which they regarded as a symbol of Britain's future attitude regarding the western front. Despite great and continuous pressure from GQG, Kitchener remained unshaken. It did not help that the French acted as though the British were obliged to concentrate every available soldier in the west.

Until there was a change in Joffre's offensive methods, Kitchener, in fact, opposed sending any more British formations across the channel, beyond what was necessary to fulfill Sir John's promise to take over stretches of the French line. He saw no reason simply to accumulate men in the trenches. He was convinced that Sir John was mismanaging his front and squandering his reinforcements. He told Asquith on February 16 that "in the last ten days Sir John's force has lost a hundred officers and about 2,600 men" with "very little that is ostensible to show for it."[1] Nor did he think that the French were justified in clamoring for additional British reinforcements to ensure the security of the line. It seemed to him that Joffre had ample reserves at his disposal. Esher had recently reported that, with over a million and a half trained men in depots, the French government was thinking about creating a reserve army of five corps.[2]

Although Kitchener felt that the Allies lacked the means to achieve a decisive victory in 1915, he deprecated a policy of passive defense in the west that would allow the Germans to leave a small force to contain the Anglo-French forces, while they concentrated their efforts in finishing off the Russians. Instead, he favored a policy of *attrition*, a term that has been defined in a variety of ways.[3] To Kitchener it meant a gradual process of wearing down the enemy. His answer to trench warfare was a step-by-step advance that focused on killing Germans rather than conquering territory. This approach contrasted with that of the generals, who mounted attacks that promised a rapid breakthrough in one bound. Setting distant objectives, as proven repeatedly, was unrealistic and had only resulted in unnecessary loss of life. As Kitchener maintained all along, the Allies would not be able to deliver the coup de grâce until 1917, when Russia had developed its vast manpower resources, Britain's munitions output had been raised to a level sufficient to support mass attacks, and the New Armies had reached their maximum strength in the field.[4] In the meantime, he was adamant that the Allies in the west should adopt a policy of attrition. It was sound strategy, much like the one Haig used with remarkable success in 1918. Kitchener was ready to assist in the wearing-down process after May 1915, when the first of the New Armies would be available as reserves to exploit any success. Whether the French, who would have to bear the brunt of the fighting, would be receptive to Kitchener's idea of a prudent attritional strategy remained to be seen.

Kitchener did not feel comfortable enough with Joffre to approach him directly with his idea. He thought of utilizing the Belgian prime minister, the Comte de Broqueville, who was currently in London. The latter knew Joffre personally, and it so happened that he was on his way to France. Invited to the War Office, he graciously agreed to act as intermediary. It is not clear if de Broqueville fully understood what Kitchener had in mind. Even if he did, he possessed too much admiration for Joffre to be a forceful defender of Kitchener's position.

Joffre's reaction to Kitchener's representations may be inferred from a remark his deputy, General Foch, uttered mockingly in the presence of Wilson and French: "You would think from Lord K.'s proposal that we were fighting negroes and not Germans."[5] On February 23, de Broqueville sent Kitchener the results of his interview with Joffre. Although paying lip service to Kitchener's novel concept, Joffre was much more interested in laying his hands on Britain's growing manpower resources, without which he could not possibly defeat the Germans. He even urged that the New Armies complete their training in France to acclimatize them to war conditions before they participated in battle.[6] Kitchener saw this as a ruse to preempt any possibility of opening a new front in the eastern Mediterranean.

Kitchener knew nothing about Joffre's long-range plans, other than that he intended to launch an attack in the near future in concert with Sir John French. As the debate over the Twenty-ninth Division intensified in the War Council, Kitchener asked French for precise details of the projected combined assault before deciding on its eventual destination.[7] Sir John answered that he would welcome the addition of the Twenty-ninth Division, but declined to supply Kitchener with the information requested lest it "detract from our object . . . to keep plans secret."[8] It would be comical, if it were not so lamentable, that while French worried that Kitchener, of all people, would leak classified material, he poured his soul out every day to his mistress in long letters that contained a wealth of military secrets.[9]

Kitchener's insistence on keeping the Twenty-ninth Division in hand for possible use in the east strained his relationship with the French. His intention to substitute a Territorial division (North Midland), instead of the Twenty-ninth, did little to mollify them. Millerand told Esher that his government was concerned about the delays and changes in the schedule of reinforcements. He thought that Allied cooperation was bound to suffer if agreements were not honored.[10] Reacting to Esher's announcement, Kitchener remarked that Millerand's complaints were not well founded. He had promised the French a certain number of troops, and it was irrelevant whether these consisted of the Twenty-ninth Division or any other division. As far as keeping engagements, Kitchener, who was still bitter over the incident, pointed to the duplicitous behavior of the French during the Antwerp relief expedition as hardly leading "me to think that they took such a rigid view."[11] The ingratitude and overbearing manner of the French was beginning to erode Kitchener's patience and goodwill. On February 27, he notified Sir John that the Twenty-ninth Division would remain in Britain and possibly be sent to support the naval operations in the Dardanelles. It seemed to him that, since the French could spare a division for the Dardanelles, their needs were not as great as they claimed.[12]

Sir John French considered the North Midland Territorial Division, which would require tutoring in trench warfare before it was fit for front-line service, an inadequate substitute for the crack Twenty-ninth Division. Accordingly, he notified Joffre that he would be unable to relieve French troops in the Ypres salient as previously agreed. In a fit of pique, Joffre cancelled his participation in the forthcoming operation.[13] French nevertheless decided to attack alone at Neuve Chapelle, eager as he was to prove the worth of British arms and to foster an offensive spirit among his men. The narrow-front attack commenced at 7:30 A.M. on March 10 after a violent bombardment lasting thirty-five minutes. Achieving complete surprise, the British easily overran the first German line and penetrated to a depth of twelve hundred yards, but delays, minor hitches, and inadequate communications proved fatal to their high hopes. German reinforcements were rushed up and halted the attack on March 13.[14]

Kitchener was exasperated at the prodigious expenditure of artillery shells and at the way Sir John had directed the operation. He made his feelings known to Asquith, who passed them on to Venetia Stanley: "Kitchener spoke to me very confidentially about French. He says he is not a really scientific soldier: a good and capable leader in the field; but without adequate equipment of expert knowledge for the huge task of commanding 450,000 men."[15]

All the same, in certain military quarters Sir John's attack was judged to have been a tactical, if not a strategic, success. It showed that the German line could be pierced and raised the prestige of the BEF as an effective fighting instrument. The French, who had treated the BEF as fit only for subsidiary duties, now manifested a desire to give it an ever-increasing part in their offensive movements. Joffre redoubled his efforts to convince Kitchener to increase Britain's military forces in France. For the French, the sense of urgency seemed greater than ever. On March 10, Kitchener had decided to divert the Twenty-ninth Division to the eastern Mediterranean, heightening their fears that the New Armies would follow when ready. They requested a conference with Kitchener so that they could reach a consensus on grand strategy. Kitchener was disinclined to go, despite appeals by Grey and Asquith that he should.[16] He was still undecided about what to do with the New Armies.[17] If he could be persuaded that Joffre's methods would force a breakthrough, he would send them to the western front, even though he lacked the stock of ammunition to meet their wants. Otherwise, he preferred to use them in a theater where less ammunition was required, either in the Dardanelles or to assist Italy if it should join the Entente. A meeting with Sir John at Dover on March 23 convinced Kitchener that he should hold talks with the French leaders before deciding on the New Armies' destination.[18]

Kitchener essentially played for time at the Anglo-French conference, which took place at Joffre's headquarters at Chantilly on March 29. By then, the naval attack against the forts at the Narrows of the Dardanelles had failed, and a military landing was being prepared for late April. Kitchener was confident that the military forces on the spot would unlock the Dardanelles to the fleet, allowing him the option to mass men in the west for an offensive in the summer.[19] Until the results of Hamilton's operations were known, Kitchener was determined to hold his cards close to his chest.

At the meeting, Kitchener resisted, amiably but firmly, the combined efforts of Joffre and French to persuade him to concentrate British strength to the fullest extent on the western front. On more than one occasion, Kitchener suddenly changed the subject to stifle discussion. The differences over strategy were not resolved, and Kitchener's only concession, intended as a sop to Joffre, was to agree to send an additional two Territorial divisions to Sir John to facilitate the relief of French troops in the Ypres salient.[20] But, he made it clear, as the following entry in French's diary shows, that he "would not send any more troops until and unless we broke the line or showed that substantial headway could be made in this theatre."[21] The talks had been held in a cordial atmosphere and went far towards improving Kitchener's relationship with the French leaders.

Kitchener reaffirmed his position two days later when he had breakfast with Sir John in London. French recorded the conversation:

> He told me that he considered Joffre and I were "on trial"—that if we showed within the next month or five weeks that we really could make "substantial advances" and "break the German" he would—so far as he was concerned—always back us up with all the troops he could send. But if we failed it would be essential that the government should look for some other theatre of operations. . . . I told him that I thought that he had put the matter very fairly and I was content to accept what he said.[22]

Kitchener had found it exacting trying to steer a middle course between the War Council's desire to send more troops to the eastern Mediterranean and the Anglo-French high command's ceaseless campaign to have all of Britain's forces deployed in Flanders. He was now giving Joffre and French every chance to shape Britain's future military policy. If they could produce a real victory on the western front in their forthcoming attack, they would settle the heated dispute in their favor.

Difficult as it was to devise a military strategy, Kitchener faced an even more daunting challenge in trying to overcome the Army's shortage of weapons and munitions. In August 1914 Kitchener inherited an ordnance branch that had been organized to supply (as recommended by a prewar committee) six or seven divisions in a limited conflict along the lines of the Boer War. Britain's armament industry, corresponding to the traditional size of its army, was small, consisting of a few state-owned factories and a handful of private manufacturers. To make matters worse, none of the factories, private or public, possessed up-to-date machinery capable of manufacturing weapons and munitions on a massive scale. In some of the factories, like the Royal Arsenal at Woolwich, shells were filled, one at a time, by hand. When manufacturers expanded their workshop space, there were often delays in starting production. Vital machinery, gauges to determine the correct size of fuses, and certain raw materials, were in short supply and had to be imported from the United States. The movement of goods between New York and London in war-time took three times longer than normal, and there were further delays when, on arrival, delivery could be held up for as much as five weeks because of port congestion.[23]

There were other problems standing in the way of increased production. The Army was uncertain about what type of shell was most effective, shrapnel or high explosive. A shrapnel shell contained several hundred lead pellets and a charge of gunpowder with a fuze timed to explode while it was still above its intended victims. Delivering its missiles in the direction it was travelling, it was deadly against unprotected troops in the open. Trench warfare, however, reduced the effectiveness of shrapnel. Under the new conditions on the western front, it was seen that high-explosive shells produced better results in chewing up barbed-wire and battering down field fortifications. The switch from shrapnel to high-explosive shells could not be accomplished, as Trevor Wilson has pointed out, "just by altering a requisition order."[24] There were formidable difficulties, not the least of which was that they required different machinery. Any advanced industrial nation would have no difficulty in producing shrapnel. If some of the shells were defective, they could not cause much harm on account of the limited quantities of gunpowder involved. The manufacture of high explosive, on the other hand, was complicated and perilous.[25] The absence of skilled and responsible workers in the plant could cause a variety of mishaps: explosions in the factories, premature detonation of shells in the gun barrel, and failure of shells to explode on impact.

Finally, the recruiting for the New Armies had dug deeply into the engineering workforce. Kitchener had urged workers with special expertise on September 8, 1914, that they would be doing their duty by remaining at their trades, and subsequently the War Office issued a poster to that effect. Nevertheless, he could not prohibit those who wanted to enlist from doing so. The absence of skilled workers in factories meant that only about one-fifth of the available machinery was used for the night shift.

As with anyone navigating through uncharted territory, Kitchener made mistakes, some of which were unforeseeable. His detractors like to dwell on his mistakes and, either through ignorance or hatred of the man, fail to look at the broad picture. They have argued that initially he underestimated the quantities of ammunition that would be required by the British Army in France. Technically, the allegation is true (no one had any idea of the amount of ammunition required in modern warfare), but that did not inhibit him from acquiring every gun, bullet, and field gun shell he could lay his hands on. Kitchener recognized on the first day he took over at the War Office that the standing munitions arrangements were inadequate, and he immediately took steps to increase the output. He called in the heads of the private British manufacturing firms and told them that the government would buy every round of ammunition they could turn out and to think in terms of years, not months, when they made their plans.[26]

Kitchener, moreover, turned to a number of American firms to supplement British munitions production. The largest order was placed with Bethlehem Steel, whose chairman, Charles M. Schwab, had offered Kitchener a million complete rounds of shells within twelve months. Before the details were finalized, Kitchener met with Schwab in the War Office early in November 1914. In the course of the discussion, Kitchener stated that the war would last five years and he wanted first option on all surplus guns and ammunition produced by Bethlehem Steel. They agreed on prices, and Kitchener's only condition was that Schwab pledge not to sell control of the company for five years. The United States was teeming with German agents and sympathizers, and Kitchener wanted to ensure that Bethlehem Steel did not become a subsidiary of Krupp. Schwab told Kitchener to draw up the contract, and he would sign it.[27]

The first orders were large enough to keep the expanding BEF supplied even beyond the expected prewar rate of expenditure. But, neither Kitchener nor anyone else on either side anticipated the gargantuan scale of the demand for shells, which began in the autumn of 1914 and escalated sharply after the onset of trench warfare. In the battle of Neuve Chapelle, as much ammunition was fired as in the entire South African War. France and Germany, with their large conscript armies, had developed the industrial capacity to make good their munitions deficiency. Britain had no such armament capacity, thanks to the government's prewar policy of restricting defense spending to the bare minimum.[28] It would take months before machinery could be imported, existing factories expanded and new ones built, and workers trained; it would take still longer before munitions could be produced on a huge scale.

Another charge against Kitchener, one that has more substance, was that the War Office was slow to act and often reluctant to accept alternative methods for the direction and supervision of munitions production. Burdened with a massive and growing volume of work, Kitchener was unable to devote enough time to setting up new channels to circumvent prewar procedures and to supervise his ordnance department closely.[29] This meant delays in taking up new ideas, conducting experimental work, introducing new designs of high explosive shells, inspecting plants that applied to be placed on the War Office list for warlike stores, transacting business, identifying new munitions sources, and applying pressure on armament firms to deliver supplies on schedule. Kitchener was much more flexible than he is given credit for. Throughout his career, as we have already noted, he showed himself to be an advocate of reform and was certainly never inhibited by the narrow framework of tradition and precedent. His error was in stubbornly refusing outside help, which made it harder to find early solutions to some of the larger problems. Until the end, he believed that whatever changes were necessary could be accomplished under the aegis of the War Office.

Kitchener's failings, however, were hardly at the root of the matter. He was a master improviser, and as everything had to be built practically from the ground up, it is virtually certain that no one else could have matched his record of accomplishment, let alone done better. The simple truth was that the production of munitions on the scale necessary to keep up with the Army's consumption was inconsistent with the state's laissez-faire policy. It required massive changes in industrial practices and labor relations, which transcended the bounds of War Office authority.[30] Strangely enough, the first one in the Cabinet to advocate a measure of state intervention was Kitchener, who wanted to set up a central control board to distribute war supplies between the two services.[31] But in the early stage of the war, the Asquith government preferred to rely on price mechanisms, instead of controls, to expand munitions output.

It was not long after the opening battles that Kitchener discovered the Army's unprecedented need for munitions. As early as September 17, he acknowledged in the House of Lords that his chief difficulty was "one of matériel rather than personnel."[32] To Sir John French, who flooded his desk with daily requests for greater quantities of munitions, he wrote in October:

> The supply of ammunition gives me great anxiety. . . . Do not think we are keeping munitions back. All we can gather is being sent, but at the present rate of expenditure we are certain before long to run short, and then to produce more than a daily allowance per gun will be impossible.[33]

The Cabinet's attention was drawn to the magnitude of the problem of armament expansion when it realized that the existing contracts would not allow a good portion of the New Armies to take the field in the spring of 1915. In October 1914, Asquith, at the urging of Lloyd George, set up a Cabinet committee on munitions to assist the War Office to expand output and expedite delivery of supplies. Serving along with Kitchener, who acted as chairman, was Lloyd George, Churchill, Walter Runciman (president of the Board of Trade), Reginald McKenna (Home Secretary), Lord Lucas (president of the Board of Agriculture), and Haldane (Lord Chancellor). The so-called Shells Committee met six times between October 12, 1914, and January 1, 1915. It increased existing orders and placed new ones, extended the War Office list of approved firms and, by promising to underwrite the costs, obtained the agreement of the heads of the four largest armament firms at home to expand their plant and facilities. An Armament Firm Committee was set up, representing the government and big armament companies on the War Office list, with power to distribute contracts for arms components among other engineering firms. By May 1915 over twenty-five hundred such firms were engaged in some aspect of arms production.[34]

Judging by the results, the work of the Shells Committee was quite good. Whether more progress could have been achieved had it continued to function after January 1, is uncertain. It was one thing to place large orders for munitions; it is quite another to ensure their promised delivery dates. It may be that the Committee had accomplished all that it could. At any rate, Kitchener brought an end to the Committee by claiming that he could no longer find time to attend its meetings.

Kitchener's resentment at the politicians' continual inquiries into military matters and interference in his department was exacerbated by Lloyd George's confrontational style. Kitchener's loathing of Lloyd George went beyond his normal dislike of politicians. He considered Lloyd George a dangerous demagogue, a man who made simplistic solutions to complex problems sound plausible. But, he feared him as much as he hated him because he was frequently the object of Lloyd George's verbal lashings, against which he had no defense. Worst still, Lloyd George did not always confine his criticism to policy differences in the heat of debates. Asquith, for example, told Venetia Stanley on April 15 that Lloyd George, in the course of an altercation with Kitchener, had let loose "some most injurious and wounding innuendoes which K. will be more than human to forget."[35] The plain truth was that Lloyd George never learned how to handle Kitchener. He made no allowances for the field marshal's unfamiliarity with the principle of Cabinet responsibility, admonishing him "that he was only one of nineteen, and must stand criticism in the same way as any other member of the Cabinet."[36] It should have been apparent to any reasonable person that, after spending a lifetime on the fringes of the Empire making decisions in solitude and expecting his subordinates to carry them out without question, the field marshal was too old to change his habits. Had Lloyd George shown greater flexibility and tried tactful persuasion, instead of steamroller methods, he would have found Kitchener willing to listen to any practical suggestion. As it was, Kitchener interpreted Lloyd George's intemperate outbursts as calling into question his competence and this, in turn, made him bitter and defensive.

The two men clashed over two related issues. In the first place, Lloyd George wanted to increase the orders placed earlier in the recognized firms by the War Office. He thought that larger orders would induce manufacturers to expand their plants and invest in new machinery, which, in turn, would expedite deliveries. Kitchener brushed aside such naive assumptions. He thought that piling up more orders was an exercise in futility, since all the factories had already overcommitted and would not be able to meet their scheduled delivery dates. Lloyd George saw this as obstructionism by a soldier lacking foresight and out of touch with the new conditions of warfare. To prove his charge, he related an incident in his memoirs that occurred in June 1915, just after the Ministry of Munitions had been established. Eric Geddes, Lloyd George's deputy director-general of munitions supply, went to see Kitchener to ask him the number of rifles and machine guns that would be required nine months hence, so that he could frame his plans accordingly. Kitchener told him that he "wanted as much of both as you can produce." When pressed by Geddes to be more precise, Kitchener thought for a moment and replied that two machine guns per battalion was the minimum and anything above four was a luxury. Geddes penned this brief statement on a scrap of paper, which Kitchener initialed, and returned to the Ministry of Munitions. After Lloyd George read the note, he turned to Geddes and said, "Take Kitchener's maximum . . . square it, multiply that result by two; and when you are in sight of that, double it again for good luck."[37] The inference here is that Lloyd George eventually intended to provide every British battalion with sixty-four machine guns.

On the surface, it would seem that Kitchener was guilty of a flagrant misjudgment, which Lloyd George had happily corrected. But, the issue is less clear-cut if seen in its true context. At the start of the war, every British battalion, like its German counterpart, was equipped with two machine guns. In August and September, the War Office ordered a total of 1,792 guns from Vickers, with the provision that they be delivered by July 1915 at the rate of 50 per week. Hitherto, Lloyd George tells us, Vickers's rate of production did not exceed twelve guns per week,[38] so that the War Office order quadrupled its highest output. In November, the War Office requested that Vickers increase its production to two hundred guns per week, that is, sixteen times the original maximum output. In February 1915, the British establishment of two machine guns per battalion was raised to four, and in that same month the War Office placed an order for two thousand more guns in the United States. This made a total of four thousand guns, an impressive figure, considering the machine gun was a defensive weapon and the British Army from March 1915 on (until March 1918) was almost always on the offensive.[39] Vickers, however, was only able to deliver 1,022 guns by June 1915, less than 60 percent of the order. The simple truth was that the War Office had already placed orders beyond the capacity of Vickers to fulfill them. Without new productive capacity, adding more orders was a waste of time.

The perception created by Lloyd George that his program would eventually equip every battalion in the Army with sixty-four machine guns is a gross distortion of what actually happened. Indeed, Lloyd George never came close to attaining that number. British battalions were limited to just under five machine guns per battalion, and no unit, except the machine gun battalion, one of which was later assigned to every division, was allotted sixty-four. Well might John Terraine write, "So the difference between Lord Kitchener's dull lack of vision and Lloyd George's war winning perspicacity turns out to be slightly less than one gun per battalion."[40]

The other area of contention between the two men was over the War Office's reluctance to spread munitions contracts. The War Office had no qualms about allowing its regular suppliers to subcontract part of their work to other engineering firms, but it was not willing to go so far as to place orders with these outside companies for complete guns and shells. Kitchener and von Donop, the MGO, were not confident that firms outside the War Office's recognized list of manufacturers possessed the expertise and trained machine operatives to produce finished guns and shells. In their view, dependence on unproven firms was likely to lead to substandard work and delays. These subcontractors could be relied on to produce simple munitions parts like casings, but not delicate items such as fuses.

By contrast, Lloyd George was convinced that the newcomers were competent enough to manufacture not only particular components, but also all types of munitions. He formed his opinion after a visit to Paris in mid-October 1914 where the French, caught like the British with inadequate munitions supplies, had developed a plan to bring in outside firms to meet the shortfall. Lloyd George met General Deville, the inventor of the famous 75mm gun and head of French ordnance, and was impressed by what he heard. Deville claimed that Britain had exceptional engineering works, with every type of machine and machine tool, and was in an even better position than France to increase its munitions supplies swiftly. He was planning to go over to Britain in a few days' time, and would be happy to provide the British authorities with any information about the French system of arms manufacture. Lloyd George noted in his memoirs that he reported "this offer to the War Office, but I never heard that it came to anything."[41] There was a reason why it did not. The War Office carefully studied Deville's proposal before rejecting it as unsafe.[42] Kitchener's fears were later justified. The French crash program of production turned out large quantities of faulty ammunition, often resulting in premature shell explosions in the gun barrels—some one thousand guns were destroyed and an additional six hundred were damaged and required repairs, to say nothing of the gunners killed or maimed.[43]

Probably the most sensible course to follow would have been somewhere between Kitchener's and Lloyd George's positions. In the beginning, Kitchener was right to increase output only through existing munitions plants. Ordinary engineering firms could not take on work immediately, as they lacked experience, but as subcontractors they gradually acquired knowledge of shell making. Because of the critical shortage of munitions, Kitchener should have risked adding some of these firms to the War Office list, as he admitted in hindsight.[44] But, to entrust men's lives to every new operation seeking munitions contracts, as Lloyd George advocated, was reckless and irresponsible There followed a two-month lull at the start of 1915, but the rivalry heated up again in March. It was apparent in the first quarter of the new year that only about a quarter of the orders placed in Britain were likely to be fulfilled on time. Munitions firms in Britain were guilty of reckless overcommitment, but it must also be said that they had to deal with problems that could not be resolved overnight or lay outside their control: restrictive practices of labor; a shortage of tradesmen and skilled workers, as well as delays caused by expansion; and the need to import machine tools and gauges from abroad. Addressing the House of Lords on March 15, 1915, Kitchener admitted that there was great cause for anxiety over the supply of war material, which was falling below the Army's needs and would continue to do so for the next few months.[45] The next day, Kitchener established an Armament Output Committee, under the chairmanship of George Booth, a successful industrialist and shipowner, who was charged with the task of overcoming the shortage of labor in the established armament factories. Booth did as he was told, although his business experience told him that the problem of arms and munitions production went beyond finding skilled workers and required spreading orders to new private engineering firms.[46]

Kitchener had not yet announced the creation of his new committee when he found himself in a life-and-death struggle to retain control over the supply of munitions. His nemesis, Lloyd George, had expected orders placed by the Shells Committee to have already borne fruit. When Kitchener revealed at a special meeting on March 5 that the delivery of rifles and all types of munitions was seriously in arrears,[47] Lloyd George attributed the delay to the War Office's missed opportunities to obtain raw materials, the pedantry and obstructionism of its experts, and inadequate supervision. The upshot was that he now set his sights on forcing the War Office to relinquish its control of arms production. As he unleashed his broadsides, he conveniently forgot that much of Kitchener's difficulties were attributable to the Treasury's parsimony before 1914, which had limited the ability of the armament industry to expand rapidly in wartime.

In response to pressure exerted by Lloyd George, Asquith agreed to appoint a War Supplies Committee to mobilize potential as well as existing sources of munitions supply. Chaired by Lloyd George, it was to be responsible to the Cabinet, rather than to the War Office, and enjoyed the right to place contracts on its own authority.[48] Kitchener, who was not even consulted about the proposed committee, was livid at the inference that he had been derelict in his duty. If he had to accept the committee, it would be on his terms or he would leave the War Office. As he needed to arm the New Armies immediately, he told Asquith that Lloyd George's committee was not to interfere with existing contracts or divert labor from War Office suppliers and subcontractors. He would welcome Lloyd George as an assistant if he would confine himself to finding more labor for existing munitions contractors.[49] Lloyd George, however, felt that these restrictions would paralyze his efforts, and, like Kitchener, threatened to resign if he did not get his way.[50]

Kitchener knew that it took more than "men of push and go" to solve the munitions shortage. He felt it would be a huge mistake to entrust armament supply to a bunch of amateurs. Their lack of technical knowledge in the various patterns of munitions and in essential machinery tools was certain to produce delays, chaos, and faulty material. His explanation that it took time to develop new means of production received little sympathy. The Cabinet generally came to believe, as Balfour observed, that "K. has only an imperfect grasp of the problem with which he has been faced for seven months."[51] But, neither Balfour nor his political colleagues had the faintest idea of what was involved in the manufacture of munitions. All, including Asquith, downplayed Kitchener's difficulties, preferring to take their cue from Lloyd George, who revealed his expertise in munitions making by claiming, as late as May 1915, that "private firms cannot turn out shrapnel because of the complicated character of the shell," but *the testimony is unanimous that the high explosive is a simple shell and that any engineering concern could easily produce it* [my italics]."[52]

Confronted by a deepening quarrel that threatened to tear apart his Cabinet, Asquith devised a compromise that only added to the confusion. On April 8, he announced the creation of a new Munitions of War Committee, with full authority to take any steps deemed necessary to ensure "the promptest and most efficient application of all the available resources of the country to the manufacture and supply" of armaments for the British Army.[53] Officially, the Armament Committee was subordinated to the new body, popularly called the Treasury Committee. Given a seat on the Treasury Committee, Booth tried unsuccessfully to act as an intermediary between Kitchener and Lloyd George. The new system was simply unworkable. Not only was the division of authority undefined, but Lloyd George was compelled to rely on the War Office for technical information if he wished to make accurate assessments of future munitions requirements. Kitchener, however, objected to providing such information on security grounds.[54] There was a terrible row in the Cabinet on April 19, and, as Hankey observed, "it required all of Asquith's dexterity to avoid an open breach between his warring colleagues."[55]

Kitchener made a last-ditch effort to strengthen his hand by persuading Percy Girouard to resign as managing director of Armstrong's at Elswick and come to the War Office to advise him, in conjunction with George Booth, on matters of munitions supply.[56] At Kitchener's insistence, Girouard joined Booth as an additional War Office representative on the Treasury Committee. Girouard, like Booth, never lost his respect and admiration for Kitchener, but the outcome of his efforts was to weaken the War Office's position in the munitions struggle. Girouard recommended that, instead of spreading contracts among small firms, the state ought to construct new, publicly owned factories in industrial areas, concentrating men and machinery in them. In this way, many of the problems associated with munitions making, such as supervision, inspection, and labor supply, would be easier to solve.

When the Treasury Committee gave the plan its blessing, Kitchener authorized Girouard and Booth to carry it out and to act "without further reference to the Secretary of State." He further conceded that in the event of differences arising between them and any government department "concerned with the supply of munitions of war or of labor for producing such munitions . . . which cannot be mutually adjusted, the instructions of the Treasury Committee . . . are to be followed."[57] Kitchener's volume of work and endless clashes with Lloyd George had worn him down, and he grudgingly accepted what Girouard was able to identify, namely that the rapid expansion of munitions production, with all of its associated technical and manpower issues, had become a task too big to be left to a subdivision of the War Office. The next logical step was to set up an independent Ministry of Munitions, empowered to control all aspects of production. In mid-May two crises that shook the political scene and brought an end to the Liberal government, hastened the process. We must now turn our attention to this story.

Confident that he had learned the lessons of trench warfare, Sir John French was eager to try again and prove that the German line could be broken in the west. This time, the plan to capture Aubers Ridge seemed to offer more hope than the previous effort, since it would be coordinated with Joffre's operations. The British role was intended to be subsidiary, the object being to pin down German forces that might otherwise be employed against the French. Kitchener questioned the wisdom of mounting another forward movement so soon after Neuve Chapelle, at which time French had claimed, falsely it must be said, that his setback was due mostly to "want of ammunition."[58] Kitchener had not been able to meet the quantity of ammunition French had requested at their meeting on March 29, so it seemed sensible to postpone the attack.[59] French, however, assured Kitchener on April 14 that his stock of ammunition was sufficient for the coming attack.[60] The following week saw the start of heavy fighting around Ypres, but French remained confident that the expenditure of artillery ammunition was not enough to hamper future operations.[61] When the fighting subsided, he again wrote to Kitchener on May 2, saying, "the ammunition will be all right."[62]

Sir John's hopes to replicate the early stages of his attack at Neuve Chapelle were shattered on May 9, the same day on which he launched his offensive. British artillery fire was inaccurate, and there was poor communication between the troops and supporting artillery, as well as a lack of heavy guns capable of destroying the well-constructed German bunkers. The result was that the advancing infantrymen were decimated before the uncut wire by withering machine gun fire. French broke off the attack that evening after his forces had suffered nearly twelve thousand casualties.[63] It was the second major British defeat in less than a week.

On April 25, Hamilton, without the assistance of the fleet's guns, had effected a landing on the Gallipoli Peninsula, but at a terrible cost. The Turks had used the interval since the naval attack to augment the size of their army and to strengthen their fortifications on the hills overlooking the beaches. Despite backbreaking efforts by British and Anzac forces, the Turks held firm, and the invasion ground to a halt. Hamilton candidly admitted on May 9 that he had failed to capture the heights, which dominated the Narrows's defenses. The task proved to be more difficult than Hamilton had supposed, and the next day he told Kitchener that the only way to get the job done was through a process of attrition. Thus, instead of a quick victory, Hamilton fell into the same sort of quagmire that existed in France, facing lines of entrenchment, possession of which could only be gained through deliberate methods of trench warfare.[64] Confident of success initially, Kitchener's disillusion deepened when he learned of the number of casualties Hamilton's army had sustained during the operations. Kitchener had counted on losses of about 10 percent, only to learn subsequently that they were closer to 30 percent.[65]

Kitchener was still nursing his disappointment when he received news of French's repulse at Aubers Ridge. Esher visited him on May 11 and found him in low spirits. Kitchener was especially frustrated with Sir John's questionable generalship. He could not understand why "with so large a preponderance of force we are unable to make a greater impression on the Germans."[66] He pointed out that Britain had five hundred fifty thousand troops in France along a line of some thirty-five miles, which was nearly four times as many men per mile of front as the French. Yet, the assault at Aubers Ridge had been beaten back with such ease that the Germans had not found it necessary to call on any reserves.

Sir John, who had been told late in March that he was on trial, did not have to be reminded that he was treading on dangerously thin ice. His response was to try to deflect attention from his tactical failure in the field by claiming that it was due to a shortage of high-explosive shells. By shifting the responsibility onto the shoulders of Kitchener, he would be pre-empting any possibility of being recalled. Accordingly, French used the military correspondent for the *Times*, Lt. Col. Charles à Court Repington, who was staying with him at GHQ, to publicize a claim that Kitchener, not he, was responsible for the unsuccessful attack. On May 14 a leading article appeared in the *Times* that attributed the army's recent failure at Aubers Ridge to a shortage of shells. The story sent shock waves throughout the country.[67]

The article contained facts and figures that only GHQ could have supplied. Kitchener told Riddell, one of the few journalist he trusted:

> It is terrible to think such a breach of discipline should have taken place in the army and that such lies, such damn lies, should have circulated. . . . No general will risk his men if he knows that his resources are inadequate for the operation proposed. These stories have been circulated to cover other matters.[68]

Although Kitchener was furious at French's treachery, he behaved with dignity and restraint, adamant that in wartime personal animosities should be put aside. His associates wanted to reply to the charges, but he prohibited them from doing so, telling them that he was out to fight the Germans, not Sir John.[69] Asquith, who refused to believe that French had inspired the story in the *Times*,[70] was more upset with Kitchener. On April 20 Asquith had made a major speech at Newcastle aimed at squashing rumors that military operations in France were being conducted without sufficient ammunition. Asquith's assertion had been based on information supplied by Kitchener, who, in turn, had been misled by French.[71] Now Asquith was made to look like a liar, and it was difficult for him not to blame Kitchener.

The Asquith administration was badly bruised by the shell controversy, but it was the altercation at the Admiralty, culminating in Sir John Fisher's resignation as first sea lord, that brought matters to a head.[72] The political background to the ministerial crisis of May, about which much has been written,[73] merits only a brief description here. When the Conservatives learned that their darling Fisher would be leaving the Admiralty and that Churchill, whom they considered unstable and a menace to the nation, would be staying, they warned of an imminent eruption on the floor of the House of Commons. On May 17, Asquith, confronted by the threat of all-out party warfare, quickly bowed to Conservative demands and agreed to form a coalition government. Asquith's reasons for capitulating are uncertain, as he enjoyed a comfortable majority in Parliament and could easily have beaten back a vote of no confidence. The most plausible explanation is that Asquith wanted to avoid party warfare, which would damage national morale and might deter Italy from fulfilling its commitment to join the Entente.[74]

While Asquith worked on the delicate task of distributing offices between the parties in the coalition, Lloyd George joined French and Lord Northcliffe, owner of the *Times* and other London dailies, in an unholy alliance aimed at driving Kitchener out of the War Office.[75] The campaign failed miserably. Although Kitchener's star was waning in certain political quarters, Asquith was shrewd enough to understand that his great popularity with the masses ruled out his removal.[76] The chief casualty of the new government was Churchill, who was replaced by Balfour at the Admiralty. Grey, like Kitchener, kept his old office. Bonar Law, the Conservative leader, became Secretary for the Colonies. Lloyd George left the Treasury to set up and direct the new Ministry of Munitions. A separate ministry had become necessary and probably should have been established a few months earlier. The rapid expansion of munitions required more and more of the nation's scarce resources—including factory buildings, machinery, skilled labor, and raw materials—and the ordnance department of the War Office lacked the personnel and organization to control this major sector of the wartime economy.[77]

Many historians continue to attribute the munitions shortage to Kitchener's indifference and mismanagement and to revere Lloyd George as a sort of miracle worker, who overnight swept away the old methods and substituted a new system capable of meeting the enormous demands of the armies.[78] Such a judgment overlooks key facts and accepts too uncritically Lloyd George's exaggerated or disingenuous claims about his achievements.[79] In the first place, Lloyd George did not, to repeat his famous anecdote, start with just "two tables and a chair."[80] He inherited much administrative machinery from the War Office, to say nothing of the practice of bringing in businessmen, which was begun by Kitchener

in spite of the Prime Minister's reservations.[81] Simply put, the organization at the Ministry of Munitions did not appear overnight, but was an
extension of what had gone on before. The ministry was ready to do business in June (formally, in July) 1915, and, as Lloyd George was in a hurry
to multiply output, a sizeable part of the initial orders was placed with
dubious firms. Not surprisingly, as Kitchener and von Donop had predicted, quality was sacrificed for quantity. Much of the early consignment
of munitions turned out to be defective, the consequences of which were
felt at the Somme, when duds littered the battlefield and shells exploded
prematurely in the breeches of the guns.[82]

Lloyd George made his share of mistakes at the Ministry of Munitions, which he never acknowledged, but he undoubtedly did his part in
stimulating production. Whether he deserves the lion's share of the credit
is by no means as plain as his biographers maintain.[83] Certainly, that judgment should not be based solely on the rapid rate of munitions expansion
in 1917 and 1918. Under Kitchener, new firms were constantly added to the
War Office list, and old ones were encouraged to expand their productive
capacity. That practice would have continued regardless of who was in
charge of munitions output.

A strong case can be made that the task of building an organization
from the ground up in the face of incredible obstacles was much more
difficult than that of improving and extending a system already in place.
When the Ministry of Munitions began to operate in June 1915, the way
had been cleared in advance by the War Office so that it knew for sure
the type and quantity of guns and shells the Army required; it benefited
from the plethora of contracts that had already been placed; and it inherited the means to conduct research, procure raw materials and machinery,
and supervise both private and state factories. Moreover, thanks to recent
legislation, it enjoyed the power, denied to the War Office, of compelling
the cooperation of labor and capital in factories producing armaments.[84]

A question far easier to answer is how well Lloyd George would have
coped with the munitions problem if he had been in charge in August
1914. Here was a man who expected the war to be over in a matter of a
few months, who had no expertise in the technical side of munitions making, and who was ready to allot contracts to fly-by-night operations. One
cannot begin to imagine the muddle and chaos that would have ensued
with disastrous, if not fatal, consequences for the Army. It is indeed fortu-
nate for Britain that munitions supply was placed in the hands of Kitchener at the outset. He was the only man in Britain to have a sense of the

amount of ammunition that the armies would require for a long war, and his makeshift arrangements, while not perfect, produced results that bordered on the miraculous. For eighteen months, the War Office supplied the expanding needs of the Army through its own arrangements. Between December 1914 and December 1915, the output of small arms ammunition increased tenfold, and the production of shells of all caliber rose twenty-seven-fold. By May 1915, the War Office presided over a network that yielded in three days the same amount of ammunition that was normally produced in one year in peacetime.[85]

After all that has been said, there is perhaps no better authority for judging Kitchener's handling of munitions production than the British Official History. While acknowledging that the supply of munitions was somewhat hampered by ingrained peacetime habits shed only slowly and reluctantly, it went on to say:

> Until [April 1916] the great and constant increase in production of war material of all kinds—not only for the original six divisions, but for the Territorial divisions, which had not been expected to take part in a Continental war, and for the divisions of the New Army—was due to the foresight of the War Office in expanding the armament factories, and placing large contracts both at home and overseas in the first months of the war. . . . During the first ten months of the war in spite of the shortage of labour and machinery, and notwithstanding the lack of housing accommodation and other inconveniences . . . the Royal Ordnance Factories and the recognized armament firms had managed to increase their output ten to twentyfold.[86]

Lord Kitchener (with walking stick) at Mudros, November 11, 1915, after an inspection. General Monro is talking to Kitchener and behind them is General Maxwell, commanding the troops in Egypt *(Imperial War Museum).*

Lord Kitchener (right) at Helles, November 12, 1915, with General Birdwood at his side, speaking to Colonel Watson, commandant of the advance base and a former ADC *(Imperial War Museum).*

Australians watching the arrival of Kitchener at Anzac on November 13, 1915 *(Imperial War Museum).*

Kitchener arriving on board a destroyer en route to Athens *(Imperial War Museum)*.

Lord Kitchener and General Cadorna (holding cigarette), Italian commander in chief, at the latter's headquarters *(Imperial War Museum)*.

Kitchener leaving a conference in Paris with Hankey *(Imperial War Museum)*.

Sir William Robertson. A first rate administrator, he reached the zenith of his career during his service as chief of the imperial staff *(U.S. Army Military History Institute).*

Sir Douglas Haig. Although a vast improvement over his predecessor, he remains legendary for his lack of imagination and callous brutality *(U.S. Army Military History Institute).*

Kitchener and Robertson on Anzac Day, 1916 *(Imperial War Museum).*

Kitchener inspecting Russian officers and men engaged in munitions work in the War Office courtyard in 1916 *(Imperial War Museum)*.

Admiral Jellicoe's farewell to Kitchener on board H.M.S. *Iron Duke (Imperial War Museum)*.

10

ARMAMENTS FOR RUSSIA

T HE Russian Army faced a munitions crisis in the spring of 1915, partly because the government had made no preparations to produce armaments for a modern war, and partly because the artillery department in Petrograd was slow to recognize that the shell shortage was as critical as reported by the generals at the front. The Russians fought the opening months of the war with munitions produced from Russian sources as well as from reserve stockpiles. By the close of 1914, they awoke to the fact that the war would be long and, in consequence, that their armies would require ammunition in great quantities. Drawing upon only a narrow circle of Russian firms, they gave no thought to extending production inside the country, for they had no faith in the capability of Russian industry to manufacture armaments. Instead, they preferred to rely on foreign manufacturers to supplement their munitions needs, which they reckoned could be done more cheaply and effectively than at home.[1]

The Russians were unable to count on France to any significant degree for, besides Schneider-Creusot, French industry was almost totally absorbed with supplying Joffre's armies. In the first week of January 1915, the grand duke asked Joffre whether he should remain on the defensive or assume the offensive, in which case he would require some of the ammunition destined for the western front. The French, facing a temporary shell shortage in the early months of 1915, did not feel that they could spare even a limited amount. Their attitude was best summarized by

Poincaré, who confided to his memoirs, "We can give nothing because we have not sufficient even for ourselves."[2]

Rebuffed by their old ally, the Russians turned to Kitchener. Because of Russia's importance to the Entente, Kitchener found it difficult to refuse them help, in spite of his own munitions requirements and back-breaking load. The Russians, however, did not make his task any easier. They used the same methods of foreign purchasing as they had in peace-time. The Russian War Ministry was compartmentalized, with certain branches, such as the Artillery Department, more or less independent and able to place orders abroad. Problems arising from such a system were exacerbated by the division of Russia into two zones, one controlled by the imperial government and the other by the *Stavka*. The front and the rear maintained only very tenuous links, owing to the strained personal relations between Grand Duke Nicholas and the War Minister, V. A. Sukhomlinov, so that when dealing with common matters like munitions, the two zones were apt to be working in the dark and at cross-purposes. The absence of a centralized agency to purchase armaments for Russia abroad, apart from hindering the Russian war effort, was a constant irritant to cordial Anglo-Russian relations.[3]

Shortly after the war broke out, a *Commission Internationale de Ravitaillement* (CIR) was created in London, under the aegis of the Board of Trade, with the object of placing Anglo-French orders with British industry. As soon as the Russians made inquiries about the possibility of purchasing British munitions, they were included in the committee as well. It was a sensible arrangement, for otherwise the Allies would be bidding against each other, causing prices to rise sharply. The presence of Russia on the CIR did not inhibit the Tsarist government from placing orders independently with firms in Britain and, later, in the United States, in direct competition with the British War Office. The CIR, however, never worked well. The head of the Russian delegation, M. V. Rutkovskii, was rarely briefed by his government on purchases made in Britain and the United States. Then, too, some departments in the Russian War Office flatly refused to order through the CIR because they were convinced that its members were taking bribes.[4]

Kitchener was eager to assist the Russians in getting a handle on their munitions difficulties, but not at the expense of the British Army. From the beginning, he had insisted on reviewing all Russian orders placed in Britain to ensure that the firms involved could carry them out without delaying the work already contracted for by the British government. In

September 1914, the Russian Ambassador in London, Count A. Benck-endorff, asked the Foreign Office whether there would be any objections if his government placed an order with Vickers for twenty antiaircraft guns.[5] The Director of Artillery at the War Office, H. Guthrie Smith, replied on behalf of Kitchener that permission would be granted on the proviso that the order did not interfere with the British war effort. He went on to say, "Vickers will probably say there will be no interference and we have no means of finding out whether this is correct or not."[6] As predicted, Vickers gave assurances that the Russian contract would not jeopardize the work being done for the British government. More Russian orders with Vickers and other British firms followed and, as long as the procedures laid down were observed, Kitchener, whatever his personal reservations, raised no objections. Too often, however, Kitchener would discover that Russian agents outside the jurisdiction of the CIR had gone behind his back and negotiated secret deals with British firms.[7]

At the beginning of January 1915, Kitchener requested through Hanbury Williams that the Russian government send a representative to London to take charge of munitions procurement.[8] To that end, Gen. Timchenko-Ruban, whose only apparent qualification was that he could speak English, was selected for the task.[9] On arrival, Timchenko-Ruban set up a new body, known as the Russian Government Committee (RGC), which included Russian delegates to the CIR. Timchenko-Ruban was authorized to terminate the practice of freelance purchasing and to funnel all future orders through his committee. Kitchener was asked to find new munitions suppliers for Russia in the United States, in collaboration with Timchenko-Ruban.[10] Kitchener expressed a willingness to do all in his power to help, but felt that his efforts would be hampered unless the Russian authorities fully disclosed their requirements.[11] Grand Duke Sergei Mikhailovitch, the former inspector-general of artillery and currently head of a new committee (called the Special Efficiency Commission for Artillery Matters), replied that it was difficult to give a thorough account of Russia's wants without knowing how much longer the war would last. He did, however, beg Kitchener to place orders in Canada and in the United States "anywhere up to 2,500,000 shrapnel, 2,500,000 explosive shells, and 1,500,000 rifles."[12]

The sense of urgency Kitchener felt deepened in February 1915, when Hanbury Williams forwarded a report in which he suspected that Russia's defeats in Poland were caused by a want of ammunition.[13] Accordingly, Kitchener instructed the Army Council to study means by which Russia's armament needs could be overcome. After intense investigation, it concluded that it could find no way, either in Britain or in the United States, to make good the shortages instantly. Its report held little hope that it could render effective help in the future unless the Russian government implemented badly overdue reforms. First, it was essential that the Russian authorities submit a "frank and full" statement regarding the estimated requirements of their army, the contracts already placed, and the munitions firms contacted for possible orders. Secondly, all purchasing in Britain and the United States would have to be vested in the hands of a single individual. It was imperative that such a person should possess the necessary expertise and authority to act on behalf of his government and be capable of checking the activities of the numerous Russian agents "who appear to be competing with one another for the same articles in the same markets and none of whom appear to be cognizant of the instructions issued to their colleagues."[14] Kitchener directed Hanbury Williams to pass on the gist of the report to Grand Duke Sergei.

As promised, Kitchener exerted every effort to procure armaments for Russia wherever he could find them. On March 8, he negotiated a contract with the Westinghouse Electric Company for one million rifles. His close business dealings with Bethlehem Steel paid dividends when on March 9 the giant firm offered him five million complete rounds of 3-inch shells, the first installment to be delivered in January 1916.[15] He tried to mediate a dispute between Russian negotiators and Kings Norton, which was holding up the manufacture of fuses. Acting on behalf of Russian authorities, Kitchener approached the Canadian government to inquire about the reputation of a Canadian syndicate (the Canadian Car and Foundry Company), with which they had signed a large contract for shells.[16] Similarly, the Russians asked Kitchener to apply pressure on Vickers, which had fallen behind on the delivery of shells and fuses.

Without an influx of foreign munitions, Kitchener knew that Grand Duke Nicholas would be compelled to remain on the defensive. The Russians had shaken off the effects of their earlier setbacks in Poland, and the grand duke had agreed to Kitchener's proposal for coordinated attacks on both fronts at the earliest possible moment.[17] Kitchener had been warned by Knox that the Russians would be incapable of undertaking such a movement during the summer without the timely arrival of their foreign orders.[18]

Kitchener felt that too much time was wasted because there was no Russian official in London invested with the authority to act without constant reference to Petrograd. At the start of March, he requested that a responsible official be sent with both a thorough knowledge of Russia's requirements and wide-ranging authority.[19] Grand Duke Sergei replied that it would be difficult to place a man in London with sufficient expertise to make decisions on his own. He knew of only one general with the necessary qualifications, but regrettably that officer did not speak English. He admitted that Timchenko-Ruban did not possess the technical knowledge for the position that he now occupied and, as a means to expedite matters, suggested direct communication between himself and Kitchener. In the interim, he begged Kitchener to do his utmost to help him ease the present shortages.[20]

When Kitchener urged Vickers to speed up the delivery of Russia's purchases,[21] he was told that Russian practices were responsible for the delays. Vickers pointed out that it could not make Russian fuses until powder for them came from Russia; that guns to test shells were late in arriving or did not come at all; that Russian blueprints came in Cyrillic and were difficult to make out; and that Russian officials negotiating contracts were overly suspicious and haggled over trivial matters, even when there was cause for urgency. While it would be unfair to discount Vickers's complaints, there can be no doubt that it contracted for more work than it could handle. Delays involved not only Russian but British orders as well.

The Russians felt let down by Vickers, which in the prewar period had supplied much of the expertise and means for creating their modern armament industry.[22] They refused to take any blame for the delayed deliveries and dismissed Vickers's excuses as without merit.[23] They were only slightly less irritated with Kitchener, who could offer them no immediate relief. That became apparent when Kitchener recommended that they accept a contract for a million Ross rifles, with half the order to be delivered by May 1916.[24] Sergei rejected the offer, saying he needed the rifles now and not in the distant future. He pointed out that he had ordered so many shells from abroad that if the war were to stop in about six months, the Russian Army would not know what to do with them. He was adamant that he needed assistance in the next few months

> which were critical ones and that he was prepared to accept anything that could be offered in the way of rifles, shells and fuses during the period that must elapse before a regular flow commences to come in

from abroad and looks on the punctual fulfillment of Vickers' contract as the saving feature of the situation.[25]

The Russians held the mistaken notion that because Britain was the world's industrial leader, it was capable of producing unlimited amounts of armaments. They resented the delays in the delivery dates by munitions firms in Britain, which they claimed had grown rich at their expense. When explanations were offered about the great demands placed on these firms, they pointed to their own achievement, the fact that despite their puny and backward industry, the output between August 1914 and April 1915 had increased hundreds of times. As they saw it, Britain's refusal to cover Russia's shortages reflected extreme selfishness and lack of appreciation for an ally that had made untold sacrifices for the common cause. This attitude led Sergei to conclude during the second half of March that reliance on foreign firms was not the answer to Russia's munitions shortages.

The aim of the new policy was to reject additional foreign offers, which could not be delivered immediately, and instead to purchase only the machinery and items required to increase domestic production. The grand duke was confident that by the autumn of 1915 increased domestic production would be equal to the Army's needs.[26] Kitchener could scarcely believe what he was told. He thought that the Russians were living in a fool's paradise if they assumed that within six months they could increase domestic production sufficiently to end their munitions shortages. On March 14, Kitchener sent a message to Grand Duke Sergei through the British Ambassador in Petrograd:

> I think it would be most unwise to limit orders owing to a possible surplus if the war stopped in six months. It is far better to have a surplus on a possible earlier termination than to risk a shortage while fighting is going on and I hope you will tell His Imperial Highness that I am doing everything possible to facilitate the manufacture of fuses ordered at Vickers and Kings Norton.[27]

Kitchener refused to let the matter drop with a simple warning. He tried again and, in response to his urgent appeal that Sergei reconsider his decision, received the following telegram from Buchanan: "Grand Duke says by the time Ross rifles start arriving in May 1916 Russia will have enough rifles."[28] Kitchener ran into the same difficulty when he recommended that the Russian government accept an offer from the American Locomotive Company for five million 3-inch shells, complete except for propellant, with delivery scheduled to begin in the autumn.[29] Sergei replied that he was not interested, as he had some ten million shells on order abroad.[30]

Kitchener received a message from Knox on April 2 telling him that Russia's artillery stock was down to two hundred rounds per gun.[31] In view of the severe nature of the shortages, Kitchener wondered if Sergei had misunderstood the offer made by the American Locomotive Company.[32] As a result, he went ahead and closed the deal on his own (subject to price negotiation), rationalizing that, if Russians remained intransigent, the British Army could always use the munitions. His concern was further aroused when Timchenko-Ruban informed him that the ten million shells on order had been placed with three firms: Vickers, Schneider-Creusot, and the Canadian Car and Foundry Company. "If these are the only outside order for shell the Russian government have got," Kitchener remarked to Buchanan, "the situation appears to be serious." Kitchener had reservations about the reliability of the Canadian outfit, and Vickers, for various reasons, was not expected to commence output before May. In these circumstances, it was improvident for the Russian government to turn its back on the offer of American Locomotive.[33] Kitchener's pleas fell on deaf ears. Buchanan forwarded Sergei's answer: "Grand Duke . . . is unwilling to give any more contracts for unfilled shell. His attitude is that no contract now can relieve pressure of the next two or three months. . . . After July he believes that conditions should commence to be normal."[34] Kitchener warned the grand duke that he would later regret passing up the deal, but his latest initiative got him no further than the previous ones.[35] It would require a spectacular enemy victory on the eastern front to bring about a new arrangement between Britain and Russia with regards to armaments.

On May 1, a powerful Austro-German force shattered the Russian front between Gorlice and Tarnow, sending what remained of the Russian Third Army fleeing in panic. Dogging the retreating Russians, the armies of the Central Powers advanced relentlessly in the spring and summer, liberating Galicia and capturing large areas of southern Poland.[36] Although the Anglo-French armies were unable to do much on the western front, except lick their wounds, the Russian collapse became daily more serious. If Russia were forced out of the war, the whole weight of the German Army would be shifted to France. That prospect, as we shall see in the next chapter, would have a decisive impact on British military planning.

Early in May, Kitchener sent Col. William E. Ellershaw, an artillery expert at the War Office, on a special mission to the *Stavka* in an effort to set up an arrangement more formal and productive than the haphazard one that had characterized dealings between Britain and Russia during the first nine months of the war. Ellershaw arrived on May 14, carrying with him a letter from Kitchener to Grand Duke Nicholas. In it, Kitchener pointed out that, according to the standard that experience had shown to be necessary on the western front, the Russian shortage of shells was at least 1.5 million rounds per month. He offered to render any assistance in his power to make good the deficiency in shells and other munitions.[37] Hanbury Williams formally presented the letter to the grand duke, who glanced at it before turning it over to his chief of staff, Gen. N. N. Ianushkevich. Hanbury Williams later had a discussion with Ianushkevich and, in the process, mentioned that Kitchener's efforts to place additional orders for Russia in the United States had been blocked by Grand Duke Sergei.[38] Ianushkevich expressed surprise over Sergei's action, but he was being disingenuous. A month earlier Sergei had written to him explaining his reasons for rejecting Kitchener's recent offers.[39]

Hanbury Williams and Ellershaw had a second meeting with Ianushkevich that evening to try to establish a new arrangement. When Hanbury Williams had seen the Emperor at Christmas, he had been told that all red tape would be eliminated and that Grand Duke Sergei would be appointed to ensure that things ran smoothly. The change had not improved matters, so now Hanbury Williams, acting on his own initiative, proposed that Kitchener be authorized by Grand Duke Nicholas to act as purchasing agent for Russia in Britain and the United States. The Russian chief of staff assented at once, subject to the approval of Grand Duke Nicholas. In a private letter to Kitchener the next day, Hanbury Williams wrote, "I hope the arrangement will thus be centralized and will work—I say hope, because there have been so many delays, and so many disappointments in connection with this matter that one feels as if one had almost got the end of one's tether in it."[40]

The proposal was welcomed by Grand Duke Nicholas, who "expressed himself most gratefully and sincerely" to the British representatives.[41] He addressed a letter to Kitchener, containing a statement of Russia's armament requirements and giving him carte blanche to act as he saw fit.[42] It was illegal under Russian law to give such authority to a foreigner but, as was pointed out, "since it is a question now whether Russia should be victorious or defeated, we will spit on these laws."[43] There were now two contradictory munitions policies in Russia, one advocated by Grand Duke Nicholas and the other by Grand Duke Sergei. It was Eller-shaw's contention that offers of munitions supply were apt to be delayed unless made personally to Grand Duke Nicholas.[44]

That the mission's work had been accomplished quickly and smoothly was in no small measure due to Ellershaw's tact, ability, and pleasant manner.[45] "We have got over some of our fences now," Hanbury Williams reported to Kitchener, " but we have the biggest fence in front of us, and that is the question of time."[46]

Although Kitchener assumed the responsibility for purchasing military armaments for Russia, he wanted to place on record the extent of the aid that the British could supply in the coming months. He was looking to protect himself because he suspected that the Russians might blame him for their setbacks. Accordingly, he sent Grand Duke Nicholas a long letter via Buchanan. George Clerk, the leading expert on Near Eastern affairs at the Foreign Office, minuted on the draft of this telegram, "Lord Kitchener is anxious that there should be something official on record, to supplement the discussions which have recently taken place between him and the Grand Duke Nicholas. Otherwise, the Russians may try to make us responsible for further retreat on their part, due to lack of ammunition."[47]

Kitchener's note to the grand duke was direct without being offensive. He assured Nicholas that he would strain every nerve to help the Russian Army through its crisis, but observed that "all existing available sources of supply are already taken up and to meet Russian requirements it will be necessary to create new sources and to erect new or convert existing manufacturing plants." He made it clear that the British government, while doing its best, could not accept any responsibility for finding the supplies within the time frame desired by Nicholas. In conveying the message, Buchanan was to remind the grand duke that in March he had offered the Russian government contracts for large deliveries from several American firms, only to be turned down. Had these contracts been accepted, substantial supplies would have been delivered in September and even more from November onwards.[48]

In the days following the agreement with Russia, a flurry of telegraphic exchanges passed between the War Office and J. P. Morgan Ltd., its purchasing agent in the United States. The officials of Bethlehem Steel were approached to see if they could manufacture shells for Russia without interfering with British orders. They responded in the affirmative, but indicated that, as their plant would have to be expanded, deliveries were unlikely to begin before a year after the contract was signed.[49] The War Office turned down the offer on the grounds that it required speedier deliveries. The War Office understood that it might not be possible to find responsible firms, such as Bethlehem Steel, which could make timely deliveries of complete shells. In that case it asked its American purchasing agent to work out a plan whereby some manufacturers would provide component parts, while others would be responsible for assembling and loading.[50]

That option did not preclude J. P. Morgan from trying to locate other firms that could supply complete shells. On May 21, it informed the War Office that Baldwin Locomotive Works had offered to supply 2.5 million complete rounds with a promise to begin delivery in January 1916. It expressed faith in the strength and efficiency of Baldwin Locomotive Works and belief that the company offered "the best source of supply available."[51] Kitchener replied that he would urge the Russians to agree to the offer, but that this order, even if accepted, would only fill a small portion of the 1.5 million complete rounds per month deemed necessary. The War Office inquired whether shell deliveries from Baldwin Locomotive Works and other suitable firms could be hastened if some of the component parts were subcontracted.[52]

From Baldwin Locomotive Works, J. P. Morgan learned that supplies could be expedited by thirty to sixty days if propellant could be obtained in September. The War Office wondered whether J. P. Morgan could persuade dependable firms, like Dupont, to expand their facilities to provide the necessary propellant. It was willing to give an assurance that, if such supplies could be obtained during the last months of the year, any additional costs within reason would be agreed to.[53] At the same time J. P. Morgan opened negotiations with E. W. Bliss Company for 18-pounder empty shell cases, cartridge cases, and primers.[54]

Kitchener called in the Russian officials in London and showed them the offer from Baldwin Locomotive Works. To his astonishment, he was told that they were not interested. Their government had already signed a contract with that firm for deliveries in April, which as yet had not been received. A preliminary War Office investigation revealed that the Russians had approached Baldwin Locomotive Works, but that negotiations had broken down. Kitchener asked J. P. Morgan on May 27 to contact

Baldwin Locomotive Works to confirm that no shell contract with Russia existed.[55] J. P. Morgan quickly attended to the matter and the following day telegraphed Kitchener that "Baldwin Locomotive Works state that they have not now nor have they ever received [an] order from Russian Government or anyone else for any kind of Russian shells."[56]

Kitchener assumed that some misunderstanding had occurred between the Russian government and its officials in London. It seemed improbable that the Russians would pass up the offer, given the worsening plight of their army. The latest information from Petrograd was grim. "Colonel Ellershaw left for London this morning," Buchanan's telegram ran, and "from what he told me, and from what I hear from other sources, I much fear that unless we or Japanese can come to Russia's assistance, Russian army may sooner or later meet with such a disaster that Germans will be able to concentrate all their forces on the western front." It was not the sort of news that Kitchener wanted to hear.[57]

Kitchener was at least encouraged by the continued good results of J. P. Morgan's initiatives. On May 28, J. P. Morgan notified the War Office that the Curtiss Manufacturing Company was prepared to supply one million complete rounds of shrapnel, with delivery to begin four months after drawings and specifications had been approved.[58] On the same day, J. P. Morgan identified General Electric Company as willing to furnish two million rounds of shrapnel and an equal number of heavy-explosive shells, but without propellant, explosives, and unleaded primers. Delivery would begin in October on the condition that drawings and specifications were promptly approved.[59] The War Office sent its American purchasing agent two telegrams on May 29. The first suggested that Baldwin Locomotive Works, General Electric Company, and Dupont should be induced to cooperate in the manufacture of shells for Russia and submit a single large offer—in the neighborhood of five million shells. Each could work on different portions of the shells, according to its equipment and access to the necessary raw materials. The second telegram amplified what was stated in the first. The War Office indicated that, anxious as it was about the state of Russia's munitions shortages, it could not close on contracts without the formal consent of the Petrograd authorities, who were invariably slow to respond. Since individual contracts were comparatively small in relation to Russia's needs, they did not usually elicit sufficiently serious consideration. The War Office felt that if the three companies named would agree to cooperate and make a single offer along the lines indicated earlier, "monthly deliveries would appear more important and it will be probably easier to get the necessary consent of the Russian authorities." Furthermore, the creation of such a powerful organization was certain to increase output and hasten deliveries. The War Office was explicit in telling J. P. Morgan that, if all went well, it was vital that deliveries should not extend beyond December 31, 1916. The note ended as follows:

> Russia's immediate necessity for shells is so great as to swamp question of future supplies and offers involving late deliveries are apt to be turned down without full consideration. Indeed it may even be difficult to get consent for deliveries as late as December 1916. War Office fully appreciate attention which you are giving to this matter and are very pleased that you have been able to get already such substantial orders.[60]

The responsibility of acquiring munitions for Russia did not change hands after the establishment of a Ministry of Munitions under Asquith's coalition government. Kitchener, in defiance of good sense, refused to concede the task to his hated enemy, Lloyd George. He was able to argue successfully "that his arrangement with the Grand Duke Nicholas was in the nature of a personal commitment." Early in June Kitchener set up a Russian Purchasing Committee (RPC) at the War Office to deal with Russia's munitions supplies. The Russian members on the RPC consisted of Rutkovskii, as well as Maj. Gen. E. Hermonius and Col. M. A. Beliaev, both of whom had been sent over in May to improve their government's chaotic purchasing methods. The British were represented by Ellershaw, Booth, U. F. Wintour (Director of Army Contracts), and Sir Edmund Wyldebore Smith (Secretary of the CIR). The key figure in the Russian delegation was Hermonius, a capable and energetic administrator. Although he could not converse in English, his liaison with the British, Beliaev, spoke the language fluently.[61]

The new committee handled most of the day-to-day work regarding munitions for Russia. There was no let up in the offers from America. J. P. Morgan telegraphed on June 5 that the Bartlett Hayward Company was prepared to supply, subject to the buyer furnishing the propellant powder, two million complete shells, with the first shipment of forty thousand rounds to begin during the fourth month after receipt of approved drawings and specifications. J. P. Morgan included a reminder to the War Office:

All companies emphasize that before anything can be done arrangements must be made to supply them with complete technical data, drawings and specifications and place them in touch with representatives of the Russian Government who will be authorized to make such modifications of specifications and inspections as may be necessary to meet American practices and methods. No contract can be signed unless this is done. Delay in doing this can only mean delay in delivery of shells.[62]

During the second week of June, Kitchener asked Hanbury Williams to give Grand Duke Nicholas personally a summary of the negotiations that he had carried on in the United States on behalf of the Russian government. Hanbury Williams reported the results of his interview:

He was very grateful to you for all the trouble you have taken and heartily approved of the lines on which you are working, but he is very sketchy on anything approaching detail and . . . was a little "peevish" about the failure to get anything to speak of hitherto from us or from France . . . and was a little inclined to lecture me upon what he seemed to consider were broken promises—and disappointed expectations . . . and desired me to carry on with the CGS. To be quite frank with you he is not of much use on these occasions—his name counts and he "matters" a lot in one way, but he doesn't "run the show" much really.[63]

Hanbury Williams, who had become exasperated at the delays caused by the Byzantine labyrinth of the Russian bureaucracy, wanted his hosts to set up an internal committee with the authority and expertise to respond instantly to the RPC at the War Office. Such a committee, he thought, should consist of representatives of Grand Duke Nicholas, the Navy, railway, and the Finance Ministry, in addition to the military and naval attachés from the British Embassy.[64] He brought up the idea when he went to see Gen. Ianushkevich. It was bad enough that Ianushkevich showed no interest in this matter, but he made it plain that his government would not entertain any offers for shells that did not guarantee delivery before October. After that date, he claimed, Russian industry would be producing 1.5 million rounds per month, which was equivalent to the full requirements of the Russian Army. Hanbury Williams urged him to accept all the American offers recommended by Kitchener and warned him of all the things that could go wrong—from local strikes and transportation problems to ships lost at sea—but to no avail. "I have no faith,"

his message to Kitchener ran, "of the declaration of their position in October and I am extremely anxious as to their position then, let alone their
position at present which is very bad."[65]

The next day Hanbury Williams tried to persuade Ianushkevich to
reconsider, again unsuccessfully. He showed the Russian general a cable
summarizing their previous interview, which he said he intended to con-
vey to Kitchener. Ianushkevich responded by giving him a draft of what
he proposed should be sent. Hanbury Williams refused to send it unless
he "altered the wording, which simply meant postponement and delay."
After further haggling, Ianushkevich took back his draft, and Hanbury
Williams left to send off his original message. In a private letter describing
his second meeting with Ianushkevich, Hanbury Williams took the occasion to bring Kitchener up to date on the gloomy military picture. He had
no way of knowing, anymore than anyone else, how long the Russians
would continue to retreat before they were able to stabilize their front. He
ended on a bitter note:

> All owing to lack of foresight, lying, dilatoriness—and even now they
> are only looking around for someone to hang. The War Minister told
> the French in September that Russia was perfectly supplied with ammu-
> nition and [had] no fear of running short—you know the result—I have
> been through very stressful times in my life in different parts of the Em-
> pire but never had such difficulties . . . to face as these, and I cannot tell
> you how grateful I feel to you for your patience with them—You will, I
> feel sure, know that I have wasted no time, and indeed have been peril-
> ously near strained relations in my arguments and insistence with these
> difficult people.[66]

Although J. P. Morgan had submitted to the War Office offers total-
ing some twenty-five million shells, the Russian authorities in the end
would sanction the purchase of only twelve million rounds. Accordingly,
the War Office telegraphed J. P. Morgan:

> After prolonged consultation with Russian delegates, War Office wish
> to arrange purchase of 12,000,000 complete rounds, either shrapnel or
> high explosive. . . . From the numerous offers which you have received
> and transmitted to us, W. O. wish you to select the best means of meet-
> ing this supply and cable us the firms you recommend should be em-
> ployed, proposed deliveries and prices. We . . . again impress upon you

most forcibly in selection of firms to be employed, speed of deliveries is the essential factor, combined of course with you being satisfied as to responsibility of firms to keep their engagements in this respect. . . . It is hoped you will be able to arrange for cooperation or combination among the bidders selected so that they may not unduly compete with each other for tools and raw materials, and if possible that their respective plant capacities may be used to greater advantage to the desired end, namely, production of largest number of complete rounds within shortest time possible.[67]

J. P. Morgan was not optimistic that even its most strenuous efforts would bear immediate fruit: "Will proceed with utmost dispatch but cannot offer encouragement that deliveries can be procured at as early date as War Office requires. Practically all preparations were based upon deliveries extending through 1916."[68] The War Office replied that it understood the conditions of the proffered contracts, but hoped that some deliveries could begin later in the current year. As an added incentive, the Russians were prepared to pay bonuses to expedite deliveries, which they counted on commencing in September or October at the latest. The War Office requested that J. P. Morgan should not close on contracts without submitting them to the War Office for final approval.[69]

For the time being, Kitchener had done all that he could to assist the Russians. He undoubtedly welcomed the respite, even though he knew that his work was far from over. How much more of his attention Russia would continue to claim was contingent on two factors: whether the armament firms in the west would be able to deliver their goods by the promised dates and whether the Russian government's prediction of self-sufficiency in munitions by October would be borne out. Only time would tell.

11

COLLAPSE OF AN
ACTIVE-DEFENSE POLICY

S a wartime government, the First Coalition had the defects, but not the merits, of its predecessor. Asquith had reached an accommodation with his Unionist opponents, not because he expected them to contribute to victory, but because he wanted to defuse political tension and involve them in the responsibility of framing policy. But, owing to the absence of a decent minimum of mutual confidence and respect between the leaders of the major parties, the coalition never operated as a cohesive body. The conduct of business became even more cumbrous and laborious than under the previous administration. Important issues, instead of being dealt with by four or five ministers, now drew the attention of twice that many. Decisions were obtained only after prolonged, heated, and exhausting discussions and, as a rule, proved to be unsatisfactory compromises.[1]

Kitchener's control of strategy, once unchallenged, began to wane in the new government. The Tories identified Kitchener with the growing fiasco in the Dardanelles and generally believed that he had mishandled the production of munitions.[2] Their distrust of his judgment was reinforced by a dislike of his style, by his secretiveness, and by the stream of complaints lodged against him by their military friends, Henry Wilson and Sir John French, and later by Lloyd George. From practically the beginning, they made no attempt to act as cordial and helpful colleagues or to make allowances for his political inexperience and peculiar habits. Instead, they badgered him for classified information (which they were incapable of keeping to themselves) and compelled him, in the manner of a barrister interrogating a hostile witness in court, to explain and defend his policies. Not surprisingly, Kitchener's effectiveness was reduced when he was forced to operate in circumstances in which his every move was scrutinized and questioned.

The coalition involved a change not only in the personnel of the Cabinet, but in the machinery for running the war. One of the first moves of the new government was to set up a special subcommittee of the Cabinet, known as the Dardanelles Committee, for the purpose of dealing with problems related to the Dardanelles campaign. Under the chairmanship of Asquith, the original members of the committee were Kitchener, Lord Crewe, and Churchill (who was kept in the Cabinet with the sinecure post of Chancellor of the Duchy of Lancaster), plus five Unionists, Bonar Law, Balfour, the Marquess of Lansdowne, Lord Curzon, and Lord Selborne.[3] Its numbers soon rose to twelve, then to fourteen. Like the War Council, it lacked executive authority. Its conclusions had to be ratified by the full Cabinet, where the arguments pro and con were often restated before a final decision was taken.

Kitchener had little use for such a committee. Instead, he wanted to replace the War Council with a smaller body to consist only of the Prime Minister, Balfour (the new first lord) and himself with Hankey as secretary. Hankey considered the suggestion impractical. Experience in recent months had shown that the heads of the service departments could not run the war without frequent consultation with other departments of state; and that, even if the Liberals could be persuaded to go along, it was a virtual certainty that the Unionists would never agree to delegate vast powers to a body on which their only representative was Balfour, whom they judged to be too closely associated with the late government. Hankey felt that such a body, as proposed by Kitchener, would cause friction and duplication of work, and that it was best to wait and see how the new Dardanelles Committee would work.[4] The Prime Minister agreed with his reasoning. Hankey's suspicions that decisions affecting the Dardanelles campaign could not be taken without reference to what was happening on other fronts proved correct. In time, the Dardanelles Committee expanded its functions to include all aspects of war policy.

The newcomers in the Cabinet felt insecure in the midst of a somewhat unfriendly environment and, with the possible exception of Balfour, knew little about the business of fighting a war. In these circumstances, it was only natural that in the beginning they make no attempt to challenge the direction of war policy set by the previous regime. Thus, the First Coalition endorsed Kitchener's policy of attrition on the western front and of pressing on with the operations in the Dardanelles.

Kitchener had no confidence that the Anglo-French armies could make any headway in the west, and he did not attribute the failure of their last offensives to either a want of men or ammunition. As he wrote in the closing days in May, "the French have an almost unlimited supply of ammunition, including H. E. and Fourteen Divisions in reserve, so if they cannot get through we may take it as proved that the lines cannot be forced."[5] That being the case, Kitchener was more determined than ever to avoid committing the New Armies to major attacks in France. He told Hankey that another premature offensive would only exhaust their own reserves and open the way for the Germans to draw reinforcements from the Russian front and inflict a crushing defeat on the Anglo-French forces in the west.[6]

Kitchener recognized that a purely passive defense, staying behind fortifications in the west, was unwise, both militarily and politically. It would take the edge off the fighting spirit of the men, surrender all initiative to the enemy, and certainly give the impression in France and Russia that they were being used as Britain's Continental cat's paw. Instead, Kitchener wanted to adopt an active defense in the west, that is, to mount small-scale assaults with limited objectives in tactically advantageous areas, and wait for the German Army to shatter itself against the Anglo-French lines.

Kitchener remained steadfast in purpose even after the Germans smashed the Russian front at Gorlice-Tarnow and Grand Duke Nicholas turned to his allies for help. On May 22, the Russian commander asked whether the Anglo-French armies intended to attack in the west or to rely on a war of attrition.[7] Kitchener favored the latter course, but Joffre, supported by Sir John French, was adamant that he intended to pursue an active and aggressive strategy.[8] Joffre wrote personally to Kitchener in an attempt to convince him that by changing tactics, a combined Anglo-French offensive would prove decisive. As his resources were stretched to the breaking point, he asked Kitchener to send over New Army divisions to permit the British to fight alongside the French, as well as to take over additional lengths of the front. He further requested a timetable for the dispatch of the New Armies to France so that he could prepare his future plans.[9]

Towards the end of May, Kitchener notified French that, other than the two divisions already promised, he proposed to withhold the New Armies from France for the immediate future. Kitchener explained that Russia's defeat in the east raised the possibility that the Germans would bring back troops for a massive assault on the Anglo-French line. He wanted to retain the New Armies as a reserve against such a contingency. Kitchener added that, at their last meeting, he had made it clear that he would dispatch the New Armies to France only if the BEF succeeded in breaking through the German line. Since that objective had not been met, he saw no purpose in simply accumulating men in the trenches.[10]

Kitchener was a bit more tactful when he charged Brig. Gen. Yarde-Buller to break the news to Joffre. Yarde-Buller was to hint that, as Allied losses had been heavy and not commensurate with gains, it would seem logical to opt for an active defense and conserve resources until German strength had been further eroded. He was also to remind Joffre that at the Anglo-French conference in Chantilly on March 29, it had been agreed that seventeen rounds per field gun per day was the minimum for the safety and support of the infantry. At present, the British could only supply eleven rounds per day for their army in the field. If more divisions were sent out, it would considerably reduce the rate of supply per gun per day. Kitchener hoped to reach the desired daily number of shells per gun in about a month, but he could not give any guarantees. Yarde-Buller was to point out that the torpedoing of a single ship carrying war supplies from the United States or the failure of munitions contractors to meet delivery dates, as was often the case, made it impossible for the government to commit to a timetable.[11]

Neither French nor Joffre, however, was prepared to cast off earlier illusions. French believed that his troops had made good progress at Festubert on May 15 before German reserves had been rushed to the threatened sector and broken up the attack. This raised his hopes that with enough men and munitions he would be able to "break thro' this tremendous crust of defence, which has been forming and consolidating through out the winter."[12] Joffre was similarly encouraged by the ongoing fighting at Artois. There his infantry made appreciable gains in the initial rush, but his reserves were too far back to exploit the success, allowing German counterattacks to recover the lost ground. By avoiding past mistakes, Joffre was confident that the next time he would break through.

During the first week in June, a French mission headed by Col. Edmond Buat, Millerand's *chef du cabinet*, arrived in London to plead Joffre's case. Buat advanced arguments to show that the German line could be forced and that the offensive should be resumed as soon as possible. He ascribed past failures to limiting the attack to a sector of the line, which had permitted the Germans to bring up reinforcements to any threatened point. Joffre now proposed to attack in two places simultaneously along a wide front. Since the Germans would not know from where the main thrust was coming, they would be unable to make full use of their reserves. France, with over two million men in the field, had reached the limit of its manpower resources. Joffre counted on Britain to supply the troops for one of the attacks.

Buat moved on to the second point. He noted that Germany had reduced its forces in the west in order to seek a decision on the Russian front. While the Russians were experiencing great difficulty at present, there was little likelihood they would be vanquished. As a result, Buat reasoned, the Allies could expect the Germans to ease up and by the middle of July send back large numbers of troops from Russia. It was therefore vital that the Allies beat the Germans in France before that occurred. Buat's emphatic language and didactic tone grated on Kitchener, who reportedly "was in one of his least sympathetic moods."[13]

Kitchener held back his comments until the next day when the French delegation returned to the War Office. He indicated that Joffre and French were too offensive minded and would exhaust themselves in futile attacks. He predicted that the deadlock would continue for some time and that the advantage would lay with the side that had husbanded its resources. His only concession was a vague promise that, if his munitions supplies permitted, he would send over the Second New Army, but not to expect it before August 15.[14]

After the French delegation left, Kitchener sent word to Sir John inviting his views on future war policy. Predictably, French concurred with Joffre on the importance of taking the offensive at the earliest possible date. French asserted that a passive defense (he evidently did not see any difference between an active and passive defense) was justifiable only if it could be proved that the German line was impenetrable. The recent attacks by the British and French armies had convinced him that this was not the case. But, to achieve a breakthrough "it is necessary to have sufficient men and ammunition to be able to attack more than one point and to keep on attacking for a prolonged period." To date, French claimed, these two requirements had been missing. On the other hand, the chances of victory would be forfeited if the British assumed a passive defense. Such a course would not only have a deplorable effect on the morale of the British Army, it would also permit the Germans to defeat the Allies one at a time.[15] There was little in what French said that Kitchener had not heard before. In response, Kitchener produced a paper in which he rejected French's arguments, adding:

> It must be remembered that casualties take place in great numbers when troops are on the offensive, so it should be our object to induce the Germans to take the offensive whenever possible. This cannot be obtained if we remain on the strict defensive, for then the Germans will contain us with a small force, and be able to put in their strength elsewhere. We have, therefore, continually to attack with the least possible loss, that is to say, by surprise attacks, and be careful not to engage in too serious operations, so as to induce the Germans to counter-attack, and thus sustain heavy casualties.[16]

Kitchener's attitude was deeply resented both at GHQ and at GQG. For Sir John, it meant that he would be neither able to participate in any major attack nor, as Joffre had requested, take over more of the line so as to free French troops for offensive operations. Equally telling, it strained Kitchener's relations with Joffre and once again raised the question of Britain's moral and military commitment to France.[17] News of Kitchener's readiness to reinforce Hamilton only exacerbated Joffre's indignation.

The inability of Hamilton's army to overcome Turkish resistance on the Gallipoli Peninsula had placed Kitchener in a dilemma. Hamilton's men were pinned to the beaches, and Kitchener could see no way they could advance, particularly in light of the Admiralty's decision to withdraw the *Queen Elizabeth* on learning of U-boat activity in the regional waters.[18] As Kitchener pondered what to do next, three options were open to him. First, he could terminate the campaign, but to do so would have such horrible political consequences that it would be justifiable only to avoid a greater disaster. Secondly, he could send large reinforcements to the Dardanelles to permit Hamilton to resume the offensive. Kitchener, however, was loath to part with troops, which might be needed to repulse an invasion of Britain or a determined effort by the Germans to pierce the Allied line in the west. Thirdly, he could provide Hamilton with sufficient reinforcements to enable him to hold on and make such progress as was possible. This had the advantage of avoiding humiliation in the Muslim world and of keeping the door open to Balkan intervention. Kitchener favored the third course, but admitted that it carried certain risks: the possibility of a blockade by German submarines; of the enemy bringing to bear sufficient effectives to compel Hamilton's force to surrender; and of an overwhelming concentration of artillery, which might render the British position untenable.[19]

The Dardanelles Committee examined these options when it held its first meeting on the afternoon of June 7. As Hankey was absent, no minutes were taken. From what Asquith later said, the Committee unanimously agreed to send Hamilton three New Army divisions "with a view to an assault during the second week in July." Churchill took the lead in urging that Hamilton be given enough fresh troops to clear the Turks from the peninsula. Some of the Tories, notably Bonar Law, entered the government with a strong prejudice against the Dardanelles operation, but they gave their reluctant assent when Selborne, one of their own, supported Churchill with powerful arguments. Kitchener, too, came out in favor of providing Hamilton with large reinforcements.[20] The change in his position was principally due to his hope of putting a quick end to an enterprise that was proving an unwelcomed drain on his resources.

In the days that followed, the tide of opinion in the Cabinet rose even higher in favor of the Dardanelles campaign. As a matter of prudence, Churchill argued that Hamilton be provided with two more divisions for his projected offensive. There was considerable support for such a move in the Dardanelles Committee. Kitchener went along with the general sentiment, believing that with no major attacks planned in the west for 1915, these additional troops would make little difference to GHQ. At the same time, Kitchener proposed to curtail temporarily the supply of ammunition to Sir John's forces to swell the amounts available for Hamilton's coming attack. The Cabinet backed Kitchener in giving the Dardanelles campaign priority over the western front.[21]

Once it became clear that the men and the ammunition required for a successful attack on the western front would not be available before the spring of 1916, GHQ reached the conclusion that, until then, it would be preferable to adopt an active defense.[22] But Joffre, as obsessive as ever, remained convinced that a supreme effort would end the war before the coming winter. He invited French to Chantilly, knowing full well that his weak-willed British counterpart could not stand up to him in a face-to-face encounter. At the meeting on June 24, Joffre ripped into the concept of passive defense, claiming that it would lead to Russia's defeat, which, in turn, "would make certain of our defeat."[23] Joffre, like French, chose to interpret Kitchener's concept of active defense as standing strictly on the defensive. As Joffre foresaw, French was quickly won over. He renounced Kitchener's suggested policy and instead consented to support Joffre's idea of a major offensive in August. It was agreed that the two commanders would send similar letters to their respective governments calling for an Anglo-French assault in the west.

Such a recommendation met with no more favor in London than it had a fortnight earlier. Kitchener produced a long memorandum on June 26 in which he scoffed at the arguments used to promote the chances of a successful summer offensive. His plea that the Allies refrain from any major operations until next spring was based on the unreadiness of the New Armies and on the importance of accumulating large supplies of guns and munitions. He was convinced that the Allies would be throwing away the chances of victory if a combined attack on the western front could not be coordinated with a Russian advance, which was impossible until the Russian armies had recovered from their successive defeats and were supplied with adequate munitions.[24] Before distributing the paper to the Cabinet, Kitchener forwarded a copy to Asquith, who wrote back, "in the main I heartily agree."[25]

Yet Kitchener and his colleagues understood that retention of the New Armies at home had to be balanced with Britain's moral and military obligation as a coalition partner. Reports from Russia continued to be grim. In mid-June Hanbury Williams notified Kitchener that, if the Germans were heavily reinforced, he doubted that the Russians could hold Riga, Warsaw, or Lemberg.[26] Knox gave a bleaker military assessment a few days later. He stressed that the military situation was less favorable than it had been at any time since the start of the war. Russian units were being battered because they lacked heavy guns, shells, and rifles.[27]

Kitchener's willingness to do what he could to help the Russians precluded sacrificing thousands of British soldiers, which he felt an offensive in the west would entail. He believed that, although the Russians showed no signs of halting their retreat, they were in no danger of a complete collapse. For the time being, Kitchener thought that the most sensible policy was to adopt an active defense in the west, while pushing on in the Dardanelles, which he hoped would also ease Russia's military plight. The question was whether such a policy would be acceptable to Britain's allies. Kitchener sensed that the Russians were likely to agree, as they could not mount an offensive before 1916 and, besides, stood to gain appreciable Ottoman territory by an Allied victory in the Dardanelles. He was much less certain, however, that the French would be willing to face another winter campaign. Kitchener had heard from a variety of sources of the growing signs of war weariness in France. There were groups calling for peace and a movement was afoot to replace both Joffre and Millerand.[28] The government felt pressure to show the public that it was making progress towards expelling the Germans from France. In these circumstances, there seemed little likelihood that Joffre could be persuaded to abandon his offensive, but Kitchener was willing to try. Consequently it was arranged to hold an Anglo-French conference at Calais on July 6.

The British Cabinet held meetings on July 2 and 3 to formulate a strategic policy for the coming conference with the French. The results amounted to a compromise between Kitchener's position and that of Joffre. While the government would not renounce Britain's freedom of action, it recognized the western front as the dominant theater of war. More importantly, it authorized Kitchener to give the French a timetable showing when the New Armies would be proceeding to France, but at the same time to emphasize that they were to be used to take over additional lengths of the line, not for offensive operations. Finally, the Cabinet agreed that it should be strongly represented to the French that they should defer major operations until 1916. If, however, they felt that it was necessary to undertake "such an operation, Sir John will lend such cooperation with his existing force as . . . will be useful for the purpose, and not unduly costly to his army."[29]

The British position was thus firmly set when Asquith, Kitchener, and the other members of the British delegation crossed over to Calais on the evening of July 5. Just before the conference, Kitchener and Joffre held private talks to settle their differences. The two soldiers reached an amicable understanding. While Kitchener promised to send over the New Armies to man the trenches, Joffre agreed that a major offensive, if considered necessary, would be undertaken by the French alone. Kitchener did his best to convince Joffre to abandon his offensive in favor of a policy of attrition. Joffre appeared to be wavering, or so Kitchener believed, when they were interrupted and told that the conference was about to begin.[30]

The Anglo-French conference, the first aimed at coordinating war policy, got under way at 10:00 A.M. It was badly organized. No agenda had been prepared, no notes were taken, and no conclusions were recorded.

Kitchener dominated the proceedings, impressing the French political authorities with his command of their language and his clear exposition of the military situation. "The French were aware of his wide popularity and power," Esher wrote. "He was personally unknown to them all except M. Millerand, and for the first time French statesmen . . . were given a taste of his quality as a man of action; patient in discussion, forceful and intrepid of speech." The French delegates bowed to Kitchener's wishes, notwithstanding their earlier inclination to support Joffre's proposal for a major offensive. There was general agreement that the Dardanelles campaign should be pushed to a successful conclusion and that a policy of attrition should be pursued on the western front. There would be small local attacks aimed at demoralizing and wearing down the enemy, but no full-scale offensive, unless the Russian Army was on the point of defeat.[31] Joffre said little after his opening remarks, and Kitchener assumed that he had been swayed by the general tenor of the discussions.[32]

Now that a joint policy had finally been settled for the western front, Kitchener could devote more attention to building up Russia's munitions supplies. Since the War Office had placed orders in the United States for twelve million shells on behalf of the Russian government, problems had emerged because of Russia's purchasing and inspection methods. The Russian government had insisted that all munitions produced in the United States for its armies be approved by its own officers before being shipped to Russia. Actually, the War Office could not have taken on the work, even if it had wanted to, as it could not provide enough inspectors familiar with munitions of Russian pattern. Thus, it was agreed that the RPC in the United States, which already possessed a staff of inspectors for orders it had already placed, should undertake all arrangements for inspection, as well as make decisions on technical matters arising in the course of manufacture.

From the beginning, the niggling methods of the RPC, headed by Maj. Gen. A. V. Sapozhnikov, created difficulties and hindered production. There were delays lasting weeks and sometimes months in the approval of drawings, specifications, and gauges. Junior inspectors were reluctant to take decisions on the innumerable technical points that inevitably arose in production, with the result that the work was held up pending the approval of senior inspectors, who were few in number. To make matters worse, Sapozhnikov showed little desire to cooperate with American firms and, at times, appeared to be deliberately obstructive. As his committee had originally been established to place munitions orders in the United States, he seemed to resent the operation of the War Office RPC as encroaching on his own functions.[33]

The War Office felt compelled to act when American firms complained loudly about the dilatory and arbitrary conduct of the Russian inspectors. Kitchener concluded that owing to the magnitude of the orders and the difficulty of communicating complicated instructions by telegraph, it would be desirable to secure from the Schneider-Creusot Works in France several experts familiar with the details of Russia's artillery specifications. When contacted, the French government placed at Kitchener's disposal a technical team, which was hurriedly dispatched to the United States in an attempt to resolve some of the difficulties in munitions production.[34] At the same time, Hermonius and Ellershaw, on Kitchener's instructions, undertook a more far-reaching effort during their visit to the United States in August. The pair spent several weeks in the country, settling outstanding technical questions and smoothing over the differences between the Russian inspectors and American contractors.[35]

While Kitchener was taking steps to put munitions purchasing for the Russians in the United States on a more businesslike footing, his agents in Russia were alerting him to disturbing developments. Kitchener had urged the grand duke to make every effort to retain Warsaw, not so much for its symbolic value, as to prevent its important railroad system from falling into German hands.[36] Knox informed Kitchener on July 4 that the pace of the German advance had not slackened and that, as a result, the Russians had decided to evacuate Warsaw before it was too late. He indicated that the abandonment of Warsaw, however lamentable, was the only practical thing to do, for "any attempt to defend it would endanger a large part of the Russian army." He tried to reassure Kitchener that Russia could never be beaten as long as its army remained "in being" and that the possession of Warsaw was no more vital to the eventual success of the Russian Army than was, for instance, "the possession of Ypres in the success of the Allies in the west."[37]

Kitchener always understood that purchasing armaments for Russia was merely the first hurdle and that another one had to be overcome before the war supplies reached the armies in the field. The railways from Archangel—the only port accessible to the western Allies—to the Russian interior were far too inadequate for what was necessary. This meant long delays in moving the huge stockpile of goods to battle zones that were sometimes thousands of miles away. Now Kitchener was finding out, to a far greater degree than he had imagined, that the difficulties of arms distribution were exacerbated immensely by the corruption and incompetence of Russian officials. It seemed that to move supplies by rail, officials at all levels had to be bribed. Private manufacturers reconciled themselves to what they considered was a necessary evil and simply added the costs to the final price of their product. The government, however, refused to stoop to such sordid practices, with the result that its freight received the lowest priority. Food and vital war supplies from Britain, France, and the United States were "piled mountain high" and rotted away because they were not, or could not, be moved inland. As no equipment existed to handle heavy cargoes, crates packed on top of one another were left in the open where they slowly sank into the soil.[38] A frustrated Blair confided to Kitchener that he held little hope that the defects along the Archangel route could be repaired:

> Enterprise is everywhere so kept down, and the paths of officialdom so devious and costly to tread, that the remedy of simple and glaring defects is almost impossible to obtain, owing to the fact that those to whom the remedying is given, in cooperation with those who have given it to them, have only one object in view, namely the filling of their own pockets.[39]

As if providing badly needed arms and munitions for Russia was not a daunting enough challenge, Kitchener received little cooperation from the very people he was trying to help. "They are a terrible people to deal with," Callwell told Henry Wilson, "and the Tsar and the Grand Duke [Nicholas] are probably the only honest men in the country."[40] British agents complained that in conversation with Russian officials, they were invariably told that things were operating smoothly when they knew the truth to be otherwise. If they suggested ways to remedy faulty practices they perceived, their advice was usually ignored. Among the most troublesome issues was a feeling that the Russians were underestimating the daily requirement of shells for their guns. It was revealed to Kitchener that Russian artillery experts had refused to accept the British formula of seventeen rounds a day per field gun, with a supply of six hundred rounds per gun in hand. They claimed that the amount was excessive and that the experience on the western front did not apply to their own theater. Moreover, they counted on long periods of virtual quiescence during the winter to build up stock reserves.[41]

British military representatives encountered another related difficulty when their requests for information about future armament requirements went unanswered because of the aversion of Russian officials to divulge classified information. Blair reported that he normally visited the artillery department three or four times a week to extract what information he could from his interviews. While the Russians had never been all that forthcoming, he had never, until now, been met with a flat refusal for information. He explained what happened during one of his talks with several high-ranking Russian officers:

> I started by trying to verify our estimates and was asked why we wanted to know about outputs. I said that we were trying to help Russia to get munitions and that it was necessary for us to know how she stood, in order to place as far as possible the necessary orders to make good such deficiencies. This was met by the retort that Colonel Knox and I had for months past been getting information as to outputs for the same purpose but that no good had come of it. They could not understand why we were so anxious to be continually verifying figures, and that doing so appeared to be the limit of our energies as nothing tangible came of them. . . . I then thought I would try a tack more likely to meet with their approval, and so commenced to inform them of their orders that Lord Kitchener had placed abroad for Russia. This, if possible, raised an even greater storm, because I was told that they were always hearing of these orders, but that nothing ever came of them beyond new estimates when deliveries were going to commence.
>
> The whole attitude of the Artillery Department is now so influenced by the fact that we have furnished them with no munitions at all yet, that I am afraid it will not only make getting information hard (this has always been the case), but I fear it may influence their willingness to allow us to place orders, which they themselves cannot place.[42]

Blair's experience was not unique, but reflected growing anti-British sentiment in the press and in the Army. More than one Russian general accused the British not only of neglect, but of perfidy. The British, it was said, were attending to their own needs before those of Russia, which was why London had been anxious to control Russia's munitions purchases abroad.[43] Briefly employed by the Foreign Office in Petrograd, Bernard Pares, a distinguished scholar and expert on Russia, submitted his observations in a report on his return to London in July. Pares stated that the failure of British munitions firms, in particular Vickers, to make deliveries, which should have begun five months earlier, had so poisoned the atmosphere as to jeopardize the harmonious relationship between Britain and Russia.[44] From Warsaw, the *Times* correspondent wrote that wherever he went, he "hear[d] nothing but protests, criticism and abuse of England." The Russians bitterly resented the inactivity of the French and British on the western front, which had permitted the Germans to increase their attacking forces in Poland. They drew unfavorable comparisons between the lax response of their allies and the way the Russian Army had gone to their aid in August 1914.[45] Hanbury Williams confirmed the widespread ill-feelings against Britain, adding that certain elements in the Army were deliberately stoking the fires "in order to excuse and cover their own muddles, and possibly to avoid an explosion of discontent in this restless country." He was certain that Grand Duke Nicholas was not involved, but thought that some members of his staff were leaking slanderous information to the press.[46]

Buchanan telegraphed London early in August, urging prompt action to counteract the impression that, with the fate of Poland in the balance, Britain was doing nothing to help Russia. He asked to be provided with the information necessary to refute the charges.[47] Kitchener, who had shown extraordinary patience in dealing with the Russians, was livid that they were now attempting to blame him for their munitions difficulties. Under arduous circumstances he had spent countless hours, on top of his own hectic schedule, in identifying new sources for them in the United States, only to have his efforts denigrated and his integrity called into question. Kitchener drew up two memos to answer charges that the British were not pulling their weight and that they had failed to provide meaningful material help to Russia. In the first memo, Kitchener pointed out that Britain had done much more for the Entente than simply keeping the sea-lanes open. Before the war Britain had promised to commit no more than 160,000 men to the Continent (actually there had been no formal pledge to commit a single soldier). At last count 2.5 million men had been recruited, and new divisions were being sent over as quickly as they could be equipped. Kitchener was adamant that no "nation that started the war with as small an army as we did could have done more than this." Besides assisting France, Britain had assumed the main burden in opening the Dardanelles in order to relieve the Russian Army of pressure on the Turkish side. Although the success of the operation would bring far greater benefit to Russia than to the Britain, the work was being pursued with resolve and at enormous cost. Kitchener ended by saying that at the root of Russia's difficulties had been its "delay in placing contracts for munitions and the fact that the Russians had fewer rifles by some millions than they had led the French to believe they possessed, and which they ought to have had."[48]

The second memorandum outlined the magnitude of British assistance to Russia. In particular Kitchener alluded to the list of articles, including explosives, that the British government had allowed Russia to import from Britain, as well as to the number of contracts the War Office had placed in the United States. He reminded the Russians that it was British credit that paid for their purchases in the United States, not to mention that it was the War Office that had provided an organization and technical experts in that country. Kitchener hinted that the Russians would have been in much less trouble if they had accepted the offers from Bethlehem Steel and the American Locomotive Company, which he had repeatedly urged them to do. Under these contracts, deliveries would have begun in September and increased substantially from November onwards.[49]

However tempted he may have been to wash his hands of the whole process, Kitchener knew that the Russians could not meet their munitions needs without his help. Nor could he continue to ignore the grand duke's call for some action by the allies in the west to assist Russia in its hour of need.[50] Kitchener was confident that in time the Russians would be able to stabilize the front on their own and, for that reason, did not want to alter his military policy. He asked Hanbury Williams to seek an interview with the grand duke to impress upon him that criticism of the western Allies by Russian officials was unfair and counterproductive; that the British and the French were "doing all they can to keep the Germans fully occupied on the western front and have prevented the enemy withdrawing troops to reinforce their eastern armies"; and that their common cause "might be jeopardized if by any rash and precipitate action the Allied forces in the west were now to become seriously weakened."[51]

Hanbury Williams replied two days later that his discussion with the grand duke had been frank and beneficial. Nicholas had been swayed by Kitchener's arguments and agreed that it was important to avoid imprudent and precipitate action on the western front. Moreover, he had been emphatic that neither he nor any member of his immediate staff had ever accused the British or the French of inactivity. Hanbury Williams confirmed that he had never heard the grand duke or his staff level the slightest criticism at the British or French armies, and he attributed the impudent press releases to junior officers. He hoped that his conversation with the grand duke would effectively check the rash statements "made by officers who are responsible for communications to the Press."[52]

So did Kitchener. A more concrete result was the grand duke's willingness to submit to his entreaty. This had exceeded Kitchener's expectations and encouraged him to think that Britain's allies might now embrace his active-defensive strategy for the remainder of the year. His optimism, however, was short-lived.

In July and August, the Germans extended peace feelers to both Russia and France, and in each case they were rebuffed. The British learned of these overtures from their allies and were assured unequivocally that they would not make peace until the war was won.[53] Still, there was no guarantee that either government would remain in power indefinitely, and there existed more than an outside chance that one or both might be replaced by parties more receptive to German offers. In France, the government was shaken by a political crisis triggered when Joffre sacked Gen. Maurice Sarrail, a republican soldier, who was a favorite of left-wing parties. The socialists were in uproar and threatened to end the *union sacrée* unless Sarrail were reinstated.[54] The British feared that the collapse of the government might open the way for Joseph Caillaux, who was thought to be opposed to the war, to return to power.

The climate inside Russia was no less turbulent. When the extent of the catastrophe at the front became known, the public clamored for a change in the nation's political leadership. The prime target of its wrath was Sukhomlinov, who was blamed for the shortages of ammunition, which the generals cited, whether true or not, as the cause of their military setbacks. To allay general discontent, the Tsar dismissed a number of unpopular ministers, including Sukhomlinov, who was replaced by Gen. Alexis Polivanov.[55] These gestures proved inadequate in the face of continual defeats, particularly after the fall of Warsaw on August 5. Amidst the criticism of the government, a rumor began to circulate in certain quarters that Russia had been enticed into a war over a dispute in which it was not involved. Questions were asked about the quiescence of the allies and about when the British Army would be ready to play a meaningful role in the war. According to Buchanan, the mood in the capital was somber; public opinion was wavering and some members of the Duma, doubtful that the Russian armies could hold out much longer, were talking about a separate peace. "I am told many reactionaries are in favour of peace," Buchanan's note read, "and the German influences at Court are working in the same direction and warning the Emperor of the dangers of revolution."[56] After a trip to the capital, Hanbury Williams made similar observations.[57] Kitchener did not have to be reminded that ten years earlier the Russian government, under less dire political circumstances than currently existed, had concluded a peace with Japan. Pressure mounted on him to do something to encourage the Russians and to convince them that the situation was not lost.

Against this background, Kitchener crossed the channel on August 16 to hold talks with Joffre at Chantilly. Ignoring the decision of the Calais conference, Joffre had gone ahead with plans for his next attack in Champagne. What he wanted from Kitchener was the full cooperation of the BEF. The offensive was necessary, Joffre insisted, to relieve pressure on the faltering Russians, and he hinted in unmistakable terms that, given the public's war weariness, a British refusal might force France to seek peace. Kitchener did not for a moment think that Joffre's attack would produce tangible results, but he felt compelled to enter into a disastrous commitment because he saw no other way to avoid a fatal rupture with the French.[58]

Back in London, Kitchener had to come to grips with the recent setback in the Dardanelles. During the first week in August, Hamilton made a surprise landing at Suvla Bay, on the far side of Gallipoli, but his chances of reaching the Narrows, by now slim at best, were lost through want of rapid exploitation. Hamilton's admission on August 17 that "his coup had so far failed" to break the stalemate was followed by a chilling request for an additional ninety-five thousand men—a tremendous number for a sideshow.[59] A disheartened Kitchener no longer held much hope that the peninsula could be captured. He conveyed his feelings to Asquith:

> To send such reinforcements as those asked for would be a very serious step to take at the present moment when an offensive in France is necessary to relieve pressure on Russia and keep the French Army and people steady. . . . I personally feel that it is not certain that even if they were sent the result would be decisive and relieve us of the Dardanelles incubus.[60]

The reasons Kitchener gave Asquith for reversing his policy and agreeing to Joffre's offensive were the same as those he offered to the Dardanelles Committee on August 20. Churchill, whose political fortunes were tied to the outcome of the Dardanelles campaign, reacted angrily when he heard

Kitchener say that it was impossible to help Hamilton in the face of the need for an offensive in France to aid Russia. Churchill insisted that the Allies lacked the necessary superiority in France and that, by gratifying their natural desire to help Russia, they risked throwing away two to three hundred thousand lives for only slight, if any, gain of ground. Kitchener admitted that there was a good deal of truth in Churchill's remarks, but that "unfortunately we had to make war as we must, and not as we should like to." When asked if he thought there was a reasonable prospect of success, Kitchener replied that the odds were against a major victory, but that continued British inactivity might drive both France and Russia into making a separate peace in the autumn.[61] Others opposed the attack and, like Churchill, were prepared to accept the political fallout. But Asquith was unwilling to risk a breach between Britain and its allies, and with his full support, Kitchener's arguments carried the day. After the meeting, Kitchener wired Hanbury Williams to inform him that a joint Anglo-French offensive "on a considerable scale" was being organized, adding, "Please tell the Grand Duke from me that we are doing our utmost to support our ally, Russia, and that when the offensive begins I can assure him that all the forces available will be utilized and the operations will be pushed with the utmost vigour."[62]

Events during the summer had conspired to frustrate Kitchener's best efforts at every turn. Convinced that no progress was possible in the west in 1915, he had pushed for an active defense policy until the following spring, when the Allies would be in a position to mount simultaneous attacks on both fronts. In the meantime he proposed to send all the troops and matériel that could be spared from the western front to reinforce Hamilton's army, which, if successful, would help Russia and prevent the Turks from spreading the war into Egypt and elsewhere. He had barely brought both the French and the Russians to his way of thinking when his plans fell apart owing to a number of reasons: the defeat of Hamilton's second major offensive; continued German gains in the east culminating in the capture of Warsaw; and growing signs of defeatism in both Paris and Petrograd, which frightened Kitchener and his colleagues "into believing that the very stability of the Entente alliance would be endangered unless they agreed to the BEF participating in the major offensive Joffre planned for the autumn."[63]

12

IMPERIAL ISSUES AND
PERIPHERAL THEATERS III

AFTER setting in motion negotiations with the Sharif of Mecca in the opening months of the war, Kitchener retained a keen interest in the British effort to generate an Arab uprising against the Ottomans. Kitchener's early exchanges with Sharif Hussein had been vague and noncommittal, little more than expressions of goodwill. He hoped that an Arab of "true race" would eventually succeed to the caliphate and pledged, in the event of a revolt organized by Mecca, to liberate the Arabs from Turkish rule, but declined to define the territorial parameters of the envisioned state.

During the first half of 1915, Kitchener's lieutenants in Egypt and the Sudan maintained contacts with Hussein, whose position had not changed; that is, he expressed a desire to form an alliance with Britain, but was reluctant to break with Turkey. His ambivalence ended, however, when he uncovered an Ottoman plan to depose him at war's end.[1] As a result, he dispatched a letter to Cairo, setting his price for fomenting an insurrection.[2] Claiming to represent all the Arab people, Hussein requested control over an independent state that embraced practically all of the Arab-speaking world east of Egypt—essentially the Arabian Peninsula, Greater Syria (including Lebanon and Palestine), and Mesopotamia. The conditions were those embodied in the so-called Damascus Protocol, an agreement negotiated between Feisal (Hussein's third son) and leaders of secret, anti-Turkish societies in Damascus, which was designed to ensure their support and his father's ascendancy in a postwar Middle East.[3]

Kitchener and his followers in Egypt were stunned by the magnitude of the demands, which also conflicted with British and French interests in the Middle East. Hussein, notwithstanding his insistence that he spoke for all Arabs, was a mere tribal chieftain, who earlier had sought only protection against being removed. The extent of Kitchener's promise to him had included only an independent state within the Arabian Peninsula. The audacity of Hussein's note bemused and annoyed Storrs. It seemed to him that the guarantee, both of an independent state and immunity from external aggression, was ample reward for someone who had been little more than an Erastian administrator for the Turks. If a sufficient number of Muslims chose him as the Caliph, "that was their business, and not ours." But Hussein's claim to wield "a general mandate as King of the Arabs for a Spiritual Pan-Araby" was wholly without merit, as he knew better than anyone else. Storrs went on to say:

> Of the great Arab peoples of North Africa some must repudiate his Sunni claims to the Caliphate: others, like Egypt and the Sudan, vastly preferred their own superior civilization. The Christians of the Lebanon could never acknowledge him, Mesopotamia was mainly Shia . . . to the South the Imam Yahya [ruler of Yemen] recognized him as nothing at all, whilst with Ibn Sa'ud on his immediate East . . . he had long been on the terms which were to lead to his final ruin and exile . . . When in addition we reflected that 90 percent of the Moslem World must call Husain a renegade and traitor to the Vicar of God we could not conceal from ourselves (and with difficulty from him) that his pretensions bordered upon the tragi-comic.[4]

After discussing Hussein's message with London by cable, McMahon sent back an evasive reply on August 30. He reiterated Kitchener's pledge in November 1914 to support an independent Arab state, but maintained that it was premature to discuss its territorial frontiers. The Sharif, however, was not so naive as to be mollified by generalities, and in his letter to Cairo on September 9 chastized the British government for its hesitation to define the boundaries of the future Arab state.

As the contents of Hussein's note were being discussed in the office of the High Commissioner, a shady twenty-four-year-old Arab staff officer in the Turkish Army, Sharif al-Faruqi, arrived in Cairo as a prisoner of war from the Gallipoli front. Faruqi had deserted his unit and deliberately crossed over to the British lines, telling his captors that he was privy to important information. He provided his British interrogators with such useful intelligence that they had decided to send him to Egypt, where his story could be verified. Brought before Clayton, Faruqi claimed that he was a member of a secret Arab military society, al-'Ahd, and that recently he had been personally involved with uniting his organization with a nationalist society in Syria, al-Fatat. He maintained that the membership of the two societies included 90 percent of the Arab officers in the Ottoman Army, as well as a wide civilian circle in Syria, both urban and rural. The aim of the organizations was the independence of the Arab countries, and they were prepared to take up arms the moment the signal was given. He thought that an understanding with the British, which they preferred, depended on London's willingness to support an Arab state within the frontiers that Hussein had outlined. He warned that unless the British gave a favorable answer within a few weeks, the Arab movement would have no alternative but to throw in its lot with Germany and the Ottoman Empire.[5]

Just who Faruqi represented is not clear, for, as it turned out, he was not a member of al-'Ahd or any other secret Arab organization. Much of the information he supplied on the Arab movements, including his statement about the strength of the one with which he was supposedly associated, was inaccurate. The story had been fabricated to give the Arabs more leverage in bargaining with the British. Faruqi gave the impression that he knew the details of the Hussein-McMahon correspondence and of Hussein's proposals to Cairo and, on that flimsy basis, gained credibility in the eyes of Clayton.[6] Although Clayton had no way of confirming or disproving Faruqi's allegations, he accepted them too uncritically when he drew up a report containing a summary of the interview.[7] Clayton assumed that, since the demands of both al-'Ahd and Hussein were identical, the Arab movement must be in close contact with the Sharif of Mecca. Thus, if the Arab societies were behind Hussein, then he was representing millions of Arabs and not only the Hejaz. Clayton concluded that Britain must seize the opportunity before it was too late. His associates in Cairo were of the same mind—the temptation on the part of British officials to grasp at floating straws appears to have arisen from their obsessive fear of a jihad. Storrs wrote to FitzGerald on October 10:

> The Arab Question is reaching an acute stage. I gather from the Sharif, as does Clayton from Faroki that they feel, rightly or wrongly, that the

time has come to choose between us and Germany. The latter promises all things but is mistrusted; the Arabs have more confidence in, and would accept much less from, us. I have thrashed the thing out at great length with Clayton, and beg you to give all possible prominence to the note being sent home by the G.O.C. in this week's bag.[8]

No sooner had Kitchener laid down Clayton's report than he received the following telegram from Maxwell:

A powerful organization with considerable influence in the Army and among Arab Chiefs, viz: the Young Arab Committee appears to have made up its mind that the moment for action has arrived. The Turks and the Germans are already in communication with them and spending money to win their support. The Arab party however is strongly inclined towards England but what they ask is a definite statement of sympathy and support even if their complete program cannot be accepted. Sherif [of] Mecca, who is in communication with the Arab party, also seems uneasy and is pressing for a declaration of policy on the part of England. If their overtures are rejected or a reply is delayed any longer the Arab party will go over to the enemy and work with them, which would mean stirring up religious feelings at once and might well result in a genuine Jehad. On the other hand the active assistance, which the Arabs would render in return for our support would be of the greatest value in Arabia, Mesopotamia, Syria and Palestine. The question is important and requires an early decision.[9]

Whether Kitchener would have endorsed the conclusions of Maxwell and Clayton if he had personally interviewed Faruqi is a question that cannot be answered. As it was, he relied on the judgment of the men on the spot, a response made much easier by his conviction that an Arab uprising was the surest means to save the Anglo-French armies facing defeat on the beaches of Gallipoli. Kitchener wired to Maxwell the next day, empowering him on behalf of the government to deal in a manner satisfactory to the Arabs, and reminding him to avoid doing anything that would alienate their traditional loyalty to Britain. Furthermore, he asked Maxwell to find out and report back to him on the details of the Arab demands.[10]

Maxwell sent Kitchener a reply three days later. He again drew attention to the fact that behind Hussein stood a large and influential Arab party, with members in the Turkish Army, which was prepared to work actively against the Turks "if a reasonable basis for negotiation" could be reached. He maintained that no time should be wasted in arriving at such an agreement; otherwise, the Arabs would join the Central Powers and the British would face more difficulties in Mesopotamia and Arabia and possibly another Turkish invasion of Egypt. Maxwell confirmed Faruqi's story that the Arab party's demands were being advanced through Hussein. It was his opinion that the Arabs' initial proposals were not set in concrete and that they would be willing to leave the door open to further bargaining. That being the case, it was time to talk to the Arabs in specific terms, rather than in coy ambiguities, eliminating "what we cannot and will not allow" and treating "the rest as a basis for negotiation." He thought that the Arabs would insist on including in their future state Mesopotamia (except for the vilayet of Basra, if the British were adamant about retaining it), Aleppo, Homs, Hama, and Damascus. In conclusion, he warned that unless the British reached an accommodation with the Arabs at once, they might find themselves confronting a "united Islam."[11]

On October 18 McMahon cabled London, summarizing the contents of Hussein's note of September 9.[12] The full text in translation was sent by surface mail and did not arrive at the Foreign Office until after the discussions on policy had taken place. Kitchener, in response to the telegrams from Maxwell and McMahon, wrote a long letter to Grey. Since, as far as I know, the document has not seen the light of day until now, it ought to be quoted at length:

> We are told that not only the Arabs in Arabia, but also the Arab officers and men in the Turkish army are ready to work against . . . the Turks, if we accept their pretensions, while if we cannot come to terms they will definitely [side] with the Germans and Turks against us. The advantages of the one are as obvious as the dangers of the other, and I would venture to suggest that no time should be lost in getting officers from Egypt and the Dardanelles with local knowledge and experience, and a representative of the French military authorities, to come to London to discuss the position and work out plans. Politically, the first thing is to settle whether we are prepared to accept in principle the idea of Arabia—even an exaggerated Arabia such as the Sherif proposes—for the Arabs. If I may express my own view, it is, as I have held since the war began, that the best solution is an independent Arabia, looking to Great

Britain as its founder and protector, and provided with territory rich and wide enough to furnish adequate revenues.

There are however two important limitations to the creation of such a state:

i. French claims and ambitions
ii. Our own advance in Mesopotamia

i. It is difficult to challenge the position which France claims, and has to some extent secured by acquiring special interest, in the northwestern portion of Arabia as now defined by the Arabs. But we cannot win the Arabs unless we can reconcile French and Arab claims, and the position must be clearly understood from both the French and Arab side from the onset, or we shall be heading straight for serious trouble. It seems to me that the line to work on is, first, to impress on our Allies the urgency of the situation and to get them to accept us as our mouthpiece, at the same time impressing on the Arabs that we speak for the Allies as a whole: and, secondly, to be ready to reorganize the priority of French commercial interests in the north west.

ii. Mesopotamia is primarily a question for India, but I do not think that a solution, which would provide for Arab independence and yet safeguard our vital interests, is necessarily impossible. Moreover, we shall have to be ready to resign acquisitions of territory in Mesopotamia if we are to get the French to give up their Syrian dreams.

There is a third difficulty, namely who is, or are, to rule this Arab empire? [This is] a question on which light can only be thrown when we reach the stage of discussion with the Arab representatives. But subject to any fresh considerations which may arise out of Sir H. McMahon's despatch . . . when we get it, I would submit that he should be told that H. M. G. agree in principle to the establishment of an independent Arabia and that we are ready to discuss the boundaries of such a state, and the measures to be taken . . . with qualified Arabian representatives without delay.[13]

On March 18, McMahon, after further talks with Faruqi, sent another telegram to Grey. From what he had learned, he was convinced that, unless the British gave them prompt and satisfactory assurances, the Arabs would join the Germans, who "have furnished them fulfillment of all their demands." The Arab party, McMahon continued, indicated that it could no "longer hesitate because they must act before Turkey receives further assistance." A copy of the telegram was immediately delivered to the War Office. Kitchener replied on March 19 that there was nothing in the report to make him alter the views he had expressed on the previous day.[14]

In trying to reach a decision, both Kitchener and Grey felt compelled to rely on the alarmist and urgent messages from Cairo. On the other hand, the Viceroy of India and the India Office were aghast at the ongoing negotiations between McMahon and Hussein. Hardinge saw in the creation of a strong Arab state only a potential source of trouble for Britain in the Middle East. Austen Chamberlain discounted the reports from Cairo as unreliable and considered it imprudent for the British government to make any specific commitments to Hussein. According to his own sources, the Sharif of Mecca was a nonentity, who could not possibly carry out his promises to unite the Arabs and spearhead an effective revolt.[15] On October 22, Chamberlain wrote to Hardinge that Kitchener and Grey accepted the proposition that, unless a definite and agreeable proposal were extended to the Sharif, there was the risk of "a genuine jihad and united Islam against us."[16] Chamberlain was evidently aware of the Foreign Office reply to McMahon sent two days earlier. The note had been drafted by Grey and approved by Kitchener. Grey's instructions were few and gave McMahon practically a free hand. He indicated that McMahon must give the necessary pledges to ensure the loyalty of the Arabs, and "I must leave you discretion in the matter as it is urgent and there is not time to discuss an exact formula." Grey was clear on one point:

> Stipulation that Arabs will recognize British interests as paramount and work under British guidance etc., should not be included unless it is necessary to secure Arab consent, as this might give impression in France that we were not only endeavoring to secure Arab interests, but to establish our own in Syria at the expense of the French.[17]

Both Kitchener and Grey regarded McMahon's impending offer to Mecca as a preliminary step, which in time would be replaced by a detailed arrangement negotiated with properly designated representatives of the Sharif.

McMahon, however, approached his task in a different spirit. His letter to Hussein on October 24 was the most substantive and controversial in the extensive correspondence. While reluctantly entering into a discussion of precise outlines of territories and frontiers, he used ambiguous and at times self-negating language to avoid making definite commitments so as to keep in step with his instructions. McMahon promised Hussein an independent Arab state that would include Syria, Mesopotamia, and Arabia, but would be limited to territories where France and Britain had no claims. McMahon proposed to exclude the vilayets of Basra and Baghdad, in view of "Britain's established position and interests," as well as the areas of Syria lying to the west of the districts of Damascus, Homs, Hama, and Aleppo. With a few proper words, the exclusion of Palestine, located south of these districts, could have been made indisputable. Only if the line Damascus, Homs, Hama, and Aleppo were extended southwards—a resolution the British later insisted was appropriate—would Palestine be excluded. Further complicating matters was a British clause protecting French future claims in the Middle East.[18] A question that has divided Middle East scholars was whether McMahon meant only to exclude Lebanon, a largely Christian region coveted by France, or if he also had in mind Palestine, where Jewish nationalists hoped to rebuild their ancient homeland.

During the following months McMahon and Hussein each exchanged three more letters. Hussein gratefully accepted McMahon's concessions, but he refused to concede western Syria, and, in exchange for British claims to the two Mesopotamian vilayets, demanded monetary compensation. McMahon, however, held firm, emphasizing that prior French interests in the Syrian littoral precluded the inclusion of that area under Arab rule. Hussein had no wish to be the cause of disrupting the Anglo-French alliance and ultimately offered a compromise. While he would not give up rights to the disputed territory, he agreed to postpone settlement of the question until after the war. McMahon appreciated the conciliatory gesture and reiterated Britain's pledge to fulfill its commitments, as far as it was free to act without detriment to the interests of its French ally. It now only remained for Hussein to rally his supporters and formally break with the Ottomans.

The second half of 1915 witnessed varying degrees of activity in the secondary theaters of war. As we noted earlier, Gen. Dobell, with the War Office's blessing, had opted to force Yaunde's surrender by interrupting the transit of supplies and ammunition through Rio Muni. Between the end of June and the start of October, there was a lull in the operations, enabling some men to proceed home on leave, while giving those remaining in the Cameroons a period of comparative rest. On July 23, Dobell telegraphed the War Office, reversing his opposition to a renewed attempt to capture Yaunde. Dobell explained that, since his letter of June 23, the unopposed occupation by the Allies of Ngaundere and Koncha (in the north) and evidence that only a handful of enemy troops remained in the region suggested that they were concentrating in the south. That being the case, the importance of Yaunde had increased. While Dobell observed that an assault against the town was no less difficult than he had previously stated, he thought that its capture might induce the enemy to surrender. Dobell doubted that the prevention of supplies, other than ammunition, would have a decisive effect. All things considered, he felt that, any operations undertaken in the dry season should be in the direction of Yaunde, their scope dependent on the resources placed at his disposal.[19]

On August 2, Kitchener drew Dobell's attention to a recent French communiqué, which had reported that, in recent operations, natives and German defenders alike were disaffected and even welcomed French forces. Intercepted German letters indicated that, without the considerable flow of supplies from Spanish territory, Yaunde would be unable to hold out. These letters also showed that, owing to native hostility, convoys destined for Yaunde required armed escorts. Kitchener asked Dobell for his opinion on how to bring about a speedy resolution to the conflict in the German colony.[20]

Dobell replied two days later, disabusing Kitchener of the notion that the Germans could be brought to their knees without a major campaign. He stated that whatever dissatisfaction existed among German troops and natives in the east did not necessarily apply to the Yaunde district. He pointed out that he and the French could interfere with the convoys heading for Yaunde, but he thought that even if all the supplies were cut off, there was no guarantee that the Germans would surrender. The only sure way to end German resistance was to capture Yaunde, and he considered that a force advancing from Edéa, reinforced with additional men and matériel, would be strong enough to accomplish this without relying on French cooperation. With his current force, he could advance as soon as the weather permitted, but in his opinion he would be held up before he reached Yaunde. In either case, lengthy preparations would be required. He requested that the War Office inform him as soon as possible whether his demands for reinforcements could be met or whether he would have to rely only on his existing army.[21]

While considering the note, Kitchener received a copy of a memorandum dated August 5, 1915, in which Delcassé questioned the wisdom of Dobell's inactivity at a time when French forces in the east under Gen.

Aymerich were making good progress. It was apparent that the French government was anxious for Dobell to resume operations against Yaunde, in concert with Aymerich's men operating from the other direction, so as to bring an end to the war in the Cameroons. Kitchener wired Dobell on August 10, concurring with him, both on the importance of Yaunde and on his proposed method of capturing it. Kitchener could not send him any reinforcements, however, but he would see whether Brig. Gen. F. H. G. Cunliffe, who had prosecuted operations in the north with Nigerian units (and was responsible to the Colonial Office), could place a battalion at his disposal.[22] Kitchener had just sent off the telegram when he received a note from Sir Frederick Lugard, Governor-General of Nigeria, who happened to be in London, suggesting that, as a preliminary to the advance on Yaunde, Dobell should cooperate with Cunliffe to clear the enemy from the Bamenda region. This would not only end the threat of enemy raids against Nigeria, but permit a considerable portion of Cunliffe's troops to take part in the march on Yaunde. Kitchener transmitted Lugard's plan to Dobell on August 14 and asked for his considered opinion.[23]

Dobell replied on August 17 that the proposal could not be carried out without jeopardizing the success of the operations against Yaunde. He asserted that any assistance Gen. Aymerich might require from him would be impossible if his forces were tied down in the northwest. In fact, he considered the whole idea impracticable. It was likely to take two months to subdue the enemy, and judging from past experience, all the troops and carriers employed would require at least an additional month's rest before they were ready to start on a further extended campaign. He concluded by saying that he would discuss the matter further with the Governor of French Equatorial Africa and Gen. Aymerich, who were coming to Duala the following week for a conference.[24] Kitchener wired back, accepting Dobell's view that the capture of Yaunde should take precedence over all other campaigns.[25]

The conference involving Dobell, Aymerich, and the Governor of French Equatorial Africa was held on August 25 and 26. Dobell's fluency in French obviated any possible misunderstandings. A final scheme was hatched for the capture of Yaunde with Dobell advancing from the west and Aymerich from the east. Both generals had been recently reinforced.[26] While Cunliffe had been unable to spare any troops as a result of ongoing operations, Kitchener had sent Dobell the Fifth Indian Light Infantry— far from the best battalion, as it had recently mutinied in Singapore—and two companies of the West Indian Regiment. The addition of Senegalese *tirailleurs* brought Aymerich's total force to two thousand. After allowing for obligatory garrisons in occupied territory, Dobell could count on about eighteen hundred rifles.[27]

Kitchener, who had been informed of the results of the conference, suggested to Dobell that he might find it beneficial to take a short spell of rest at Dakar (in Senegal) before the start of operations. Dobell, however, felt it would not be opportune for him to be absent while preparations were reaching an advanced stage. The campaign got under way early in October, just as the rains were diminishing. Along the way British forces were successful almost everywhere. They reached Yaunde on January 1, 1916, only to find, much to their disappointment, that all the German troops and officials had fled southwards. British columns took up the pursuit, but were unable to overtake them before they crossed over into neutral Spanish territory. By then, the only remaining stronghold held by the Germans was at Mora, in the northernmost corner of the protectorate. It withstood a number of attacks and a long period of investment before lowering the German flag on February 18, 1916, at which time the conquest of the Cameroons was complete.[28]

In German East Africa, where Lettow-Vorbeck's name struck fear in the British rank and file, as Rommel's would in a later war, there appeared to be no end in sight to the fighting. Throughout 1915 the British showed little enterprise or initiative, confining themselves mostly to a passive defense of the Uganda Railway. With the British force broken up into a line of detachments, any major enterprises were out of the question. On the rare occasions when columns of several battalions were formed to undertake some minor operation, other than the coup at Bukoba, little was accomplished. The nature of the war took its toll on the commanding officer, Maj. Gen. Tighe, and he began to drink heavily. He became irritable, jumpy, and was unapproachable much of the time. "Poor man," said Meinertzhagen. "I am terribly sorry for him as his condition will only get worse and mean his eventual removal."[29]

Kitchener was kept abreast of what was happening at headquarters by Brig. Gen. W. Malleson, a first-rate soldier who was once a staff officer in his Intelligence Department in India. Malleson corresponded regularly with Kitchener and was scathing in his criticism of Tighe and his staff.[30] This could not help but dim Kitchener's confidence in Tighe's judgment.

On August 2, and again on the August 14, Tighe cried out to the War Office for additional troops. He claimed that the Germans, thanks to the supplies of munitions from German blockade runners and the salvage of guns from the *Königsberg* (a destroyed cruiser), had seriously altered the balance of military strength in their favor. He thought that German strength might be raised to twenty thousand, and he contrasted this figure with his own reliable infantry, which, owing to ever-increasing sickness, had been reduced to four thousand men.[31] He warned that should the enemy make a determined attack, which he regarded as quite possible, he was not sure he could hold his own. Kitchener did not respond immediately to Tighe's representations, for at the time he was more concerned with events in France and in the Dardanelles than in East Africa. But from a different quarter came the prospect of assistance for Tighe's badly overextended force.

The fall of German Southwest Africa in July 1915 had set free South African forces for service elsewhere. In August, the South African government offered to recruit men so as to raise to a total of eight hundred the strength of its regiment (2/Rhodesia) in East Africa, which had been badly depleted by sickness. Kitchener gladly welcomed the offer. A decision for more extensive South African participation was postponed, pending general elections in the Union in October.[32] Nevertheless it was reasonably certain that, in the near future, a considerable number of South African troops would be available. This gave Kitchener hope that eventually he would have the resources necessary to hold the troublesome Lettow-Vorbeck in check. But exactly how this should be done was a question he left to Lt. Gen. Archibald Murray, the new chief of the imperial general staff.[33]

In a memorandum dated October 8, Murray considered that as the Germans possessed both superior numbers and strategic advantage, they were capable of invading British East Africa and, if successful, the "moral effect throughout Africa would probably be so great that our military liabilities would be very largely increased in that continent." To head off such a contingency and to secure the British position permanently, he advocated the subjugation of the German colony, for which he estimated that ten thousand troops would be required.[34] Kitchener rejected the idea of invading German East Africa, which in his opinion would require many more troops than Murray had estimated. He did not want all the forces freed by the conquest of other German colonies used as reinforcements in East Africa. But, while he was away, a subcommittee of the CID, called together to consider the question of future operations in East Africa, approved of Murray's recommendations at its meeting on November 12. It expressed the opinion that, since the transport of troops would take time and the rainy season in the area affected would begin early in April, it was "desirable to move the Union Government to proffer further assistance to make sure of success during the few weeks that will be available for active operations."[35] The Cabinet accepted the conclusions of the subcommittee, and on November 22 decided to give Gen. Horace Smith-Dorrien[36] the command of the projected expedition against German East Africa.

Mesopotamia was the one place in the summer of 1915 where subsidiary operations seemed to be progressing effortlessly. In April 1915 the expeditionary force was placed under the command of Gen. Sir John Nixon, a bold and fearless cavalryman. His arrival marked a turning point in the campaign. Although London favored a defensive strategy, Nixon was under the impression, after discussing his orders with Gen. Duff, Commander in Chief of the Indian Army, that he was to plan for an eventual advance on Baghdad. But the adhesion of the Arabs, one of the principal conditions set by Kitchener for so ambitious an undertaking, had not been met. As Callwell explained to a brother officer at the time, "Our local people have entirely misread public opinion in that quarter because the Arabs are by no means on our side. Quite the contrary."[37] Another important point, which was disregarded, was the state of the Indian Army. After Kitchener left India, his successors lacked his drive, with the result that Army reforms proceeded at a much slower pace. No less significant was the parsimony of the financial overlords. After the Anglo-Russian convention of 1907, the Indian government, assuming that its army was unlikely to have to fight other than on the northwest frontier, slashed the military budget again and again. In short, in 1914, the Indian Army lacked the training, logistical support, and equipment to undertake a campaign abroad on any considerable scale.[38]

Kitchener would have been happy to see Nixon remain at Qurna. If Nixon were allowed to push forward with an understrength force, he would have to overcome a numerically superior enemy, not to mention imperfect lines of communications and a terrain that was barren and inhospitable. But the War Office was not in charge of the campaign, and the authorities in Delhi and London gave their guarded assent each time Nixon asked for permission to advance. Chamberlain found it difficult to overrule the advice of the soldiers on the spot, particularly when one easy victory was quickly followed by another, and Hardinge hoped that by dealing the Turks a hard blow in Mesopotamia, Britain would ensure the loyalty of the Arabs.[39] By the end of September, British forces had reached the town of Kut-al-Amara on the Tigris, following heavy fighting.[40]

After Nixon captured Kut, he became obsessed with the prospect of pushing on to Baghdad, a distance of less than a hundred miles. Maj. Gen. Charles Townshend, who would actually be conducting the advance, was much less enthusiastic, concerned as he was over the extension of his supply lines, the exhaustion of his men, and his heavy losses resulting from sickness and recent fighting. With roughly one division at his disposal, he warned Nixon that he would require two additional divisions to capture and hold Baghdad. Reinforcements were not immediately available, but Nixon, who was sure that the Turks were practically beaten, believed that Townshend had an adequate force for the job. Although the fabled city of the Arabian Nights had no military value, there were strong political arguments in favor of advancing. The British were badly in need of a concrete victory in the fall of 1915, especially to counter the effects of the debacle in the Dardanelles. Delhi was at first wary of approving the march, but it soon succumbed to Nixon's optimism and the temptation to pull off a spectacular propaganda coup.[41] It was now up to London to make the final decision.

At Asquith's request, Kitchener called upon the General Staff to investigate the feasibility of an advance on Baghdad. On October 6, and again on October 12, the General Staff produced two memoranda in which it stated that any attempt to capture and hold Baghdad with the forces presently available to Townshend was to court disaster. It estimated that the Turks could assemble sixty thousand men within a few weeks to recapture Baghdad. It would not justify an advance on Baghdad, unless Townshend were reinforced by two divisions.[42]

The Dardanelles Committee met on October 14 and, notwithstanding the General Staff recommendation, was unable to reach a definite agreement.[43] As a result, Asquith directed the Admiralty War Staff and the War Office General Staff to prepare a joint appreciation of the question, which they submitted on October 19. The combined staffs acknowledged that capture of the city would have a profound moral effect throughout the east, but that a subsequent enforced retirement would outweigh this advantage. Still, they felt that for the British Army to remain where it was would also be regarded as a confession of failure in the Muslim countries. Its conclusion was that Townshend, if reinforced by two divisions, should be able to capture and hold Baghdad.[44] The responsibility for supplying the reinforcements would have to be borne by India, since Kitchener had told Chamberlain that he could spare no troops from either Egypt or France.[45]

The joint paper was before the Dardanelles Committee when it met on October 21 to consider the matter. Three options offered themselves to the members. The first was to consolidate at Kut and advance no further; the second was to make a raid on Baghdad and to withdraw immediately to Kut; and the third was to capture and permanently occupy the city. Curzon favored the first option, Kitchener the second, and Asquith, Bonar Law, Grey, Churchill, and Balfour the third. Kitchener was in accord with Curzon's view that to retreat from Baghdad because sixty thousand Turks were advancing towards it would result in a loss of British prestige. Kitchener's solution was to conduct a quick raid on the city to destroy supplies and anything of military value, followed by a return to Kut. Such an operation would require no reinforcements and could be carried out without serious risks. It would weaken the enemy and would not hurt British prestige, since the withdrawal would be immediate and voluntary. On the other hand, Kitchener observed, to refrain from moving forward and "seize what was practically in our grasp would make all the local population think that we were afraid to do it."[46]

There was no real support for Kitchener's position. The majority in the Dardanelles Committee wanted, to quote Bonar Law, "a victory now badly and as cheaply as possible, but that we should have to take some risks to achieve success." Given the go-ahead on October 24, Nixon instructed a reluctant Townshend to march on Baghdad. Two divisions were to be sent as reinforcements, but no precise date was given for their arrival.

By failing to coordinate ends and means, the politicians followed the same practice in Mesopotamia as in the Dardanelles. They were so attracted by the political advantages to be derived that they gave insufficient consideration to the requirements of the distant advance. But so far, the Mesopotamian operation had been favored by good fortune. It remained to be seen whether this campaign could achieve its ends by continuing to flout the odds or whether it would run out of luck and encounter the same fate as the other one in the Mediterranean.

13

TORMENTED WAR LORD

B RITISH prospects in the Dardanelles seemed dim after the failure of Hamilton's landing at Suvla Bay in August. Kitchener's commitment to support Joffre's fall offensive also meant that he would have to deny Hamilton the reinforcements he had requested, at least for the foreseeable future. On the evening of August 20, Kitchener wired Hamilton that he could expect some replacements, but no new divisions.[1] It was unrealistic to think that Hamilton, with such meager support and with an army that was weary and dispirited, could achieve tangible results. Kitchener reckoned that Hamilton would be able to hold his position until after the offensive on the western front, when it might be possible to bolster his force with a few fresh divisions.

Aware that the Turks could more than match any reinforcements he might send to the Dardanelles, Kitchener no longer considered it possible for the British Army to capture the peninsula and push on to Constantinople. Accordingly, he scaled back his objectives, limiting the Army's future role to helping the fleet get through the Narrows, after which its work would be completed.[2] Under this new plan, even if the Army had managed to reach the Narrows (which would have been highly unlikely), Kitchener must have known that the Navy alone could not bring the Turks to their knees. But he was bitter at the Navy, which had dragged him into this quagmire and essentially left him in the lurch. He would have been well advised in the closing days of August to have cut his losses and abandoned the enterprise. But he feared that such a move would condemn large numbers of Hamilton's men to death or imprisonment and that a catastrophe of this magnitude would have a devastating effect on British prestige throughout the Muslim world.

Just when it seemed that things could not get any bleaker, the Dardanelles operation received a promise of new life. On August 31, the French government, which had never shown much interest in the Dardanelles campaign, made an unexpected offer to land an army, under the command of Gen. Sarrail, on the Asiatic side of the straits.[3] Sarrail's force would consist of four divisions sent from France, plus the two serving at Gallipoli. It was proposed that Sarrail, acting independently, would march on the Turkish forts at Chanak, in conjunction with a renewed attack by Hamilton on the peninsula.

Kitchener found it especially strange that, on the eve of Joffre's major offensive, the French authorities should propose to send four more divisions to the Dardanelles. Only a fortnight before, Joffre, in the process of trying to convert him to the merits of a joint offensive, had indicated that he intended to strike with maximum force. If Joffre allowed troops to be dispatched from France, presumably this meant that he had decided to postpone his operation. Whatever the French motive, Kitchener welcomed their new-found resolve, which was bound to help Hamilton's operations.

The French announcement evoked great excitement in London, and there was no longer talk of evacuating the peninsula. Kitchener told the Dardanelles Committee on September 3 that he was not certain what had occasioned the French change of attitude. He imagined that perhaps they were prepared to make a big effort to resolve the campaign, so that British troops in the eastern Mediterranean could be transferred to France. This would serve the dual purpose of bringing relief to Russia and, once the campaign was over, of strengthening the French line. Kitchener proposed to instruct Sir John to send two divisions from France to replace the two French divisions on Gallipoli. The strength of the Turkish garrison on the Asiatic shore was estimated to be no more than two divisions, or twenty thousand men.[4] If a reinforced Hamilton was permitted to make another push, at the same time that Sarrail advanced on Chanak, the British Cabinet was reasonably confident that the campaign could be brought to a successful end.

These hopes were blasted as quickly as they had risen. Sir John, arriving in London on September 6, reported that Joffre fully intended to carry on with his offensive. If this was true, Kitchener wondered, what was the status of the French expedition to the Dardanelles? Neither he nor his colleagues would contemplate the idea of attacking simultaneously in France and in the Dardanelles. It was evident that if the Allies divided their strength between the two theaters, they ran a good risk of meeting with failure in both. The Cabinet concluded that Kitchener should proceed to France to find out precisely the intentions of the French authorities. On September 11, Kitchener met Millerand, Joffre, and Sarrail at Calais, where it was tentatively decided that the four French divisions should begin to embark at Marseilles on October 10 and that the operations on either side of the straits should commence in the middle of November.[5] Joffre had gone along with the French government's plan because his position was not so secure as to leave him impervious to political pressure. But his grudging assent was subject to certain conditions. The four divisions would be released only after his offensive in Champagne was over, and not at all if it succeeded.

After the meeting, Kitchener learned of the circumstances that had suddenly awakened the French government's interest in the Dardanelles. On receiving news of Hamilton's failure at Suvla Bay, the French government had seen an opportunity to kill two birds with one stone. It would send enough troops to finish the job and, at the same time, solve its political dilemma by providing Sarrail with an important command outside of France.[6] Joffre told Kitchener in private that he had no confidence in Sarrail's leadership or in the success of the Asiatic operation, which he felt would certainly require more than six divisions. Kitchener was not pleased with the results of the conference, but felt that any attempt on his part to force the issue would fracture the alliance. From what he later told Hamilton, he doubted that the French scheme would ever materialize. Kitchener reasoned that, even if the leading French divisions embarked on the fixed date, they could not arrive on the scene before the fierce winter storms made a landing impossible. As it happened, the whole plan collapsed under the pressure of events in the Balkans.

While the lamentable drama over the French divisions was playing out, Bulgaria, coaxed by both sides since the start of the war, signed a secret military convention with Germany and Austria-Hungry on September 6 and a fortnight later began to mobilize. The Central Powers aimed to overwhelm Serbia and open direct communications with Constantinople. If successful, they would be able to bring in heavy artillery and make Hamilton's position on the peninsula untenable and, later, conceivably reactivate the front along the Suez Canal.

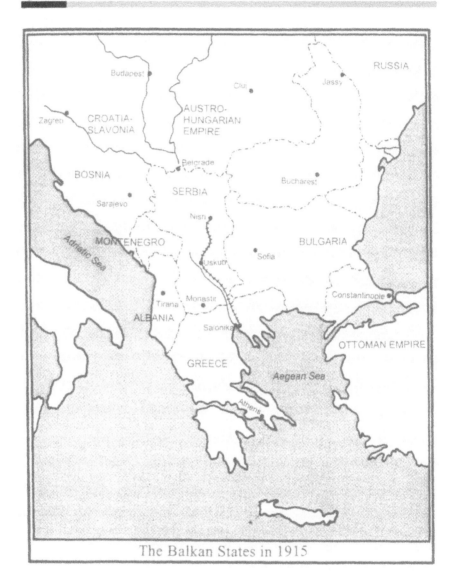

The Balkan States in 1915

Serbia, about to be attacked simultaneously from the north and east, looked to Greece for immediate assistance.[7] The Greek prime minister, Venizelos, was ready to stand by his country's alliance with Serbia, providing the British and the French deployed one hundred fifty thousand men on the Bulgarian frontier.[8] For the Entente, it seemed at first glance a small price to pay to save an ally and to enlist a new one. The French government leaped at the offer, proposing to divert the troops earmarked for the Dardanelles.

Kitchener, however, was more cautious. As a military maneuver to bring direct aid to Serbia, there was little chance that an Allied expedition could achieve its goal. Hostile forces, poised to strike from two directions, were certain to overrun Serbia before any effective aid, other than that offered by the Greeks, could possibly arrive. On the other hand, if the object was to bring Greece into the war, then the Anglo-French landing was justified. But where were the requisite troops to come from? A large-scale offensive on the western front was pending, and no significant number of troops could be transferred from Sir John's command until the operations were over. As matters stood, it was impossible to send more than a few divisions immediately, and these could only come from Gallipoli. Estimating that the Central Powers could bring to bear 450,000 troops against Serbia, Kitchener thought that, in addition to Greece's 180,000-man army, the Allies would require no fewer than 300,000 men.[9] A General Staff appreciation, more or less dictated by Kitchener, was prepared for the Dardanelles Committee. Not surprisingly, it weakened the case for involvement by implying there was little chance of saving Serbia, even with Greek assistance. It was adamant that an Allied force of three hundred thousand men, in addition to the Greek Army, would be needed to save Serbia from an Austro-German onslaught in the north and protect the lines of communications with Salonica. It observed that, if only one hundred fifty thousand men were sent, these troops should be confined to assist the Greek Army in protecting the Serbian flank and in securing the lines of communications with Salonica.[10] In case the last option was adopted, Kitchener sought to define the perimeters within which he would find it feasible to open a second front in the eastern Mediterranean.

At the meeting of the Dardanelles Committee on September 24, Kitchener read out the General Staff appreciation, but it was practically ignored.[11] As in the past, Britain's alliance with France and Russia restricted its options. The French, having promised the Greeks their half of the one hundred fifty thousand men, made no secret that they expected the British to do the same. Petrograd reinforced the French position by urging that strong measures be taken against Bulgaria. Hence, the committee hesitated no longer and unanimously agreed to follow the French and send seventy-five thousand troops.[12] The next day Kitchener informed Hamilton that two British divisions and one French division must be withdrawn from the Dardanelles and sent to Salonica.

The British Foreign Office held a glimmer of hope that Bulgaria, where mobilization was reported to be highly unpopular with the public, might hesitate before taking the final plunge. Consequently, Grey persuaded his colleagues to deny Serbia's request to launch a preemptive strike against Bulgaria.[13] The Serbs had wanted to use their central position to crush Bulgaria and then turn westward to fight the Austro-Germans. Kitchener felt that the idea was not strategically sound. He calculated that, even if the Serbian Army defeated the Bulgarians, it would be so weary and depleted that it would easily succumb to the Austro-German onslaught. He advised the Serbs (through his liaison officers attached to the Serbian Army) to avoid ill-considered action against Bulgaria and, instead, to seek refuge in the mountains to the north until the Allies arrived. As he pointed out:

> Serbia would be playing into German hands by precipitating hostilities with Bulgaria and at the present juncture any such action would be most unwise while we are arranging to send troops to Salonika in order to enable the Greeks to support Serbia. The Serbians should ensure their country from attack from the north and not allow their feeling with regard to Bulgaria to precipitate matters.[14]

Everything depended on the attitude of Greece, where the pro-Entente Venizelos was locked in a fierce struggle with King Constantine, who was the Kaiser's brother-in-law. The fact that the Allies were sending troops to Salonica from Gallipoli suggested to Constantine that they no longer intended to force the straits, strengthening his conviction that the Central Powers would win the war. During the last week in September the Greek government went back and forth on its offer to the Allies, depending on whether Venizelos or Constantine was in the ascendancy. The mixed signals from Athens created confusion in British councils, which in turn led to incessant and lengthy meetings. Prolonged absences from the War Office meant that Kitchener could not devote the necessary time to do his work. Frustrated and feeling helpless, he complained bitterly to Hankey, who recorded the following in his diary:

> For three-quarters of an hour he rampaged against the Cabinet, whence he had just returned, declaiming particularly against the irresponsible members—Churchill in particular, also Lord Curzon, Lord Selborne and Lloyd George. Also against the Dardanelles Committee. He said

so much time was wasted in arguing with these people that he simply couldn't get time to do his work at the War Office. He was almost in a hysterical condition; he even talked seriously of resigning.[15]

Hankey's ominous impression of Kitchener at the start of October was that he was "in a very queer state," and he feared that the field marshal was on the verge of a nervous breakdown.[16] Kitchener's anxieties were exacerbated by his excessive workload (at least partially of his own making), by the potential dangers of opening a new front, by his uncertainty of what to do with regards to the Dardanelles campaign, and by two other factors, which also had the effect of fueling his already deteriorating relations with his colleagues.

The first involved the latest battle on the western front. Sir John's attack at Loos, as the British part of the Allied offensive in the west, was winding down in dismal failure with losses exceeding fifty thousand men. By keeping his reserves too far back, French had prevented Haig from exploiting a break-in, which eventually led to a German counterattack and unnecessary slaughter.[17] Although the battle had been badly mismanaged in the field, Kitchener could not escape criticism for having sanctioned it.

The second issue was tied to the first. The manpower losses at Loos rekindled demands in the Cabinet for the introduction of conscription. It was a contentious issue and fought more or less along party lines. The Liberals opposed conscription on the grounds that it was contrary to democratic principles. The Tories saw it as the only effective and fair way to meet the needs of the Army and the economy. Given Kitchener's immense popularity with the public, the government would have been compelled to adopt universal military service if he had thrown his weight behind it. The Tories looked to Kitchener to give the lead and force the issue. Had he done so, life for him in the Cabinet would have been easier, as his principal antagonists also happened to be ardent conscriptionists. But, Kitchener was not one to allow political expediency to take precedence over patriotic duty. He stood loyally by the Prime Minister, who had convinced him that compulsion was premature and would divide the nation. In so doing, Kitchener brought down the full wrath of the Conservatives on his head.[18]

Kitchener's isolation from his colleagues became complete during the final months of 1915. His aloofness, secretiveness, lack of candor, and autocratic behavior often exasperated them. Undoubtedly they would have suffered in silence if his management of the war had produced positive results. But, the war was going badly for Britain, and each time a military defeat occurred, for which he was held responsible as the supreme war-lord, his reputation took a blow.[19] An influential section of the Cabinet came to see his methods as the principal cause of the setbacks, and conse-quently their remaining faith in his judgment quickly vanished.

Kitchener was as sick of his Cabinet colleagues as they were with him. He often felt that he was waging a war on two fronts, one against the Germans and the other against the politicians. He complained that he spent more time at meetings and preparing for them than in attending to his duties at the War Office. He despaired at the backbiting and confusion that reigned in the upper councils of war. He could not understand how his colleagues could be so adamant on issues about which they obviously knew little. Their attention shifted back and forth, often influenced by daily impressions, and their decisions were neither farsighted nor took into consideration the larger aspects of the war.

Much of the Cabinet's ills can be laid at Asquith's doorstep. Before 1914 he had shown great skill in handling able, though willful, Cabinet colleagues and in delaying decisions on contentious issues until compro-mises had been reached. However, his wait-and-see approach was more of a liability in war, when events sometimes required instant decisions. What was needed was a thrusting figure in command. Asquith failed to pull the Cabinet together, as Churchill would do in his coalition during World War II. In particular, he made no effort to rein in Lloyd George, whose mischievous conduct sowed dissention and confusion, and, bit by bit undermined Kitchener's management of the war. In the previous Lib-eral government, Asquith had frequently come to Kitchener's rescue by cutting off questions or rephrasing in a more cogent way ideas that he had expressed awkwardly. But, Asquith was himself under attack in the cur-rent administration and, with his natural instinct for self-preservation, simply left Kitchener to fend for himself.[20] For Kitchener, interaction with politicians, never a pleasant task, became an ordeal. The harassment, cross-examinations, and demands for lengthy explanations, even on trivial matters, in the Cabinet and in the Dardanelles Committee robbed him of his vigor and inhibited his capacity for bold, firm, and clear-headed ac-tion, which had characterized his early conduct of the war. He became indecisive, frequently changed his mind, and lost touch with his war aims.

Kitchener was partially at fault for his own predicament. Struggling against his colleagues and maintaining an inhuman workload, he did not have enough time to devote to the big problems of the war. As Churchill pointed out, the absence of an effective general staff left Kitchener "to face the rushing, swirling torrent of events with no rock of clear, well-thought-out doctrine and calculation at his back."[21] On more than one occasion, he was forced to reverse a decision because of some development that a trained general staff would have anticipated and provided for.

In late September, the Cabinet, having lost confidence in Kitchener's strategic vision, passed a resolution while he was in France, instructing him to reconstitute the General Staff.[22] Asquith realized that things would stay the same unless he found a new CIGS. His choice fell on Archibald Murray, French's former chief of staff. Murray was sent home when his health broke down and, until his latest appointment, had been serving as deputy CIGS. Asquith sent Kitchener a delicately worded note, notifying him of the Cabinet's decision and requesting that Wolfe-Murray be replaced by Archibald Murray.[23] Kitchener, on his return, grudgingly implemented the desired changes.

In the meantime, the Balkans continued to take center stage. On October 3, the uncertain outlook in Greece improved, when Venizelos asked the Allies to land at Salonica as soon as possible. The next day the Dardanelles Committee met to discuss what to do next. There was a suspicion that Joffre was unaware of the French government's promise to send half of the one hundred fifty thousand men requested by Greece, and, moreover, plans for the role of the Anglo-French troops and their conveyance needed to be worked out.[24] Arrangements were accordingly made for Kitchener and Balfour to meet Joffre and the two French service ministers, Millerand and Victor Augagneur, on October 5 at Calais. Here the British ministers discovered that Joffre was not only cognizant, but also approved, at least outwardly, of his government's offer to assist Serbia. Joffre and Kitchener agreed that each side would immediately furnish sixty-four thousand men, with the remainder to be made good at a later date. Kitchener proposed to send three additional divisions from France to Salonica as soon as the joint offensive in France was over. Balfour indicated that he would provide transportation for the French as well as for the British divisions. The only discordant note was over a plan after the landing—Joffre wanted the Allied force to move swiftly north into the heart of Serbia, but Kitchener refused to do so until he was certain that the Greeks were irrevocably committed to the Entente and the lines of communications were secured.[25]

Trying to define the exact role of the Anglo-French expedition in the

Balkans proved to be an exercise in futility in view of the events that were taking place concurrently in Greece. On October 5, ironically, as the British Tenth Division and a French division arrived at Salonica, Constantine repudiated the invitation issued to the Allies and dismissed Venizelos. As the motive for the Allied expedition to Salonica had entirely disappeared, Kitchener hastily countermanded the movement orders of the Tenth Division and directed its commander, if he had already left, to return to Lemnos.[26] The Dardanelles Committee on October 6 overruled Kitchener, but agreed to hold back the remaining troops, until the Greek political picture was in clearer focus.[27]

The next day the proceedings of the Dardanelles Committee were more chaotic and divisive than usual. A majority of ministers believed that Allied help could not arrive in time to establish ties with Serbia, against which an attack was expected any day. But a few die-hard ministers led by Lloyd George, whose old enthusiasm for a Balkan campaign had been revived, persisted in arguing that prompt action could yet save the Serbs. As Lloyd George appeared to have come up against a stone wall, he urged the Prime Minister to remit the question to the newly revitalized General Staff. Asquith responded by proposing to ask for the considered judgment of the combined staffs of the War Office and Admiralty.[28]

In the afternoon of October 7, Kitchener went over to 10 Downing Street to attend a conference with René Viviani (prime minister), Millerand, and Victor Augagneur (minister of marine). The French ministers, having agreed that one hundred fifty thousand men would be insufficient to accomplish the desired goals, now suggested that the Allies send an army of four hundred thousand, with France supplying sixty-seven thousand and the British the remainder. Kitchener rejected the suggestion outright, adamant that he would not commit a sizeable contingent to the Balkans without Greek cooperation. As the Viviani Government had not apprised Joffre of its latest proposal, it was decided that Kitchener should cross over to France and confer with the French commander.[29]

When Kitchener returned to the War Office after the meeting, he was unaware that the Austro-German offensive against Serbia had begun on the night of October 6–7. Within twenty-four hours, the Central Powers were in possession of Belgrade. Several days later, Bulgaria abandoned its wobbly neutrality and invaded from the southwest, driving a wedge between the Serbian Army and the Anglo-French forces in southern Greece. Given the military reality, there was no longer any point in keeping the Anglo-French troops in Salonica, galling as it may have been to abandon Serbia to its fate. Kitchener, Asquith, and the majority in the Cabinet favored leaving Salonica, but they were fiercely opposed by Lloyd George, Sir Edward Carson (attorney general), and later Bonar Law.[30]

During heated debates, Lloyd George sought to use Kitchener as a scapegoat for the unfolding tragedy in the Balkans. He accused Kitchener of gross irresponsibility and wanton indifference towards Serbia. Why, he asked rhetorically, had the War Office failed to make the slightest preparation against an invasion of the Balkans? What particularly aroused his ire was Kitchener's failure to double the carrying capacity of the single-track from Salonica to Uskub in Serbia, as directed by the War Council the previous February. He thundered in an I-told-you-so vein that some months ago he had warned against the very disaster that was now occurring in the Balkans and held that it was Kitchener's irresolution and want of foresight that had prevented timely action.[31]

To begin with, Lloyd George's partial recollection of events overlooked the factors that had caused the Balkan project to founder in February—the fierce animosities among the states in the area, which posed an insuperable obstacle to uniting them as one, and the refusal of Greece to act unless Romania became involved. Nor was Kitchener involved in or responsible for the negotiations that allowed Bulgaria to fall into the grasp of the Central Powers. The other charges against Kitchener were equally without merit. Lloyd George ignored the fact that the requisite engineers and building materials to increase and improve the transport facilities between Salonica and Uskub could only be obtained at the expense of the western front, where they were already at a premium. He disregarded the distance between the two places, some 245 miles (391.2 kilometers to be precise) and the topography of the region, which is mostly mountainous.[32] To conduct surveys, double the line where possible, construct sidings, and increase the rolling stock would have required years, not months. Then, too, the project would have been vulnerable to damage or destruction by enemy raids, unless it had been protected by a fairly considerable force. Finally, although Lloyd George may not have thought that it mattered, it was illegal to occupy a neutral country.

Kitchener was exceedingly sensitive to the dangers of creating a new front at a time when his resources were stretched to the breaking point. Understandably, he did not want to be dragged by the politicians into another Gallipoli, with an inferior force that would ultimately be thrown back and bottled up against the coast. All along he had known that Britain alone would be unable to stop a determined German bid to break through to Constantinople. Resources determine policy, and Kitchener had none to spare. He hoped that any major military effort to counteract enemy designs in the Balkans would be undertaken by Bulgaria or Romania. When Foreign Office initiatives failed to entice either state and the Greeks went back on their latest offer, Kitchener realized that with such troops as the Allies could muster, an expedition to save Serbia was doomed before it began.

Kitchener lacked the ability to articulate convincingly either the flaws that he recognized in Lloyd George's thinking or his own reasons for writing off Serbia, whereas Lloyd George and Carson were such masters of rhetoric that they could make a ludicrous scenario seem plausible. They had no difficulty in outmaneuvering Kitchener in debate and at times made him look foolish, particularly when an issue came up for the first time and caught him off guard. On such occasions he retreated into sullen silence or rambled incoherently. A case in point occurred on October 8, when the Cabinet held a rather tumultuous meeting. The discussion centered on the rival claims of Gallipoli and the Balkans, when Lloyd George suddenly asked Kitchener if any intelligence report had been received of the threatened Austro-German advance on Serbia. Kitchener replied that up to the moment of his departure for the meeting, he was unaware that any such information had come in. Lloyd George thought that news might have arrived since then, and he suggested that the Prime Minister's secretary check with the War Office. Back came the reply that a telegram announcing the Austro-German attack had been received late in the afternoon on the day before.[33] Stunned and somewhat embarrassed, Kitchener offered no excuses.

In Kitchener's defense, he had been away from the War Office for most of the day on October 7, and when he had returned, no one had shown him the telegram. In a time of crisis, such omissions unfortunately occur. The fact that Kitchener's attention was not immediately drawn to the announcement had no adverse repercussions whatsoever, but the incident was damaging in the eyes of his colleagues and strengthened Lloyd George's assertion that he had lost control of the direction of the war.

As instructed by the Dardanelles Committee, Kitchener left for Chantilly on October 8 to hold talks with Joffre over the new situation that had arisen in the Balkans. The meeting at GQG occurred the next day. Kitchener maintained that an army of two hundred fifty thousand was needed to save Serbia and that an additional one hundred fifty thousand would be required if the Allies planned to initiate a major offensive in the Balkans. Joffre's position was that the Allies could not afford to wage great campaigns simultaneously in the west and in the Balkans. He admitted that Serbia was beyond help, but that it was still possible to save the Serbian Army. In his opinion, the Anglo-French force should confine its activities to securing Salonica as a base, maintaining communications with the Serbian Army, and covering the right of the Serbian Army against Bulgaria. For such a defensive role, he thought that one hundred fifty thousand men would suffice. But he warned that should a more substantial effort be required at a later date, the responsibility for sending more men must be borne by the British government alone.[34] Kitchener had no faith in Joffre's plan, but he promised to submit it to the Dardanelles Committee, which he did on October 11. Set against this document was the report of the combined military and naval staffs, which slammed the door on British involvement in the Balkans. Instead, they recommended renewing pressure on the western front where decisive results could be obtained. Failing this, they favored a renewed attempt on the Dardanelles, with eight more British divisions from France. The Navy was prepared to join the action and accept heavy losses.

The combined staff appreciation did little to unite the divergent views in the Dardanelles Committee. As there was no interest in more frontal attacks in the west, the choice boiled down to either the Dardanelles or the Balkans. Kitchener left no doubt as to which of the two he favored. Although he understood the strategic ramifications of a Serbian defeat, quite apart from the political and human costs, he simply did not have the troops to prevent it. On the other hand, he was adamantly opposed to the abandonment of Gallipoli, making the far-fetched claim that it "would be the most disastrous event in the history of the Empire." Asquith and most of the ministers supported a renewed attempt on Gallipoli before German supplies could reach Turkey by the overland route.

By contrast Lloyd George and Carson, now joined by Bonar Law, hammered away on the importance of a rescue mission. Basing his case strictly on political considerations, Lloyd George asserted that if Britain turned its back on Serbia, it would be sending a signal to the whole of the East that it could not be counted on to protect its friends and "that Germany was the country to be followed." Kitchener's rejection of the mission to rescue Serbia provoked an angry clash with Lloyd George. To break the impasse, the Dardanelles Committee accepted the Prime Minister's recommendations: that substantial forces be withdrawn from France as soon as Joffre's offensive was over and sent to Egypt to await their ultimate destination; and that a specially selected general be dispatched to the Near East to study and advise as to whether the troops should be used in Gallipoli or in the Balkans.[35]

On returning to the War Office, Kitchener wired Hamilton, asking for an estimate of his army's losses in case it became necessary to withdraw. Hamilton replied that he might lose as much as half his force if compelled to evacuate under the fire of Turkish guns.[36] That assessment strengthened Kitchener's resolve against evacuation, but it sealed Hamilton's fate as commander of the Mediterranean Expeditionary Force (MEF). The Dardanelles Committee concluded that he was too deeply committed to the enterprise to give an objective evaluation. Hamilton's recall had been in the air for sometime. The Cabinet's expectation of success, reinforced by Hamilton's optimism, had intensified its disappointment in the results of the August landing. The remaining confidence in his leadership vanished, when disturbing reports drifted back to London of the muddled manner in which the offensive had been conducted.[37] Kitchener had the Suvla Bay operation reviewed by a committee of four generals, and their report amounted to an indictment of Hamilton's leadership.[38] Much as Kitchener hated to—he was the last one to hold out—he had no alternative but to approve of Hamilton's recall. Gen. Sir Charles Monro, the shrewd and capable commander of the Third Army in France, was appointed in Hamilton's place. He was to report on whether Gallipoli should be abandoned or another effort made to carry it.[39] When Hamilton left the peninsula on October 17, Birdwood assumed temporary command of the MEF.

Monro was still in London when Kitchener asked Birdwood for an appreciation of the situation on Gallipoli.[40] Birdwood replied that rapid progress was out of the question, owing to the impossibility of a flank attack, although he thought it was possible to make some headway on the northern front at Suvla, if the units were brought up to strength and supplemented by plenty of ammunition and two fresh divisions sent out from England. But the best way to end the operation was to hold the Turks on the peninsula, while a large force landed on the Asiatic side and marched on Chanak.[41] As Birdwood's assessment had considered only offensive action, Kitchener wired back, inquiring whether the Army could hold out against repeated attacks by the Turks, reinforced by German artillery and munitions.[42] Birdwood's answer was not encouraging. In his view, unless the Turks were driven inland, which would require heavy reinforcements in men and munitions, he doubted that the Army could withstand prolonged strain.[43]

Any possibility that more troops might be sent to the Dardanelles was seriously prejudiced by the intervention of the French. The Viviani Government had packed off Sarrail to the Balkans, but, owing to Joffre's resistance, was unable to provide him with large forces. The plight of Serbia was becoming more desperate with each passing day, and Sarrail could do little on his own, as the British troops, instead of advancing northwards, showed every intention of staying at Salonica during the winter months. The socialists in Parliament, worried that Sarrail's campaign would end in disaster, warned Viviani of political repercussions, unless more Allied divisions were committed to the Balkans. Although the Viviani Government easily beat back a vote of no confidence in the chamber, it was significant that a hundred left-wing deputies abstained.[44]

In London, the number of abstentions was interpreted as a sign of growing war weariness, renewing fears that the collapse of the Viviani Ministry might propel the peace-minded Caillaux to power.[45] The British Embassy in Paris confirmed that political chaos might ensue if the British wavered in their support of Serbia.[46] Millerand, who arrived in London on October 15, played on these fears after a meeting with Lloyd George. Realizing that he could count on a number of supporters in the Cabinet, the French minister of war left no doubt that unless the British continued to send more troops to the Balkans, the Viviani Government would be compelled to resign and the Alliance itself would be endangered.[47] Kitchener was reluctant to commit more than the division already at Salonica, but did not exclude sending out additional troops destined for Egypt if circumstances so warranted. What little military rationale remained evaporated, when the Bulgarians took Uskub on October 22, cutting the Salonica-Nish Railway and isolating the Serbian Army.[48] On October 24, Kitchener received a strongly worded message from the French military attaché in London, urging that the troops withdrawn from the western front be sent directly to Salonica, since any delay would ensure the destruction of the Serbian Army.

The next day Kitchener brought the note to the attention of the Dardanelles Committee, explaining that it was couched in such a way as to suggest that the French position was based less on strategic grounds than on political considerations. In these circumstances, Kitchener wondered if Britain's refusal to comply with French demands would spell the doom of the Viviani Administration. Selborne and Chamberlain argued that it was not worth embarking on a hopeless campaign just to prevent the downfall of the French government. For Kitchener, domestic issues could not be divorced from strategy. There was more at stake, he replied, than to preserve a tottering government. "It was to save the Alliance; that if we were to break with France the war would be over." Despite the sense of urgency, the Dardanelles Committee put off a decision pending the results of consultations between Murray and Joffre.[49]

The British did not know that Joffre, who for months had resisted all attempts to divert forces from the western front, had become a late convert to the Balkan enterprise. Joffre was astute enough to understand that if Sarrail's supporters were not mollified, the government would fall, and consequently, his own position would be threatened. Since his resources in men and munitions were required to fight for the survival of France, where the Germans were installed barely fifty miles from Paris, he expected Kitchener to supply the bulk of the forces for the Balkans.[50] He proposed to Murray, when they met at Chantilly on October 27, that the British should send four additional divisions to Salonica. When Murray found the idea unacceptable, Joffre left for London to plead his case personally with the British government.[51]

At a conference at 10 Downing Street, Joffre argued that a major effort should be undertaken to prevent the destruction of the Serbian Army, observing that if the Central Powers could be held up, Greece might still come in on the side of the Allies. He was not asking the British to do anything more than play a defensive role. While Sarrail's three divisions moved northwards in an attempt to reestablish communications with the Serbian Army, the five British divisions would simply be guarding Salonica and the railway as far as the Serbian border. Joffre made more of an impact after the meeting when, during informal conversation, he stated bluntly that the retention of his post as commander in chief, and even the permanence of the alliance itself, would depend on the British government's reply. According to Kitchener, Joffre had pointed a pistol at the Cabinet when he said, "If you back out of Salonica it is the end of the Entente." Buckling under what Churchill called "this outrageous threat," the Cabinet agreed to dispatch four more divisions to the Balkans with the understanding that if communications with the Serbs could not be reopened and maintained, the whole Allied force would be withdrawn.[52] At the time, the British did not understand the implications of their commitment. A precedent had been established that maintaining the existing regime in France overrode all other considerations. This meant that the

British would be abdicating their right to an equal voice in determining Allied strategy whenever their proposed action threatened to add to the instability of French domestic politics.

Ironically, Joffre's political victory came too late to save Viviani. By the time he returned to Paris a new ministry under Aristide Briand had been formed. Briand had long championed a front in the Balkans, less on military grounds than as a base to expand France's interests in the Mediterranean. His political survival rested upon continued Allied presence in the Balkans. Britain was now trapped in a morass solely to ensure French postwar preponderance in the eastern Mediterranean.[53]

Kitchener's promise to the French practically predetermined the fate of the Dardanelles before Monro's report was received. Arriving in Mudros on October 27, Monro proceeded to interview the divisional commanders and to inspect the widely separated fronts on the peninsula. Waiting impatiently in London, Kitchener telegraphed Monro, "Please send me as soon as possible your report on the main issue at the Dardanelles, namely, leaving or staying."[54] In a well-reasoned statement relayed to the War Office on October 31, Monro recommended that in view of the lateness of the season, the exhaustion of the troops, and the imminent arrival of German supplies, the peninsula should be evacuated.[55]

Kitchener's reaction to the report was one of consternation, for he remained unalterably opposed to evacuation. He could not accept the heavy losses that would occur in the course of withdrawal, which Monro estimated at between 30 and 40 percent of the total force. Added to this was his old fear, which if anything had intensified, of the impact a major defeat would have on Muslim opinion in Egypt and India. In hindsight he may have overestimated the danger of Muslim disaffection, but with authorities in Cairo and Delhi reminding him that any erosion of British prestige might provoke serious internal disturbances, it is difficult to blame him for realizing it and taking what precautions he could to avert it. In Egypt, intelligence reported that German agents were trying to bribe the Senussi with arms and money to rise against the British. An incident in late August lent credence to the rumors. As Maxwell intensified his security arrangements on the western frontier, he intercepted a packet of letters in which the Senussi incited Muslim potentates and journalists in Arabia and India to a holy war against the British. Since most of his troops were involved in the defense of the canal, Maxwell could only rely on a few semitrained battalions for internal police duties. Well might he worry, as confronting his security forces were some twelve million Muslims, most of whom, in his words, "do not love us."[56] Similar concern about German intrigues and native unrest were expressed by the government of India. Hardinge wrote on September 10:

> Among those who, like myself, are in a position to know, there can be no doubt that the situation in India is slowly but surely deteriorating and, so long as the war lasts, is likely to continue to do so. The constant repetition of attacks on our frontier, the sulkiness of the Mahomedans, the plots hatched outside with ramifications in India, and the cases of sedition in native regiments, all tend to show steady deterioration.[57]

In the midst of the debate over the fate of the Gallipoli expedition, practically all of the Cabinet ministers, in an informal meeting, came to the conclusion that Kitchener ought to be removed from the War Office on the grounds that he lacked candor and was a poor guide on matters of strategy. Two of the leading members, Lloyd George and Bonar Law, went so far as to threaten to resign unless the Prime Minister took immediate action. Asquith realized that his shaky government would never survive Kitchener's dismissal. He toyed with the idea of making Kitchener, among other things, commander in chief of all British forces outside of France. Kitchener turned down all suggestions aimed at getting rid of him, as he did not want either to weaken national unity or leave the running of the war to incompetent, self-seeking politicians. But he did consent to go out to Gallipoli to judge for himself whether Monro was right in suggesting evacuation.[58] This appeased Kitchener's enemies, who hoped that he would not come back.

Kitchener stopped in Paris to hold talks with Briand and Gen. Joseph Galliéni, the new minister of war, before proceeding to Mudros, via Marseille, on board the *Dartmouth*.[59] He arrived on November 10, and his first words to Birdwood, who was on hand to greet him, were, "I can't tell you how glad I am to have you with me again, Birdie, and to be away from all those bloody politicians." Birdwood later remarked, "I always remember how he squeezed my arm and pressed it. He was normally so very undemonstrative."[60] Kitchener was then taken to the flagship, *Lord Nelson*. He spent the rest of the day and much of the next in consultation with de Robeck, Birdwood, Monro, Maxwell, and McMahon. Kitchener asked Birdwood if he could break through with the forces at his disposal. Birdwood replied that he could not do so, unless reinforced by three or four fresh divisions. Kitchener did not feel that he could spare that number of divisions at the moment, and de Robeck did not make thing easier for him by asserting that another naval attempt would achieve nothing. What finally swayed Kitchener was Maxwell's suggestion, which was endorsed by Monro and McMahon, that the withdrawal from Gallipoli should first be preceded by a landing in Ayas Bay, near Alexandretta.[61] The object of the new front would not only cushion the political impact of evacuation, but would also cut Turkish rail communications, thus protecting Egypt and assisting operations in Mesopotamia by preventing the eastward flow of Ottoman troops.

Kitchener telegraphed his provisional conclusion to Asquith on the evening of August 11. Subject to a full inspection of the peninsula, he was inclined to favor abandoning Suvla and Anzac, but retaining a presence at Helles to save face. As a means of ensuring the safety of Egypt, he recommended a fresh landing in Ayas Bay with the troops from Suvla and Anzac.[62] Asquith was startled by the unexpected proposal and at once consulted the military experts at the War Office. The General Staff advised against the scheme on the grounds that Egypt could best be defended along the line of the canal and that it would require more troops than Kitchener had estimated.[63] That was also the view of the Cabinet. A series of telegrams passed between Asquith and Kitchener, who was exasperated by the rebuff. A report that the Germans were laying plans to attack the Suez Canal fueled his fears for the safety of Egypt and was the principal cause of his persistent plea in favor of the Ayas Bay landing. The final nail in the coffin of the projected operation was driven by the French, who for political reasons did not want British troops near Syria.[64]

Kitchener examined the British positions in the peninsula on November 12 to 14 and was disheartened by the impregnable nature of the Turkish defenses. After he had inspected Anzac, he turned to Birdwood and said, "Thank God Birdie, I came to see this for myself. . . . I had no idea of the difficulties you were up against."[65] He telegraphed his overall impressions to Asquith on the November 15: "The country is much more difficult than I imagined and the Turkish positions . . . are natural fortresses . . . which, if not taken by surprise at first, could be held against very serious attack by larger forces than have been engaged."[66]

Kitchener's final report was delayed, when his attention was diverted by new developments in the Balkans. The Anglo-French advance into Serbia had been effectively blocked by the Bulgarians, foreclosing any possibility of linking up with the Serbs.[67] Under pressure from the Germans, the Greek government hinted that it would disarm the Allied troops if they fell back across the Greek frontier. On November 16, Kitchener hurriedly gathered his personal belongings and set off for Salonica, where he held a long conversation with Sarrail the next day. The French general explained that he had insufficient troops to break through to the Serbs and warned that if the Greeks acted on their threat, he would require three hundred thousand men to guarantee the security of his base at Salonica.[68]

Kitchener was subsequently granted an interview with King Constantine on November 20, at which he threatened reprisals in the event any unfriendly measures were initiated against the retreating Allied force. Kitchener brushed aside Constantine's strong protest that the Allies had violated Greece's neutrality by reminding him that they had come in response to an invitation extended by a lawfully constituted government. Kitchener went on to say that Britain would eventually triumph over Germany because it would be able to put a vastly superior army in the field, and he warned of serious consequences if a single Allied soldier in Greece were harmed in any way. Constantine was made to understand that he could not commit a hostile act against the Entente without putting Greek ports and seaborne trade alike at the mercy of the Royal Navy. As the Kaiser's brother-in-law, Constantine was in a difficult position, but whatever his personal feelings, he pledged that he would not interfere with the Allied troops if they returned to Greece.[69]

Back in Mudros, Kitchener telegraphed London on November 22 to the effect that, in view of the likelihood of German assistance, which would make the British positions untenable, there was no alternative but to leave the peninsula. He therefore recommended evacuating Anzac and Suvla, but retaining Helles for the time being. He regretted that he and the government had prevented a resumption of the offensive at Suvla by denying Hamilton's request for reinforcements in August. A thrust from that point might have turned the Kilid Bahr position and enabled the fleet to pass through the straits, thus changing entirely the situation in the east. No such operation occurred because of the mistaken policy that had been pursed in the Balkans at the dictation of France, and now it was too late to attempt it.[70] The next day Asquith replied that the War Committee (the successor to the Dardanelles Committee[71]) favored total evacuation and that the matter was being referred to the Cabinet for confirmation.

Kitchener left for England on November 24, after rejecting a suggestion from the Prime Minister that he should return to Egypt to counter the moral effects of evacuation. He traveled by way of Italy, which had joined the Entente in May 1915.[72] Here he visited the front, spoke to several leading politicians, and was introduced to King Victor Emmanuel, who presented him with the Grand Cordon of St. Maurice and St. Lazarus. While in Rome, he found time to see an old friend, Sir James Rennell Rodd, the British Ambassador, to whom he confided his troubles. He described the protracted discussions that occurred on practically every question that came up for consideration and the consequent delays in reaching a decision. He also referred to the hostility of some of his colleagues, who sought to use him as a scapegoat when things went awry in an effort to oust him from office. Under the circumstances he did not think that it would be possible for him to continue in office.[73]

On reaching London on November 30, Kitchener went straight to 10 Downing Street and submitted his resignation as secretary for war. Asquith was not anxious to see Kitchener leave the government at this juncture, given that the string of disasters in 1915 had rendered his own position precarious. He persuaded Kitchener to return to the War Office by appealing to his sense of duty.[74] Asquith told Kitchener that he had notified French that he was to be recalled from France.[75] He presumed that Douglas Haig would be his logical successor. Kitchener was not unhappy to see French removed, a step he had been deterred from taking in May because of the Prime Minister's objections.[76] Asquith further announced that he wanted Sir William Robertson, French's exceptionally able chief of staff, to replace Murray as CIGS and act as the government's principal adviser on strategy. He suggested that Kitchener arrange to meet Robertson, who was currently in London, and try to work out the conditions under which he would accept the post of CIGS as soon as French laid down his command.[77]

Kitchener had set his sights on Robertson since mid-1915, recognizing at long last that he required a top level CIGS to relieve him of staff work. Kitchener hesitated to ask for his services because of his contentious relations with Sir John French. According to Sir George Arthur, Kitchener had been willing to wait for Robertson, as he was convinced that it was only a matter of time before French was recalled home.[78] After the fiasco at Loos, Asquith had come to the belated conclusion that French would have to go.

Kitchener had no inkling that Robertson would prove to be so tough a negotiator when they met at his home on the evening of November 30. Robertson, who barely knew Kitchener, admitted later that he could not help but be influenced by the prevailing gossip that the War Office chief

centralized all authority in his hands and would not allow the General
Staff to carry out its proper duties. Robertson made it clear that he wanted
to be free to formulate strategy and manage the General Staff; otherwise,
he hoped he would be permitted to remain in France. Kitchener admitted
his faults, but assured Robertson that he was "not at all the kind of 'K'
some people think I am."[79] He indicated that he would take no action that
would endanger their working together smoothly, stressing that he would
be more than happy to rid himself of some of the chores he had hitherto
been compelled to take on. Robertson was impressed by Kitchener's candor and willingness to extend himself to reach an accommodation. Nevertheless, to avoid any future misunderstanding, Robertson asked for a
delay, so that he could set down in writing the ground rules of their professional relationship. Kitchener consented and the two men shook
hands.[80]

During Kitchener's absence, new developments at home and abroad
had added to the confusion and deepened divisions in the Asquith Cabinet. Curzon led a group in the Cabinet, which succeeded in blocking rati-
fication of the War Committee's recommendations that Gallipoli should
be evacuated.[81] Vice Adm. Rosslyn Wemyss, who had replaced de Robeck
in command of the fleet in the Dardanelles, announced the Navy's readiness to support the Army if another attempt was made to capture the peninsula. On top of this came disturbing news that Townshend's imperial
force in Mesopotamia had met unexpected difficulties and was in grave
peril.

Townshend had moved out of Aziziya on November 14 without the
promised reinforcements. He encountered little resistance until he ran up
against a heavily fortified Turkish position near Ctesiphon, twenty miles
from Baghdad. His attack failed (November 22–26), and he lost forty-five
hundred men, a third of his total strength of some fourteen thousand.
Lacking the resources to continue his assault, Townshend fell back on Kut
with the Turks in pursuit. On reaching the town, Townshend, convinced
that his weary men could march no more, prepared to withstand a siege.[82]

The sudden downturn in Britain's fortunes in Mesopotamia dominated War Committee and Cabinet proceedings during the opening days
of December. Kitchener, executing a dramatic volte-face, grasped eagerly
at the Admiralty's offer to cooperate in another bid to open the straits. In
a memorandum to the Cabinet, dated December 2, Kitchener mentioned
that since his report of November 22, two factors had caused him to
change his mind: first, the possibility that troops would shortly be avail-

able from Salonica; and second, that Townshend's setback made it imperative to deny the Turks a victory on the peninsula.[83]

Kitchener's constant shilly-shallying did nothing to improve his standing in the Cabinet. By his own admission, another offensive in the Dardanelles was at best a long shot to drive the Turks from the high ground they occupied. The proper course for him to have taken, after he had personally inspected the fronts and seen what the Army was up against, would have been to hold firmly to his recommendation to evacuate the peninsula. A noisy minority, led by Curzon, drew attention to the political and diplomatic complications arising from any withdrawal as the chief reason for staying on. It is unfortunate that Kitchener allowed such considerations to override military logic. As Philip Magnus has correctly observed, it was "the act of a passenger in a feeble team, rather than that of a leader of men in a critical situation."[84] Kitchener's turnaround reinforced the pro-Dardanelles position and gave rise to the possibility that the campaign might yet be rescued from extinction. But before the matter could be pursued further, it was necessary to reach an understanding with the French over Salonica.

The British did not reckon, however, on having to take on the Russians as well. Petrograd, like Paris, placed great importance on maintaining an Allied presence at Salonica. In fact, in late November 1915 Russian military authorities had handed Hanbury Williams a memorandum calling for a joint offensive by the Anglo-French Army at Salonica and Russian forces in Bessarabia. The object was for the Anglo-French troops to occupy Serbia before driving in concert with the Russians into Hungary.[85] This absurd scheme was never seriously considered by either the British or the French. Nevertheless, on December 2 Count Benckendorff sent a note to the Foreign Office, stressing the necessity of preventing the Germans from crushing the Balkan states one by one.[86] At the same time, the Russian chief of staff appealed to Joffre, arguing that the retention of Salonica tied down enemy forces, which otherwise would be used to impede Russia's offensive in Galicia. The contents of the letter were immediately conveyed to Kitchener.[87] Grey was worried about the effects on Anglo-Russian relations that a withdrawal from Salonica would cause. He wrote to Kitchener on December 4:

> If you come to any decision with the French today I think the Russians ought to be told at once. . . . It would be much better to break the news to them through Hanbury Williams. They will take it much better if

they understand it is based solely on military grounds and communicated directly to their GHQ. . . . I am sure they will resent it less than
if it reaches their GHQ through the diplomatic channel.[88]

On the same day, Asquith, Kitchener, and Balfour crossed over to
Calais, where they met Briand, Joffre, Galliéni and Adm. Marie Jean
Louis Lacaze, the new minister of marine. Kitchener was in good form,
demonstrating a sense of resolution that had been missing in recent
weeks. He pointed out that the condition of British participation in the
Salonica campaign had not been fulfilled: Serbia was beyond saving and
communications with the Serbian Army could not be reestablished. The
Anglo-French force was now in great danger, and the only sensible course
was to withdraw immediately. Kitchener then announced that, if it was
decided to remain at Salonica, he would have to resign, as he had no intention of shouldering the responsibility for a military disaster. Kitchener's arguments were buttressed by a firm statement read out by Asquith.
Joffre remained silent, while Briand, after an emotional speech explaining
the advantages of remaining at Salonica, reluctantly capitulated.[89]

For the British it proved to be a hollow victory. The conference had
barely ended when a report arrived that the Bulgarians had attacked Sarrail's forces. When Briand returned to Paris, he faced a Cabinet crisis.
The socialists were up in arms, claiming that their hero had been left in
the lurch. They threatened to leave the Cabinet. Briand hurriedly sent
Albert Thomas, the Minister of Munitions and a friend of Lloyd George,
to London in a desperate attempt to reverse the Calais agreement. The
French could not have secured a more effective ally than the tenacious
Lloyd George to do their bidding. In the War Committee Lloyd George
brushed aside Kitchener's view that military consideration dictated that
the troops reembark from Salonica without delay, focusing instead on the
need to avoid a breach in the Alliance. Any impression that the British
were deserting the French would bring down the Briand ministry and create a political crisis that would endanger France's continued participation
in the war. Just as Kitchener had persuaded the Cabinet to support Joffre's
disastrous autumn offensive by underlining Britain's obligations to its allies, so Lloyd George used the same arguments to block the Anglo-
French retreat from the Balkans.[90]

Working effectively behind the scenes, the French complemented
Lloyd George's efforts. At a major Allied military conference at Chantilly
(December 6–8), a Joffre-guided resolution designed to force London to

give way over Salonica passed with only one dissension, the British representative.[91] Bertie warned the Foreign Office on December 6 that a British withdrawal from Salonica would be badly received in France and probably would result in the fall of Briand.[92] In retrospect, Hankey wrote, "The risks of so serious a quarrel with our Allies were too grave to be run, especially on an issue on which opinion in the Cabinet itself was divided."[93] The decision to remain at Salonica destroyed any hope Kitchener entertained of continuing operations in the Dardanelles. On December 7 the Cabinet finally decided to evacuate Suvla and Anzac, but to retain Helles for the immediate future.[94]

On December 8 the War Committee, to preserve harmony in the Alliance, decided to send Kitchener and Grey to Paris with plenary powers to settle the Balkan matter as best they could.[95] Kitchener did not look forward to the mission. His presence and that of Grey in Paris would be a tacit admission that the British had succumbed to French pressure. Kitchener and Grey met Briand and Galliéni, and from the start of the negotiations, there was no question that the Balkan sideshow would continue for the present at any rate. Kitchener and Grey indicated that their main concern was to arrange with the French government how the British troops could best support French forces and secure the Anglo-French base. The eventual fate of Salonica, it was agreed, would be determined by the course of events. According to Kitchener, their visit had dissipated many of the ill feelings harbored by the French government and averted a ministerial crisis.[96]

Before leaving for Paris, Kitchener had received a memorandum from Robertson, setting down in detail his views on the division of their respective responsibilities. His conditions, much more stringent than Kitchener had anticipated, may be summarized as follows: that the CIGS should be the only channel through which the War Committee receive all advice on matters concerning military operations; that the CIGS should have direct access to the field commanders and sign all operational orders under the authority of the War Committee; and that the Secretary for War, besides administrating the War Office, should confine himself to feeding, clothing, and equipping the Army.[97] Robertson's terms would give him powers never before (or since) accorded to the post of CIGS.

Kitchener found the document offensive, and made up his mind to resign. He was very weary and dispirited by ongoing attacks on his professional judgment and refused to submit to further indignities. "They want to use my name," he told Esher, "and deprive me of authority."[98] Friends who saw him periodically were shocked at how much he had aged during the last few months. He had lost weight, his hair was turning white, and the lines in his face had deepened.

Kitchener went to 10 Downing Street and recommended that the government accept Robertson's proposals, but added that he did not wish to remain at the War Office in so diminished a capacity. Instead, he felt he could be more useful as generalissimo of British forces at home and overseas. Asquith asked for time to think it over.[99] What Asquith wanted was a solution that would leave Kitchener without real authority, but in a position of eminence, so that the government could use him as a protective umbrella.

Robertson had no wish to force Kitchener's resignation. "I am an unknown man in the country," he informed Maj. Clive Wigram, the King's equerry. "K. with me would be a great help. Without him I would be nobody in the eyes of the public."[100] While Robertson wanted Kitchener to remain at the War Office, he was equally determined to carry on the CIGS's duties without being interfered with or overruled. When Kitchener and his party crossed the channel to discuss Salonica with French leaders, Robertson joined them at Calais and accompanied them to Paris. Robertson begged Kitchener not to resign and offered to modify the offending paragraphs in his memorandum. Esher took it upon himself to mediate their differences. He rewrote and amended the original draft numerous times before arriving at a formula acceptable to the disputants. Robertson got what he wanted most: independence from Kitchener and assurance that he would be the government's sole military adviser. He made only two minor concessions to Kitchener. Operational orders would go out under the authority of the Secretary for War, not the War Committee. Moreover the humiliating paragraph limiting the power of the Secretary of State was eliminated.[101] Kitchener told Esher when he accepted the final draft, "I hope Robertson understands that, much as I dislike the plan, now that I have agreed, I mean to carry it out."[102]

Before Robertson could take up his duties, Kitchener was confronted with an issue that had initially arisen while he was on a fact-finding mission to the Dardanelles. In November 1915, as discussed in an earlier chapter, the War Committee had decided to supersede Tighe, designating Smith-Dorrien to take charge of a new expedition against German East Africa. In a memorandum for the War Office, Smith-Dorrien asked for considerable reinforcements in men, heavy guns, transport vehicles, and airplanes. His plan of campaign, as far as could be formed in advance, was to eject the Germans from British territory around Kilimanjaro, together with a landing at Dar es Salaam, and an advance on the enemy's rear. If carried out in sufficient strength, Smith-Dorrien thought there was a good chance that this envelopment movement would put an end to the conflict in German East Africa. He did not expect to begin operations in earnest until the summer of 1916, as it was desirable to wait until the rainy season was over and to give the South African troops time to acclimatize and gain familiarity with East African bush fighting.[103]

Kitchener disapproved of the expedition, loath as he was to divert troops and supplies that might be needed for the western front. "I had constant interviews with him in an effort to get guns, aeroplanes and sufficient troops," Smith-Dorrien would write in his memoirs, "but obtaining them was like squeezing blood out of a stone."[104] Kitchener turned to the General Staff to assess Smith-Dorrien's plan. In a paper dated December 10, Murray considered unfeasible the idea of conquering the whole of German East Africa. As a practical proposition, however, he favored an expedition that would wrest certain rich portions of the German colony adjacent to British East Africa, so that Britain would be in a better position to claim these, should it choose, at the end of hostilities. He believed that the fifteen thousand troops the South African government was prepared to send to British East Africa, together with those already there, would be adequate for such active operations.[105]

Kitchener was as unhappy with Murray's memorandum as he had been with Smith-Dorrien's. In a formal dissent, inserted at the conclusion of Murray's appreciation, he wrote:

> The scheme for offensive operations in the centre of Africa is, in my opinion, a very dangerous project in the present state of the war when we require to concentrate all our efforts on defeating the Germans in Europe. No one, I presume, supposes that a success in East Africa will have any effect on the war, and the sending out of a General of the standing of Sir Horace Smith-Dorrien to conduct military operations there and to conquer territory which, when it was at our disposal, we refused after due examination,[106] seems to me an unwise proceeding. If we win this war, we can easily acquire any portion of East Africa we desire to possess. If we lose it, the lives of the troops we are now sending to conquer this territory will be purely wasted. The country, I know from personal experience,[107] is an extremely difficult one, and I fear that the forces as constituted will prove inadequate. The general military pol-

icy now advocated may, therefore, lead us to place South African troops in positions they will be liable to disaster from which we shall not be able to extricate them, as our troops will be fully engaged elsewhere. I think that the recent example we have had of similar proceedings based on wrong premises in Mesopotamia should teach us to be cautious in undertaking operations of this nature. In my opinion an offensive-defensive policy in East Africa is incumbent upon us, and, though I agree that to carry out this policy certain increases to the forces now protecting the East African Colony are advisable and necessary, I am opposed at the present stage of the war to the principles of conquest in German East Africa which have been put forward in the above paper.[108]

But Kitchener's opinion no longer commanded the respect it once did. The government overruled his objections and on December 18 formally appointed Smith-Dorrien to command the expedition.[109] The general left for East Africa by way of the Cape of Good Hope, but on the first day of the voyage he fell ill with a chill, which soon developed into pneumonia. Feeling better by the time he reached South Africa, he insisted on picking up his work before he was fully recovered. As a result, he suffered a relapse so severe he was compelled to resign his appointment and return to Britain. He was replaced by Lt. Gen. Jan C. Smuts of South Africa. As Kitchener had predicted, East Africa would prove to be a quagmire, drawing in more and more troops and supplies. For the rest of the war, Smuts and his successors chased Lettow-Vorbeck across German and Portuguese East Africa, but they were never able to corner their quarry, whose force never exceeded fifteen thousand men. The German leader was still evading his pursuers when the armistice came. His tenacity had cost the British 18,626 casualties, not including those admitted to hospitals owing to disease, and tied down an army of at least 160,000 men, some of whom could have been used more profitably on other fronts.[110]

Kitchener's effort to limit the scope of the future operations in East Africa was his last direct involvement in strategic questions before Robertson assumed the post of CIGS on December 21. On the previous day Kitchener had received word that the evacuation of Suvla and Anzac had been carried out without the loss of a single man. The days leading up to the retirement had been sheer torture. "I pace my room at night," he confided to Asquith, "and see the boats fired at and capsizing, and the drowning men."[111] Needless to say, he was immensely relieved to hear the good news. Under Monro's leadership, plans had been prepared with thoroughness and care, in sharp contrast to the mistakes and muddles that had characterized every earlier stage of the Gallipoli enterprise.[112] A week later the Cabinet, spurred on by Robertson, agreed to the evacuation of Cape Helles as well. Although the operation was undertaken at the worse possible time of the year, the last men were safely removed from Cape Helles on January 8, 1916. Contrary to all expectations, the evacuation of Gallipoli caused neither loss of life, nor much damage to British prestige.

The successful withdrawal from Gallipoli was the one bright spot in what had been a terrible year for Kitchener and Britain. It can be argued that Kitchener was hardly at fault for the nation's misfortunes. In the first place, the problems resulting from the nation's unpreparedness for a major conflict were exacerbated by the onset of trench warfare. Then too, the constant intervention of the Cabinet, as well as Britain's obligations to its allies, made it impossible for Kitchener to follow his war script. Yet, as the supreme warlord, he was blamed whenever things went wrong. Coinciding with the Cabinet's ill-advised sideshows were French's badly bungled operations on the western front, with each setback contributing in varying degree to the erosion of Kitchener's once immense reputation in government circles. Cumulatively, these defeats affected Kitchener's health and brought his standing in the Cabinet to its nadir by year's end.

14

THE FINAL PHASE

BROKEN in health and spirit at the close of 1915, Kitchener staged a remarkable rally in the opening months of the new year. With the arrival of Robertson, much of the burden of responsibility was lifted from his shoulders, and he was able to visit friends and spend more time at Broome Park, where he found solace working in his garden or took pleasure mingling among, and talking to, wounded soldiers whom he had invited to recuperate on his estate. In the Cabinet, he was no longer the object of personal attacks. In fact, the politicians got the shock of their life when they discovered that the man they had chosen to smite Kitchener had no interest in doing so[1] and, moreover, was bent on reorienting Britain's strategy in a direction of which they disapproved, was less forthcoming, and, in some ways, was more inflexible and difficult to deal with than the Secretary for War. As a result, they tried to bring Kitchener back, hoping to neutralize Robertson's influence in the War Committee. It was all in vain. Kitchener and Robertson worked together happily and without strain. Kitchener grew to like Robertson, who treated him with deference, was an admirable administrator, single-minded, shrewd, and aboveboard. While he did not always agree with Robertson, he supported him unequivocally in the War Committee. Kitchener knew that any hint that he and Robertson stood apart would open the way for the civilians to gain control of strategy and undermine Britain's commitment to the land campaign in France and Flanders. Together they formed an unbeatable combination because of the political risks of overruling them both.

Kitchener and Robertson had much in common. They were both cautious and conventional, rather than imaginative. They were united in their dislike of politicians in whose company their limited fluency placed them at a disadvantage. They understood that coalition warfare imposed restrictions on Britain's freedom of action. They shared a belief that no victory or peace satisfactory to Britain's interest could be achieved without defeating the German Army on the western front. They held firm to the notion that there was no magic formula for winning the war and that attrition engagements, while costly and devoid of dramatic results, were necessary to wear down the Germans and make final victory possible.

There was, however, a fundamental difference in their strategies. Although both Kitchener and Robertson favored what later became known as the "bite and hold" concept—intense bombardment, an infantry advance confined to readjust the line, consolidation of gains, and preparations to inflict maximum casualties on the Germans when they counterattacked—they differed in their belief as to how it should be applied. Kitchener favored attacks on narrow fronts with limited objectives to deny the German Army respite, and to gradually sap its strength and morale. Robertson considered such an approach inadequate. Instead, he preferred to deliver major blows with more distant objectives. A series of these, carefully prepared and coordinated with the French and, if possible, the Russians, were, in his view, the only way to ensure the enemy's defeat.[2]

Their difference in the degree of British military activity influenced their position on the issue of conscription. Kitchener wanted to delay the advent of compulsion as long as possible. Aside from loyalty to Asquith, he worried that a mass influx of conscripts in 1916 would drain Britain's reservoir of manpower, so that when the right moment arrived, he would not have enough men to deliver the knockout blow. On the other hand, Robertson had long supported national military service to augment the size of the British Army rapidly. "Don't try to hurry things so," Kitchener would reply whenever Robertson brought up the subject. "What we should aim at is to have the largest army in Europe when the terms of peace are being discussed, and that will not be in 1916 but in 1917."[3]

On December 28, a week after becoming CIGS, Robertson sought to gain the approval of the War Committee that France and Flanders should be regarded as the main theater of war and that the British Army should participate in combined operations with its allies in the spring of 1916.[4] The endorsement of the War Committee would accord with plans formulated by an Allied general staff conference earlier that month at Chantilly, which had prescribed synchronized and sustained offensives on three fronts—an attack on the German line in France and Flanders, matched by an Russian thrust from the east, and an Italian drive against the Austro-Hungarians—to be preceded by a series of minor wearing-out operations.[5] Robertson admitted that casualties would be high and there was no guarantee that the German line would be broken. Still, he thought that chances of success had improved because the Allies would be deploying more men, guns, and ammunition, as well as attacking simultaneously.

Kitchener stood alongside Robertson in defending the planned offensive. Although Kitchener's estimate of the war's duration remained constant, his military policy had undergone a change since August 1914. Kitchener assumed in the beginning that between 1914 and 1916 the Continental powers would fight each other to a stalemate in a series of costly battles. In the meantime Britain would provide its allies with money and supplies, but its direct military commitment would be restricted to sending only such troops as were necessary to prevent a defeat in the west.

The advent of trench warfare did not induce a modification in Kitchener's outlook. The troops sent over were confined to engaging in minor wearing-down operations and to taking over more of the French line, so as to permit Joffre to conduct large offensives. It was seen that by the spring of 1917, Britain, as the only belligerent with large and fully equipped reserves of manpower, would be able to win the war for the Entente. During the first year of the war, Kitchener staged a careful balancing act, trying to avoid a complete Continental commitment without alienating Britain's allies.

Kitchener hoped in 1915 that the Germans would wear themselves out by counterattacking the strongly entrenched line in the west. However, they were not so obliging. While adopting a defensive posture in the west, they had turned eastwards and inflicted an almost fatal defeat on Russia. As the year ended, Kitchener feared that if the British continued to hold back, the French and especially the Russians might opt to leave the war. With the political solidarity of the Entente at stake, Kitchener recognized that Britain had no option but to bear a heavier share of the fighting in 1916. For that reason he agreed with Robertson that Britain must participate fully in the combined offensive planned at Chantilly, although he did not believe that a breakthrough was possible.[6]

The Cabinet, however, was reluctant to rubber-stamp the recommendation of its military advisers, who were careful not to raise hopes that the Entente would be able to inflict such a crushing defeat on the Germans as to drive them to make peace by the end of 1916. Both Lloyd George and Balfour objected to the idea of a big offensive on the grounds that German defenses were too strong and that the result would be another costly Allied defeat. Kitchener reminded them of the dire consequences that might ensue if Britain refused to cooperate with its allies. Bonar Law made one of his rare telling points when he asked rhetorically how, if the views of the General Staff were rejected, Britain could hope to defeat the Germans. In the end, the War Committee accepted the western front as the primary theater, but hedged on the other issue, only going as far as to agree to prepare to carry out an offensive next spring "in close cooperation with the allies."[7]

The equivocation of the War Committee about the offensive made it almost certain that Balfour and Lloyd George would return to the charge at the next meeting on January 13. As the debate resumed, Kitchener was left alone to plead the War Office's case. Robertson said practically nothing. Mindful of his limited forensic skills, his habitual practice at the War Committee—one that Kitchener perhaps should have adopted from the outset—was to offer his advice and then refuse to debate.[8] At any rate, Kitchener's strength was never in the power of his words. Because of Balfour's persistence, the War Committee's earlier conclusion was revised to read that every effort should be made to prepare a massive assault in the west in the spring, "although it must not be assumed that such offensive operations are finally decided on."[9] The amendment served no purpose, unless the dissenters could offer a convincing alternative course. But no one could generate any interest in eccentric operations in view of Britain's humiliations in the Balkans, Mesopotamia, and the Dardanelles at the hands of non-German forces.

Although the Cabinet's focus was drawn back to the western front, there remained a nagging uneasiness among its most influential members that the plan for a spring offensive was premature and bound to repeat the futile assault at Loos. Kitchener was able to show in a private meeting with Balfour on January 21 that the latter and other Cabinet ministers had misinterpreted the strategic policy of the General Staff. Balfour thereupon set forth Kitchener's explanation in a paper that he distributed to the War Committee. Intended to correct a misapprehension "probably shared by all my civilian colleagues on the Committee," it ran as follows:

> I had supposed that Lord Kitchener's plan was to attempt to bring the war to a close by a repetition in the spring of the kind of attack on the

German trenches which has been already tried but has so far failed; the only important difference being that the new attempt was to be made on a much wider front, and with a much larger supply of heavy artillery. I had, however, the advantage of a conversation with Lord Kitchener on Friday, which shows me that I was mistaken, and that his present plan is of an essentially different character. He has no desire (if I understand him rightly) to repeat the Champagne experiment, and is keenly alive to the danger of any operations, which could cause a heavier wastage among the French and British than among the German and Austrian troops opposed to them. His scheme is of a different character, and involves not so much an attempt to break through the German lines, as an attempt to exhaust their reserves by carrying operations of the type which are now being employed at the front, though on a much more formidable scale; as well as by other means to be devised by the Generals on the spot. He thinks it highly probable that this may compel a retirement of the German forces to the line of the Meuse, not because their front will have been broken by assault, but because the increasing shortage of men will make it impossible for them to keep up a sufficient reserve to hold their present defensive positions.

While this heavy and continuous pressure was being exercised on the west, his hope is that the Russians would be able gradually to accumulate a force with which, some time in the summer, they might be able to gain vital successes in the east; the result of the double operation (if successful) being to bring the Central Powers to terms before the end of the year.[10]

The note quieted the dissenting voices in the War Committee for the time being. At the end of January, Lloyd George, while attending a conference in Paris, gained the impression that Joffre intended to launch a general offensive along the lines of his costly Champagne attack in 1915. But, his concerns were based on skimpy data and were brushed aside when he expressed them in the War Committee on his return.[11] While reconciling himself to the inevitable, Lloyd George tried to get the offensive postponed to June on the ground that he could not supply the BEF with heavy guns and ammunition before that period. Kitchener and Robertson, however, claimed that in view of the shaky position of Britain's allies, it was vital that the BEF participate in Joffre's general offensive, even if its preparations were not completed.

A new and unexpected development disrupted Anglo-French planning when the Germans unleashed a ferocious assault against the ancient fortress of Verdun. The attack, begun on February 21, was designed to bleed the French Army white and break its morale. With the fate of France, many thought, hanging in the balance, the purpose of the impending offensive on the Somme River changed from applying pressure on the Germans to relieving the pressure on the defenders at Verdun. There was yet another alteration in the plan. Originally the joint operations in the Somme sector had called for the French to make the main effort. However, when more and more French divisions were removed from the area and rushed to Verdun, Joffre sought to limit the extent of French collaboration. That became apparent to Robertson when he visited Joffre in March. An unhappy Robertson reported afterwards that apparently Joffre "has no idea of ever taking the offensive if he can get other people to take it for him." What was even worse, the plans for concerted action by the Allied powers appeared to be breaking down: The Russians favored an early start; the Italians, short of heavy guns and munitions, wanted an indefinite delay; and the French, staggering under the weight of the German assault at Verdun, wanted the British to carry most of the burden.[12] Kitchener's earlier support for the general offensive began to wane.[13] He doubted that Joffre would participate to any appreciable extent in the joint operations, and he also distrusted the ability of Britain's other allies to carry out their end of the bargain. He thought that it was in the interest of Britain to wait until the autumn or perhaps early 1917.[14] He welcomed the German strike against Verdun, for he was convinced that the longer the attack went on, the more likely the enemy was to use up its reserves. The delay would also permit the British to accumulate more men, munitions, and guns. Thus, a carefully prepared counterattack, delivered after the Germans had sustained massive casualties at Verdun, might achieve a breakthrough.

Coalition warfare, however, persisted in imposing restrictions on Britain's ability to control its conduct of the war. The siege against Verdun had induced Joffre to request that Sarrail, in charge of both the French and British forces, submit an offensive plan with the view of immobilizing German divisions in the Balkans. Far from supporting an offensive in the Balkans, which would have required massive reinforcements, Robertson, like Kitchener, wanted the Anglo-French divisions at Salonica transferred to the western front. He exploded when he learned that Sarrail had recommended an ambitious drive aimed at taking Sofia. "I studied the Balkan question for years," Robertson told Joffre. "The region is hell." As a result, Joffre told Sarrail to drop the idea of marching on Sofia and merely to threaten an attack in order to contain the enemy.[15] Distrustful of the French, Robertson sought to tie Sarrail's hands by reducing the force under his command. At a War Committee meeting on March 23, Robertson, backed by Kitchener, argued that the British contingent at Salonica should be reduced by one division because the existing garrison was considerably in excess of the number necessary to hold the port. Overriding the objections of Lloyd George, who claimed that it would have a demoralizing effect on the Russians and deter Romania from joining the Entente, the War Committee authorized Robertson to raise the issue with the French at the forthcoming Allied conference in Paris.[16]

Asquith, Kitchener, and Robertson attended the Allied conference, which took place in the final week of March. During a break in the proceedings, the British representatives asked to meet separately with their hosts to discuss the question of reducing Britain's presence at Salonica. On arriving at the meeting (held at the Quai d'Orsay) the British delegates found to their disgust that the slippery French had brought along the Russian Ambassador, Count A. P. Isvolsky, and Gen. Galinski. The British relied on Kitchener's prestige to plead their case. The Secretary for War pointed out that of the nearly 220,000 Allied troops in the Balkans, 118,000 were British, a sum considerably greater than their original contribution of 75,000. Thus, the government proposed to withdraw one division immediately, leaving about one hundred thousand British troops at Salonica. His justification was that it was essential to be as strong as possible on the western front, particularly in light of the severe losses suffered recently by the French Army.

Briand spoke out against the idea of reducing the garrison, claiming that the addition of one division to the troops on the western front would make little difference. Joffre agreed with Briand's position. He maintained that he had successfully resisted the German onslaught at Verdun and that the withdrawal of troops from Salonica would give the impression that he had failed, thereby losing the moral effect that he had recently gained. Robertson weighed in by stating that there were more troops in Salonica than were required for defense, yet a hugely insufficient number, by Joffre's own calculations, for an offensive. For the previous five or six months, more than two hundred thousand men had languished at Salonica without firing a shot. They had failed to bring in either Romania or Greece or to prevent the Germans from withdrawing most of their divisions from the Balkans. Joffre reacted with an extreme outburst and hinted that the

British were looking for an excuse to go back on their promise to participate in the summer offensive. Given an opportunity to speak, both Isvolsky and Galinski rallied behind the French. With the French refusing to yield an inch and tempers heating up, Asquith thought it best to bring the meeting to a close. He indicated that Britain's whole desire was to do everything possible to win the war and that, in their opinion, concentrating all available troops in France would best serve Allied interests. If, however, the French government was of a different mind, there was nothing more to say.[17] The manner in which the French had sidestepped key issues strengthened Kitchener's conviction that their insistence on remaining at Salonica was based not on any sound military reason, but on a desire to build an eastern Mediterranean empire.[18]

The frustration the British felt on leaving the conference would deepen in the months that followed. Time and time again, the British would plead with the French to abandon the sideshow in the Balkans to no avail. For the Allied Army there, the real war was waged against the malaria-carrying mosquito, and it saw no dramatic action until the Central Powers began to collapse in the autumn of 1918.[19] The size of the Allied Army swelled to six hundred thousand by 1917, draining men and supplies from more important areas of operations. As this huge force was contained by a mere one hundred fifty thousand Bulgarians, it is no wonder that the Germans jokingly referred to Salonica as "the largest internment camp in the world."

In Mesopotamia, the British faced a different dilemma, namely, how to relieve their encircled garrison at Kut. In February 1916 responsibility for the conduct of operations was transferred from the Indian government to the War Office. All rescue efforts to reach Townshend's men were turned back, and on April 25, 1916, Kitchener authorized British negotiators to open talks with the Turks. Kitchener was prepared to offer the Turks up to £1 million as ransom for the release of the Anglo-Indian defenders at Kut.[20] When the Turks rejected the offer, Townshend decided against holding out any longer and surrendered his starving and exhausted force of ten thousand on April 29.[21] Although the fall of Kut had been expected, the news still came as something of a shock to the British public. Not since the surrender of Cornwallis at Yorktown had so large a British force been captured. Asquith relied on Kitchener to placate the dejected nation with a soothing message.[22]

The surrender of Kut did not provoke a general Arab uprising as had been feared. Events closer to home quickly smothered memories of the military disaster. For Kitchener there were plenty of other distractions. In fact, while he and Robertson were struggling to find a way to free the garrison at Kut, they were faced with another hurdle at home. The War Committee, or at least some of its members, continued to have misgivings about the offensive on the Somme. It kept postponing a decision, but at the start of April, Haig, who had succeeded French as commander in chief of the BEF the previous December, forced its hand. Deeming it unseemly for the British Army to remain idle while the Germans destroyed the French Army at Verdun, Haig asked the CIGS in a letter dated April 4 for permission to proceed with the attack.[23]

Robertson fully supported Haig, as he would repeatedly during their association whether he agreed with him or not. Kitchener's relations with Haig were cordial and friendly if not warm. Haig, for all his faults, was better educated, possessed a firmer grasp of his profession, and was more temperamentally stable than his predecessor. He also showed more tact in his dealings with Kitchener. He always provided Kitchener with a guard of honor whenever he visited GHQ, took him on tours of the front, and generally treated him as a valued guest and superior. When Kitchener called on Haig at GHQ after the Allied conference in March, he warned him "to beware of the French and to husband the strength of the British Army in France."[24] Haig assured him that he would.

Robertson discussed Haig's note with Kitchener, but exactly what he said to win him over is unknown. Presumably Robertson assured Kitchener that Haig would set modest goals and use tactics designed to keep British losses to a minimum, while maximizing German casualties.

Haig's request was discussed in the War Committee on April 7. Kitchener claimed that Haig's part in the general attack, if he understood it correctly, involved intensifying the operations that were currently going on along his line. Alluding to a recent conversation with Albert Thomas, Lloyd George was convinced that Joffre had in mind an offensive "on a very big scale." Kitchener did not think that Joffre was stupid enough to repeat earlier mistakes—he gave the French general more credit than he deserved. Robertson chimed in by saying that Haig "would adjust the kind of fight which he intended to put up according to circumstances." If he were satisfied that the French intended to leave all the fighting to him, "then he would shut down at once." Robertson emphasized that Haig "was perfectly alive to the situation, and would not do any foolish thing." In the end, the War Committee reluctantly gave Haig authorization for the offensive.[25] Its members had succumbed to the pressure. As William

J. Philpott has recently noted, they "had no real control over strategy on the western front, their action as usual being determined more by alliance considerations than from knowledge or understanding of the military position in that theatre."[26]

It now remained for Haig to draw up the plans and prepare for the battle. Kitchener had no reason to suspect that Haig would misuse the BEF. Kitchener did not know, however, that Haig was aiming for a decisive victory and had no intentions of adopting cautious, methodical methods and a policy of limited objectives. Haig evidently did not understand that Britain lacked the resources to achieve his grandiose objective. The arrangement, which placed Robertson in charge of overall strategy, had created a buffer between Kitchener and British GHQ. Since Haig was not directly responsible to Kitchener, he neither disclosed his plans nor paid much heed to his admonition. Robertson, according to his most recent biographer, was equally deceived.[27] Perhaps so, but Robertson ought to have done more than simply trust Haig "not to do anything rash."[28] The two generals, unlike Kitchener and French, were on good terms, and Robertson was in a position to ensure that Haig understood the distinction between a campaign that would intensify the process of attrition and one that aimed at breaking through the German line. His failure to lay down guidelines set the stage for one of the bloodiest and most tragic British defeats of the war.

The government's commitment to the Somme offensive made it imperative to find more men for the Army. According to a memorandum produced by Robertson on March 21, 1916, the current intake of recruits was barely enough to meet normal wastage in France, let alone to allow for reinforcements to other theaters or for reserves in case of a great battle.[29] Since the autumn of 1915, Asquith had taken a series of half measures, including the drafting of bachelors, to appease Lloyd George and the Unionists and to save his ministry.[30] But, by mid-April it was apparent to Robertson that conscription must be extended to married men as well if a western strategy was to be implemented. Behind the scenes, he pressured Kitchener and lobbied politicians and the press to induce the government to accept full conscription. Kitchener would have preferred to wait until the autumn before reaching for the married men, but he had no real alternative other than to fall in line with Robertson.[31] His reputation in the Army would have been finished if he had held out. With the defection of Kitchener, Asquith bowed to the inevitable, and in May a bill conscripting all able-bodied men passed through both houses of Parliament and gained the royal assent.

Kitchener's activities in the first six months of 1916 were not confined merely to routine War Office work and to providing vital support for Robertson in the inner councils of war. Although the Cabinet had shorn Kitchener of many of his responsibilities, it continued to look to him to take the lead in formulating policy for the Middle East.

In December 1915 Sykes, back from a tour of the Middle East and India, proposed the creation of an Arab Bureau as an instrument to shape a uniform Arab policy by inducing cooperation among the various government departments. It was his hope that this agency would be independent, based in Cairo, and under his own direction.[32] Such an organization would have eliminated needless delays, confusion, interdepartmental rivalry, and duplication of work.[33] The idea met with a cool reception from the India government, which was not keen on the creation of any agency empowered to intrude into areas within its jurisdiction. In January 1916, Asquith called an interdepartmental conference at Whitehall to consider setting up a division to take charge of Arab affairs.[34] The upshot was that the conference accepted Sykes's proposal, but with major modifications. An Arab Bureau was to be established, but instead of being a separate body, it was to be merely a section of the Cairo Intelligence Department. Kitchener and the Foreign Office had insisted on this arrangement because they did not wish to surrender control in determining Middle East policy.[35]

The Arab Bureau did not begin to function for several months after January and took no part in the McMahon-Hussein negotiations. When the correspondence ended early in 1916, McMahon had not committed Britain to any specific course of action beyond assurances of an independent Arab state. One Arab nationalist dissatisfied with the way the British were conducting the negotiations was Aziz Ali al-Masri, founder and leader of al-'Ahd. It seemed to him that the British wanted Arab help to defeat the Turks, but were unwilling to pay the price. Early in February 1916, al-Masri wrote directly to Kitchener, the man whose personal intervention before the war had played a significant part in saving him from the gallows. He indicated that those for whom he spoke wanted freedom from the Turks, which they realized could only be accomplished with Britain's help. Although they were anxious to form a close alliance with the British, they did not want to be governed by them directly or indirectly through a protectorate. He warned that any attempt by foreigners to invade Arab territory would throw the Arabs in the arms of the Turks and serve only the interests of Germany. On the other hand, an Arab state, with its people left free to exercise full and genuine independence, would be an invaluable friend to Britain. Backed by a large and modern army, it would be in a position to thwart any hostile force on the way to India or Egypt. He concluded by saying that the time to act had come and that he hoped his proposals would find favor with the British authorities.[36]

There is no evidence that Kitchener wrote back to al-Masri but, if he did, it is safe to assume that his answer was couched in vague and non-committal terms. Never for a moment did he imagine that the region could or should be independent in the modern sense of the word. His concept of a Middle East under Britain's tutelage contrasted sharply with the one envisaged by al-Masri and Arab nationalists. Indeed, at the time, Kitchener was supervising active negotiations with the French regarding the postwar Middle East.

In the fall of 1915 the Foreign Office, at Kitchener's prodding, invited the French government to send representatives to London to discuss the frontiers of Syria, as well as to define their interests in the area. By then Kitchener had realized that with the British proposing to establish a protectorate in Mesopotamia, it was highly unlikely that the French would "abandon their dreams in Syria, even in return for compensation in Africa."[37] That being the case, it was necessary to delineate French aspirations, not only to be free to deal with Hussein, but also to avoid Anglo-French conflict over claims in the Ottoman Empire. Sir Arthur Nicolson headed the British delegation, while Georges Picot acted as the chief spokesman for the French. By the end of the year, the talks had deadlocked, as a result of which the Foreign Office replaced Nicolson with Mark Sykes, in effect turning over the responsibility to Kitchener.[38]

Sykes had the dual task of trying to satisfy the French and fulfilling Kitchener's mandate of securing British influence or control over Ottoman possessions strategically placed on the land routes to Egypt and India. As with his earlier service on the de Bunsen committee, he did not deal directly with Kitchener. In the evening he reported the details of the day's negotiations to FitzGerald and from him received Kitchener's directions. Writing to Sir George Arthur after Kitchener's death, Sykes described the arrangement: "[O]ne worked a sort of triangular equation, I acted, FitzGerald spoke, he inspired."[39] Still, it was an awkward system and one that invited misunderstandings about what Sykes was instructed to demand and what he was told he could concede. Oddly enough, Sykes preferred to work through FitzGerald, as this statement from the afore-mentioned letter attests: "The less I saw of him [Kitchener] the easier it was to do what he required; you will understand this, but I am afraid—except poor FitzGerald—no one else could."[40]

Central to Kitchener's plan for Britain's domination of the postwar east was the creation of a French sphere that would provide Britain with a shield against a Russian attack from the north. For that reason, he favored conceding to the French a zone that would adjoin and run parallel to Russia, extending from the Mediterranean coast in the west all the way to Mosul in the east. The final Sykes-Picot draft was roughly based on the recommendations of the de Bunsen committee. The most notable difference was that the committee had included Mosul, believed to be rich in oil deposits, within the British sphere. Kitchener did not relish handing over Mosul to the French, but in doing so, he was placing them in the front line. The city was located in an area where the Russians might be expected to attack one day.[41] On February 4, 1916, Kitchener, Grey, and representatives of the India Office approved the agreement Sykes had negotiated with Picot.[42]

The Sykes-Picot agreement is one of the most controversial documents of the war, for it appears to contravene some of the pledges Britain had made to Hussein. That the two understandings often tallied is often overlooked, but it is equally true that there were quite substantial differences on three main points: First, Hussein was not told about the enclave containing the ports of Haifa and Acre, which the Sykes-Picot agreement accorded to the British; second, Hussein was led to believe that the interior of Syria would be wholly independent, but, as it turned out, the French, with Britain's blessing, were to have a measure of supervision over it; and finally, McMahon was unclear about the future status of Palestine, but, according to the deal between Sykes and Picot, part of it was to be placed under an international administration.[43]

To what extent Kitchener was aware of the incompatibility between the commitments to Hussein and those to the French must remain a matter of conjecture. Magnus believes that, while Kitchener had personally supervised every detail of the arrangement worked out with the French, he did not devote equal attention to the negotiations with the Arabs.[44] There are others who feel that Kitchener, preoccupied with a host of problems, not the least of which was trying to counteract the repercussions of British defeats in Gallipoli and Mesopotamia, was too busy to compare carefully the promises made to the Arabs with the Sykes-Picot agreement. In my opinion, both assumptions are off the mark. Kitchener had not only supervised the British end of the negotiations with Picot, but he was also at a meeting in the Foreign Office on February 4, 1916, when the final draft was accepted. An examination of the archives, furthermore, shows that Kitchener had read all the letters exchanged between McMahon and Hussein, as well as analyses of the correspondence by a host of Middle East experts both in London and Cairo. He could not help but know of the implicit promise to grant the Arabs Damascus and its hinterland. The probable explanation is that Kitchener did not think that the differences were all that great, however significant they appear by today's standards. There would be ample opportunity at the peace negotiations to repair the conflicting accords and, if necessary, for London to impose an arrangement. Presumably, Kitchener recognized that it would not benefit the British if, in securing the adhesion of the Sharif, they alienated France. In terms of winning the war, the French were far more important than Hussein, a tribal chief bringing with him limited resources and an uncertain prospect of subverting Ottoman rule.

Hussein had been warned about French designs in Syria, but he was apparently unaware of the extent to which the British had gone to accommodate them. How would he have reacted if he had known? It is a safe bet that he would have protested vigorously, but it is equally certain that ultimately he would not have turned his back on the British. Hussein was ill placed to charge the British with perfidy and betrayal, as many Arab nationalists have since done.[45] At best, he was himself guilty of playing both ends against the middle. While he was negotiating with Cairo, he was carrying on parallel talks with Constantinople, seeking to reach an accommodation with the Turks that would assure both autonomy for Hejaz and hereditary succession for his line.[46] In any case, his policy was one of stalling, avoiding a break with Constantinople, and collecting bribes from both sides. Suspecting, however, that he was in imminent danger of being ousted by the Ottomans threw him into hasty and improvised action and drove him to strike first. On June 5, 1916, he formally proclaimed the independence of his kingdom and raised the standard of revolt. Unaware of the real reason for the rebellion, the British congratulated themselves for what they considered to be their own handiwork—their "tactic of dangling vague but grandiose prospects of future glory" in front of Hussein.[47]

Another area that continued to absorb Kitchener's attention was Russia, without the help of which, he was convinced, the Entente stood little chance of winning the war. The summer of 1915 had been disastrous for the Russian armies, which, in the face of the Austro-German juggernaut, had been compelled to abandon one fortress after another. It must have seemed to Kitchener as if the Russian retreat would never end. By September, the Central Powers had advanced three hundred miles at the farthest point, occupied Russian Poland, taken an estimated one million prisoners, and inflicted almost as many casualties. Kitchener was concerned not by the loss of territory, itself insignificant considering the vast expanse of Russia, but by the possibility that the Russian Army might collapse. His informants in Russia had warned him about the shortcomings of Russian commanders, the massive corruption pervading both the political and military systems, the inadequacy of the transport network, the woeful shortages of weapons, ammunition, and supplies of every kind, and the sinking morale among the rank and file.

Grand Duke Nicholas was not a great soldier, but he had conducted the retreat with considerable skill, avoiding encirclement and preserving most of his armies. But the magnitude of the Russian disaster cried out for a scapegoat, and in these circumstances, it was inevitable that the axe should fall on the Commander in Chief. Dismissing the grand duke, the Tsar assumed personal command of the Russian armies and left for the front on September 5. The actual direction of the war fell on the new chief of staff, Gen. Mikhail Alekseev, whose reputation as a scientific soldier was offset by his bland personality, inability to delegate work, and indecision.[48] Kitchener regretted the departure of the grand duke, whom he respected as a hard-working, honest, and capable soldier. He agreed with his men on the spot that the Tsar was taking a great gamble by tying himself directly to the direction of the war.

The change in command happily coincided with the slackening pace of the Austro-German offensive. The forces of the Central Powers were weary after their rapid advance and had outrun their supplies. With winter approaching, Gen. Erich Falkenhayn, the Supreme German Commander, closed down the operation at the end of September. He had no wish to repeat Napoleon's mistake. Battered though the Russian armies were, they had not been destroyed and were still in the war. The front stabilized along a six-hundred-mile line that stretched from Riga on the Baltic to Czernowitz on the Romanian border.

Kitchener appreciated that what the Russians needed above all was breathing space, while their armies reorganized and reequipped. As he was anxious to find out the state of their armies, he sent Wolfe-Murray on a fact-finding mission to Russia in November 1915. Wolfe-Murray's report on November 21 was encouraging. He had visited three fronts and inspected infantry units that he estimated were at between 50 and 60 percent of full establishment. All the same, wherever he went, he had been impressed by the confidence and esprit de corps of both officers and men, all of whom seemed persuaded that they "will be able to drive the Germans back when they are fully armed and equipped." The Russians, he added, had learned from past mistakes. They had constructed prepared lines of defense in the rear in case they were driven out of their positions at the front. The only problem area he could detect was in the operation of the railway system, where excessive congestion, owing to mismanagement, frequently inhibited the movement of goods.[49]

Wolfe-Murray also indicated that the Russian armies were well supplied: Artillery ammunition was said to be adequate for defensive purposes, and no limit was placed on its expenditure. This revelation must have seemed odd to Kitchener, given that the Russian authorities had recently made demands for weapons and munitions that were inordinately large. In any case there was a limit to what the British could produce, and it was impossible for them to equip the Russians and the New Armies simultaneously. Kitchener was willing to go far to help the Russians, but not to the extent of siphoning off huge quantities of armaments earmarked for the New Armies.

Nevertheless, Kitchener could not ignore the plight of the Russians, even though he was annoyed by their frequent hints that the British were being selfish or parsimonious. They grumbled that of all the orders placed abroad on their behalf, only a fraction had come in—1.3 million rounds by the end of 1915—and the total number of rifles for the same period was equally dismal according to a reliable study.[50] It was hardly Kitchener's fault that the Russians were excessively tardy in acknowledging their munitions shortages, with the result that armament manufacturers could not attend to their requests until they had cleared the backlog of orders. He could not be blamed if firms had accepted more contracts than they could handle. Nor could he be held accountable for the manner in which the Russians conducted business. He had taken great pains to cut through their Byzantine practices in placing orders. Yet, they resisted adapting to new procedures, took forever to reach decisions, and proved difficult and uncooperative in dealings with arms manufacturers in the United States.[51] It was apparent that a new arrangement would have to be worked out with them.

In the autumn of 1915, Kitchener tried to persuade the Ministry of Munitions to limit its armament purchases in the United States to what the military authorities considered necessary. As matters stood, the War Office could do little to assist Russia. According to von Donop, British armament firms were fully occupied with meeting "the 'minimum' needs of the British army for 1916."[52] As for the United States, factories there also were occupied fully with British orders. Supplies for Russia might, however, be forthcoming if the Ministry of Munitions released resources beyond the requirements of the British Army.[53] Lloyd George's ministry deemed the proposal impractical on the grounds that there was no scientific way to calculate Britain's future needs or to ensure that contractors made deliveries on time. The general attitude was that Britain would not be hampered by having too many guns, but that it could lose the war by having too few. In short, Russia would have to be content only with such resources as did not impinge on British needs, real or potential.[54]

No less important to Kitchener than procuring supplies for Russia was the need to coordinate Russia's military plans with those of its allies on the western front. It was counterproductive for each commander in chief to initiate operations on his own front whenever he deemed it desirable, regardless of whether it was strategically sound. The object for the Allies should be to treat the war as a common front and to attack simultaneously after devising a plan that offered the best opportunity to defeat the enemy. During the summer of 1915, Kitchener approached the Russian high command, which after some hesitation—loath as always to disclose its future plans—agreed to discuss the matter with the British and French military attachés. However, the French military attaché, General de Laguiche, out of a desire to magnify his own position at the expense of his British counterpart, refused to assist in any such combined effort, saying that he could obtain or impart all information he wished through the medium of the grand duke himself. De Laguiche was able to ingratiate himself with Nicholas by representing Joffre as commander of both the BEF and the French Army. When the grand duke was replaced, de Laguiche lost his high standing at the *Stavka*, and the new administration showed itself more receptive to suggestions of inter-Allied cooperation.[55] The upshot was that in November and December a series of conferences was held at Chantilly, aiming to ensure that Allied policy in 1916 would be better coordinated than in the past.

At the close of 1915, Kitchener surrendered control of strategy to Robertson, but retained responsibility for the purchase of munitions for Russia. Through Hanbury Williams and others, he kept abreast of Russia's munitions needs and of events in the country. If he detected a problem, such as the unsatisfactory state of Russia's railway system, he asked for more details and urged that the matter be brought to the attention of the Emperor.[56] Whenever a War Office representative went on a mission to Russia to gather information, Kitchener requested that a personal message from him be delivered to the Emperor and to the High Command. A case in point was Callwell's visit in February 1916, when he carried with him an exposition of Kitchener's "views as to the future" and a hint that Britain's command of the seas did not mean that it could provide Russia with unlimited shipping or freely undertake operations in distant theaters.[57] The Russians were more receptive to advice or criticism from Kitchener than from any other Allied official. They held him in awe, partly because of his accomplishments at home and partly because of his relentless efforts on behalf of Russia. Callwell recorded the following after an interview with the Tsar:

> Of Lord Kitchener and his work he spoke with admiration, and he asked me many questions about the New Armies, their equipment, their training, their numbers and so on. He talked with wonder of what our great War Minister had accomplished in the direction of transforming the United Kingdom into a first-class military Power in less than a year. In this respect he, however, merely reflected the opinion held in military circles right throughout Russia; one heard on all hands eulogy of the miracles that had been accomplished in this direction. His Imperial Majesty was also most appreciative of what our War Office was doing towards assisting the Russians in the all-important matter of war material, and he asked me to convey his thanks to all concerned for their loyalty and good offices.[58]

All in all, Kitchener felt better about Britain's improved relations with Russia in the early months of 1916. Agreement had been reached, not only for inter-Allied military cooperation, but also on a mechanism to provide financial aid to Russia and on a new method to control the purchase of its munitions abroad. The new Russian military regime was more sensitive than the previous one to the importance of anticipating future munitions needs and the length of time that must elapse between the placing of orders and the date of delivery. Other Allied countries, like France and Japan, took some weight off Britain's shoulders by supplying more of Russia's armament requirements. Thus, the reduction of contentious issues, or the creation of regular means of dealing with them, resulted in a level of harmony that had not existed since the start of the war.[59]

By the spring of 1916, conditions in the Russian Army, in respect to munitions and morale, had improved enough to permit the *Stavka* to launch an unscheduled and, as it turned out, ill-fated offensive against the Central Powers in the Lake Naroch region. Designed to ease pressure on the French at Verdun, it was undertaken without informing the British authorities in advance. The incident annoyed Kitchener and Robertson, who questioned whether the Russians could be relied on to adhere to the agreement reached earlier at Chantilly. Inside the *Stavka*, the battle at Lake Narotch shook the confidence of Russian planners, many of whom became convinced that victory could be achieved only after they had attained an overwhelming superiority in matériel. Russia's burgeoning military needs were fueled by requests for large amounts of goods unrelated to the war effort. "They want us to put a big bag of money on their doorsteps," Knox reported, "and then run away."[60] The British, however, were unable to aid Russia to the desired extent because of their increasing independence on the United States for loans and war matériel. The Russians were under the impression that Britain possessed infinite manufacturing capacity and inexhaustible credit. When their demands often went unanswered, they attributed it unjustly to their ally's insensitivity.[61]

Russia's continuing demands for further credits prompted the Chancellor of the Exchequer, Reginald McKenna, to raise the issue in the War Committee on May 4. McKenna indicated that the country was approaching a financial crisis. He noted that £54 million granted to Russia the previous September had already been spent on new contracts, that a further loan of £24.7 million had been urgently requested, and that inquiries about obtaining an additional £24 million had recently reached his office, making a total of £102 million. Added to this figure were the ever-increasing requests from France for huge loans. If more money were lent to Russia, Britain would be unable to meet its own liabilities and would face bankruptcy. He issued a stern warning that "if we go on at the present rate," the moment "will come when I shall have to state to this Committee that in three or four months' time we must make peace."

Kitchener agreed that, while some check must be imposed on Russia, Britain could not stop lending it money altogether. He recommended that a committee be set up to control Russia's purchases, canceling its less pressing needs. Such an expedient, McKenna judged, would prove unworkable. Instead, he recommended sending an emissary of the highest status to Russia to determine its armies' most vital needs and to explain the "essential connection between British finance and the cause of the Allies as a whole." The idea caught on immediately, and one or two names were bandied about before McKenna turned to Kitchener and asked him if he would be interested in heading a mission. Kitchener asked for time to think it over, even though he was eager to go.[62]

Kitchener had been worried by reports received through the French government at the end of April that there was a serious shortage of munitions in Russia. The French had reason to believe that despite this shortage, the Russians intended to mount an offensive in the near future, and the fear in Paris was that they would waste what ammunition they had and repeat earlier defeats.[63] Kitchener looked upon the proposed mission not only as a means to reach an understanding with the Russians over finance and supplies, but also to iron out strategic differences and ascertain the condition of their armaments.

With security notoriously lax in London, Benckendorff picked up rumors that the Cabinet was thinking of sending Kitchener to Russia and relayed this information to Petrograd. On May 14, Kitchener, to his surprise, received a formal invitation from the Tsar to visit Russia.[64] Kitchener thanked the Tsar for his gracious invitation, but a final decision was postponed pending Asquith's return from Ireland, where he had been drawn by events arising out of the Easter Rebellion.[65] On May 26, the Cabinet sanctioned Kitchener's mission, and on the same day he communicated his acceptance of the Tsar's invitation. Kitchener planned on staying a week in Russia, where he hoped to visit the *Stavka* and a portion of the front, before moving on to Petrograd to deal with the outstanding questions.[66]

Kitchener looked forward to his Russian trip, which would afford him relief from the labors of his office and from a renewed wave of political criticism directed against his methods of running the war. On May 31, Sir Ivor Herbert MP, undoubtedly at the instigation of the Conservative leadership, which had not forgiven Kitchener's stand on conscription, moved that the salary of the Secretary of State for War be reduced by £100—the traditional procedure for the House of Commons to open a censure debate on a particular minister. Herbert and his allies portrayed Kitchener as incompetent, obstinate, and wholly lacking in brains. In an eloquent speech, punctuated by loud cheers and applause, Asquith defended Kitchener, emphasizing his list of accomplishments and reproving his critics. The motion was easily defeated. Forewarned of the attack, Kitchener sprang a surprise. He announced, through H. J. Tennant, the Undersecretary for War, that he would he happy to meet members of the House on Friday, June 2, for an informal briefing session. It was a rare event when Kitchener spoke in public. He avoided it as much as possible for a number of reasons: his knowledge that he was no orator, his secretive nature, and his fear that in the course of a debate he might inadvertently reveal classified information. The meeting was originally scheduled to take place in the War Office, but so many MPs expressed a desire to attend that it was moved to a large committee room in the House.[67]

Accompanied by Robertson, Kitchener was in his field marshal's blue undress uniform when he arrived at Westminster shortly before 11:30 A.M. on June 2. He strode into the committee room, put on his spectacles, and addressed the packed assembly from a carefully prepared statement. He opened his remarks by reminding the members that his previous work in life "had not been of a kind to make me into a ready debater nor to prepare me for the various turns and twists in argument," and he hoped that they would "overlook any of my shortcomings in this respect."[68] He proceeded to discuss the huge problems he faced at the outset, particularly in raising, clothing, and equipping the New Armies, and the means by which most of these had been solved or nearly so. He explained that he had refrained from taking the lead in urging compulsion because such a question of social change "running counter to the most ancient traditions of the British people" was for the Cabinet, not himself, to decide. His speech, delivered calmly but confidently, was a brilliant defense of his administration. At the end, he took questions from the floor, answering frankly and cordially, which surprised and charmed his critics. Kitchener had feared that he might be heckled and get flustered, but he had carried the House with him, evoking prolonged applause. A vote of thanks, proposed by a Labor MP and seconded by the very man who had initiated the censure proceedings, passed unanimously.[69]

Kitchener, having handled a potentially embarrassing situation with the skill of a seasoned politician, left the House in the highest of spirits. That evening he visited 10 Downing Street to bid the Prime Minister farewell and took a boyish delight in telling him of his happy encounter with the parliamentarians.[70] The Cabinet ministers, however, were less than happy over Kitchener's personal triumph, which had capped an upturn in his political fortunes. He had regained much of his influence in the Cabinet because of his partnership with Robertson, his standing with parliamentarians was as high as ever, and he continued to dominate Allied conferences, as well as to enjoy the immense confidence of his sovereign and that of the British public. One Cabinet minister lamented that, in his view, Kitchener "was more firmly seated than ever."[71]

Kitchener spent Saturday morning at the War Office, then left to lunch with the King. That afternoon, he motored to Broome Park with FitzGerald. Renovations on the mansion were nearing completion and furniture was gradually filling the rooms. After attending Sunday service at Barham Church, he worked part of the morning in his sunken rose garden, at the center of which he intended to place an ornate fountain with four bronze statues at the corners of the square. In the afternoon, he was back at the War Office, where he took care of some personal matters and put his signature to a pile of official papers. Business done, he asked Arthur to have tea with him and to accompany him in his car to the station.

At King's Cross, Kitchener boarded a special carriage, which had been attached to the overnight express to Edinburgh. On arrival early next morning, he and his party continued on to Thurso and, from there, a short sea journey in pouring rain took them across Pentland Firth to the naval base at Scapa Flow. Adm. Jellicoe, who only a few days before had engaged the German High Sea Fleet in an indecisive battle off the coast of Jutland, welcomed them, as they were piped aboard his flagship, the *Iron Duke*. Kitchener told Jellicoe the purpose of his mission to Russia and insisted that he must be back in Britain in three weeks' time. He did not think that he could achieve much, but looked forward to his forthcoming trip as a sort of holiday. Jellicoe later wrote, "The strain of the last two years, he confessed, had been very great, adding that he had felt that he could not have gone on without this break, which he welcomed very much."[72]

After lunch, Kitchener was taken on a tour of the vast battleship. He watched the various drills going on, inspected gun turrets, and was shown the operating techniques of the wireless telegraph. Although Kitchener's visit had been kept secret, the sailors recognized him as soon as they caught sight of him and, wherever he went, greeted him with spontaneous ovations.

All day the weather was miserable with the rains coming down in torrents. The water was rough, for a gale was blowing from the northeast. Kitchener was a good sailor, and he would not wait until the heavy winds moderated, as Jellicoe had suggested. The planned northeasterly route from Scapa Flow made it impossible for the escorting destroyers heading into the extreme force of the gale to keep up with Kitchener's designated cruiser, the *Hampshire*. Instead, Jellicoe selected a westabout passage, sailing through the Pentland Firth, then north, close to the western coast of the Orkney Islands. Jellicoe's reasoning was that this course would provide a lee from the gale, allowing the destroyers to keep pace with the *Hampshire* and to screen it against submarine attack.[73] Jellicoe did not know that on the night of May 28, 1916 (just before the battle of Jutland), a German U-boat, commanded by Kurt Beitzen, had laid a group of mines off the west coast of the Orkneys, along the route he had chosen for the *Hampshire*. The U-boat's object was to block one of the exits from Scapa Flow. The German fleet was preparing to enter the North Sea, where it was certain to be intercepted by the Royal Navy. The fewer units of the Royal Navy it encountered, the better its chances of success.

Shortly after 4:00 P.M. Kitchener left the flagship and transferred to the *Hampshire* on a small trawler. At 4:45 P.M. the *Hampshire* slipped from its moorings, sailed out of Scapa Flow towards the stormy waters of the Pentland Firth, and an hour later met its two escorting destroyers, *Unity* and *Victor*. As the ships turned northwest along the coast, the gale increased in violence and shifted. Instead of the lee from the island, the group faced the fury of the gale head on with the result that the destroyers fell further and further behind the faster and more powerful cruiser. Since it was unlikely that enemy submarines would be operating in such heavy seas, Capt. H. J. Savill, commander of the *Hampshire*, ordered the destroyers to return to base—a regrettable decision as it turned out.[74] Continuing alone on course and pitching steeply in the huge waves, the *Hampshire* was about a mile and a half off Marwick Head, when it was rocked by a violent explosion around 7:40 P.M. and heeled over to starboard.

Kitchener emerged from his cabin and made his way to the quarterdeck. The blast had torn a hole in the cruiser's bottom between the bows and bridge, and there was no hope that it could be saved. Worst still, the lifeboats that were lowered were smashed on the side of the ship by the fury of the enormous waves. Kitchener looked on impassively, while preparations were made to abandon the ship. Savill called on Kitchener to get into one of the lifeboats, but either he did not hear him or saw no point in doing so. A quarter of an hour after the explosion, the stern suddenly rose high and the ship almost somersaulted, as it slipped beneath the waves. Out of more than six hundred men on board, only twelve on two

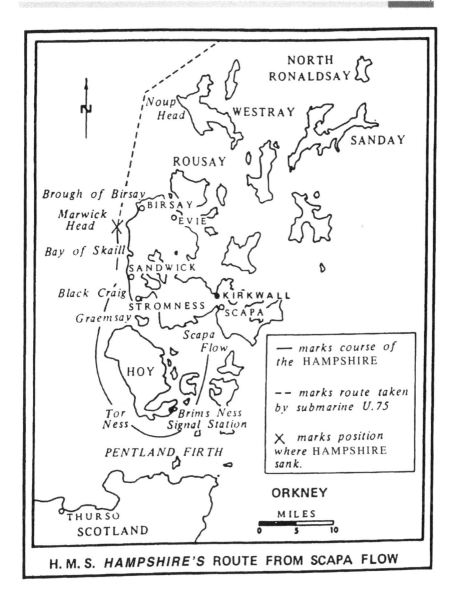

H. M. S. *HAMPSHIRE'S* ROUTE FROM SCAPA FLOW

carley rafts managed to reach the rockbound shore alive. FitzGerald's body was recovered, but Kitchener's was never found.

News of Kitchener's death reached London at midday on June 6, provoking a mixture of stunned disbelief and monumental despair. Before the announcement, the public assumed he was still in London, as his trip to

Russia had been a closely guarded secret. Not since the death of Queen Victoria had there been such a national outpouring of grief. Lloyd George would write two decades later, "The tidings of the German advance of March 1918 did not send such a shudder of despair through Britain as did the news of the tragic end of this remarkable man."[75] For many, the shock, heightened by the uncertainty of the outcome of the war, was simply too great to accept. As Trevor Royle has observed, "it seemed that the center had been torn out of their lives, that a rock-like presence had crumbled, leaving them alone in a world which was suddenly unsure and unsafe."[76] Stores closed for the rest of the day, the blinds at the War Office and the Admiralty were drawn, and throughout the country flags were lowered to half-mast. London was deluged by messages of condolences from every corner of the Allied and neutral worlds.

A memorial service, attended by the King and Queen, Kitchener's family and friends, eminent representatives of the services, and members of Parliament, was held at St Paul's Cathedral on June 15, 1916. The mood was somber and restrained. As was to be expected, friends and dignitaries delivered touching eulogies, emphasizing Kitchener's patriotism, dedication, and qualities as a man. His colleagues were equally generous in their tributes, even if they did not mean most of what they said. They avoided any hint of criticism, concentrating instead on his triumphs, his leadership, and his role in creating the means to fight and win the war. Balfour's speech, one of the most eloquent, ended on a fitting note: "He died, as he lived, in work which he was doing for his country."[77]

15

KITCHENER'S LEGACY IN THE GREAT WAR

ITCHENER was an enigma to his contemporaries and has remained a puzzle to historians. To this day, there are aspects of his life that are unknown or unclear to us. He was antisocial and rarely gave interviews or committed his feelings to paper. He discouraged close acquaintance, and only a few chosen friends were privy to his innermost thoughts. Even if he had survived the war, it is unlikely that he would have written his memoirs in retirement. Secure in himself, at no time did he feel the need to justify his actions, content to leave that to the judgment of history. In a note intended for Esher, written shortly before he died (but never completed), Kitchener said, "I believe that, in time—though perhaps not in our time—facts will establish themselves and will prove themselves the true witness of those who had steadfastly looked to the larger issues of the war."[1]

Posterity's treatment of Kitchener, at least so far, has been unkind. The war was barely over when Sir John French lashed out at Kitchener in his book *1914*, but most of his wild accusations were so obviously untruthful and easily refutable that the old cavalryman was rebuffed by critics, emerging with his character and reputation irreparably damaged. Less than two years later, Kitchener's fair-weather friend, Lord Esher, produced *The Tragedy of Lord Kitchener*, a mean-spirited and disparaging account of the field marshal's tenure at the War Office. Esher, who, as Lord

Derby has observed, was trusted by Kitchener and owed much to him, "seemed to go out of his way to pick out all that was detrimental to Kitchener in the administration of the War Office and nothing that was good."[2] Specifically, Esher claimed that physically and mentally the field marshal was past his prime, that complicated and interwoven detail overwhelmed him, and that he wavered and proved indecisive in military matters. One wonders how Esher could reconcile this unflattering portrait of Kitchener with the many entries in his war diary singing the praise of the field marshal[3] and with what he told Balfour in January 1916, "My journals of the War are assuming formidable proportions. Looking back through them, you will be surprised to see how well K. comes through this ordeal."[4] Since denigrating Kitchener had become fashionable in high political circles, Esher had no compunction about betraying his friend's memory, if he could advance closer to the center of power.

Open season for attacking Kitchener came with the publication of the memoirs and recollections of his colleagues. It was easy to blame him for most of the mistakes committed by the government, as he could not answer the charges brought against him. To be sure, like any man in a position of responsibility, Kitchener made mistakes, some, it must be added, because so much of what was required had to be improvised owing to the nation's unpreparedness. It is equally true that he was, to some extent, hampered by his own operating methods. Nevertheless, his occasional misjudgments pale in comparison to his accomplishments. Much of the criticism of Kitchener was unwarranted, born of personal dislike for his personality, authoritarian style, and prejudices.

In a selectively documented case, Churchill tried hard to convince an uninformed British public that but for Kitchener, the Dardanelles campaign would have succeeded. Balfour, who, according to a close friend, regarded verbal dexterity as a measure of a person's intelligence,[5] described Kitchener "as a stupid man," able to accomplish only "little things."[6] Probably the most damaging blow to Kitchener's reputation came at the hands of Lloyd George. According to his peculiar thesis, Kitchener's stock of vitality had been burned out by great tasks accomplished under a tropical sun, that is, in conditions alien to men born and bred in temperate climates. There were moments of blinding light, like the creation of the New Armies, but these were rare and followed by long periods of utter darkness. Kitchener was castigated for his secretive ways, for his imperious assumption of complete authority, for being a plodding soldier unreceptive to advice, and for his inability to grapple with the complexities of a global war.

However, with rare exception, all those who had worked closely with Kitchener and knew him best thought differently of his character and ability. In his memoirs, Storrs would write in stirring Churchillian prose about his former boss:

> By any who had the good fortune to enjoy in close association his confidence, his ready and humorous adoption of constructive suggestions and the free hand he accorded, with entire absence of fussing over detail, for their carrying out, his loyal and constant support . . . he will . . . be gratefully remembered as the Perfect Chief.[7]

Callwell called him "the greatest of our War Ministers."[8] "Kitchener was a great man," was Booth's conclusion. "He was inexplicable at times, but he really knew the big things."[9] Robertson, who did not realize how valuable Kitchener's help was until deprived of it, would recall in 1921 that the field marshal gave him much constructive assistance at the War Office and in the councils of war and that he "had the wonderful knack of being right in the things that really mattered." Robertson went on to say:

> Like some other great men Lord Kitchener was exacting, and had no use whatever for those who raised petty difficulties at a time when prompt action was required; while . . . he was as ready to listen to the advice of his department heads as were any of the seven Secretaries of State under whom I have worked. Nor did he disclose any sign of that ruthless and domineering disposition attributed to him by those who wished to injure his good name. On the contrary, he was a kind and delightful chief to serve, once his ways were understood; and I know that he many times stood up against opposition in high quarters so as to protect officers who were threatened with unfair treatment.[10]

These laudatory assessments of Kitchener have had little impact on the modern scholarly community, which generally holds him in low esteem. With a few exceptions, most historians view him as a bungler who mismanaged a great war, sharing the blame with incompetent generals for callously sacrificing an entire generation of Britain's young men to no good purpose. John Gooch considers Kitchener's appointment as secretary for war "a grave mistake—perhaps Asquith's greatest during his wartime period of office."[11] Kitchener's stewardship of the War Office, John Grigg writes, "turned out to be disastrous."[12] To Paul Guinn, Kitchener "was an ageing ignorant man armed only with a giant reputation."[13] William Philpott is in step with the prevailing consensus "that Kitchener was not the right man for the job."[14] The list is endless.

What I find puzzling among Kitchener's detractors is why they merely gloss over his record of accomplishments as if they were inconsequential, while dwelling on, and at times magnifying, his mistakes. Nor do they take into consideration the complexities of events, the limited scope for decisive influence, and, in the final analysis, what mistakes would have been made by the Cabinet had someone other than Kitchener been at the War Office. In some cases it is sheer ignorance, but many of these writers have spent a good part of their careers studying World War I. One recent Kitchener biographer believes that the deeds of the man considered the "apotheosis of the Victorian hero" while alive "now strike a discordant note" in a country that has rejected its imperial past.[15] Be that as it may, it is clearly improper to evaluate a historical figure by standards other than those of his age—just as it would be inappropriate, for example, to debunk George Washington's presidency because he owned slaves. At any rate, such critical judgments as cited immediately above are disproved by the broad facts. Kitchener's contribution to the war was not merely significant, it was decisive.

Recognizing that the existing military organization was wholly inadequate for the type of war Britain faced, Kitchener persuaded the government and the public to prepare for a prolonged struggle. He took immediate steps to build a continental-sized army, found the means to train, house, and equip the recruits, and laid the foundation for a gigantic expansion of armaments and munitions. He envisaged that the New Armies would reach their peak strength in 1917, by which time the Continental powers would have exhausted themselves in a series of battles of attrition. Britain, with its army relatively intact, would be in a position to win the war and impose its own terms on Allies and enemies alike. Thus, the period between 1914 and 1917 would be one of preparation, holding the Alliance together, husbanding Britain's manpower, and helping whittle down Germany's strength.

During the months that Kitchener was in total control of Britain's war effort, he won high praise from his colleagues. Asquith would tell Venetia Stanley, "My own opinion of K's capacity increases daily: I think he is a really fine soldier, and he keeps his head and temper, and above all equability wonderfully, considering how all three are tried."[16] Even Lloyd George admitted early in 1915 that Kitchener was "a big man and the best for the job."[17]

The vast, if undefined, powers Kitchener exercised in the opening months of the war were not derived officially from Parliament, but delegated to him informally by the Cabinet. Had Kitchener been allowed to continue to formulate policy, the evidence strongly suggests that he would have pushed for an active-defensive posture in the west in the spring of 1915, while arranging with the Admiralty a limited, but practical, operation against a soft area of the Ottoman Empire. A sideshow, such as the proposed landing at Alexandretta, where the local population could have rendered assistance, might have drained Ottoman resources without the sacrifice of much British blood. Unfortunately for Kitchener, his strategy began to unravel when the politicians decided to take an active part in determining the future course of the war. Outgunned by the politicians' rhetoric, Kitchener tried his best to block their dangerous ideas or repair their blunders—such as his ill-advised effort to pull the Admiralty's chestnuts out of the Dardanelles fire—as he struggled unsuccessfully to hold his strategy together. As 1915 wore on, with one military defeat following another, the politicians saw this as evidence of Kitchener's mismanagement, rather than the outcome of their interference, and reacted by stripping him of much of his power.

Kitchener was to some extent at fault for the view held by his colleagues that his strategy was incoherent. Secretive by nature and distrustful of their discretion, he would not take them into his confidence, so that his military pronouncements seemed oracular in nature, rather the product of reasoned judgment. But much of the blame lay with the politicians themselves, who wanted instant results and closed their ears to calls for patience. Distraught that the generals were throwing away British lives in the grim war of attrition in the west, the politicians, brilliant at their own game, but novices when it came to strategy, looked for a way to strike the enemy from another direction and deliver a blow that would end the war quickly and cheaply. It was no use for Kitchener to tell them that there was no shortcut to victory, that the war could only be won by defeating the German Army on the western front, and that in the wearing-down process, heavy casualties had to be anticipated and endured. Unless the Allies were willing to pay the piper and attack the Germans, a victory would have to be postponed indefinitely, perhaps permanently.

The politicians felt that Germany could be brought down, to use

Lloyd George's words, by eliminating its "props" or allies, an approach that had no relation to reality. It was Germany that propped up its allies, not the other way around. The Cabinet's collective insight led to a series of unrelated and incoherent peripheral operations, begun without a thorough analysis of probable consequences and costs and fought with leftover forces. The three sideshows in the east—the Dardanelles, Mesopotamia, and Salonica—together with the colonial campaign in East Africa, absorbed well over a million men and contributed nothing to the defeat of Germany.

What was needed at the helm during this period was a commanding prime minister. Asquith allowed the same leisurely methods of discussion in the inner councils of war as he had in the Cabinet in time of peace. He never understood that a major war could not be run effectively by committee. Well might Lord Sydenham, a contemporary of Asquith, write in hindsight, "A fluctuating Committee of eleven or twelve members, largely preoccupied with other work, for the most part unaccustomed to study naval and military questions, and depending ultimately on the acquiescence of the whole Cabinet, is necessarily incapable of directing the greatest of wars."[18] Men of powerful mentality and ardent temperament, such as Churchill and Lloyd George, required a restraining hand to curb their more erratic impulses before leading others down the primrose path. It was Asquith's responsibility to step in when things threatened to get out of hand and impose his will. By throwing his support unequivocally behind Kitchener, he would have averted delays, confusion, acrimony, and unsound adventures, which consumed massive resources that would have been better employed elsewhere.

Kitchener's influence over strategy waned not only because of Asquith's lack of leadership, but because he had no way of controlling events on the Continent. He was compelled to rely on an incompetent and choleric commander in chief, whom he could not replace. He was further hampered by the need to reconcile national interests and alliance obligations. It was a difficult balancing act. Kitchener believed, somewhat unrealistically, that it was possible to leave the brunt of the fighting to the French and Russians, while the British Army engaged in defensive attrition and waited for the Germans to dash themselves to pieces against carefully prepared positions. He overestimated the resilience and patience of his Allies, who chafed at British inaction, while the enemy remained in occupation of large parts of their territory. By the autumn of 1915, the need to hold the Entente together in the face of German peace overtures induced Kitchener to commit large numbers of British forces to future military operations in the west. Still, had Kitchener returned from his Russian journey, it seems unlikely, given his determination to avoid squandering British lives for no purpose, that he would have tolerated the slaughter that occurred in 1916 and 1917 under Haig's offensive attrition policy.

On the whole Kitchener enjoyed cordial relations with both the French and Russians. In his interaction with the demanding French generals, his fluency in their language and commanding personality stood him in good stead. "That he was not always successful is only to be expected," wrote one historian, "although without his guiding hand it might be surmised that Great Britain's policy would have been both less consistent and less forcibly championed."[19] Since Russia was the linchpin of Kitchener's strategy, he was unflagging in his determination to provide its army with armaments from western countries. While the Russians were slow to place orders, rarely made their needs clear, and clung to purchasing methods so chaotic as to preclude close liaison with the War Office over munitions, Kitchener showed extraordinary patience with them and eventually earned their respect and gratitude.

After all that has been said, what should we make of Kitchener's legacy as secretary for war? It is my contention that the stream of criticism heaped on Kitchener by contemporaries and modern writers is wholly unjustified. On the contrary, he deserves high praise. Indeed, if we take into account that the nation was unprepared for a long conflict and that he was confronted with many unprecedented obstacles, his record of achievements is all the more remarkable. In August 1914, he provided badly needed unity to a nation that had become disillusioned with its political leadership after several years of social and industrial disturbances and inspired the same sort of confidence that Churchill provided a quarter of a century later. He set the proper tone for Britain's wartime relations with its allies. By overruling French during the retreat from Mons in the fall of 1914, he prevented the British Army from leaving the battle line—which would have precluded the victory at the Marne and led to the defeat of the Entente. Valuable material aid to Russia, initiated by Kitchener and continued after his death, may have kept its army in the field longer than it otherwise would have. But, Kitchener's greatest contribution to the Entente was the development, to an extent previously unimagined, of Britain's military resources. Within eighteen months of the outbreak of the war, he built, out of a nation customarily reliant on sea power, a mass army capable of holding its own against the soldiers of the greatest military power in Europe. It was this army that sustained the Entente in the latter stages of the war, stepping into the breach left by the collapse of Russia and the exhaustion of France. While it would be a fallacy to point to any single person as having won the war, it can be fairly claimed that Kitchener did more than any other individual to bring about the defeat of Germany. One thing is indisputable: Without Kitchener, the Entente would have lost the war.

Notes

Chapter 1: The Making of a Warlord

1. The eldest, Henry Chevallier, was born in 1846, followed two years later by a daughter, Frances, nicknamed "Millie." The third son, Arthur, came in 1852, and six years later the family was completed with the arrival of Frederick Walter.

2. Philip Magnus, *Kitchener: Portrait of an Imperialist* (London: John Murray, 1958), 5–7.

3. Trevor Royle, *The Kitchener Enigma* (London: Michael Joseph, 1985), 18–21.

4. George H. Cassar, *Kitchener: Architect of Victory* (London: William Kimber, 1977), 23–24.

5. Magnus, *Kitchener*, 13–20.

6. Dr. Samuel Daiches, *Lord Kitchener and His Work in Palestine* (London: Luzac and Co., 1915), 11.

7. For an account of Kitchener at work, see John Macdonald, "Fellah Soldiers, Old and New: A Reminiscence and a Moral," *Nineteenth Century* 44 (1898): 582–590.

8. Cited in Magnus, *Kitchener*, 50.

9. When Gladstone recognized that Egypt had lost control of the Sudan, he proposed to cut his losses, determined not to be drawn into further adventures. Still, Britain held some responsibility for the safety of Egyptian garrisons scattered in the Sudan who were likely to be slaughtered unless evacuated. Accordingly, Gladstone selected Charles "Chinese" Gordon, a popular hero, for this mission. Gordon, however, was not the man to carry out an inglorious retreat and, disobeying his instructions, decided to defend Khartoum.

10. Cited in Magnus, *Kitchener*, 58.

11. The entire document can be seen in Sir George Arthur, *Life of Lord Kitchener*, vol. 1 (London: Macmillan and Co., 1920), 116–124.

12. Royle, *Kitchener Enigma*, 78–81.

13. E. S. Grew, *Field Marshal Lord Kitchener: His Life and Work for the Empire*, vol. 1 (London: Gresham Publishing Co., 1920), 147.

14. The Mahdi died of unknown causes shortly after the fall of Khartoum.

15. Royle, *Kitchener Enigma*, 89.

16. Arthur, *Lord Kitchener*, vol. 1, 165–167.

17. Earl of Cromer, *Modern Egypt*, vol. 2 (London: Macmillan and Co., 1908), 86–88.

18. Kitchener admitted as much to one of his subordinates. See John Pollock, *Kitchener* (London: Constable, 2001), 170–171.

19. Magnus, *Kitchener*, 66.

20. Cited in Royle, *Kitchener Enigma*, 93.

21. Royle, *Kitchener Enigma*, 107–108.

22. Cassar, *Kitchener*, 73–74.

23. Arthur, *Lord Kitchener*, vol. 1, 210–212.

24. Ronald Wingate, *Wingate of the Sudan* (London: John Murray, 1955), 114.

25. Magnus, *Kitchener*, 120–122.

26. The most recent study of the battle is Philip Ziegler's *Omdurman* (New York: Alfred A. Knopf, 1974).

27. Lt. Col. Charles à Court Repington, *Vestigia* (Boston: Houghton Mifflin Co., 1919), 160.

28. Ziegler, *Omdurman*, 223–227.

29. Patricia Wright, *Conflict on the Nile: The Fashoda Incident of 1898* (London: William Heinemann, 1972), pt. 3; Wingate, *Wingate*, 118–121; David L. Lewis, *The Race to Fashoda* (London: Bloomsbury, 1988), 222–225.

30. Cassar, *Kitchener*, 102–107.

31. There are plenty of accounts of the South African War, but the best single volume, in my view, is Thomas Packenham, *The Boer War* (New York: Random House, 1979).

32. Arthur, *Lord Kitchener*, vol. 2, chs. 61–70.

33. Predictably, there are differences of opinion among scholars as to which of the two men was right. David Dilkes, *Curzon in India*, vol. 2 (New York: Taplinger, 1969), chs. 4, 7–9, and Peter King, *The Viceroy's Fall: How Kitchener Destroyed Curzon* (London: Sidgwick and Jackson, 1986), pt. 2, have argued forcibly on behalf of Curzon. Kitchener is defended with equal fervor by Arthur, *Lord Kitchener*, vol. 2, chs. 71–73, and by his most recent biographer, Pollock, *Kitchener*, 286–326.

34. Pollock, *Kitchener*, 329–42.

35. Philip Mason, *A Matter of Honour: An Account of the Indian Army, Its Officers and Men* (New York: Holt, Reinhart and Winston, 1974), 399.

36. Royle, *Kitchener Enigma*, 227–232.

37. Royle, *Kitchener Enigma*, 232–233.

38. Pollock, *Kitchener*, 351, 353, 360, 364–365; Magnus, *Kitchener*, 257–258.

39. The CID had been established in 1903 as the cabinet's advisory and consultative body on matters relating to home and imperial defense.

40. Peter Mansfield, *The British in Egypt* (New York: Holt, Reinhart and Winston, 1972), ch. 18; Lord Lloyd, *Egypt since Cromer*, vol. 1 (London: Macmillan and Co., 1933), ch. 10.

41. Cited in Magnus, *Kitchener*, 274–275.

Chapter 2: War Plans

1. George H. Cassar, *Kitchener: Architect of Victory* (London: William Kimber, 1977), 170.

2. Minutes of the CID, July 14, 1914, CAB 2/3. Kitchener's opinion is best summarized in the following statement: "It would put us in the position of a continental nation with a land frontier, and we should be faced with all the disadvantages which land frontiers entail."

3. Ronald Storrs, *Orientations* (London: Nicholson and Watson, 1945), 124; Sir George Arthur, *Life of Lord Kitchener*, vol. 3 (London: Macmillan and Co., 1920), 2.

4. Michael and Eleanor Brock, eds., *H. H. Asquith: Letters to Venetia Stanley* (Oxford: Oxford University Press, 1982), 138.

5. "If we stood aside," Grey observed, "our moral position would be such as to have lost us all respect."

6. Asquith to Kitchener, August 3, 1914, Kitchener papers, PRO 30/57/76; Storrs, *Orientations*, 125.

7. In March 1914 sixty officers of the Third Cavalry Brigade, stationed at the Curragh, outside Dublin, opted for dismissal rather than commit themselves to coercing Ulster into accepting Home Rule. Jack Seely, the Secretary for War, gave written assurances that they would not be compelled to do so. The government repudiated the agreement, which led Seely to resign. The Chief of the General Staff, Sir John French, having persuaded the mutineers to return to duty on the strength of a document they had accepted as representing cabinet policy, felt he had no alternative but to tender his resignation as well.

8. Lady Violet Bonham Carter, *Winston Churchill: An Intimate Portrait* (New York: Harcourt, Brace and World, 1965), 257.

9. J. A. Pease (Lord Gainford), "War Reminiscences," Gainford papers, vol. 42, 9. His war memoirs, as of this writing, remain unpublished.

10. A soldier-politician, Seely had already arranged to join the BEF when Asquith invited him to return to his old post. He served on the western front, as commander of a Canadian cavalry brigade, until 1918 when he was gassed and retired from the Army with the rank of major general.

11. Riddell diary, August 6, 1914, Riddell papers, ADD 62974.

12. The absurd allegation was based on an innocuous statement Haldane made while on a visit to Berlin in 1912 in which he referred to Germany as his spiritual home.

13. Milner diary, August 4, 1914, Milner papers; Cassar, *Kitchener*, 174.

14. Oliver Viscount Esher, ed., *Journals and Letters of Reginald Viscount Esher,* vol. 2 (London: Nicholson and Watson, 1934), 298.

15. George H. Cassar, *Asquith As War Leader* (London: Hambledon Press, 1994), 39–40.

16. Cassar, *Kitchener*, 176.

17. Brock and Brock, eds., *Letters to Venetia Stanley*, 157.

18. Robert Blake, *The Unknown Prime Minister* (London: Eyre and Spottiswoode, 1955), 227; Bonham Carter, *Winston Churchill*, 257; Maj. Gen. C. E. Callwell, *Experiences of a Dug-Out, 1914–1918* (London: Constable, 1920), 80; J. M. Bourne, *Britain and the Great War, 1914–1918* (London: Edward Arnold, 1989), 139: Lord Beaverbrook to author, during an interview in September 1962.

19. Bonham Carter, *Winston Churchill*, 257; A. F. S. Oliver, *Ordeal by Battle* (London: Macmillan and Co., 1915), 354–355.

20. On the subject of British prewar planning, see S. R. Williamson, *The Politics of Grand Strategy: Britain and France Prepare for War, 1904–1914* (Cambridge: Harvard University Press, 1969); Paul Kennedy, ed., *The War Plans of the Great Powers, 1880–1914* (London: Allen and Unwin, 1979); John Gooch, *The Plans of War: The General Staff and British Military Strategy, c. 1900–1916* (London: Routledge and Kegan Paul, 1974); William J. Philpott, *Anglo-French Relations and Strategy on the Western Front, 1914–1918* (New York: St. Martin's Press, 1996), ch. 1.

21. Kitchener had not approved of the prewar semimilitary conversations between the French and British general staffs. In 1909 he told his former subordinate Henry Rawlinson that "he did not like this, as we had no plan of our own, and it would mean inevitably that we should be tacked on to a French plan." See Maj. Gen. Sir Frederick Maurice, *The Life of General Lord Rawlinson of Trent* (London: Cassell, 1928), 96.

22. Wilson diary, August 5, 1914, Wilson papers; Haig diary, August 5, 1914, Haig papers; Minutes of the Council of War, August 5, 1914, CAB 42/1/2; Lord Hankey, *The Supreme Command, 1914–1918*, vol. 1 (London: Allen and Unwin, 1961), 169–172; Winston S. Churchill, *The World Crisis*, vol. 1 (New York: Charles Scribner's Sons, 1951), 248–251; Viscount French of Ypres, *1914* (London: Constable, 1919), 3–5.

23. Brock and Brock, eds., *Letters to Venetia Stanley*, 158; Cassar, *Asquith*, 40.

24. Minutes of the Council of War, August 6, 1914, CAB 42/1/3.

25. Cassar, *Kitchener*, 230–231.

26. David French, *British Strategy and War Aims, 1914–1916* (London: Allen and Unwin, 1986), 12–13; P. Towle, "The European Balance of Power in 1914," *Army Quarterly and Defence Journal* 104 (1974): 333–342; Keith Neilson, "Watching the 'Steamroller': British Observers and the Russian Army before 1914," *Journal of Strategic Studies* 8 (1985): 199–217.

27. Esher diary, October 9, 1914, Esher papers.

28. David Lloyd George, *War Memoirs*, vol. 1 (London: Odhams Press, 1938), 38.

29. During the years preceding 1914, French military planners had decided to put their faith in an offensive of unbridled fury as a prescription for victory. They believed that the absence of an offensive spirit had led to their defeat in the war of 1870–1871. The psychology of an all-out offensive (*offensive à l'outrance*) lay at the heart of Plan XVII, which the high command intended to implement at the start of the campaign.

30. Keith Neilson, *Strategy and Supply: The Anglo-Russian Alliance* (London: Allen and Unwin, 1984), 8–9.

31. Charles à Court Repington, *The First World War, 1914–1918*, vol. 1 (Boston: Houghton Mifflin Co., 1921), 21.

32. Reginald Viscount Esher, *The Tragedy of Lord Kitchener* (London: John Murray, 1921), 35; Arthur, *Lord Kitchener*, vol. 3, 7n.

33. Esher diary, October 9, 1914, Esher papers.

34. Brian Bond, *The Victorian Army and the Staff College, 1854–1914* (London: Eyre Methuen, 1972), 300–301.

35. Composed of the Secretary for War, the Parliamentary Undersecretary, the Financial Secretary, and the heads of the four military departments, its purpose was to discuss and determine all questions of military policy.

36. Creedy to Dardanelles Commission, April 3, 1917, CAB 19/33.

37. Asquith to Dardanelles Commission, March 29, 1917, CAB 19/33.

38. Callwell, *Expereiences*, 58; Gooch, *Plans of War*, 299; Sir George Arthur, *General Sir John Maxwell* (London: John Murray, 1932), 131.

39. Trevor Wilson, *The Myriad Faces of War* (Cambridge: Polity Press, 1986), 201; C. E. W. Bean, *The Official History of Australia in the War of 1914–1918*, vol. 1 (Sydney: Angus and Robertson, 1935), 202–203; Dominick Graham and Shelford Bidwell, *Coalitions, Politicians and Generals* (London: Brassey's, 1993), 65; Brig. Gen., C. F. Aspinall-Oglander, *Military Operations: Gallipoli*, vol. 1 (London: William Heinemann, 1929), 46–47; Dardanelles Commission, *First Report* (London: HMSO, 1917), 12–13; Callwell, *Experiences*, passim.

40. Arthur to Dardanelles Commission, May 1, 1917, CAB 19/33.

41. Kitchener to Duff, September 16, 1914, WO 33/714.

42. Duff to Kitchener, September 17, 1914, and Maxwell to Kitchener, September 26, 1914, both telegrams in WO 33/714.

43. Edward David, ed., *Inside Asquith's Cabinet: From the Diaries of Charles Hobhouse* (London: John Murray, 1977), 231.

44. Callwell to Wilson, January 1, 1916, Wilson papers, HHW 2/75/75.

45. Lloyd George, *War Memoirs*, vol. 1, 298.

46. Churchill, *World Crisis*, vol. 1, 253.

47. David French, *British Economic and Strategic Planning, 1905–1915* (London: Allen and Unwin, 1982), chs. 2–5.

48. Bourne, *Britain*, 138.

49. Viscount Grey of Fallodon, *Twenty-five Years*, vol. 2 (New York: Frederick A. Stokes Co., 1925), 71.

50. Asquith does not even mention this important measure in his summary of cabinet proceedings, which he habitually sent to the King.

51. Lord Beaverbrook, *Politicians and the War, 1914–1916*, (London: Oldbourne Book Co., 1960), 173.

52. Maj. Gen. C. E. Callwell, *Field Marshal Sir Henry Wilson: His Life and Diaries*, vol. 1 (London: Cassell, 1927), 178.

53. The average annual intake of recruits between 1908 and 1913 was 29,626. See Peter Simkins, "The Four Armies, 1914–1918," in *The Oxford Illustrated History of the British Army*, ed. David Chandler (Oxford: Oxford University Press, 1994), 242.

54. The most recent works on Kitchener's army are Peter Simkins, *Kitchener's Army* (Manchester: Manchester University Press, 1988); Ray Westlake, *Kitchener's Army* (Tunbridge Wells: Nutshell Publishing Co., 1989); and A. J. Smithers, *The Fighting Nation* (London: Leo Cooper, 1994).

55. Simkins, *Kitchener's Army*, ch. 2; Brig. Gen. Sir James E. Edmonds, *Military Operations: France and Belgium, 1914*, vol. 2 (London: Macmillan and Co., 1929), 17–18.

56. Bourne, *Britain*, 180–181; Churchill, *World Crisis*, vol. 1, 253; R. J. Q. Adams and Philip P. Poirier, *The Conscription Controversy in Great Britain, 1900–1918* (London: Macmillan and Co., 1987), 57; Peter Fraser, *Lord Esher* (London: Hart-Davis, MacGibbon, 1973), 263–264; Stephen Koss, *Haldane: Scapegoat for Liberalism* (New York: Columbia University Press, 1969), 119–120; Simkins, "Four Armies," 244.

57. Grey, *Twenty-five Years*, vol. 2, 70–71.

58. Bonham Carter, *Winston Churchill*, 259.

59. Ian F. W. Beckett, "The Territorial Force," in *A Nation in Arms: A Social History of the British Army in the First World War*, ed. Ian F. W. Beckett and Keith Simpson (Manchester: Manchester University Press, 1985).

60. See for example the letter to the *Times*, August 14, 1914.

61. Lloyd George, *War Memoirs*, vol. 1, 232–233.

62. Kenneth O. Morgan, ed., *Lloyd George Family Letters, 1885–1936* (Cardiff: University of Wales, 1973), 169.

63. The *Times*, August 15, 1914.

64. Cassar, *Kitchener*, 198–201.

65. See for example Richard Burdon Haldane, *An Autobiography* (New York: Doubleday, Doran and Co., 1929), 297; Correlli Barnett, *Britain and Her Army, 1509–1970* (New York: Morrow and Co., 1970), 378; Philip Magnus, *Kitchener: Portrait of an Imperialist* (London: John Murray, 1958), 279, 289–290.

66. Esher diary, August 13, 1914, Esher papers.

67. Simkins, *Kitchener's Army*, 46.

68. Arthur, *Lord Kitchener*, vol. 3, 9; French, *British Strategy*, xiii.

69. Repington, *First World War*, vol. 1, 22.

70. The importance of Russia in Kitchener's overall plan is admirably laid out in Keith Neilson, "Kitchener: A Reputation Refurbished?" *Canadian Journal of History* 15 (1980): 207–227.

Chapter 3: Imperial Issues and Peripheral Theaters

1. Sir Julian S. Corbett, *Naval Operations*, vol. 1 (London: Longmans and Green, 1920), 131–132; Lord Hankey, *The Supreme Command, 1914–1918*. vol. 1 (London: Allen and Unwin, 1961), 168; Michael and Eleanor Brock, eds, *H. H. Asquith: Letters to Venetia Stanley* (Oxford: Oxford University Press, 1982), 158; Asquith to George V, August 6, 1914, CAB 41/35/26.

2. Field Marshal Sir William Robertson, *Soldiers and Statesmen, 1914–1918*, vol. 1 (London: Cassell, 1926), 171.

3. Byron Farwell, *The Great War in Africa, 1914–1918* (New York: W. W. Norton and Co., 1986), 183.

4. Farwell, *Great War in Africa*, ch. 1.

5. Brig. Gen. F. J. Moberly, *Military Operations: Togoland and the Cameroons* (London: HMSO 1931), chs. 2–5.

6. Col. R. Meinertzhagen, *Army Diary, 1899–1926* (London: Oliver and Boyd, 1960), 83–84, 109.

7. Farwell, *Great War in Africa*, 105–107.

8. Meinertzhagen, *Army Diary*, 103–105.

9. Leonard Mosley, *Duel for Kilimanjaro: An Account of the East African Campaign, 1914–1918* (London: Weidenfeld and Nicolson, 1963), ch. 3; Lt. Col. Charles Hordern, *Military Operations: East Africa*, vol. 1 (London: HMSO, 1941), chs. 4–6; Farwell, *Great War in Africa*, ch. 13.

10. Hordern, *East Africa*, vol. 1, 100–101.

11. Hordern, *East Africa*, vol. 1, 100–101.

12. Meinertzhagen, *Army Diary*, 110.

13. Kitchener to Wapshare, December 4, 1914, WO 33/714.

14. Hordern, *East Africa*, vol. 1, 120–127.

15. Meinertzhagen, *Army Diary*, 112–113.

16. Wapshare to Kitchener, January 19, 1915; Kitchener to Wapshare, January 21, 1915, both telegrams in WO 33/714.

17. Wapshare to Kitchener, January 23, 1915, WO 33/714.

18. Kitchener to Wapshare, January 24, 1915, WO 33/714.

19. David French, *British Strategy and War Aims, 1914–1916* (London: Allen and Unwin, 1986), 48.

20. Cited in French, *British Strategy*, 25.

21. Cited in Elie Kedourie, *In the Anglo-Arab Labyrinth* (Cambridge: Cambridge University Press, 1976), 29.

22. Lt. Col. P. G. Elgood, *Egypt and the Army* (Oxford: Oxford University Press, 1924), 122ff, describes the routes open to the Turks.

23. Cheetham to Foreign Office, August 6, 1914, FO 371/2162/36525; Cheetham to Foreign Office, August 29, 1914, FO 371/2169/44613.

24. "Note from the Advisor of the Interior to His Majesty's Acting Consul-General on the General Situation in Egypt," n.d., but enclosed with a telegram dated September 7, 1914, FO 407/183.

25. Graham to Tyrell (Grey's private secretary), October 25, 1914, Grey papers, FO 800/48.

26. Graham to Kitchener, October 24, 1914, Kitchener papers, PRO 30/57/45/QQ49; see also Maxwell to Kitchener, October 22, 1914, WO 33/714.

27. Kitchener to Grey, October 23, 1914, FO 371/1969/62659.

28. Kitchener to Cheetham (via Foreign Office), October 23, 1914, FO 371/1969/62659.

29. Kitchener to Cecil, November 3, 1914, Grey papers, FO 800/48.

30. Cheetham to Kitchener, November 5, 1914, FO 800/48.

31. Kitchener to Grey, November 6, 1914, Grey papers, FO 800/102.

32. Graham to Kitchener, November 7, 1914, Grey papers, FO 800/48; Graham to Kitchener, November 8, 1914, Kitchener papers, PRO 30/57/45/QQ58. See also Storrs to FitzGerald, November 11, 1914, Kitchener papers, PRO 30/57/45/QQ62.

33. Cheetham to Kitchener, November 7, 1914, Grey papers, FO 800/48.

34. Brock and Brock, eds., *Letters to Venetia Stanley*, 171; Asquith to George V, August 17, 1914, CAB 41/35/31.

35. The two German cruisers were allowed sanctuary in Constantinople after eluding a British squadron in the Mediterranean. Using this turn of fortune to best advantage, the Germans then presented the warships to Turkey as replacements for the two Turkish dreadnoughts sequestered by Britain.

36. Winston S. Churchill, *The World Crisis*, vol. 1 (New York: Charles Scribner's Sons, 1951), 529–532.

37. Dardanelles Commission, Supplement to First Report.

38. Brig. Gen. C. F. Aspinall-Oglander, *Military Operations: Gallipoli*, vol. 1 (London: William Heinemann, 1929), 41–43.

39. Kitchener to GOC, Egypt, August 30, 1914, WO 33/714.

40. Elgood, *Egypt*, 58.

41. For additional information on Maxwell, see Sir George Arthur, *General Sir John Maxwell* (London: John Murray, 1932).

42. Lt. Gen. Sir George Macmunn and Cyril Falls, *Military Operations: Egypt and Palestine*, vol. 1, (London: HMSO, 1928), 14–15.

43. Maxwell to Kitchener, September 29, 1914, WO 33/714.

44. Cheetham to Grey, September 22, 1914, FO 371/1971/48402.

45. Kitchener to Maxwell, September 23 and October 22, 1914, WO 33/714.

46. A. J. Barker, *The Bastard War: The Mesopotamian Campaign of 1914–1918* (New York: Dial Press, 1967), 22; Mesopotamian Commission, *Report* (London: HMSO, 1917), 12; Brig. Gen. F. J. Moberly, *The Campaign in Mesopotamia, 1914–1918*, vol. 1 (London: HMSO, 1923), ch. 5.

47. For the events leading to Turkey's involvement in the war, see Ulrich Trumpener, *Germany and the Ottoman Empire, 1914–1918* (Princeton: Princeton University Press, 1968); and Y. T. Kurat, "How Turkey Drifted into World War I," in *Studies in International History*, ed. K. Bourne and D. C. Watts (London: Longmans, 1967).

48. Moberly, *Campaign in Mesopotamia*, vol. 1, chs. 6–7; Barker, *Bastard War*, ch. 1.

49. Briton C. Busch, *Britain, India and the Arabs, 1914–1921* (Berkeley: University of California Press, 1971), 23ff.

50. Kitchener minute, n.d. but c. December 5, 1914, FO 371/2144/61439.

51. Peter Mansfield, *The British in Egypt* (New York: Holt, Rinehart and Winston, 1972), 207.

52. Lord Lloyd, *Egypt since Cromer*, vol. 1 (London: Macmillan and Co., 1933), 194–196; John Marlowe, *A History of Modern Egypt and Anglo-Egyptian Relations, 1800–1956* (Hamden: Archon Books, 1965), 215–217.

53. Kitchener's dislike of Abbas dated back to the period when he was sirdar of the Egyptian Army. See Philip Magnus, *Kitchener: Portrait of an Imperialist* (London: John Murray, 1958), 83–88, 272–274.

54. Grey to Cheetham, September 11, 1914, FO 407/183.

55. Asquith to George V, November 14, 1914, CAB 41/35/59.

56. Kitchener to Maxwell, November 14, 1914, WO 33/714.

57. Maxwell to Kitchener, November 17, 1914, WO 33/714.

58. Grey to Cheetham, November 18, 1914, Grey papers, FO 800/48.

59. Lloyd, *Egypt*, vol. 1, 197.

60. Asquith to George V, November 18, 1914, CAB 41/35/60.

61. Aziz Ali al-Masri, founder and leader of *al-'Ahd*, a secret society of Arab Army officers, was arrested and convicted on trumped-up charges in Constantinople early in 1914. He was pardoned following the intercession of Kitchener and the Foreign Office and allowed to return to Egypt. George Antonius, *The Arab Awakening* (London: Hamish Hamilton, 1938), 119–120.

62. Antonius, *Arab Awakening*, 126–127; Jukka Nevakivi, "Lord Kitchener and the Partition of the Ottoman Empire," in *Studies in International History*, 318; Elizabeth Monroe, *Britain's Moment in the Middle East, 1914–1971* (Baltimore: John Hopkins University Press, 1981), 27.

63. Randall Baker, *King Husain and the Kingdom of Hejaz* (Cambridge: Olander, 1979), 46.

64. C. Ernest Dawn, *From Ottomanism to Arabism* (Urbana, Ill.: University of Illinois Press, 1973), 61.

65. Kitchener to Grey, February 6, 1914, FO 141/460/1198; Bruce Westrate, *The Arab Bureau* (University Park, Pa.: University of Pennsylvania Press, 1992), 14; Ronald Storrs, *Orientations* (London: Nicholson and Watson, 1945), 122–123; Sir George Arthur, *Life of Lord Kitchener*, vol. 3 (London: Macmillan and Co., 1920), 153–154.

66. Baker, *King Husain*, 47–48.

67. Storrs memorandum, April 19, 1914, FO 141/460/1198.

68. Storrs, *Orientations*, 148–149.

69. Grey to Cheetham, September 24, 1914, FO 141/460/1198.

70. Cheetham to Foreign Office, October 17, 1914, FO 371/2140/60661.

71. Kitchener to Cheetham, October 18, 1914, FO 371/2140/60661.

72. Cheetham to Foreign Office, October 26, 1914, FO 371/2140/6358; Kedourie, *Anglo-Egyptian Labyrinth*, 16.

73. Cheetham to Foreign Office, November 9, 1914, FO 371/2141/69074.

74. Elie Kedourie, *England and the Middle East: The Destruction of the Ottoman Empire* (London: Mansell Publishing, 1956), 23.

75. Kitchener was referring to Abdul Aziz Ibn Saud, Emir of Nejd, who, along with other Arab leaders, had in the past considered taking up arms against the Sultan.

76. Kitchener to Foreign Office, November 9, 1914, FO 371/2141/69074.

77. Cheetham to Foreign Office, October 31, 1914, FO 371/2139/65589.

78. Grey to Cheetham, October 31, 1914, FO 371/2139/65589.

79. Kedourie has reproduced and carefully analyzed the two letters in *Anglo-Arab Labyrinth*, 17–20.

80. Kitchener to Grey, October 31, 1914, Grey papers, FO 800/102.

81. David Fromkin, *A Peace to End All Peace* (New York: Henry Holt, 1989), ch.10.

82. An Arab nationalist, he interviewed both Hussein and Abdullah in compiling his classic study.

83. Antonius, *Arab Awakening*, 133–134.

84. Cheetham to Foreign Office, December 10, 1914, FO 371/2139/81133.

85. C. E. W. Bean, *The Official History of Australia in the War of 1914–1918*, vol. 1 (Sydney: Angus and Robertson, 1935), 111–112.

86. Kitchener to Maxwell, December 18, 1914, WO 33/714.

87. Maxwell to Kitchener, November 20, 1914, WO 33/714; Macmunn and Falls, *Egypt and Palestine*, vol. 1, 20.

88. Minutes of the War Council, November 25, 1914, CAB 42/1/4.

89. Maxwell to Kitchener, November 25, 1914, WO 33/714.

Chapter 4: Stumbling Colossus

1. Keith Neilson, *Strategy and Supply: The Anglo-Russian Alliance, 1914–1917* (London: Allen and Unwin, 1984), passim.

2. Ward Rutherford, *The Tsar's War, 1914–1917* (Cambridge: Ian Faulkner Publishing, 1992), 22.

3. Norman Stone, *The Eastern Front, 1914–1917* (New York: Charles Scribner's Sons, 1975), 145–146.

4. Maj. Gen. Sir C. E. Callwell, *Experiences of a Dug-Out, 1914–1918* (London: Constable and Co., 1920), 46–47.

5. Neilson, *Strategy and Supply*, 29.

6. David Lloyd George, *War Memoirs*. vol. 1 (London: Odhams Press, 1938), 938.

7. Neilson, *Strategy and Supply*, 29, 32; Callwell to Wilson, July 14, 1915, Wilson papers, HHW 2/75/53.

8. Stone, *Eastern Front*, 144.

9. Callwell, *Experiences*, 282.

10. Accurate figures for military spending by the powers during the immediate prewar period were unavailable so that British estimates were not entirely accurate. As it was, expenditures for the Army in Russia, although amounting to about one-third of the nation's budgets, were still proportionately less than in Germany or France.

11. Knox Dispatch A, September 3, 1914, WO 106/1045; Michael and Eleanor Brock, eds., *H. H. Asquith: Letters to Venetia Stanley* (Oxford: Oxford University Press, 1982), 214.

12. Stone, *Eastern Front*, ch. 4.

13. Buchanan to Grey, September 18, 1914, FO 371/2095/50911.

14. Grey to Buchanan, September 19, 1914, FO 371/2095/50911; two letters from Kitchener to Grey, September 20, 1914, FO 371/2095/51213.

15. Buchanan to Grey, September 24, 1914, FO 371/2095/52753; Buchanan to Grey, September 24, 1914, FO 371/2095/52478.

16. Grey to Buchanan, September 25, 1914, FO 371/2095/52753.

17. Stone, *Eastern Front*, 96–101.

18. FitzGerald to Grey, October 6, 1914, FO 371/2095/56275.

19. Hanbury Williams, Dispatch 3, October 9, 1914, FO 371/2095/65033.

20. This issue is explored in depth in the next chapter.

21. Kitchener to Buchanan (via Foreign Office), October 4, 1914, FO 371/2095/55811.

22. Buchanan to Grey, October 11, 1914, FO 371/2095/58217.

23. Buchanan to Grey, October 8, 12 and 15, 1914, FO 371/2095/57137, 58681, 59971; Hanbury Williams to Kitchener (via Buchanan), October 12, 1914, FO 371/2095/65033; Hanbury Williams Dispatch P, December 12, 1914, WO 106/1101.

24. Kitchener to Grey, October 13, 1914, FO 371/2095/58929.

25. Bertie to Grey, October 14, 1914, FO 371/2095/59142.

26. Edward David, ed., *Inside Asquith's Cabinet: From the Diaries of Charles Hobhouse* (London: John Murray, 1977), 197, 199; Asquith to George V, October 22, 1914, CAB 41/35/54.

27. Kitchener to Grey, October 13, 1914, Grey papers, FO 800/102.

28. Kitchener to Grey, October 13, 1914, Grey papers, FO 800/102.

29. Buchanan to Grey, October 15, 1914, FO 371/2095/59973.

30. Grey to Buchanan, October 17, 1914, FO 371/2095/59973; Hanbury Williams Dispatch 10, October 16, 1914, FO 371/2095/69395.

31. Stone, *Eastern Front*, 95–100.

32. David French, *British Strategy and War Aims, 1914–1916* (London: Allen and Unwin, 1986), 45.

33. Keith Neilson, *Britain and the Last Tsar* (Oxford: Oxford University Press, 1995), 344.

34. C. J. Smith, "Great Britain and the 1914–15 Straits Agreement with Russia : The British Promise of November 1914," *American Historical Review* 70 (1965): 1015–1034.

35. L. L. Farrar, *Divide and Conquer: German Efforts to Conclude a Separate Peace, 1914–1918* (New York: Columbia University Press, 1978), 7ff.

36. For more details of the fighting around Lódz, see W. Bruce Lincoln, *Passage through Armageddon* (New York: Simon and Schuster, 1986), 86–88; Stone, *Eastern Front*, 105ff.

37. Buchanan to Foreign Office, November 19 and 21, 1914, FO 371/2171/72812, 73843; Buchanan to Foreign Office, November 22, 1914, FO 371/2447/73883.

38. Hanbury Williams, Dispatch K, November 24, 1914, WO 1101/87289; Hanbury Williams, Dispatch M, November 28, 1914, WO 1101/87289; Hanbury Williams Dispatch O, December 2, 1914, WO 1101/87289; Knox, Dispatches E and F, November 26 and 29, 1914, both in WO 106/1048.

39. Buchanan to Foreign Office, December 4, 1914, FO 371/2095/78627.

40. Kitchener to Buchanan, December 4, 1914, FO 371/2095/78627.

41. Hanbury Williams, Dispatch Q, December 6, 1914, WO 106/1101.

42. Buchanan to Foreign Office, December 5, 1914, FO 371/2095/79063.

43. Knox, Dispatch F, December 10, 1914, WO 106/1048.

44. Hanbury Williams, Dispatch U, December 13, 1914, WO 106/1101; Buchanan to Grey, December 15, 1914, FO 371/2095/82761.

45. Buchanan to Grey, December 18, 1914, FO 371/2095/83997.

46. Hanbury Williams to Kitchener, December 20, 1914, Kitchener papers, PRO 30/57/67.

47. Knox, Dispatch H, December 21, 1914, WO 106/1049.

48. Grey to Buchanan, December 18, 1914, FO 371/2095/83996.

49. Lincoln, *Passage through Armageddon,* 90.

50. Callwell to Wilson, December 23, 1914, Wilson papers, HHW 2/75/32.

51. Bertie Memorandum (reporting previous day's luncheon discussion with Kitchener), December 18, 1914, Bertie papers, FO 800/177.

52. Kitchener to Grey, December 20, 1914, Grey papers, FO 800/102; Grey to Buchanan, December 21, 1914, Grey papers, FO 800/74.

53. Hanbury Williams, Dispatch Y, December 24, 1914, WO 106/1102.

54. Kitchener to French, December 18, 1914, French papers, 75/46/11.

55. Brock and Brock, eds., *Letters to Venetia Stanley*, 331–332, 335; George H. Cassar, *Kitchener: Architect of Victory* (London: William Kimber, 1977), 263.

56. David, ed., *Inside Asquith's Cabinet*, 213–214.

57. Viscount French of Ypres, *1914* (London: Constable and Co., 1919), 334–336; Brock and Brock, eds., *Letters to Venetia Stanley*, 335–336; Cassar, *Kitchener*, 261.

58. French to Kitchener, December 28, 1914, Kitchener papers, PRO 30/57/48.

59. Maj. Gen. Sir Alfred Knox, *With the Russian Army, 1914–1917*, vol. 1 (London: Hutchinson and Co., 1921), 18–19.

60. Maurice Paléologue, *An Ambassador's Memoirs*, trans. F. A. Holt. vol. 1 (New York: George H. Doran Co., 1927), 221–222.

61. French, *1914*, 335–336; Callwell to Wilson, December 26, 1914, Wilson papers, HHW 2/75/34; Asquith to George V, December 31, 1914, CAB 41/35/65.

62. Neilson, *Strategy and Supply*, 61.

Chapter 5: The Early Test of Leadership

1. David French, *British Strategy and War Aims, 1914–1916* (London: Allen and Unwin, 1986), 20.

2. Archibald Murray, "Notes of a Conversation with Lord Kitchener," WO 79/62.

3. Brig. Gen. Sir James E. Edmonds, *Military Operations: France and Belgium, 1914*, vol. 1 (London: Macmillan and Co., 1922), 10.

4. Field Marshal Sir William Robertson, *Soldiers and Statesmen, 1914–1918*, vol. 1 (London: Cassell and Co., 1926), 41–43.

5. Tim Travers, "The Army and the Challenge of War," in *The Oxford History of the British Army*, ed. David Chandler (Oxford: Oxford University Press, 1994), 216–217, 220.

6. Edmonds was among some of Murray's critics who used that term. Haig was not much kinder. He called Murray an old woman.

7. Edmonds memoirs (unpublished), Edmonds papers, III/8/2–3.

8. See n. 7 in ch. 2.

9. See George H. Cassar, *The Tragedy of Sir John French* (Newark: University of Delaware, 1985), 79–80.

10. Cassar, *Sir John French*, 81.

11. Kitchener to Roberts, September 6, 1901, Roberts papers, 7101–23–33.

12. The letter can be seen in Sir George Arthur, *Life of Lord Kitchener*, vol. 3 (London: Macmillan and Co., 1920), 24.

13. Kitchener to Roberts, January 17, 1902, Roberts papers, 7101–23–33.

14. Edmonds memoirs, Edmonds papers, III/3/30.

15. The most recent book on Hamilton is John Lee, *A Soldier's Life: General Sir Ian Hamilton, 1853–1947* (London: Macmillan and Co., 2000).

16. Esher diary, August 21, 1914, Esher papers. Esher's record of a conversation with Kitchener.

17. John Terraine, *Mons* (London: Leo Cooper, 1991), 37.

18. Viscount French of Ypres, *1914* (London: Constable and Co., 1919), 13–15; Edmonds, *France and Belgium, 1914*, vol. 1, appendix 8.

19. Terraine, *Mons*, 57.

20. French to Kitchener, August 17, 1914, Kitchener papers, PRO 30/57/49.

21. Maj. Gen. Sir C. E. Callwell, *Experiences of a Dug-Out, 1914–1918* (London: Constable and Co., 1920), 57.

22. Michael, and Eleanor Brock, eds., *H. H. Asquith: Letters to Venetia Stanley* (Oxford: Oxford University Press, 1982), 172 n. 5.

23. Callwell, *Experiences*, 57.

24. Sir George Arthur, *Not Worth Reading* (London: Longmans, Green and Co., 1938), 213–214.

25. Maj. Gen. Sir Edward Spears, *Liaison 1914* (New York: Stein and Day, 1968), 56ff; Barbara Tuchman, *The Guns of August* (New York: Macmillan Co., 1962), passim.

26. William J. Philpott, *Anglo-French Relations and Strategy on the Western Front, 1914–1918* (New York: St. Martin's Press, 1996), 17.

27. French to Kitchener, August 17, 1914, Kitchener papers, PRO 30/57/49.

28. Brock and Brock, eds., *Letters to Venetia Stanley*, 179.

29. Brock and Brock, eds., *Letters to Venetia Stanley*, 190–191.

30. Kitchener to French, August 19, 1914, WO 33/713.

31. Kitchener to French, August 20, 1914, French papers, 75/46/11.

32. French to Kitchener, August 21, 1914, Kitchener papers, PRO 30/57/49.

33. Kitchener to French, August 22, 1914, French papers, 75/46/11.

34. French to Kitchener, August 22, 1914, Kitchener papers, PRO 30/57/49.

35. Arthur, *Lord Kitchener*, vol. 3, 33–34.

36. Spears, *Liaison*, 173–174.

37. Terraine, *Mons,* and David Ascoli, *The Mons Star* (London: Harrap, 1981), are two good accounts of the BEF's clash at Mons and its subsequent retreat.

38. French to Kitchener, August 24, 1914, Kitchener papers, PRO 30/57/49.

39. Brock and Brock, eds., *Letters to Venetia Stanley*, 191

40. Edward David, ed., *Inside Asquith's Cabinet: From the Diaries of Charles Hobhouse* (London: John Murray, 1977), 184.

41. David, ed., *Inside Asquith's Cabinet*, 184; Brock and Brock, eds., *Letters to Venetia Stanley*, 191; Emmott diary, August 25, 1914, Emmott papers; Pease diary, August 24, 1914, Gainford papers, vol. 39.

42. Kitchener to French, August 25, 1914, WO 33/713.

43. French to Kitchener, August 25, 1914, WO 33/713.

44. Kitchener to French, August 26, 1914, WO 33/713.

45. Field Marshal Joseph Joffre, *The Personal Memoirs of Joffre*, trans. Col. T. Bentley Mott. vol. 1 (New York: Harper and Brothers, 1932), 189–192.

46. Joffre, *Memoirs*, vol. 1, 195–196; Spears, *Liaison*, 228–233; Cassar, *Sir John French*, 126–127.

47. French telegrams to Kitchener, August 27, 1914, WO 33/713.

48. A. J. Smithers, *The Man Who Disobeyed* (London: Leo Cooper, 1970), 190–206; Edmonds, *France and Belgium, 1914*, vol. 1, chs. 7–9; Tuchman, *Guns of August*, 355–358; Cassar, *Sir John French*, 119–123.

49. French to Kitchener, August 28 and 29, 1914, WO 33/713.

50. Brock and Brock, eds., *Letters to Venetia Stanley*, 202–203.

51. Terraine, *Mons*, 160–165.

52. Cassar, *Sir John French*, 128–129.

53. Ascoli, *Mons Star*, 127–128; Terraine, *Mons*, 174–176.

54. Arthur, *Lord Kitchener*, vol. 3, 44–45.

55. Joffre, *Memoirs*, vol. 1, 222–223.

56. Spears, *Liaison*, 287.

57. Terraine, *Mons*, 180.

58. Clive diary, August 29, 1914, Clive papers.

59. Robb to Kitchener, August 30, 1914, WO 33/713.

60. Kitchener to French, August 30, 1914, WO 33/713.

61. French to Kitchener, August 30, 1914, WO 33/713.

62. French to Kitchener, August 30, 1914, WO 33/713.

63. Kitchener to French, August 31, 1914, WO 33/713.

64. Brock and Brock, eds., *Letters to Venetia Stanley*, 209.

65. Asquith to George V, August 31, 1914, CAB 41/35/38; Pease diary, August 31, 1914, Gainford papers, vol. 39; Emmott diary, August 31, 1914, Emmott papers; Brock and Brock, eds., *Letters to Venetia Stanley*, 209.

66. Kitchener to French, August 31, 1914, WO 33/713.

67. French to Kitchener, 31 August 1914, WO 33/713.

68. Cited in Archie Hunter, *Kitchener's Sword-Arm: The Life and Campaigns of General Sir Archibald Hunter* (Staplehurst: Spellmount, 1996), 220.

69. Pease diary, August 31, 1914, Gainford papers, vol. 39; Brock and Brock, eds., *Letters to Venetia Stanley*, 212–213; George H. Cassar, *Asquith As War Leader* (London: Hambledon Press, 1994), 48; Asquith to George V, September 1, 1914, CAB 41/35/42.

70. Kitchener to French, September 1, 1914, WO 33/713.

71. Grey to Kitchener, August 31, 1914, Kitchener papers, PRO 30/57/77. The letter was misdated. It was written during the early hours of September 1.

72. General Charles Huguet, *L'Intervention Militaire Britannique en 1914* (Paris: Berger-Levrault, 1928), 101.

73. Terraine, *Mons*, 190–191.

74. French, *1914*, 100.

75. Kitchener to French, September 1, 1914, French papers, 75/46/11.

76. Joffre, *Memoirs*, vol. 1, 242–243.

77. French to Kitchener, September 4, 1914, Kitchener papers, PRO 30/57/49.

78. Kitchener to French, September 5, 1914, French papers, 75/46/11.

79. Cassar, *Sir John French*, 140–142.

80. Bertie to Grey, September 5, 1914, Grey papers, FO 800/ 56A.

81. Kitchener to French, September 5, 1914, WO 33/713.

82. Spears, *Liaison*, 407–408, 413–418.

83. Cassar, *Sir John French*, 144–149.

84. Parliamentary Debates, *House of Lords*, September 17, 1914, vol. 17, col. 735.

Chapter 6: From Antwerp to the Close of 1914

1. Lord Hankey, *The Supreme Command, 1914–1918*, vol. 1 (London: Allen and Unwin, 1961), 194.

2. Winston S. Churchill, *The World Crisis*, vol. 1 (New York: Charles Scribner's Sons, 1951–1955), 363.

3. Villiers to Foreign Office, September 29, 1914, WO 32/5086/1. The telegram is misdated and was actually sent the next day.

4. Michael and Eleanor Brock, eds., *H. H. Asquith: Letters to Venetia Stanley* (Oxford: Oxford University Press, 1982), 258; Martin Gilbert, *Winston S. Churchill: The Challenge of War, 1914–1916*, vol. 3 (Boston: Houghton Mifflin Co., 1971), 101.

5. Gilbert, *Churchill*, 101.

6. Bertie to Foreign Office, September 30, 1914, WO 32/5086/2.

7. Foreign Office to Bertie, telegram sent at 11:30 A.M., October 1, 1914, WO 32/5086/3; Brock and Brock, eds., *Letters to Venetia Stanley*, 258; Edward David, ed., *Inside Asquith's Cabinet: From the Diaries of Charles Hobhouse* (London: John Murray, 1977), 193.

8. Toward the end of September, Sir John arranged to transfer the BEF from the Aisne, where it was wedged in between two armies, to its original place on the extreme left of the Allied line. The move was designed to shorten the BEF's supply lines and provide naval assistance when required.

9. The messages were compiled in a packet entitled "Correspondence in Regard to the Fall of Antwerp" (WO 32/5086), and designation was given whether they were sent by telegram or by telephone. All telegrams between Kitchener and Dallas were transmitted through the Foreign Office personnel (Grey in London and Villiers in Antwerp). See also Sir George Arthur, *Not Worth Reading* (London: Longmans, Green and Co., 1938), 221.

10. Dallas to Kitchener, telephone messages during the afternoon and at 8 P.M., and telegram sent at 10:15 P.M., all on October 1, 1914, WO 32/5086/5, 8, 9.

11. Bertie to Foreign Office, telegram sent at 1:14 P.M., received at 3.40 P.M., October 1, 1914, WO 32/5086/6; William J. Philpott, *Anglo-French Relations and Strategy on the Western Front, 1914–1918* (New York: St. Martin's Press, 1996), 37.

12. Brock and Brock, eds., *Letters to Venetia Stanley*, 259.

13. Kitchener to Dallas, telegram sent at 1:30 P.M., October 2, 1914, WO 32/5086/14.

14. Foreign Office to Bertie, telegram sent at 12:30 P.M., October 2, 1914, WO 32/5086/12.

15. Bertie to Foreign Office, telegram sent at 12:15 P.M., received at 2:10 P.M., October 2, 1914, WO 32/5086/16.

16. The total number, including irregulars, was closer to one hundred thousand.

17. Bertie to Foreign Office, telegram sent at 12:15 P.M., received at 2:10 P.M., October 2, 1914, WO 32/5086/16.

18. Villiers to Foreign Office, telegram sent at 8:20 P.M., received at 10 P.M., October 2, 1914, WO 32/5086/20.

19. Viscount Grey of Fallodon, *Twenty-five Years*, vol. 2 (New York: Frederick A. Stokes Co., 1925), 81.

20. Dallas to Kitchener, telegram sent at noon, received at 1:20 P.M., October 2, 1914, WO 32/5086/13.

21. Churchill, *World Crisis*, vol. 1, 369.

22. Grey, *Twenty-five Years*, vol. 2, 81–82.

23. Grey, *Twenty-five Years*, vol. 2, 82–83.

24. Grey to Villiers, telegram sent at 12:45 A.M., October 3, 1914, WO 32/5086/21.

25. Bertie to Foreign Office, telegram sent at 11 P.M., October 2, received 12:55 A.M., October 3, 1914, WO 32/5086/26.

26. Kitchener to Bertie, telegram sent at 9:40 A.M., October 3, 1914, WO 32/5086/26.

27. Bertie to Kitchener, telegram sent at 12:30 P.M., October 3, 1914, WO 32/5086/29; Kitchener to Bertie, telegram sent at 4:30 P.M., October 3, 1914, WO 32/5086/32; Bertie to Kitchener, telegrams sent at 5:25 P.M., 8 P.M., and 11 P.M., October 3, 1914, WO 32/5086/35, 36, 36A and 39.

28. Kitchener to Dallas, telegram sent at 2:15 P.M., October 3, 1914, WO 32/5086/30.

29. Churchill to Kitchener, telegram sent at 5:50 P.M., October 3, 1914, WO 32/5086/33.

30. Churchill to Kitchener, telegram sent at 6:53 P.M., October 3, 1914, WO 32/5086/38; Churchill, *World Crisis*, vol. 1, 372–374.

31. Foreign Office to Villiers, October 4, 1914, WO 32/5086/45.

32. Bertie to Kitchener, telegram sent at 11 A.M., received at 1:35 P.M., October 4, 1914, WO 32/5086/48.

33. Churchill sent a cable to Asquith on October 5, offering to resign his post to take command of the British forces at Antwerp. Asquith, who had lost the capacity to be surprised by Churchill's unpredictable behavior, replied at once without consulting the Cabinet. Although expressing warm appreciation for Churchill's mission, Asquith turned down his offer on the grounds that he could not be spared from the Admiralty. When Asquith read Churchill's telegram in the Cabinet, only Kitchener refrained from breaking out in laughter.

34. David, ed., *Inside Asquith's Cabinet*, 194–195; Asquith to George V, October 5, 1914, CAB 41/35/49; Brock and Brock, eds., *Letters to Venetia Stanley*, 262–263.

35. Brig. Gen. Sir James E. Edmonds, *Military Operations: France and Belgium, 1914*, vol. 2 (London: Macmillan and Co., 1925), appendix 8.

36. Philpott, *Anglo-French Relations*, 43.

37. Kitchener to French, telegram sent at 1:39 P.M., October 2, 1914, WO 32/5086/15.

38. French to Kitchener, telegrams sent at 7:40 P.M., October 2, and at 7:20 P.M., 3 October 1914, WO 32/5086/19, 34.

39. Field Marshal Joseph Joffre, *The Personal Memoirs of Joffre*, trans. Col. T. Bentley Mott. vol. 1 (New York: Harper and Brothers, 1932), 305.

40. George H. Cassar, *Kitchener: Architect of Victory* (London: William Kimber, 1977), 245.

41. Philpott, *Anglo-French Relations*, 43–45; Joffre, *Memoirs*, vol. 1, 305–306; Lt. Gen. E. J. Galet, *Albert King of the Belgians in the Great War*, trans. Sir Ernest Swinton (Boston: Houghton Mifflin Co., 1931), 231.

42. Galet, *Albert King*, 222–225; Churchill, *World Crisis*, vol. 1, 384–386.

43. Churchill to Kitchener, telegram sent at 10:30 P.M., October 6, 1914, WO 32/5086/78.

44. Kitchener to Rawlinson, telegram sent at 8 A.M., October 7, 1914, WO 32/5086/80.

45. Rawlinson to Kitchener, telephone call in the late afternoon or early evening, October 7, 1914, WO 32/5086/90.

46. French to Kitchener, telegram sent at 6:30 P.M., October 7, 1914, WO 32/5086/89.

47. Kitchener to Bertie, telegram sent at 9:15 A.M., October 7, 1914; Bertie to Kitchener, telegram sent at 1:55 A.M., October 8, 1914, WO 32/5086/81, 92.

48. Kitchener to Bertie, telegram sent at 9:20 A.M., October 8, 1914, WO 32/5086/94.

49. Kitchener to French, October 11, 1914, French papers, 75/46/11.

50. Much of the public criticism centered on Churchill's use of untrained recruits in defense of the fortress. Most of the naval division got away, but in the confusion and darkness, two battalions inadvertently crossed into Holland and were interned.

51. Brock and Brock, eds., *Letters to Venetia Stanley,* 275.

52. Churchill to Kitchener, September 13, 1914, Kitchener papers, PRO 30/57/72.

53. Gilbert, *Churchill,* vol. 3, 35–36.

54. David French, *British Strategy and War Aims, 1914–1916* (London: Allen and Unwin, 1986), 44.

55. Minutes of the CID, October 7, 1914, CAB 2/3.

56. For the CID investigations see John Gooch, *The Plans of War: The General Staff and British Military Strategy, c. 1900–1916* (London: Routledge and Kegan Paul, 1974), 166, 284–285, 293–295.

57. Hankey, *Supreme Command,* vol. 1, 216.

58. Gilbert, *Churchill,* vol. 3, 138.

59. Cited in Cassar, *Kitchener,* 257.

60. Brock and Brock, eds., *Letters to Venetia Stanley,* 281; See also David, ed., *Inside Asquith's Cabinet,* 200–201.

61. Churchill, *World Crisis,* vol. 1, 490–491; Cassar, *Kitchener,* 258.

62. Marshal F. Foch, *Memoirs,* trans, Col. T. Bentley Mott (London: William Heinemann, 1931), 183–184; Report of Kitchener's visit, November 2, 1914, Asquith papers, vol. 7; Raymond Poincaré, *Au Service de la France,* vol. 5 (Paris: Plon-Nourrit, 1928), 411–412; Joffre, *Memoirs,* vol. 1, 318–319.

63. Brock and Brock, eds., *Letters to Venetia Stanley,* 302.

64. David, ed., *Inside Asquith's Cabinet,* 205.

65. Cassar, *Kitchener,* 249–250.

66. Wilson diary, November 6, 1914, Wilson papers; Joffre, *Memoirs,* vol. 1, 319.

67. Kitchener to French, December 9, 1914, French papers, 75/46/11; Churchill to French, December 8, 1914, French papers, 75/46/11.

68. Edmonds, *France and Belgium, 1915,* vol. 1, 15.

69. Philpott, *Anglo-French Relations,* 55; George H. Cassar, *The Tragedy of Sir John French* (Newark, Del.: University of Delaware Press, 1985), 186–187.

70. Sir George Arthur, *Life of Lord Kitchener,* vol. 3 (London: Macmillan and Co., 1920), 87.

71. Edmonds, *France and Belgium, 1915,* vol. 1, 15.

72. Hankey, *Supreme Command,* vol. 1, 260.

73. Philip Magnus, *Kitchener: Portrait of an Imperialist* (London: John Murray, 1958), 306.

74. Gilbert, ed., *Companion to Churchill,* vol. 3, pt. 1, 331–332.

75. Cassar, *Kitchener,* 261–262.

76. Mary Soames, *Clementine Churchill* (Boston: Houghton Mifflin Co., 1979), 141.

77. Cassar, *Kitchener,* 263.

78. Hankey, *Supreme Command,* vol. 1, 237–239; Dardanelles Commission, *First Report* (London: HMSO, 1917), 5–6; H. H. Asquith, *Memories and Reflec-*

tions, vol. 2 (London: Cassell, 1928), 87: George H. Cassar, *Asquith As War Leader* (London: Hambledon Press, 1994), 54–55.

79. For example, he poured his heart out to Sir George Riddell, who kept a detailed record of their conversation. *Lord Riddell's War Diary, 1914–1918* (London: Nicholson and Watson, 1933) is a shortened edition of his unpublished diaries for the period.

80. Hankey to Dardanelles Commission, September 19, 1916, CAB 19/33.

81. Riddell diary, November 19, 1914, Riddell papers, ADD 62974.

82. The Earl of Derby, "K," in *The Lord Kitchener Memorial Book*, ed. Sir Hedley Le Bas (London: Hodder and Stoughton, 1917).

Chapter 7: Drawn into the Dardanelles Vortex

1. Viscount Grey of Fallodon, *Twenty-Five Years*, vol. 1 (New York: Frederick A. Stokes Co., 1925), 71–72.

2. Kitchener to French, January 2, 1915, Kitchener papers, PRO 30/57/50.

3. Lord Rawlinson, "Notes on the Situation of the Allied Forces in Flanders at the Beginning of 1915," December 29, 1914, Creedy papers, WO 159/3/1.

4. Lt. Gen. Sir George Macmunn and Cyril Falls, *Military Operations: Egypt and Palestine*, vol. 1 (London: HMSO, 1928), 20–21; Maj. Gen. Sir C. E. Callwell, *Experiences of a Dug-Out, 1914–1918* (London: Constable and Co., 1920), 62–63; Sir Llewellyn Woodward, *Great Britain and the War of 1914–1918* (London: Methuen, 1967), 95–96; Sir George Arthur, *General Sir John Maxwell* (London: John Murray, 1932), 153–154.

5. Churchill to Asquith, December 29, 1914, in *Companion to Churchill*, vol. 3, pt. 1, 343–345.

6. Lord Hankey, *The Supreme Command, 1914–1918*, vol. 1 (London: Allen and Unwin, 1961), 244–250.

7. David Lloyd George, *War Memoirs*, vol. 1 (London: Odhams Press, 1938), 219–226.

8. Kitchener to French, January 2, 1915, Kitchener papers, PRO 30/57/50.

9. William J. Philpott, *Anglo-French Relations and Strategy on the Western Front, 1914–1918* (New York: St. Martin's Press, 1996), 60.

10. French to Kitchener, January 3 and 4, 1915, Kitchener papers, PRO 30/57/50.

11. David French, *British Strategy and War Aims, 1914–1916* (London: Allen and Unwin, 1986), xi–xii; David Woodward, *Lloyd George and the Generals* (Newark, Del.: University of Delaware Press, 1983), 28–29; Victor Bonham-Carter, *Soldier True: The Life and Times of Field Marshal Sir William Robertson* (London: Frederick Muller, 1963), 107–109; Trevor Wilson, *The Myriad Faces of War* (Cambridge: Polity Press, 1986), 104–105.

12. Hanbury Williams Dispatch B1, December 30, 1914, WO 106/1103; Dardanelles Commission, *First Report* (London: HMSO, 1917), 15.

13. Martin Gilbert, *Winston S. Churchill: The Challenge of War, 1914–1916*, vol. 3 (Boston: Houghton Mifflin Co., 1971), 232–233.

14. Brig. Gen. C. F. Aspinall-Oglander, *Military Operations: Gallipoli*, vol. 1 (London: William Heinemann, 1929), 52–53.

15. There is a good, brief description of the battle of Sarikamish in Edward J. Erickson, *Ordered to Die: A History of the Ottoman Army in the First World War* (Westport, Conn.: Greenwood Press, 2001), 54–60.

16. Hanbury Williams Dispatch C1, January 5, 1915, WO 105/1103.

17. Minutes of the War Council, January 7, 1915, CAB 42/1/11.

18. Minutes of the War Council, January 8, 1915, CAB 42/1/12; Hankey, *Supreme Command*, vol. 1, 260–262.

19. The letter is reproduced in full in Sir George Arthur, *Life of Lord Kitchener*, vol. 3 (London: Macmillan and Co., 1920), 90–94.

20. Philpott, *Anglo-French Relations*, 59.

21. "An Appreciation," n.d., but early January 1915, Creedy papers, WO 159/3/2. The document appears to have been written in response to French's note of January 4, 1915.

22. Dardanelles Commission, *First Report*, 16–17.

23. Dardanelles Commission, *First Report*, 17–18.

24. Formed after the outbreak of the war, it consisted of, among others, the First Lord, the First Sea Lord, the Chief of the Staff (Vice Adm. Sir Henry Oliver), the Admiral of the Fleet (Sir Arthur Wilson), and the Naval Secretary (Commodore de Bartolomé).

25. Battenberg was hounded out of office because of his German name.

26. A. J. Marder, *From the Dreadnought to Scapa Flow*, vol. 2 (London: Oxford University Press, 1965), 214.

27. Asquith set up a commission of inquiry in July 1916 to examine the causes of the failure of the Dardanelles operation. It held eighty-nine sittings over the next eighteen months and took evidence from all those in the planning and execution of the campaign, except Kitchener, who had gone down with the *Hampshire* on June 5, 1916. The commission released two (or three if the brief supplement to the first report is counted) heavily censored reports in 1917. The full proceedings were never published, but became available to researchers on January 1, 1968.

28. Churchill to Dardanelles Commission, September 28, 1916, CAB 19/33. Churchill gave a similar version in *The World Crisis*, vol. 2 (New York: Charles Scribner's Sons, 1951), 103.

29. Testimony provided to the Dardanelles Commission by Arthur (December 1, 1916), Creedy (December 4, 1916), von Donop (December 4, 1916), and Cowans (March 30, 1917), CAB 19/33. Arthur also submitted a written statement to the commission, CAB 19/28.

30. Von Donop to Dardanelles Commission, December 4, 1916, CAB 19/33.

31. Creedy to Dardanelles Commission, January 4, 1917, CAB 19/33.

32. Churchill to Dardanelles Commission, December 1, 1916, CAB 19/33.

33. Dardanelles Commission, *First Report*, 3.

34. Minutes of the War Council, May 14, 1915, CAB 42/2/19.

35. Hankey, *Supreme Command*, vol. 1, 265–266.

36. Minutes of the War Council, January 13, 1915, CAB 42/1/16.

37. Keith Neilson, *Strategy and Supply: The Anglo-Russian Alliance, 1914–1917* (London: Allen and Unwin, 1984), 63. See also Reginald Viscount Esher, *The Tragedy of Lord Kitchener* (London: John Murray, 1921), 91.

38. Churchill to Kitchener, January 20, 1915; Churchill to Kitchener and Grey, January 26, 1915; both letters are in *Companion to Churchill*, vol. 3, pt. 1, 433, 458.

39. John Grigg, *Lloyd George: From Peace to War, 1912–1916*, (London: Methuen, 1985), 204.

40. George H. Cassar, *Asquith As War Leader* (London: Hambledon Press, 1994), 63.

41. Cassar, *Asquith*, 64.

42. Oliver Viscount Esher, ed., *Journals and Letters of Reginald Viscount Esher*, vol. 3 (London: Nicholson and Watson, 1938), 208–209.

43. Esher, ed., *Journals*, vol. 3, 210.

44. Minutes of the War Council meeting at 11.30 A.M., January 28, 1915, CAB 42/1/26.

45. Churchill, *World Crisis*, vol. 2, 163–164.

46. Field Marshal Sir William Robertson, *Soldiers and Statesmen, 1914–1918*, vol. 1 (London: Cassell and Co., 1926), 103.

47. George B. Leon, *Greece and the Great Powers, 1914–1917* (Thessaloniki: Institute for Balkan Studies, 1974), 108–109.

48. Callwell to Robertson, January 30, 1915, Robertson papers, I/8/1.

49. Minutes of the subcommittee of the War Council, meeting at 4 P.M., January 28, 1915, CAB 42/1/27.

50. Minutes of the War Council, meeting at 6:30 P.M., January 28, 1915, CAB 42/1/28.

51. Churchill, *World Crisis*, vol. 2, 176–177.

52. George H. Cassar, *The French and the Dardanelles* (London: Allen and Unwin, 1971), 34–40; David Dutton, "The Balkan Campaign and French War Aims in the Great War," *English Historical Review* 94 (1979): 100–101; Leon, *Greece and the Great Powers*, 101–102.

53. Woodward, *Lloyd George*, 37–38.

54. Hankey, *Supreme Command*, vol. 1, 277.

55. French, *British Strategy*, 72–73.

56. Hankey, *Supreme Command*, vol. 1, 277.

57. Macmunn and Falls, *Egypt and Palestine*, vol. 1, ch. 3; Erickson, *Ordered to Die*, 69–71. Erickson claims that Turkish losses amounted to about thirteen hundred.

58. Minutes of the War Council, February 9, 1915, CAB 42/1/33.

59. David Dutton, *The Politics of Diplomacy: Britain and France in the Balkans in the First World War* (London: I. B. Tauris Publishers, 1998), 28; Neilson, *Strategy and Supply*, 68–69; Leon, *Greece and the Great Powers*, 109–121; Hankey, *Supreme Command*, vol. 1, 278–279.

60. Gilbert, *Churchill*, vol. 3, 286–287.

61. Minutes of the War Council, February 9, 1915, CAB 42/1/33.

62. John Presland, *Deedes Bey* (London: Macmillan and Co., 1942), 233–234.

63. Minutes of the War Council, February 16, 1915, CAB 42/1/35.

64. For a detailed examination of the French side of the campaign, see Cassar, *The French and the Dardanelles.*

65. Lt. Gen. Sir Henry Sclater (adjutant-general under Kitchener) to Dardanelles Commission, February 16, 1917, CAB 19/33.

66. Churchill to Kitchener, February 13, 1915, in *Companion to Churchill*, vol. 3, pt. 1, 524 n. 2.

67. Margot Asquith diary, February 19, 1915, cited in *Companion to Churchill*, vol. 3, pt. 1, 524.

68. Michael, and Eleanor Brock, eds., *H. H. Asquith: Letters to Venetia Stanley* (Oxford: Oxford University Press, 1982), 436.

69. Margot Asquith diary, February 19, 1915, cited in *Companion to Churchill*, vol. 3, part 1, 524–525.

70. Churchill to Asquith, February 17, 1915, in *Companion to Churchill*, vol. 3, part 1, 518.

71. Churchill to Kitchener, February 19, 1915 in *Companion to Churchill*, vol. 3, part 1, 525.

72. Minutes of the War Council, February 19, 1915, CAB 42/1/36.

73. Besides the leading British newspapers of the day, the statement can be seen in Hankey, *Supreme Command*, vol. 1, 282–283.

74. A. J. P. Taylor, ed., *Lloyd George: A Diary by Frances Stevenson* (New York: Harper and Row, 1971), 50.

75. See for example Brock and Brock, eds., *Letters to Venetia Stanley*, 374.

76. Cassar, *Asquith*, 68.

77. Lady Violet Bonham Carter, *Winston Churchill: An Intimate Portrait* (New York: Harcourt, Brace and World, 1965), 294.

78. Minutes of the War Council, February 24, 1915, CAB 42/1/42.

79. Aspinall-Oglander, *Gallipoli*, vol. 1, 74–75.

80. Minutes of the War Council, February 24 and 26, 1915, CAB 42/1/42, 47.

81. George H. Cassar, "Kitchener at the War Office," in *Facing Armageddon*, ed. Hugh Cecil and Peter Liddle (London: Leo Cooper, 1996), 41–42.

82. Cassar, *Asquith*, 77–78.

83. General Sir Ian Hamilton, *Gallipoli Diary*, vol. 1 (New York: George H. Doran Co., 1920), 2–6.

84. Kitchener's instructions to Hamilton are reproduced in full in Ian B. M. Hamilton, *The Happy Warrior: A Life of General Sir Ian Hamilton* (London: Cassell, 1966), 279–281.

85. David Fromkin, *A Peace to End All Peace* (New York: Henry Holt, 1989), 86.

86. General Staff, "The Question of Employing Forces Elsewhere than in the Western Theatre of War," n.d. but written at the end of January 1915, possibly for the War Council meeting on January 28. WO 106/1523.

87. Birdwood correspondence with Kitchener during the first half of March 1915, Kitchener papers, PRO 30/57/61.

88. Maxwell to Kitchener, March 8, 1915, Kitchener papers, PRO 30/57/55.

89. British policy makers believed, almost without exception, that the lengthy military preparations required in mounting an attack against a first-class European power would be unnecessary in a confrontation with Turkey. See David French, "The Origins of the Dardanelles Campaign Reconsidered," *History* 68 (1983): 213–215.

90. Carden had suffered a nervous breakdown.

91. There are many accounts detailing the naval operations, but the best, in my view, is Paul G. Halpern, *The Naval War in the Mediterranean, 1914–1918* (Annapolis: Naval Institute, 1987).

92. Dardanelles Commission, *First Report*, 37.

93. Dardanelles Commission, *First Report*, 37.

94. Churchill, *World Crisis*, vol. 2, 545.

95. The total strength of the Turkish defenders in April is difficult to determine. Two very recent books based on Turkish primary sources, Erickson, *Ordered to Die*, and Tim Travers, *Gallipoli 1915* (Charleston: Tempus, 2001), do not give a figure, although they identify the units and their disposition. In *Five Years in Turkey* (Annapolis: Naval Institute, 1927), 64, Liman von Sanders, who commanded the Turkish Army on the Gallipoli Peninsula, placed its overall strength at around sixty thousand. But, as Travers has shown, von Sanders's memoirs vary at times from the actual facts, and the number of troops at his disposal was probably higher.

Chapter 8: Imperial Issues and Peripheral Theaters II

1. Kitchener to Grey, November 1, 1914, Grey papers, FO 800/102.

2. Briton C. Busch, *Britain, India and the Arabs, 1914–1921* (Berkeley: University of California Press, 1971), 65–66; Elie Kedourie, *Into the Anglo-Arab Labyrinth* (Cambridge: Cambridge University Press, 1976), 34–36; Lord Lloyd, *Egypt since Cromer*, vol. 1 (London: Macmillan and Co., 1933), 213.

3. Michael G. Ekstein, "Russia, Constantinople and the Straits," in *British*

Foreign Policy under Sir Edward Grey, ed. F. H. Hinsley (Cambridge: Cambridge University Press, 1977), 431–434; Keith Neilson, *Britain and the Last Tsar* (Oxford: Clarendon Press, 1995), 358–359.

4. David French, *British Strategy and War Aims, 1914–1916* (London: Allen and Unwin, 1986), 82.

5. Storrs to FitzGerald, March 8, 1915, Kitchener papers, PRO 30/57/45/QQ18.

6. David Fromkin, *A Peace to End All Peace* (New York: Henry Holt, 1989), 143.

7. Kedourie, *Anglo-Arab Labyrinth,* 33.

8. Grey's minute on Kitchener's letter of November 14, 1914, Grey papers, FO 800/102.

9. Fromkin, *A Peace,* 93–94.

10. George H. Cassar, *Asquith As War Leader* (London: Hambledon Press, 1994), 70; V. H. Rothwell, *British War Aims and Peace Diplomacy, 1914–1918* (Oxford: Clarendon Press, 1971), 18–19.

11. Minutes of the War Council, March 10, 1915, CAB 42/2/5.

12. French, *British Strategy,* 82.

13. Kitchener, "The Future Relations of the Great Powers," April 21, 1915, CAB 37/127/34.

14. Kitchener, "Alexandretta and Mesopotamia," March 16, 1915, CAB 42/2/10.

15. Minutes of the War Council, March 10, 1915, CAB 42/2/5.

16. McMahon to Kitchener, February 4, 1915, Kitchener papers, PRO 30/57/47/QQ15.

17. Kitchener, "Alexandretta and Messopotamia," CAB 42/2/10.

18. Minutes of the War Council, March 19, 1915, CAB 42/2/14; The Admiralty, "Alexandretta and Mesopotamia," March 17, 1915, CAB 42/2/11; H. B. Jackson, "Alexandretta. Its Importance As a Future Base," March 18, 1915, CAB 42/2/18; Sir A. Hirtzel, "Note by the Secretary, Political Department, India Office," March 14, 1915, CAB 37/126/14; "Note by Sir E. Barrow on the Defence of Mesopotamia," CAB 37/126/14; Michael and Eleanor Brock, eds., *H. H. Asquith: Letters to Venetia Stanley* (Oxford: Oxford University Press, 1982), 509–510; Cassar, *Asquith,* 75–76; Keith Neilson, "For Diplomatic, Economic, Strategic and Telegraphic Reasons: British Imperial Defence, the Middle East and India," in *Far Flung Lines,* ed. Greg Kennedy and Keith Neilson (London: Frank Cass, 1996).

19. Roger Adelson, *Mark Sykes: Portrait of an Amateur* (London: Jonathan Cape, 1975), passim.

20. Sykes to Arthur, September 12, 1916, Kitchener papers, PRO 30/57/91.

21. The report was never published, but can be found, along with its appendixes, in CAB 27/1.

22. Jukka Nevakivi, "Lord Kitchener and the Partition of the Ottoman Em-

pire, 1915–1916," in *Studies in International History*, ed. K. Bourne and D. C. Watts (London: Longmans, 1967), 325–326.

23. Minutes of the War Council, March 10, 1915, CAB 42/2/5.

24. Kitchener, "Alexandretta and Messopotamia," CAB 42/2/10.

25. Kitchener did not own a home or flat in London. He lived first at a residence at 2 Carleton Gardens, then in the middle of March 1915 accepted the King's offer of York House, St James's Place, for the remainder of the war.

26. Sykes to Arthur, September 12, 1916, PRO 30/57/91.

27. Busch, *Britain, India and the Arabs*, ch. 2, passim.

28. Randall Baker, *King Husain and the Kingdom of Hejaz* (New York: Oleander, 1979), 57.

29. Lt. Gen. Sir George Macmunn and Cyril Falls, *Military Operations: Egypt and Palestine*, vol. 1 (London: HMSO, 1928), 65–67, 221–22.

30. Hardinge to Crewe, February 16, 1915, Kitchener papers, PRO 30/57/69.

31. Minutes of the War Council, February 24, 1915, CAB 42/1/42.

32. A. J. Barker, *The Bastard War: The Mesopotamian Campaign of 1914–1918* (New York: Dial Press, 1967), ch. 2.

33. Brig. Gen. F. J. Moberly, *Military Operations: Togoland and the Cameroons, 1914–1916* (London: HMSO, 1931), 255–256; Harcourt to Kitchener, March 30, 1915, Creedy papers, WO 159/20.

34. Dobell to War Office, April 11, 1915, WO 33/748.

35. Kitchener to Dobell, April 14, 1915, WO 33/748.

36. Moberly, *Togoland and the Cameroons*, 259–264.

37. Moberly, *Togoland and the Cameroons*, 271–284.

38. Dobell to War Office, June 8 and 12, 1915, WO 33/748.

39. Kitchener to Dobell, June 15, 1915, WO 33/748.

40. Dobell to War Office, June 23, 1915, WO 33/748.

41. General Paul von Lettow-Vorbeck, *East African Campaigns* (New York: R. Speller, 1957), 56–57.

42. Leonard Mosley, *Duel for Kilimanjaro: An Account of the East African Campaign, 1914–1918* (London: Weidenfeld and Nicolson, 1963), 97.

43. Kitchener to Wapshare, January 12, 1915, WO 33/714.

44. Wapshare to Kitchener, January 19, 1915, WO 33/714.

45. Wapshare to Kitchener, January 26, 1915, WO 33/714.

46. Colonel Kitchener to War Office, March 18, 1915, WO 33/858.

47. Duff to Kitchener, March 20, 1915, WO 33/714.

48. Kitchener to Duff, March 23, 1915, WO 33/714.

49. Duff to Kitchener, March 25, 1915, WO 33/714.

50. War Office to Wapshare, April 3, 1915, WO 33/858.

51. Wapshare to War Office, April 10, 1915, WO 33/858.

52. Kitchener to Wapshare, April 12, 1915, WO 33/858.

53. Col. R. Meinertzhagen, *Army Diary, 1899–1926* (Edinburgh: Oliver and Boyd, 1960), 123.

54. War Office to Tighe, April 17, 1915, WO 33/ 858.

55. Tighe to War Office, April 20, 1915, WO 33/858.

56. War Office to Tighe, May 4, 1915, WO 33/858.

57. Kitchener to Tighe, May 14, 1915, WO 33/858.

58. Tighe to War Office, May 20, 1915 and June 2, 1915, WO 33/858.

59. Kitchener to Tighe, June 3, 1915, WO 33/858.

60. Lt. Col. Charles Hordern, *Military Operations: East Africa*, vol. 1 (London: HMSO, 1941), 152–153.

Chapter 9: Mounting Troubles

1. Michael and Eleanor Brock, eds., *H. H. Asquith: Letters to Venetia Stanley* (Oxford: Oxford University Press, 1982), 434

2. Esher to Kitchener, February 13 and 15, 1915, Kitchener papers, PRO 30/57/59.

3. David French has an excellent article on the subject. "The Meaning of Attrition, 1914–1916," *English Historical Review* 103 (1988): 385–405.

4. William J. Philpott, *Anglo-French Relations and Strategy on the Western Front, 1914–1918* (New York: St. Martin's Press, 1996), 75.

5. Wilson diary, February 28, 1915, Wilson papers.

6. De Broqueville to Kitchener, February 23, 1915, Kitchener papers, PRO 30/57/57.

7. Kitchener to French, telegram, 9.55 A.M., February 24, 1915, Kitchener papers, PRO 30/57/57.

8. French to Kitchener, telegram, 6.47 P.M., February 24, 1915, Kitchener papers, PRO 30/57/57.

9. The Imperial War Museum possesses French's letters to his paramour, Mrs. Winifred Bennett.

10. Esher to Kitchener, February 21, 1915, Kitchener papers, PRO 30/57/59.

11. Kitchener to Esher, February 22, 1915; Esher to Kitchener February 27, 1915, both in Kitchener papers, PRO 30/57/59.

12. Kitchener to French, February 27, 1915, French papers, 7/4(2); French diary, February 28, 1915, French papers.

13. Joffre to French, March 7, 1915, WO 158/13.

14. George H. Cassar, *The Tragedy of Sir John French* (Newark, Del.: University of Delaware Press, 1985), 210–214.

15. Brock and Brock, eds., *Letters to Venetia Stanley*, 488.

16. George H. Cassar, *Kitchener: Architect of Victory* (London: William Kimber, 1977), 300–302.

17. Sir Ian Hamilton, *Gallipoli Diary*, vol. 1 (New York: George H. Doran Co., 1920), 4–5.

18. French diary, March 23, 1915, French papers; Cassar, *Sir John French*, 217–218.

19. Philpott, *Anglo-French Relations*, 76.

20. Henry Wilson, "Notes on Meeting at Chantilly," March 29, 1915, Creedy papers, WO 159/7; French diary, March 29, 1915, French papers.

21. French diary, March 29, 1915, French papers.

22. French diary, March 30, 1915, French papers.

23. Cassar, *Kitchener*, 334–338.

24. Trevor Wilson, *The Myriad Faces of War* (Cambridge: Polity Press, 1986), 218.

25. Ian V. Hogg, *The Guns, 1914–1918* (New York: Ballantine Books, 1971), 16–17.

26. Cassar, *Kitchener*, 333.

27. Sir George Arthur, *Life of Lord Kitchener*, vol. 3 (London: Macmillan and Co., 1920), 271; A. F. Petch (agent for Bethlehem Steel) to Arthur, January 22, 1917, Kitchener papers, PRO 30/57/91.

28. David French, *British Economic and Strategic Planning, 1905–1915* (London: Allen and Unwin, 1982), 15.

29. Chris Wrigley, "The Ministry of Munitions: An Innovatory Department," in *War and the State*, ed. Kathleen Burke (London: Allen and Unwin, 1982), 36–37.

30. Wrigley, "Ministry of Munitions," 39; French, *British Economic*, ch. 10, passim.

31. Duncan Crow, *A Man of Push and Go* (London: Hart-Davis, 1965), 71.

32. Parliamentary Debates, *House of Lords*, September 7, 1914, vol. 17, col. 736.

33. Arthur, *Lord Kitchener*, vol. 3, 74.

34. Great Britain, *History of the Ministry of Munitions*, vol. 1 (London: HMSO, 1920), ch. 4, pt. 1; R. J. Q. Adams, *Arms and the Wizard: Lloyd George and the Ministry of Munitions* (College Station: Texas A & M University Press, 1978), 19–20.

35. Brock and Brock, eds., *Letters to Venetia Stanley*, 544.

36. A. J. P. Taylor, ed., *Lloyd George: A Diary by Frances Stevenson* (New York: Harper and Row, 1971), 7.

37. David Lloyd George, *War Memoirs*, vol. 1 (London: Odhams Press, 1938), 359–360.

38. Lloyd George, *War Memoirs*, vol. 1, 357.

39. John Terraine, *The Smoke and the Fire: Myths and Anti-Myths of War, 1861–1945* (London: Sidgwick and Jackson, 1980), 137.

40. Terraine, *Smoke and Fire*, 138–139.

41. Lloyd George, *War Memoirs*, vol. 1, 92.

42. Cassar, *Kitchener*, 336.

43. Wilson, *Myriad Faces of War*, 218.

44. W. A. S. Hewins, *The Apologia of an Imperialist* (London: Constable and Co., 1929), vol. 2, 26.

45. Parliamentary Debates, *House of Lords*, March 15, 1915, vol. 18, col. 719–724.

46. Crow, *Man of Push and Go*, 91–92.

47. Minutes of the meeting, March 5, 1915, MUN 5/6/170/22.

48. "Provisional Conclusions of the Proposed Committee on War Supplies," March 22, 1915, Lloyd George papers, C/14/3/4; Asquith to Lloyd George, March 22, 1915, Lloyd George papers, C/6/11/36; Asquith to Kitchener, March 23, 1915, Kitchener papers, PRO 30/57/82.

49. Kitchener to Asquith, March 25, 1915, Kitchener papers, PRO 30/57/82; Kitchener to Lloyd George, March 26, 1915, Kitchener papers, PRO 30/57/82.

50. Lloyd George to Kitchener, March 25, 1915, Kitchener papers, PRO 30/57/82; Brock and Brock, eds., *Letters to Venetia Stanley*, 514.

51. Cited in Lloyd George, *War Memoirs*, vol. 1, 108.

52. Lloyd George, *War Memoirs*, vol. 1, 121–122; Lloyd George to Asquith, May 19, 1915, Asquith papers, vol. 14.

53. Asquith, Memorandum on the Munitions of War Committee, April 8, 1915, Kitchener papers, PRO 30/57/82.

54. Cassar, *Kitchener*, 345.

55. Lord Hankey, *The Supreme Command, 1914–1918*, vol. 1 (London: Allen and Unwin, 1961), 311; David, ed., *Inside Asquith's Cabinet*, 235–236.

56. *History of Ministry of Munitions*, vol. 1, pt. 3, 61.

57. Crow, *Man of Push and Go*, 111.

58. Cited in Hankey, *Supreme Command*, vol. 1, 312.

59. David French, "The Military Background to the 'Shell Crisis' of May 1915," *Journal of Strategic Studies* 2 (1979): 201; Cassar, *Sir John French*, 232.

60. Kitchener to Asquith, April 14, 1915, Asquith papers, vol. 14.

61. French to Kitchener, April 29, 1915, WO 32/5/155.

62. The full letter can be seen in Arthur, *Lord Kitchener*, vol. 3, 235–236.

63. Cassar, *Sir John French*, 233–235.

64. There are more books written about Gallipoli in the English-speaking world than on any other campaign in World War I. Michael Hickey, *Gallipoli* (London: John Murray, 1995), is among the better recent books, but in my view, Robert Rhodes James, *Gallipoli* (London: Batsford, 1965), is still the best single-volume study

65. British losses amounted to some fourteen thousand, whereas the War Office had calculated the number of likely casualties for the landing and capture of the peninsula at about five thousand.

66. Esher diary, May 11, 1915, Esher papers.

67. Cassar, *Sir John French*, 240–241; French, "'Shell Crisis' of May 1915," 201–202.

68. Riddell diary, May 27, 1915, Riddell papers, ADD 62975.

69. Cassar, *Kitchener*, 356.

70. Asquith clung to that illusion until 1919, when French admitted his part in the shell crisis in his book *1914*.

71. Stephen Koss, *Asquith* (London: A. Lane, 1976), 181; Roy Jenkins, *Asquith* (London: Collins, 1978), 357.

72. For a detailed explanation of the disagreement between Churchill and Fisher, see Martin Gilbert, *Winston S. Churchill: The Challenge of War, 1914–1916*, vol. 3 (Boston: Houghton Mifflin Co., 1971), 417ff, and Arthur J. Marder, *From the Dreadnought to Scapa Flow*, vol. 2 (London: Oxford University Press, 1965), ch. 11.

73. See, for example, Lord Beaverbrook, *Politicians and the War, 1914–1916* (London: Oldbourne Book Co., 1960), bk. 1, ch. 8; Trevor Wilson, *The Downfall of the Liberal Party, 1914–1945* (London: Collins, 1966), 53–64; Jenkins, *Asquith*, 355–362; R. J. Q. Adams, *Bonar Law* (Stanford: Stanford University Press, 1999), 181–188; Cameron Hazlehurst, *Politicians at War* (London: Jonathan Cape, 1971), pt. 3; George H. Cassar, *Asquith As War Leader* (London: Hambledon Press, 1994), ch. 6.

74. Cassar, *Asquith*, 98.

75. David R. Woodward, *Lloyd George and the Generals* (Newark, Del.: University of Delaware Press, 1983), 51–52; Stephen Inwood, "The Role of the Press in English Politics during the First World War, with Special Reference to the Period 1914–1916" (Ph. D. thesis, Oxford University, 1971), 217–218.

76. Cassar, *Kitchener*, 366ff; Cassar, *Asquith*, 102–103.

77. Wrigley, "Ministry of Munitions," 39.

78. See especially Adams, *Arms and the Wizard*.

79. As a rule, memoirs of high-ranking public and military officials must be approached with caution, and none more so than Lloyd George's *War Memoirs*, as they are nauseatingly self-serving and peppered with half-truths and out-and-out lies.

80. Lloyd George, *War Memoirs*, vol. 1, 146.

81. Crow, *Man of Push and Go*, 69.

82. Edmonds wrote in his memoirs, "Lloyd George knew nothing whatever about munitions. He hustled the factories . . . to produce quantities that he might quote in the House of Commons, and to the public regardless of quality and this was the cause of the defective ammunition which handicapped the Army at the battle of the Somme," Edmonds papers, III/10/15.

83. See for example John Grigg, *Lloyd George: From Peace to War, 1912–1916* (London: Methuen, 1985), 256.

84. The Treasury Agreement and especially the Munitions of War Act gave the new ministry the authority to take control of firms deemed essential for the production of munitions. In these places, the rights of labor were seriously curtailed. Strikes were forbidden, a system of arbitration was laid down to settle disputes, and restrictive practices in the workshops were suspended to permit dilution of skilled workers by semiskilled and unskilled personnel.

85. War Office, *Statistics of the Military Effort of the British Empire during the*

Great War (London: HMSO, 1922), 466ff; Great Britain, *History of the Ministry of Munitions,* vol. 1, pt. 1, appendixes 3 and 4, 146–150.

86. Brig. Gen. Sir James E. Edmonds, *Military Operations: France and Belgium, 1915,* vol. 1 (London: Macmillan and Co., 1922–1938), 49–50.

Chapter 10: Armaments for Russia

1. Norman Stone, *The Eastern Front, 1914–1917* (New York: Charles Scribner's Sons, 1975), 150.

2. Raymond Poincaré, *Au Service de la France,* vol. 6 (Paris: Plon-Nourrit, 1930), 4–5.

3. Keith Neilson, *Strategy and Supply: The Anglo-Russian Alliance, 1914–1917* (London: Allen and Unwin, 1984), 53–54.

4. Neilson, *Strategy and Supply,* 51–53.

5. Benckendorff to Foreign Office, September 15, 1914, FO 368/1085/49832.

6. Guthrie Smith to Foreign Office, September 18, 1914, FO 368/1085/49832.

7. Hanbury Williams Dispatch I, January 15, 1915, WO 106/1105.

8. Hanbury Williams to Kitchener, January 3, 1915, Kitchener papers, PRO 30/57/67.

9. Buchanan to Foreign Office, January 12, 1915, FO 371/2447/4777.

10. Buchanan to Foreign Office, January 24, 1915, FO 371/2447/9016.

11. FitzGerald to Grey, January 25, 1915, FO 371/2447/9016.

12. Buchanan to Foreign Office, January 26, 1915, FO 371/2447/9932.

13. Hanbury Williams Dispatch XI, February 18, 1915, WO 106/1110.

14. Brade to Foreign Office, February 27, 1915, FO 371/2447/23509.

15. Neilson, *Strategy and Supply,* 74–75.

16. For the complete story see Keith Neilson, "Russian Foreign Purchasing in the Great War: A Test Case," *Slavonic and East European Review* 60 (1982): 572–590.

17. Beckendorff to Kitchener, March 11, 1915, PRO 30/57/85.

18. Buchanan to Foreign Office, March 11, 1915, FO 371/2447/28459.

19. "Memorandum on the Steps Taken by the British Government to Assist the Russian Government in Procuring Supplies," August 11, 1915, FO 371/2454/110274; FitzGerald to Foreign Office (for Buchanan), March 10, 1915, FO 371/2147/27712.

20. Buchanan to Grey, March 6, 1915, FO 371/2147/26298.

21. Foreign Office to Buchanan, March 13, 1915, FO 371/2447/29292.

22. Neilson, *Strategy and Supply,* 75.

23. Buchanan to Foreign Office, March 9, 1915, FO 371/2447/27712.

24. Kitchener to Buchanan, March 10, 1915, FO 371/2447/27712.

25. Buchanan to Foreign Office, March 12, 1915, FO 371/ 2447/29292.

26. Neilson, *Strategy and Supply*, 75–76.

27. Kitchener to Buchanan, March 14, 1915, FO 371/2447/29292.

28. Buchanan to Foreign Office, March 18, 1915, FO 371/2447/31388.

29. Kitchener to Buchanan, March 26, 1915, FO 371/2447/35305; "Memorandum on the Steps Taken by the British Government to Assist the Russian Government Procure Supplies," August 11, 1915, FO 371/2454/110274.

30. Buchanan to Foreign Office, March 31, 1915, FO 371/2447/37362.

31. Buchanan to Foreign Office, April 2, 1915, FO 371/2447/38485.

32. Kitchener to Buchanan, April 8, 1915, FO 371/2447/38485.

33. Kitchener to Buchanan, April 9, 1915, FO 371/ 2447/42142.

34. Buchanan to Foreign Office, April 13, 1915, FO 371/2447/42913.

35. Kitchener to Buchanan, April 13, 1915, FO 371/2447/4116; Buchanan to Foreign Office, April 14, 1915, FO 371/2447/44041.

36. The details of the campaign from the Russian side can be followed in Ward Rutherford, *The Tsar's War, 1914–1917* (Cambridge: Ian Faulkner Publishing, 1992) or Stone, *Eastern Front.*

37. Kitchener to Nicholas, April 29, 1915, MUN 4/1296.

38. Hanbury Williams to Kitchener, May 15, 1915, Kitchener papers, PRO 30/57/67.

39. Neilson, *Strategy and Supply*, 87.

40. Hanbury Williams to Kitchener, May 15, 1915, Kitchener papers, PRO 30/57/67.

41. Hanbury Williams to Kitchener, May 19, 1915, Kitchener papers, PRO 30/57/67.

42. Nicholas to Kitchener, May 19, 1915, MUN 4/1296.

43. Knox Dispatch W, May 26, 1915, WO 106/1061. The statement was made by Ianushkevich.

44. Neilson, *Strategy and Supply*, 103.

45. Hanbury Williams to Kitchener, May 24, 1915, Kitchener papers, PRO 30/57/67.

46. Hanbury Williams to Kitchener, May 19, 1915, Kitchener papers, PRO 30/57/67.

47. Clerk's note on draft of telegram sent, May 21, 1915, FO 371/2448/645664.

48. Kitchener to Buchanan, May 21, 1915, FO 371/2448/645664.

49. J. P. Morgan to Morgan, Grenfell, May 20, 1915, MUN 4/270.

50. Morgan, Grenfell to J. P. Morgan, May 20, 1915, MUN 4/270.

51. J. P. Morgan to Morgan, Grenfell, May 21, 1915, MUN 4/270.

52. Morgan, Genfell to J. P. Morgan, May 21, 1915, MUN 4/270.

53. Morgan, Grenfell to J. P. Morgan, May 21, 1915, MUN 4/270.

54. Morgan, Grenfell to J. P. Morgan, May 25 and 27, 1915, MUN 4/270.

55. Morgan, Grenfell to J. P. Morgan, May 27, 1915, MUN 4/270.

56. J. P. Morgan to Morgan, Grenfell, May 28, 1915, MUN 4/270.

57. Buchanan to Foreign Office, May 27, 1915, FO 371/2448/67703.

58. J. P. Morgan to Morgan, Grenfell, May 28, 1915, MUN 4/270.

59. J. P. Morgan to Morgan, Grenfell, May 28, 1915, MUN 4/270.

60. Morgan, Grenfell to J. P. Morgan, May 29, 1915, both telegrams in MUN 4/270.

61. Neilson, *Supply and Strategy*, 100–102.

62. J. P. Morgan to Morgan, Grenfell, June 5, 1915, MUN 4/270.

63. Hanbury Williams to Kitchener, June 13, 1915, Kitchener papers, PRO 30/57/67.

64. Hanbury Williams to Kitchener, June 13, 1915, Kitchener papers, PRO 30/57/67.

65. Hanbury Williams to Kitchener, June 16, 1915, Kitchener papers, PRO 30/57/67.

66. Hanbury Williams to Kitchener, June 17, 1915, Kitchener papers, PRO 30/57/67.

67. Morgan, Grenfell to J. P. Morgan, June 17, 1915, MUN 4/270.

68. J. P. Morgan to Morgan, Grenfell, June 19, 1915, MUN 4/270.

69. Morgan, Grenfell to J. P. Morgan, June 19, 1915, MUN 4/270.

Chapter 11: Collapse of an Active-Defense Policy

1. Winston S. Churchill, *The World Crisis*, vol. 2 (New York: Charles Scribner's Sons, 1951), 402; John Grigg, *Lloyd George: From Peace to War, 1912–1916* (London: Methuen, 1985), 308; Trevor Wilson, *The Myriad Faces of War* (Cambridge: Polity Press, 1986), 205–206; George H. Cassar, *Asquith As War Leader* (London: Hambledon Press, 1994), 111.

2. George H. Cassar, *Kitchener: Architect of Victory* (London: William Kimber, 1977), 368.

3. Paul Guinn, *British Strategy and Politics* (Oxford: Clarendon Press, 1965), 84; Dardanelles Commission, *Final Report* (London: HMSO, 1918), 24; David French, *British Strategy and War Aims, 1914–1916* (London: Allen and Unwin, 1986), 104.

4. Lord Hankey, *The Supreme Command, 1914–1918*, vol. 1 (London: Allen and Unwin, 1961), 337.

5. Kitchener to Wolfe Murray, n.d., but late May 1915, Creedy papers, WO 159/3.

6. Hankey to Asquith, n.d., but probably on May 29, 1915, the day of his interview with Kitchener, WO 159/7.

7. French diary, May 22, 1915, French papers.

8. Wilson diary, May 22, 1915, Wilson papers.

9. Joffre to Kitchener, May 27, 1915, Kitchener papers, PRO 30/57/57.

10. Esher diary, May 21, 1915, Esher papers; Esher to Kitchener, May 23, 1915, Kitchener papers, PRO 30/57/59.

11. Kitchener to Yarde-Buller, May 29, 1915, Creedy papers, WO 159/7; "Notes for Discussion with General Joffre," n.d., Creedy papers, WO 159/7.

12. French to Winifred Bennett, May 24, 1915, French papers.

13. Esher diary, June 11, 1915, Esher papers.

14. "Note of a Meeting Held at the War Office," June 8, 1915, Creedy papers, WO 159/7; Note by Kitchener, June 9, 1915, Creedy papers, WO 159/7; Cassar, *Kitchener*, 374–375.

15. French to Kitchener, June 11, 1915, Kitchener papers, PRO 30/57/50.

16. "Reason for Offensive in Flanders," n.a., but definitely Kitchener, June 12, 1915, Kitchener papers, PRO 30/57/58.

17. William J. Philpott, *Anglo-French Relations and Strategy on the Western Front, 1914–1918* (New York: St. Martin's Press, 1996), 78.

18. For Kitchener's reaction to the withdrawal of the *Queen Elizabeth*, see Cassar, *Kitchener*, 361–363.

19. Kitchener, "The Dardanelles," May 28, 1915, CAB 37/128/27.

20. Brig. Gen. C. F. Aspinall-Oglander, *Military Operations: Gallipoli*, vol. 2 (London: William Heinemann, 1932), 57–60; Hankey, *Supreme Command*, vol. 1, 340–341.

21. Sir Llewellyn Woodward, *Great Britain and the War of 1914–1918* (London: Methuen, 1967), 84; Minutes of the Dardanelles Committee, June 25, 1915, CAB 42/3/5.

22. Brig. Gen. Sir James E. Edmonds, *Military Operations: France and Belgium, 1915*, vol. 2 (London: Macmillan and Co., 1936), 117.

23. Robertson, Minutes of the Military Conference at Chantilly, June 24, 1915, Robertson papers, I/5/14.

24. Kitchener, "An Appreciation of the Military Situation in the Future," June 26, 1915, CAB 37/130/27.

25. Asquith to Kitchener, June 26, 1915, Kitchener papers, PRO 30/57/76.

26. Hanbury Williams to Kitchener, June 14, 1915, Lloyd George papers, D/17/6/17.

27. Knox Dispatch Z, June 16, 1915, WO 106/1063.

28. French, *British Strategy*, 105–106.

29. J. A. Spender and Cyril Asquith, *The Life of Herbert Henry Asquith, Lord Oxford and Asquith*, vol. 2 (London: Hutchinson and Co., 1932), 182; Cassar, *Asquith*, 116–117; French, *British Strategy*, 107.

30. Cassar, *Kitchener*, 381; Stamfordham (summary of an interview with Asquith) to George V, July 9, 1915, Royal Archives, GV Q981/3.

31. Hankey, *Supreme Command*, vol. 1, 348–349; Cassar, *Kitchener*, 381–382; Crewe to Bertie, July 8, 1915, Bertie papers, FO 800/161; Reginald Viscount Esher, *The Tragedy of Lord Kitchener* (London: John Murray, 1921), 139–140.

32. Callwell to Wilson, July 9, 1915, Wilson papers, HHW 2/75/51.

33. "Difficulties of Inspection in Connection with Contracts Placed in

America on Behalf of the Russian Government," n.s., November 15, 1915, MUN 7/149; "Difficulties in Inspection," n.s., n.d., MUN 4/1296.

34. "Minutes of the Sub-Committee on Russian Munitions," n.s., July 1, 1915; "Instructions for the Guidence of Lieutenant Dumontier and M. Lamere . . . in the United States," n.s., n.d., (but July 1915), both in MUN 7/149.

35. "Report upon the Contracts for Munitions Placed . . . on Behalf of the Russian Government," MUN 4/1296.

36. Callwell to Wilson, June 24, 1915, Wilson papers, HHW 2/75/48; Hanbury Williams to Kitchener, July 9, 1915, Kitchener papers, PRO 30/57/67.

37. Knox Dispatch A1, July 4, 1915,WO 106/1064.

38. Lt. Gen. Nicholas N. Golovin, *The Russian Army in the World War* (New Haven: Yale University Press, 1931), 199–200; Maj. Gen. Sir Alfred Knox, *With the Russian Army, 1914–1917*, vol. 1 (London: Hutchinson and Co., 1921), 335–336; M. V. Rodzianko, *The Reign of Rasputin: An Empire's Collapse* (Gulf Breeze, Fla.: Academic International Press, 1973), 142–143. Rodzianko was President of the Russian Duma.

39. Blair to Kitchener, "Notes on the Archangel Route," July 27, 1915, WO 106/996.

40. Callwell to Wilson, June 24, 1915, Wilson papers, HHW 2/75/48.

41. Callwell to Wilson, July 28, 1915, Wilson papers, HHW 2/75/58.

42. Blair Dispatch LXXVI, August 26, 1915, WO 106/999.

43. Knox Dispatch A1, July 4, 1915, WO 106/1064; Hanbury Williams to Kitchener, July 9, 1915, Kitchener papers, PRO 30/57/67.

44. Pares, "Memorandum on Russian Munitions," July 1915, Lloyd George papers, D/12/2/5.

45. Buchanan to Grey, August 3, 1915, Grey papers, FO 800/75.

46. Hanbury Williams to Kitchener, August 11, 1915, Kitchener papers, PRO 30/57/67.

47. Buchanan to Grey, August 3, 1915, Grey papers, FO 800/75.

48. Kitchener memorandum, August 5, 1915, sent to Buchanan via Foreign Office the following day, FO 371/2454/107794.

49. Kitchener, "Memorandum on the Steps Taken by the British Government to Assist the Russian Government in Procuring Supplies," August 11, 1915, FO 371/2454/110274.

50. Grand Duke Nicholas to Kitchener, July 17, 1915, Kitchener papers, PRO 30/57/67.

51. Kitchener to Hanbury Williams, August 4, 1915, WO 33/832.

52. Hanbury Williams to Kitchener, August 6, 1915, WO 33/842.

53. The details may be followed in L. L. Farrar, *Divide and Conquer* (New York: Columbia University Press, 1978), chs. 2 and 3.

54. Jan K. Tanenbaum, *General Maurice Sarrail, 1859–1929* (Chapel Hill: University of North Carolina Press, 1974), 58ff; George H. Cassar, *The French and the Dardanelles* (London: Allen and Unwin, 1971), 157–158.

55. Ward Rutherford, *The Tsar's War, 1914–1917* (Cambridge: Ian Faulkner Publishing, 1992), ch. 13.

56. Buchanan to Foreign Office, August 19, 1915, FO 371/2454/115774.

57. Hanbury Williams to Kitchener, August 18, 1915, WO 33/832.

58. Cassar, *Kitchener*, 388; Asquith to George V, August 20, 1915, CAB 41/36/ 30.

59. Hamilton to Kitchener, August 17, 1915, Hamilton papers, 5/7.

60. Kitchener to Asquith, August 17, 1915, Creedy papers, WO 159/7.

61. Minutes of the Dardanelles Committee, August 20, 1915, CAB 42/3/16.

62. Kitchener to Hanbury Williams, August 20, 1915, FO 371/2450/116873.

63. David, French, "The Meaning of Attrition, 1914–1916," *English Historical Review* 103 (1988): 395.

Chapter 12: Imperial Issues and Peripheral Theaters III

1. David Fromkin, *A Peace to End All Peace* (New York: Henry Holt, 1989), 174.

2. This was the beginning of the now famous Hussein-McMahon correspondence, which can be found in CAB 21/154, among other places. The reference to McMahon's comments on the first letter to the Foreign Office is FO 371/ 2486/117236.

3. Eliezer Tauber, *The Arab Movements in World War I* (London: Frank Cass, 1993), 62–65.

4. Ronald Storrs, *Orientations* (London: Nicholson and Watson, 1945), 153.

5. Fromkin, *A Peace*, 176–177; Tauber, *Arab Movements*, 70–74; Elie Kedourie, *Into the Anglo-Arab Labyrinth* (Cambridge: Cambridge University Press, 1976), 73–76.

6. Fromkin, *A Peace*, 177.

7. Kedourie, *Anglo-Arab Labyrinth*, 76.

8. Storrs to FitzGerald, October 10, 1915, Kitchener papers, PRO 30/57/47/ QQ46.

9. Maxwell to Kitchener, October 12, 1915, FO 371/248/150309.

10. Kitchener to Maxwell, October 13, 1915, FO 371/248/150309.

11. Maxwell to Kitchener, October 16, 1915, FO 371/2486/152729.

12. McMahon to Foreign Office, October 18, 1915, FO 371/2486/152901.

13. Kitchener to Grey, October 18, 1915, FO 371/2486/152901.

14. Kitchener to Foreign Office, October 19, 1915, FO 371/2486/153045.

15. Isaiah Friedman, *The Question of Palestine, 1914–1918* (London: Routledge and Kegan Paul, 1973), 72–73.

16. Chamberlain to Hardinge, October 22, 1915, Hardinge papers, vol. 121.

17. Grey to McMahon, October 20, 1915, FO 371/2486/1552203.

18. The text is carefully analyzed in Kedourie, *Anglo-Arab Labyrinth*, 97ff.

19. Dobell to War Office, July 23, 1915, WO 33/748.

20. War Office to Dobell, August 2, 1915, WO 33/748.

21. Dobell to War Office, August 4, 1915, WO 33/748.

22. War Office to Dobell, August 10, 1915, WO 33/748.

23. War Office to Dobell, August 14, 1915, WO 33/748.

24. Dobell to War Office, August 17, 1915, WO 33/748.

25. War Office to Dobell, August 18, 1915 WO 33/748.

26. Brig. Gen. F. J. Moberly, *Military Operations: Togoland and the Cameroons, 1914–1916* (London: HMSO, 1931), 320–321.

27. Moberly, *Togoland and the Cameroons*, 317; Byron Farwell, *The Great War in Africa, 1914–1918* (New York: W. W. Norton and Co., 1986), 68.

28. Farwell, *Great War in Africa*, 68–71.

29. Col. R. Meinertzhagen, *Army Diary, 1899–1926* (Edinburgh: Oliver and Boyd, 1960), 158.

30. Meinertzhagen, *Army Diary*, 154.

31. Tighe to War Office, August 2 and 14, 1915, WO 33/858.

32. GOC, South Africa, to War Office, September 3, 1915, WO 33/858.

33. The circumstances leading to Murray's appointment will be examined in the next chapter.

34. Murray, "The Military Situation in British East Africa," October 8, 1915, CAB 42/4/5.

35. "Report of a Meeting of the Sub-Committee of the Committee of Imperial Defence on the Future Operations in East Africa," November 12, 1915, CAB 42/5/16.

36. An excellent officer, Smith-Dorrien had been dismissed by Sir John French, who had not forgiven him for the rear guard action at Le Cateau, fought on his own initiative. During the German gas attack at Ypres in April 1915, a difference of opinion over what strategy to adopt gave French a pretext to get rid of an undesirable subordinate.

37. Callwell to Robertson, March 5, 1915, Robertson papers, I/8/12b.

38. A. J. Barker, *The Bastard War: The Mesopotamian Campaign of 1914–1918* (New York: Dial Press, 1967), 14–16.

39. David French, *British Strategy and War Aims, 1914–1916* (London: Allen and Unwin, 1986), 144–145.

40. Barker, *Bastard War*, chs. 3–4.

41. The debate over whether or not to advance to Baghdad can be followed in Mesopotamia Commission, *Report* (London: HMSO, 1917), 20–28, and Paul K. Davis, *Ends and Means: The British Mesopotamian Campaign and Commission* (Cranbury: Associated University Presses, 1994), ch. 6.

42. Murray, "Appreciation by the General Staff of the Balkans and Dardanelles Situation," October 6, 1915, annexed to the minutes of the Dardanelles

Committee, October 7, 1915, CAB 42/4/4; Brig. Gen. F. J. Moberly, *The Campaign in Mesopotamia, 1914–18,* vol 2 (London: HMSO, 1924), 18–19.

43. Minutes of the Dardanelles Committee, October 14, 1915, CAB 42/4/9.

44. "The Present and Prospective Situation in Syria and Mesopotamia," annexed to the minutes of the Dardanelles Committee, October 21, 1915, CAB 42/4/15.

45. Moberly, *Campaign in Mesopotamia,* vol. 2, 12.

46. Minutes of the Dardanelles Committee, October 21, 1915, CAB 42/4/15.

Chapter 13: Tormented War Lord

1. Dardanelles Commission, *Final Report* (London: HMSO, 1918), 52.

2. George H. Cassar, *Kitchener: Architect of Victory* (London: William Kimber, 1977), 393.

3. The French decision was based on political as well as on military considerations. The episode is related in detail in George H. Cassar, *The French and the Dardanelles* (London: Allen and Unwin, 1971), ch. 8.

4. Minutes of the Dardanelles Committee, September 3, 1915, CAB 42/3/23.

5. "Note of a Conference held at the Terminus Hotel, Calais," September 11, 1915, CAB 28/1.

6. Hankey diary, September 11, 1915, Hankey papers.

7. The early events relating to the Salonica campaign are fully described in Roy A. Prete, "Imbroglio Par Excellence: Mounting the Salonica Campaign, September–October 1915," *War and Society* 19 (2001): 47–70.

8. Under the terms of the 1913 treaty, Greece was obligated to take Serbia's part in case of an attack by Bulgaria. Serbia, in turn, had to concentrate one hundred fifty thousand men opposite the Bulgarian frontier. As Serbia was unable to do so, Venizelos asked the French and British to provide the force.

9. Hankey diary, September 23, 1915, Hankey papers; Cassar, *Kitchener,* 398–399.

10. "Appreciation of the Situation in the Balkans by the General Staff, War Office," September 24, 1915, CAB 42/3/29.

11. Hankey diary, September 24, 1915, Hankey papers.

12. Minutes of the Dardanelles Committee, September 24, 1915, CAB 42/3/30.

13. Lord Hankey, *The Supreme Command, 1914–1918,* vol. 1 (London: Allen and Unwin, 1961), 418.

14. Kitchener to Colonel Philips, September 25, 1915, WO 33/832.

15. Hankey diary, September 30, 1915, Hankey papers.

16. Hankey diary, October 1, 1915, Hankey papers.

17. George H. Cassar, *The Tragedy of Sir John French* (Newark, Del.: University of Delaware Press, 1985), 262–270.

18. Kitchener's part in the conscription controversy may be followed in Cassar, *Kitchener*, ch. 21.

19. David Lloyd George, *War Memoirs*, vol. 1 (London: Odhams Press, 1938), 298.

20. George H. Cassar, *Asquith As War Leader* (London: Hambledon Press, 1994), 121–122.

21. Winston S. Churchill, *The World Crisis*, vol. 2 (New York: Charles Scribner's Sons, 1951), 173.

22. Asquith to George V, September 23, 1915, CAB 41/36/45.

23. Asquith to Kitchener, September 23, 1915, Kitchener papers, PRO 30/57/76.

24. Minutes of the Dardanelles Committee, October 4, 1914, CAB 42/4/2.

25. "Note by Lord Kitchener of a Conference Held at Calais on October 5, 1915," annexed to the minutes of the Dardanelles Committee of October 6, 1915, CAB 42/4/3; Cyril Falls, *Military Operations: Macedonia*, vol. 1 (London: HMSO, 1933), 42.

26. Kitchener to Hamilton, October 6, 1915, WO 33/747.

27. Minutes of the Dardanelles Committee, October 6, 1915, CAB 42/4/3.

28. Minutes of the Dardanelles Committee, October 7, 1915, CAB 42/4/4.

29. Hankey diary, October 7, 1915, Hankey papers.

30. Hankey diary, October 7 and 8, 1915, Hankey papers; David Dutton, *The Politics of Diplomacy: Britain and France in the Balkans in the First World War* (London: I. B. Tauris Publishers, 1998), 49–50.

31. Memorandum by Lloyd George, October 14, 1915, CAB 37/136/9; Minutes of the Dardanelles Committee, October 11 and 14, 1915, CAB 42/4/6,9; Lloyd George, *War Memoirs*, vol. 1, 295–297.

32. I am grateful to George Contis, a native of Greece, for supplying this information to me.

33. Lloyd George, *War Memoirs*, vol. 1, 294, 311.

34. "Summary of General Joffre's Note to Secretary of State for War," October 9, 1915, annexed to the minutes of the War Committee, October 11, 1915, CAB 42/4/6; Hankey, *Supreme Command*, vol. 1, 429.

35. Minutes of the Dardanelles Committee, October 11, 1915, CAB 42/4/6.

36. Brig. Gen. C. F. Aspinall-Oglander, *Military Operations: Gallipoli*, vol. 2 (London: William Heinemann, 1932), 383, 385–386.

37. Robert Rhodes James, *Gallipoli* (London: B. T. Batsford, Ltd., 1965), 312–316.

38. Cassar, *Kitchener*, 406.

39. Dardanelles Commision, *Final Report*, 53.

40. Kitchener to Birdwood, October 19, 1915, WO 33/747.

41. Birdwood to Kitchener, October 21, 1915, WO 33/747.

42. Kitchener to Birdwood, October 23, 1915, WO 33/747.

43. Birdwood to Kitchener, October 26, 1915, WO 33/747.

44. Jan K. Tanenbaum, *General Maurice Sarrail, 1856–1929* (Chapel Hill: University of North Carolina Press, 1974), 71.

45. David French, *British Economic and Strategic Planning, 1905–1915* (London: Allen and Unwin, 1982), 142.

46. Bertie to Grey, October 23, 1915, FO 371/2270.

47. Dutton, *Politics of Diplomacy,* 53–54.

48. Tanenbaum, *Sarrail,* 72.

49. Minutes of the Dardanelles Committee, October 25, 1915, CAB 42/4/17.

50. Tanenbaum, *Sarrail,* 73–74.

51. Cassar, *French and the Dardanelles,* 209; *Les Armées Françaises dans la Grande Guerre,* tome viii, vol. 1 (Paris: Imprimerie Nationale, 1923), 163; Raymond Poincaré, *Au Service de la France,* vol. 7 (Paris: Plon-Nourrit, 1931), 201–202, 207.

52. "Notes of a Conference . . . Held at 10 Downing Street," October 29, 1915; Memoranda by Joffre and Kitchener, October 29 and 30, 1915, all in CAB 28/1; Minutes of the Dardanelles Committee, October 30 1915, CAB 42/4/20; Hankey diary, October 29 and 30, 1915, Hankey papers; Churchill, *World Crisis,* vol. 2, 504–505.

53. David Dutton, "The Balkan Campaign and French War Aims in the Great War," *English Historical Review* 94 (1979): 97–113.

54. Aspinall-Oglander, *Gallipoli,* vol. 2, 401.

55. The telegram is quoted in full in Aspinall-Oglander, *Gallipoli,* vol. 2, 402–404.

56. Maxwell to Kitchener, August 30, 1915, Hamilton papers, 5/7; French, *British Strategy,* 143–144; Sir George Arthur, *General Sir John Maxwell* (London: John Murray, 1932), ch. 24.

57. Cited in David French, *British Strategy and War Aims, 1914–1916* (London: Allen and Unwin, 1986), 144.

58. Cassar, *Asquith,* 132–133; Martin Gilbert, *Winston S. Churchill: The Challenge of War, 1914–1916,* vol. 3 (Boston: Houghton Mifflin Co., 1971), 558–559; Hankey diary, November 1, 1915, Hankey papers.

59. Cassar, *Kitchener,* 418–419.

60. Cited in Philip Magnus, *Kitchener: Portrait of an Imperialist* (London: John Murray, 1958), 363.

61. Rhodes James, *Gallipoli,* 330–331.

62. The telegrams exchanged between Kitchener and Asquith can be found in the Asquith papers, vol. 121.

63. Aspinall-Oglander, *Gallipoli,* vol 2, 415–416.

64. Asquith to Kitchener, November 14, 1915, Asquith papers, vol. 121; "Conference tenu au Ministère des Affairs Etrangères à Paris," November 17, 1915, CAB 28/1.

65. Field Marshal Lord Birdwood, *Khaki and Gown* (London: Ward, Lock and Co., 1942), 280.

66. Dardanelles Commission, *Final Report*, 56.

67. Tanenbaum, *Sarrail*, 76–78.

68. General Sarrail, *Mon Commandement en Orient* (Paris: Flammarion, 1920), 44; George B. Leon, *Greece and the Great Powers, 1914–1917* (Thessaloniki: Institute for Balkan Studies, 1974), 289.

69. Cassar, *Kitchener*, 424–425; Sir George Arthur, *Life of Lord Kitchener*, vol. 3 (London: Macmillan and Co., 1920), 201–204.

70. Aspinall-Oglander, *Gallipoli*, vol. 2, 421–422.

71. The Dardanelles Committee was deemed too large and divided to make effective decisions. The War Committee, which formally replaced it on November 11, was smaller, consisting of six or seven members depending on whether Grey, who was always present, should be included. Asquith, Kitchener, Balfour, Lloyd George, Bonar Law, and McKenna were announced as the official members.

72. French, *British Strategy*, 84–87.

73. Sir James Rennell Rodd, *Social and Diplomatic Memoirs, 1902–1919*, vol. 3 (London: Edward Arnold, 1925), 279–280.

74. Magnus, *Kitchener*, 367.

75. The political moves behind the scene are fully described in Cassar, *Sir John French*, ch 14.

76. Cassar, *Sir John French*, 244.

77. Magnus, *Kitchener*, 367.

78. Arthur to Dardanelles Commission, May 1, 1917, CAB 19/33.

79. General Sir William Robertson, "Lord Kitchener at the War Office," in *The Lord Kitchener Memorial Book*, ed. Sir Hedley Le Bas (London: Hodder and Stoughton, 1917).

80. Victor Bonham-Carter, *Soldier True: The Life and Times of Field Marshal Sir William Robertson* (London: Frederick Muller, 1963), 137; Field Marshal Sir William Robertson, *Soldiers and Statesmen, 1914–1918*, vol. 1 (London: Cassell and Co., 1926), 164–165; Field Marshal Sir William Robertson, *From Private to Field Marshal* (Boston: Houghton Mifflin Co., 1921), 236–237.

81. Marquess of Zetland, *The Life of Lord Curzon*, vol. 3 (London: E. Benn, 1928), 130–132; Dardanelles Commission, *Final Report*, 57; Curzon's two memoranda entitled "The Evacuation of Gallipoli," November 25 and 30, 1915, CAB 37/138/12, 22.

82. Brig. Gen. F. J. Moberly, *Campaign in Mesopotamia, 1914–18*, vol. 2 (London: HMSO, 1924), chs. 14–17; A. J. Barker, *The Bastard War: The Mesopotamian Campaign of 1914–1918* (New York: Dial Press, 1967), chs. 4 and 5.

83. Minutes of the War Committee, December 2, 1915, CAB 42/6/2; Asquith to George V, December 3, 1915, CAB 41/36/53; Aspinall-Oglander, *Gallipoli*, vol. 2, 436n.

84. Magnus, *Kitchener*, 369.

85. Memorandum, n.a., November 22, 1915, Robertson papers, I/9/33. Murray was of the opinion that the Russian project "presents far greater difficulties than

an offensive in [the] Western theatre, and its success would be both less immediate and less valuable." "A Note by the General Staff on General Alexeieff's Suggested Plan of Campaign," December 10, 1915, annexed to the minutes of the War Committee on December 13, 1915, CAB 42/6/7.

86. Benckendorff to Foreign Office, December 2, 1915, FO 371/2457/184297.

87. Captain Doumayrou (French liasion officer at the War Office) to Kitchener, n.d., but early December 1915, Kitchener papers, PRO 30/57/57.

88. Grey to Kitchener, December 4, 1915, Kitchener papers, PRO 30/57/77.

89. "Summary of a Conference Held at Calais," December 5, 1915; "Note on the Anglo-French Conference at Calais," December 6, 1915; both in CAB 28/1; Memorandum by Bertie, December 6, 1915, Bertie papers, FO 800/172; H. H. Asquith, *Memories and Reflections*, vol. 2 (London: Cassell and Co., 1928), 111.

90. Dutton, *Politics of Diplomacy*, 72–74; Woodward, *Lloyd George*, 67–68; Minutes of the War Committee, December 6, 1916, CAB 42/6/4.

91. "General Staff Conference at Chantilly," December 6, 1915, WO 106/1454; Brig. Gen. Sir James E. Edmonds, *Military Operations: France and Belgium, 1916*, vol. 1 (London: Macmillan and Co., 1932), 6–8.

92. French, *British Strategy*, 151.

93. Hankey, *Supreme Command*, vol. 2, 462.

94. Dardanelles Commission, *Final Report*, 58.

95. Minutes of the War Committee, December 8, 1915, CAB 42/6/6.

96. Kitchener to Asquith, December 10, 1915, Kitchener papers, PRO 30/57/76.

97. Memorandum by Robertson, December 5, 1915, Kitchener papers, PRO 30/57/55.

98. Oliver Viscount Esher, ed., *Journals and Letters of Reginald Viscount Esher*, vol. 3 (London: Nicholson and Watson, 1938), 295.

99. Cassar, *Asquith*, 137.

100. Robertson to Wigram, December 11, 1915, Royal Archives, George V Q. 838/61.

101. Esher, ed., *Journals*, vol. 3, 294–296; Bonham-Carter, *Soldier True*, 139; Robertson, *From Private*, 237–243.

102. Reginald Viscount Esher, *The Tragedy of Lord Kitchener* (London: John Murray, 1921), 184.

103. Smith-Dorrien, "Appreciation of the Situation in East Africa," December 1, 1915, Smith-Dorrien papers, 87/47/8.

104. Gen. Sir Horace Smith-Dorrien, *Memories of Forty-Eight Years' Service* (New York: E. P. Hutton and Co., 1925), 483.

105. "An Appreciation by the General Staff on the Situation in East Africa," December 10, 1915, Murray papers, 79/48/3/33.

106. Kitchener is referring to the Anglo-German treaty in 1890, which gave the British everything they had set their heart on in East Africa.

107. Kitchener had visited German East Africa in 1885.

108. "Minute by the Secretary of State for War," December 14, 1915, Murray papers, 79/48/3/33.
109. Kitchener to Smith-Dorrien, December 18, 1915, Smith-Dorrien papers, 87/47/8.
110. British casualties during the East African campaign vary from study to study. The figures cited in the text are based on War Office, *Statistics of the Military Effort of the British Empire during the Great War, 1914–1920* (London: HMSO, 1922), 292–303.
111. Arthur, *Lord Kitchener*, vol. 3, 185.
112. Rhodes James, *Gallipoli*, 338–342.

Chapter 14: The Final Phase

1. Reginald Viscount Esher, *The Tragedy of Lord Kitchener* (London: John Murray, 1921), 189.
2. David Woodward, *Field Marshal Sir William Robertson* (Westport: Praeger, 1998), passim; J. M. Bourne, *Britain and the Great War, 1914–1918* (London: Edward Arnold, 1989), 146–147. While I do not always agree with the authors, some of the material for the above paragraphs was gleaned from their studies.
3. Field Marshal Sir William Robertson, *From Private to Field Marshal* (Boston: Houghton Mifflin Co., 1921), 264.
4. Minutes of the War Committee, December 28, 1915, CAB 42/6/14; Robertson, "Note for the War Committee by the Chief of the Imperial Staff, with Reference to the General Staff Paper dated December 16, 1915," December 23, 1915, annexed to the minutes of the War Committee of December 28; Sir Llewellyn Woodward, *Great Britain and the War of 1914–1918* (London: Methuen, 1967), 82–83.
5. "Military Conference of the Allies Held at the French Headquarters, December 6–8, 1915," CAB 28/1.
6. Brig. Gen. John Charteris, *At GHQ* (London: Cassell, 1931), 137.
7. Minutes of the War Committee, December 28, 1915, CAB 42/6/14; "Note for the War Committee by the Chief of the Imperial General Staff," December 23, 1915, annexed to the minutes of the War Committee of December 28.
8. Woodward, *Robertson*, 30.
9. Minutes of the War Committee, January 13, 1916, CAB 42/7/5.
10. Note by Balfour, January 25, 1916, CAB 42/7/12.
11. Minutes of the War Committee, February 3, 1916, CAB 42/8/1.
12. Woodward, *Robertson*, 41; Minutes of the War Committee, March 21, 1916, CAB 42/11/6.
13. David Lloyd George, *War Memoirs*, vol. 1 (London: Odhams Press, 1938), 319.

14. Oliver Viscount Esher, ed., *Journals and Letters of Reginald Viscount Esher*, vol. 4 (London: Nicholson and Watson, 1938), 17; Minutes of the War Committee, April 7, 1916, CAB 42/12/5.

15. Jan K. Tanenbaum, *France and the Arab Middle East, 1914–1920* (Philadelphia: American Philosophical Society, 1978), 89–90.

16. Minutes of the War Committee, March 23, 1916, CAB 42/11/9.

17. "Resumé of a Discussion at the Foreign Office, Paris . . . Regarding the Withdrawal of Troops from Salonica," March 27, 1916, CAB 28/1.

18. Haig diary, March 29, 1916, Haig papers.

19. Besides the official history, the Balkan operations are described in Alan Palmer, *The Gardeners of Salonika* (New York: Simon and Schuster, 1965).

20. Aubrey Herbert, *Mons, Anzac and Kut* (London: Edward Arnold, 1919), 228ff; Paul K. Davis, *Ends and Means: The British Mesopotamian Campaign and Commission* (Cranbury, N.J.: Associated University Presses, 1994), 166–167.

21. The story of the defence of Kut is detailed in Ronald Millar, *Death of an Army: The Siege of Kut, 1915–1916* (Boston: Houghton Mifflin, 1970).

22. Kitchener's speech in the House of Lords was printed in full in the *Times*, May 5, 1916.

23. Haig to Robertson, April 4, 1916, annexed to the minutes of the War Committee, April 7, 1916, CAB 42/12/5.

24. Haig diary, March 29, 1916, Haig papers.

25. Minutes of the War Committee, April 7, 1916, CAB 42/12/5.

26. William J. Philpott, *Anglo-French Relations and Strategy on the Western Front, 1914–1918* (New York: St. Martin's Press, 1996), 85.

27. Woodward, *Robertson*, 42.

28. Lt. Col. Court à Court Repington, *The First World War, 1914–1918*, vol. 1 (Boston: Houghton Mifflin Co., 1921), 196.

29. "Memorandum by the Chief of the General Staff Regarding the Supply of Personnel," March 21, 1916, CAB 42/11/8.

30. George H. Cassar, *Asquith As War Leader* (London: Hambledon Press, 1994), 145–165.

31. Kitchener's involvement in the conscription controversy may be followed in George H. Cassar, *Kitchener: Architect of Victory* (London: William Kimber, 1977), ch. 21.

32. Roger Adelson, *Mark Sykes: Portrait of an Amateur* (London: Jonathan Cape, 1975), 198.

33. Bruce Westrate, *The Arab Bureau* (University Park, Pa.: University of Pennsylvania Press, 1992), 23–24.

34. "Establishment of An Arab Bureau in Cairo: Report of an Inter-Departmental Conference," January 10, 1916, CAB 42/7/4.

35. H. V. F. Winstone, *The Illicit Adventure* (London: Jonathan Cape, 1982), 197–198.

36. Al-Masri to Kitchener, February 5, 1916, Kitchener papers, PRO 30/57/48.

37. Kitchener to Foreign Office, November 5, 1915, FO 371/2486/164659.

38. David Fromkin, *A Peace to End All Peace* (New York: Henry Holt, 1989), 189.

39. Sykes to Arthur, September 12, 1916, Arthur papers, PRO 30/57/91. These form part of the Kitchener collection and consist mostly of material Arthur assembled for his biography of Kitchener.

40. Sykes to Arthur, September 12, 1916, Arthur papers, PRO 30/57/91.

41. Jukka Nevakivi, *Britain, France and the Arab Middle East, 1914–1920* (London: Athlone Press, 1969), 25–44; Jan K. Tanenbaum, *France and the Arab Middle East, 1914–1920* (Philadelphia: American Philosophical Society, 1978), 10–14; Isaiah Friedman, *The Question of Palestine, 1914–1918* (London: Routledge and Kegan Paul, 1973), ch. 7; Fromkin, *A Peace*, 190–195; Elie Kedourie, *Into the Anglo-Arab Labyrinth* (Cambridge: Cambridge University Press, 1976), ch. 5.

42. Foreign Office, "Arab Question," February 4, 1916, CAB 37/142/10.

43. Elizabeth Monroe, *Britain's Moment in the Middle East, 1914–1971* (Baltimore: John Hopkins University Press, 1981), 32–33.

44. Philip Magnus, *Kitchener: Portrait of an Imperialist* (London: John Murray, 1958), 314–315.

45. See, for example, Suleiman Mousa, "'A Matter of Principle': King Hussein of the Hejaz and the Arabs of Palestine," *International Journal of Middle East Studies* 9 (1978): 183–194.

46. Randall Baker, *King Husain and the Kingdom of Hejaz* (New York: Oleander, 1979), 59.

47. Fromkin, *A Peace*, 218.

48. Ward Rutherford, *The Tsar's War, 1914–1917* (Cambridge: Ian Faulkner Publishing, 1992), 168–169.

49. Wolfe-Murray (via military attaché) to Kitchener, November 21, 1915, WO 33/832.

50. Norman Stone, "Organizing an Economy for War: The Russian Shell Shortage, 1914–1917," in *War Economy and the Military Mind*, eds. Geoffrey Best and Andrew Wheatcroft (London: Croom Helm, 1976), 10.

51. Keith Neilson, *Strategy and Supply: The Anglo-Russian Alliance, 1914–1917* (London: Allen and Unwin, 1984), 172, gives a good summary of the catalogue of complaints that American manufacturers had registered with the British. A more detailed version is available in "Difficulties of Inspection in Connection with the Contracts Placed in America on Behalf of the Russian Government," n.s., November 15, 1915, MUN 7/149.

52. Von Donop to Grey, October 27, 1915, Nicolson papers, FO 800/380.

53. U. F. Wintour (Director of Army Contracts) to Christopher Addison (Parliamentary Secretary to the Ministry of Munitions), September 9, 1915, MS Addison Dep. C40; Nicolson (reporting a conversation with Wintour) to Grey, October 28, 1915, Nicolson papers, FO 800/38.

54. Neilson, *Strategy and Supply,* passim.

55. Guy MacCaw (Hanbury William's assistant) Aide Memoire, n.d., but October 1915, Kitchener papers, PRO 30/57/67.

56. Hanbury Williams to Kitchener, January 14, 1916, Kitchener papers, PRO 30/57/67; Kitchener to Hanbury Williams, January 14, 1916, Grey papers, FO 800/102; Hanbury Williams to Kitchener, January 21, 1916, Grey papers, FO 800/102;

57. Hanbury Williams to Kitchener, January 26, 1916, Kitchener papers, PRO 30/57/67.

58. Maj. Gen. Sir C. E. Callwell, *Experiences of a Dug-Out, 1914–1918* (London: Constable and Co., 1920), 247–248.

59. Neilson, *Strategy and Supply,* 133–134.

60. Maj. Gen. Sir Alfred Knox, *With the Russian Army, 1914–1917,* vol. 2 (London: Hutchinson and Co., 1921), 419.

61. Neilson, *Strategy and Supply,* ch. 5.

62. Minutes of the War Committee, May 4, 1916, CAB 42/13/4; McKenna, "Russian Credits," May 2, 1916, annexed to the minutes of the meeting.

63. Lord Hankey, *The Supreme Command, 1914–1918,* vol. 2 (London: Allen and Unwin, 1961), 506.

64. Stamfordham to Kitchener, May 14, 1916, Royal Archives, GV Q2554/31; Kitchener's reply on same date, Royal Archives, GV Q939/2; Kitchener to Hanbury Williams, May 16, 1916, Kitchener papers, PRO 30/57/67.

65. The militant extremists Sinn Fein took advantage of Britain's absorption with the war to stage an uprising in Dublin on Easter Monday 1916. A republic was declared, but after a week of fierce fighting, the insurgents were defeated. Fifteen of their leaders were executed, an act that created terrible bitterness in Ireland and encouraged the growth of extreme nationalism.

66. War Office to Knox, June 1, 1916, WO 33/832.

67. Magnus, *Kitchener,* 376.

68. The speech is printed in full in Sir George Arthur, *Life of Lord Kitchener,* vol. 3 (London: Macmillan and Co., 1920), 326–342.

69. Arthur, *Kitchener,* vol. 3, 342–343.

70. H. H. Asquith, *Memories and Reflections,* vol. 2 (London: Cassell and Co., 1928), 84.

71. Peter Fraser, *Lord Esher* (London: Hart-Davis, MacGibbon, 1973), 325.

72. Viscount Jellicoe, *The Grand Fleet, 1914–1916* (New York: George H. Doran Co., 1919), 419.

73. Jellicoe, *Grand Fleet,* 420–421; Jellicoe, Report on Kitchener's death, June 7, 1916, Arthur papers, PRO 30/57/85.

74. Trevor Royle, *The Kitchener Enigma* (London: Michael Joseph, 1985), 368–371.

75. Lloyd George, *War Memoirs,* vol. 1, 455.

76. Royle, *Kitchener,* 377.

77. The speech can be found among the press clippings in the Arthur papers, PRO 30/57/ 94.

Chapter 15: Kitchener's Legacy in the Great War

1. Kitchener to Esher, May 24, 1916, Kitchener papers, PRO 30/57/59.

2. Randolph S. Churchill, *Lord Derby: "King of Lancashire"* (London: Heinemann, 1959), 191.

3. For example, on the first anniversary of Kitchener's death, when friction between civilians and soldiers was acute in Lloyd George's war cabinet and when the nation's fortunes seemed to be sinking deeper, Esher would write, "I wish we could invoke his [Kitchener's] presence out of the waters for a brief season at this juncture. Then the war might have for us a happy ending." Oliver Viscount Esher, ed. *Journals and Letters of Reginald Viscount Esher,* vol. 4 (London: Nicholson and Watson, 1938), 123.

4. Esher to Balfour, January 25, 1916, Balfour papers, ADD 49719.

5. Letter written to the *Times,* November 17, 1936.

6. Blanche E. C. Dugdale, *Arthur James Balfour* (London: Hutchinson, 1936), vol. 2, 157.

7. Ronald Storrs, *Orientations* (London: Nicholson and Watson, 1945), 127.

8. Maj. Gen. Sir C. E. Callwell, *Experiences of a Dug-Out, 1914–1918* (London: Constable and Co., 1920), 82.

9. Duncan Crow, *A Man of Push and Go* (London: Hart-Davis, 1965), 137–138.

10. Field Marshal Sir William Robertson, *From Private to Field Marshal* (Boston: Houghton Mifflin Co., 1921), 287–288.

11. John Gooch, *The Plans of War: The General Staff and British Military Strategy, c. 1900–1916* (London: Routledge and Kegan Paul, 1974), 299.

12. John Grigg, *Lloyd George: From Peace to War, 1912–1916* (London: Methuen, 1985), 157.

13. Paul Guinn, *British Strategy and Politics, 1914 to 1918* (Oxford: Clarendon Press, 1965), 32.

14. William J. Philpott, *Anglo-French Relations and Strategy on the Western Front, 1914–1918* (New York: St. Martin's Press, 1996), 52.

15. Trevor Royle, *The Kitchener Enigma* (London: Michael Joseph, 1985), 391.

16. Michael and Eleanor Brock, eds., *H. H. Asquith: Letters to Venetia Stanley* (Oxford: Oxford University Press, 1982), 306.

17. Lord Riddell, *Lord Riddell's War Diary, 1914–1918* (London: Nicholson and Watson, 1933), 52.

18. Lord Sydenham, *My Working Life* (London: John Murray, 1927), 322.

19. Philpott, *Anglo-French Relations,* 52.

Bibliography

Manuscript Sources, Departmental Records, Public Record Office, London

Cabinet
Foreign Office
Ministry of Munitions
War Office

Private Collections*

* The location is London unless otherwise indicated.
Addison papers, Bodleian Library, Oxford.
Asquith papers, Bodleian Library, Oxford.
Balfour papers, British Library.
Beaverbrook papers, House of Lords Record Office.
Bertie papers, Public Record Office; copies in British Library.
Bonar Law papers, House of Lords Record Office.
Carnock (Nicolson) papers, Public Record Office.
Chamberlain papers, Birmingham University Library.
Clive papers, Liddell Hart Centre for Military Archives, King's College.
Creedy papers, Public Record Office.
Crewe papers, Cambridge University Library.
Edmonds papers, Liddell Hart Centre for Military Archives, King's College.
Emmott papers, Nuffield College, Oxford.
Esher papers, Churchill College Library, Cambridge.
French papers, Imperial War Museum.
Gainford (Pease) papers, Nuffield College, Oxford.
George V papers, Royal Archives, Windsor.
Grey papers, Public Record Office.
Haig papers, National Library of Scotland, Edinburgh.

345

Hamilton papers, Liddell Hart Centre for Military Archives, King's College.
Hankey papers, Churchill College Library, Cambridge.
Hardinge papers, Cambridge University Library.
Kitchener papers, Public Record Office.
Lloyd George papers, House of Lords Record Office.
Milner papers, Bodleian Library, Oxford.
Murray papers, Imperial War Museum.
Paget papers, British Library.
Rawlinson papers, Churchill College Library, Cambridge.
Roberts papers, National Army Museum.
Robertson papers, Liddell Hart Centre for Military Archives, King's College.
Smith-Dorrien papers, Imperial War Museum.
Wilson papers, Imperial War Museum.

Official Publications

Aspinall-Oglander, Brig. Gen. C. F. *Military Operations: Gallipoli.* 2 vols. London: William Heinemann, 1929–1932.
Bean, C. E. W. *The Official History of Australia in the War of 1914–1918.* vol. 1. Sydney: Angus and Robertson, 1935.
Corbett, Sir Julian S. *Naval Operations.* vol. 1. London: Longmans, Green and Co., 1920.
Dardanelles Commission. *First Report and Final Report.* London: HMSO, 1917–1918.
Edmonds, Brig. Gen. Sir James E. *Military Operations: France and Belgium.* vols. for 1914 to 1916. London: Macmillan and Co., 1932–1938.
Falls, Cyril. *Military Operations: Macedonia.* vol. 1. London: HMSO, 1933.
France, Ministère de la Guerre, Etat Major de l'Armée. Service Historique. *Les Armies Françaises dans la Grande Guerre.* tome viii. vol. 1. Paris: Imprimerie Nationale, 1923.
Great Britain. *History of the Ministry of Munitions.* vol. 1. London: HMSO, 1920.
Hordern, Lt. Col. Charles. *Military Operations: East Africa.* vol. 1. London: HMSO, 1941.
Macmunn, Lt. Gen. Sir George, and Cyril Falls. *Military Operations: Egypt and Palestine.* vol. 1. London: HMSO, 1928.
Mesopotamia Commission. *Report.* London: HMSO, 1917.
Moberly, Brig. Gen. F. J. *Military Operations: Togoland and the Cameroons, 1914–1916.* London: HMSO, 1931.
————. *The Campaign in Mesopotamia, 1914–18.* vols. 1 and 2. London: HMSO, 1923–1924.
Parliamentary Debates. *House of Lords* for 1914–1916.

War Office. *Statistics of the Military Effort of the British Empire during the Great War, 1914–1920.* London: HMSO, 1922.

Primary and Secondary Sources

Adams, R. J. Q. *Arms and the Wizard: Lloyd George and the Ministry of Munitions, 1915–1916.* College Station, Tex.: Texas A & M University Press, 1978.
———. *Bonar Law.* Stanford: Stanford University Press, 1999.
Adams, R. J. Q., and Philip P. Poirier. *The Conscription Controversy in Great Britain, 1900–1918.* London: Macmillan Press, 1987.
Addison, Christopher. *Four and a Half Years.* vol. 1. London: Hutchinson and Co., 1934.
Adelson, Roger. *Mark Sykes: Portrait of an Amateur.* London: Jonathan Cape, 1975.
Antonius, George. *The Arab Awakening.* London: Hamish Hamilton, 1938.
Arthur, Sir George. *General Sir John Maxwell.* London: John Murray, 1932.
———. *Life of Lord Kitchener.* 3 vols. London: Macmillan and Co., 1920.
———. *Not Worth Reading.* London: Longmans, Green and Co., 1938.
Ascoli, David. *The Mons Star.* London: Harrap, 1981.
Asquith, H. H. *Memories and Reflections.* 2 vols. London: Cassell and Co., 1928.
Baker, Randall. *King Husain and the Kingdom of Hejaz.* New York: Oleander, 1979.
Ballard, Brig. Gen. C. R. *Kitchener.* London: Faber and Faber, 1930.
Barker, A. J. *The Bastard War: The Mesopotamian Campaign of 1914–1918.* New York: Dial Press, 1967.
Barnett, Correlli. *Britain and Her Army, 1509–1970.* New York: Morrow and Co., 1970.
Beaverbrook, Lord. *Politicians and the War, 1914–1916.* London: Oldbourne Book Co., 1960.
Birdwood, Field Marshal Lord. *Khaki and Gown.* London: Ward, Lock and Co., 1941.
Blake, Robert, ed. *The Private Papers of Douglas Haig, 1914–1919.* London: Eyre and Spottiswoode, 1952.
———. *The Unknown Prime Minister.* London: Eyre and Spottiswoode, 1955.
Bond, Brian. *The Victorian Army and the Staff College, 1854–1914.* London: Eyre Methuen, 1972.
Bonham-Carter, Victor. *Soldier True: The Life and Times of Field Marshal Sir William Robertson.* London: Frederick Muller, 1963.
Bonham Carter, Lady Violet. *Winston Churchill: An Intimate Portrait.* New York: Harcourt, Brace and World, 1965.
Bourne, J. M. *Britain and the Great War, 1914–1918.* London: Edward Arnold, 1989.

Brock, Michael, and Eleanor, eds. *H. H. Asquith: Letters to Venetia Stanley*. Oxford: Oxford University Press, 1982.

Busch, Briton C. *Britain, India and the Arabs, 1914–1921*. Berkeley: University of California Press, 1971.

Callwell, Maj. Gen. Sir C. E. *Experiences of a Dug-Out, 1914–1918*. London: Constable and Co., 1920.

———. *Field Marshal Sir Henry Wilson: His Life and Diaries*. vol. 1. London: Cassell and Co., 1927.

———. *Stray Recollections*. vol. 2. London: Edward Arnold Co., 1923.

Cassar, George H. *Asquith As War Leader*. London: Hambledon Press, 1994.

———. *The French and the Dardanelles*. London: Allen and Unwin, 1971.

———. *Kitchener: Architect of Victory*. London: William Kimber, 1977.

———. *The Tragedy of Sir John French*. Newark, Del.: University of Delaware Press, 1985.

Charteris, Brig. Gen. John. *At GHQ*. London: Cassell and Co., 1931.

Churchill, Randolph S. *Lord Derby: "King of Lancashire."* London: Heinemann, 1959.

Churchill, Winston S. *The World Crisis*. vols. 1–3. New York: Charles Scribner's Sons, 1951–1955.

Cooper, Duff. *Old Men Forget*. London: Hart-Davis, 1953.

Cromer, Earl of. *Modern Egypt*. vol. 2. London: Macmillan and Co., 1908.

Crow, Duncan. *A Man of Push and Go*. London: Hart-Davis, 1965.

Daiches, Samuel. *Lord Kitchener and His Work in Palestine*. London: Luzac and Co., 1915.

David, Edward, ed. *Inside Asquith's Cabinet: From the Diaries of Charles Hobhouse*. London: John Murray, 1977.

Davis, Paul K. *Ends and Means: The British Mesopotamian Campaign and Commission*. Cranbury, N.J.: Associated University Presses, 1994.

Dawn, C. Ernest. *From Ottomanism to Arabism*. Urbana, Ill.: University of Illinois Press, 1973.

Dugdale, Blanche E. C. *Arthur James Balfour*. vol. 2. London: Hutchinson and Co., 1936.

Dutton, David. *The Politics of Diplomacy: Britain and France in the Balkans in the First World War*. London: I. B. Tauris Publishers, 1998.

Ehrman, John. *Cabinet Government and War, 1890–1940*. London: Cambridge University Press, 1958.

Elgood, Lt. Col. P. G. *Egypt and the Army*. London: Oxford University Press, 1924.

Erickson, Edward J. *Ordered to Die: A History of the Ottoman Army in the First World War*. Westport, Conn.: Greenwood Press, 2001.

Esher, Oliver Viscount, ed. *Journals and Letters of Reginald Viscount Esher*. vols. 3 and 4. London: Nicholson and Watson, 1938.

Esher, Reginald Viscount. *The Tragedy of Lord Kitchener*. London: John Murray, 1921.

Farrar, L. L. *Divide and Conquer*. New York: Columbia University Press, 1978.

Farwell, Byron. *The Great War in Africa, 1914–1918*. New York: W. W. Norton and Co., 1986.

Foch, Marshal F. *Memoirs*, trans. Col. T. Bentley Mott. London: William Heinemann, 1931.

Fraser, Peter. *Lord Esher*. London: Hart-Davis, MacGibbon, 1973.

French, David. *British Economic and Strategic Planning, 1905–1915*. London: Allen and Unwin, 1982.

———. *British Strategy and War Aims, 1914–1916*. London: Allen and Unwin, 1986.

French of Ypres, Viscount. *1914*. London: Constable and Co., 1919.

Friedman, Isaiah. *The Question of Palestine, 1914–1918*. London: Routledge and Kegan Paul, 1973.

Fromkin, David. *A Peace to End All Peace*. New York: Henry Holt, 1989.

Galet, Lt. Gen. E. J. *Albert King of the Belgians in the Great War*, trans. Sir Ernest Swinton. Boston: Houghton Mifflin Co., 1931.

Gilbert, Bentley B. *David Lloyd George: Organizer of Victory, 1912–1916*. vol. 2. London: B. T. Batsford, Ltd., 1992.

Gilbert, Martin. *Winston S. Churchill: The Challenge of War, 1914–1916*. vol. 3. Boston: Houghton Mifflin Co., 1971, and *Companion* volumes. London: Heinemann, 1972.

Golovin, Lt. Gen. Nicholas N. *The Russian Army in the World War*. New Haven: Yale University Press, 1931.

Gooch, John. *The Plans of War: The General Staff and British Military Strategy, c. 1900–1916*. London: Routledge and Kegan Paul, 1974.

Graham, Dominick, and Shelford Bidwell. *Coalitions, Politicians and Generals*. London: Brassey's, 1993.

Grew, E. S. *Field Marshal Lord Kitchener: His Life and Work for the Empire*. vol. 1. London: Gresham Publishing Co., 1916.

Grey of Fallodon, Viscount. *Twenty-five Years*. vol. 2. New York: Frederick A. Stokes Co., 1925.

Grigg, John. *Lloyd George: From Peace to War, 1912–1916*. London: Methuen, 1985.

Guinn, Paul. *British Strategy and Politics, 1914 to 1918*. Oxford: Clarendon Press, 1965.

Haldane, Richard B. *An Autobiography*. New York: Doubleday, Doran and Co., 1929.

Halpern, Paul G. *The Naval War in the Mediterranean, 1914–1918*. Annapolis: Naval Institute, 1987.

Hamilton, Sir Ian. *Gallipoli Diary*. 2 vols. New York: George H. Doran Co., 1920.

Hamilton, Ian B. M. *The Happy Warrior: A Life of General Sir Ian Hamilton.* London: Cassell, 1966.

Hankey, Lord. *The Supreme Command, 1914–1918.* 2 vols. London: Allen and Unwin, 1961.

Hazlehurst, Cameron. *Politicians at War.* London: Jonathan Cape, 1971.

Herbert, Aubrey. *Mons, Anzac and Kut.* London: Edward Arnold and Co., 1919.

Hewins, W. A. S. *The Apologia of an Imperialist.* vol. 2. London: Constable and Co., 1929.

Hickey, Michael. *Gallipoli.* London: John Murray, 1995.

Hogg, Ian V. *The Guns, 1914–1918.* New York: Ballentine Books, 1971.

Howard, Michael. *The Continental Commitment.* London: Maurice Temple Smith, Ltd., 1972.

Huguet, Gen. Charles. *L'Intervention Militaire Britannique en 1914.* Paris: Berger-Levrault, 1928.

Hunter, Archie. *Kitchener's Sword-Arm: The Life and Campaigns of General Sir Archibald Hunter.* Staplehurst: Spellmount, 1996.

Inwood, Stephen. "The Role of the Press in English Politics during the First World War, with Special Reference to the Period 1914–1916." Oxford: Ph.D. thesis, 1971.

Jellicoe, Viscount. *The Grand Fleet, 1914–1916.* New York: George H. Doran Co., 1919.

Jenkins, Roy. *Asquith.* London: Collins, 1978.

Joffre, Marshal. *Personal Memoirs,* trans. Col. T. Bentley Mott. 2 vols. London: Harper and Brothers, 1932.

Kedourie, Elie. *England and the Middle East: The Destruction of the Ottoman Empire, 1914–1921.* London: Mansell Publishing, 1956.

———. *Into the Anglo-Arab Labyrinth.* Cambridge: Cambridge University Press, 1976.

Knox, Maj. Gen. Sir Alfred. *With the Russian Army, 1914–1917.* 2 vols. London: Hutchinson and Co., 1921.

Koss, Stephen E. *Asquith.* London: A. Lane, 1976.

———. *Haldane: Scapegoat for Liberalism.* New York: Columbia University Press, 1969.

Lennox, Lady Algernon G., ed. *The Diary of Lord Bertie of Thame, 1914–1918.* vol. 1. London: Hodder and Stoughton, 1924.

Leon, George B. *Greece and the Great Powers, 1914–1917.* Thessaloniki: Institute for Balkan Studies, 1974.

Lettow-Vorbeck, Gen. Paul von. *East African Campaigns.* New York: R. Speller, 1957.

Lewis, David L. *The Race to Fashoda.* London: Bloomsbury, 1988.

Lincoln, W. Bruce. *Passage through Armageddon.* New York: Simon and Schuster, 1986.

Lloyd, Lord. *Egypt since Cromer.* vol. 1. London: Macmillan and Co., 1933.

Lloyd George, David. *War Memoirs.* vol. 1. London: Odhams Press, 1938.

Louis, William Roger. *Great Britain and Germany's Lost Colonies, 1914–1919.* Oxford: Clarendon Press, 1967.

Magnus, Philip. *Kitchener: Portrait of an Imperialist.* London: John Murray, 1958.

Mansfield, Peter. *The British in Egypt.* New York: Holt, Rinehart and Winston, 1972.

Marder, Arthur J. *From the Dreadnought to Scapa Flow.* vols. 1 and 2. London: Oxford University Press, 1961–1965.

Marlowe, John. *A History of Modern Egypt and Anglo-Egyptian Relations, 1800–1956.* Hamden, Conn.: Archon Books, 1965.

Mason, Philip. *A Matter of Honour: An Account of the Indian Army, Its Officers and Men.* New York: Holt, Reinhart and Winston, 1974.

Maurice, Maj. Gen. Sir Frederick. *The Life of General Lord Rawlinson of Trent.* London: Cassell and Co., 1928.

Meinertzhagen, Col. R. *Army Diary, 1899–1926.* Edinburgh: Oliver and Boyd, 1960.

Monroe, Elizabeth. *Britain's Moment in the Middle East, 1914–1971.* Baltimore: John Hopkins University Press, 1981.

Morgan, Kenneth O. *Lloyd George Family Letters, 1885–1936.* Cardiff: University of Wales, 1973.

Mosley, Leonard. *Duel for Kilimanjaro: An Account of the East African Campaign, 1914–1918.* London: Weidenfeld and Nicolson, 1963.

Neilson, Keith. *Britain and the Last Tsar.* Oxford: Clarendon Press, 1995.

———. *Strategy and Supply: The Anglo-Russian Alliance, 1914–1917.* London: Allen and Unwin, 1984.

Nevakivi, Jukka. *Britain, France and the Arab Middle East, 1914–1920.* London: Athlone Press, 1969.

Oliver, A. F. S. *Ordeal by Battle.* London: Macmillan and Co., 1915.

Packenham, Thomas. *The Boer War.* New York: Random House, 1979.

Paléologue, Maurice. *An Ambassador's Memoirs,* trans. F. A. Holt. vol. 1. New York: George H. Doran Co., 1927.

Palmer, Alan. *The Gardeners of Salonika.* New York: Simon and Schuster, 1965.

Philpott, William J. *Anglo-French Relations and Strategy on the Western Front, 1914–1918.* New York: St. Martin's Press, 1996.

Poincaré, Raymond. *Au Service de la France.* vols. 5–8. Paris: Plon-Nourrit, 1928–1931.

Pollock, John. *Kitchener.* London: Constable and Co., 1998.

Presland, John. *Deedes Bey.* London: Macmillan and Co., 1942.

Repington, Lt. Col. Court à Court. *The First World War, 1914–1918.* vol. 1. Boston: Houghton Mifflin Co., 1921.

———. *Vestigia.* Boston: Houghton Mifflin Co., 1919.

Rhodes James, Robert. *Gallipoli.* London: B. T. Batsford, Ltd., 1965.

Riddell, Lord. *Lord Riddell's War Diary, 1914–1918.* London: Nicholson and Watson, 1933.

Robbins, Keith. *Sir Edward Grey.* London: Cassell, 1971.

Robertson, Field Marshal Sir William. *From Private to Field Marshal.* Boston: Houghton Mifflin Co., 1921.

————. *Soldiers and Statesmen, 1914–1918.* 2 vols. London: Cassell and Co., 1926.

Rodd, Sir James Rennell. *Social and Diplomatic Memoirs, 1902–1919.* vol. 3. London: Edward Arnold Co., 1925.

Rodzianko, M. V. *The Reign of Rasputin: An Empire's Collapse.* Gulf Breeze, Fla.: Academic International Press, 1973.

Roskill, Stephen. *Hankey: Man of Secrets.* vol. 1. London: Collins, 1970.

Rothwell, V. H. *British War Aims and Peace Diplomacy, 1914–1918.* Oxford: Clarendon Press, 1971.

Royle, Trevor. *The Kitchener Enigma.* London: Michael Joseph, 1985.

Rutherford, Ward. *The Tsar's War, 1914–1917.* Cambridge: Ian Faulkner Publishing, 1992.

Sanders, Liman von. *Five Years in Turkey.* Annapolis: United States Naval Institute, 1927

Sarrail, Gen. M. *Mon Commandement en Orient.* Paris: Flammarion, 1920.

Simkins, Peter. *Kitchener's Army.* Manchester: Manchester University Press, 1988.

Smith-Dorrien, Gen. Sir Horace. *Memories of Forty-Eight Years' Service.* New York: E. P. Hutton and Co., 1925.

Smithers, A. J. *The Fighting Nation: Lord Kitchener and his Armies.* London: Leo Cooper, 1994.

————. *The Man Who Disobeyed.* London: Leo Cooper, 1970.

Soames, Mary. *Clementine Churchill.* Boston: Houghton Mifflin Co., 1979.

Spears, Maj. Gen. Sir Edward. *Liaison 1914.* New York: Stein and Day, 1968.

Spender, J. A., and Cyril Asquith. *Life of Herbert Henry Asquith, Lord Oxford* and *Asquith.* vol. 2. London: Hutchinson and Co., 1932.

Stone, Norman. *The Eastern Front, 1914–1917.* New York: Charles Scribner's Sons, 1975.

Storrs, Ronald. *Orientations.* London: Nicholson and Watson, 1945.

Sydenham, Lord. *My Working Life.* London: John Murray, 1927.

Tanenbaum, Jan K. *France and the Arab Middle East, 1914–1920.* Philadelphia: American Philosophical Society, 1978.

————. *General Maurice Sarrail, 1856–1929.* Chapel Hill: University of North Carolina Press, 1974.

Tauber, Eliezer. *The Arab Movements in World War I.* London: Frank Cass, 1993.

Taylor, A. J. P., ed. *Lloyd George: A Diary by Frances Stevenson.* New York: Harper and Row, 1971.

Terraine, John. *Douglas Haig.* London: Hutchinson and Co., 1963.

———. *Mons*. London: Leo Cooper, 1991.

———. *The Smoke and the Fire: Myths and Anti-Myths of War, 1861–1945*. London: Sidgwick and Jackson, 1980.

Travers, Tim. *Gallipoli 1915*. Charleston: Tempus, 2001.

Tuchman, Barbara W. *The Guns of August*. New York: Macmillan Co., 1962.

Turner, John. *British Politics and the Great War*. New Haven: Yale University Press, 1992.

Warner, Philip. *Kitchener: The Man Behind the Legend*. New York: Atheneum, 1986.

Wesseling, H. L., *Divide and Rule: The Partition of Africa, 1880–1914*, trans. Arnold J. Pomerans. Westport, Conn.: Praeger, 1996.

Westrate, Bruce. *The Arab Bureau*. University Park, Pa.: University of Pennsylvania Press, 1992.

Williamson, S. R. *The Politics of Grand Strategy: Britain and France Prepare for War, 1904–1914*. Cambridge: Harvard University Press, 1969.

Wilson, Trevor. *The Myriad Faces of War*. Cambridge: Polity Press, 1986.

Wingate, Sir Ronald. *Wingate of the Sudan*. London: John Murray, 1955.

Winstone, H. V. F. *The Illicit Adventure*. London: Jonathan Cape, 1982.

Woodward, David R. *Field Marshal Sir William Robertson: Chief of the Imperial General Staff in the Great War*. Westport, Conn.: Praeger, 1998.

———. *Lloyd George and the Generals*. Newark, Del.: University of Delaware Press, 1983.

Woodward, Sir Llewellyn. *Great Britain and the War of 1914–1918*. London: Methuen, 1967.

Wright, Patricia. *Conflict on the Nile: The Fashoda Incident of 1898*. London: Heinemann, 1972.

Zetland, Marquess of. *The Life of Lord Curzon*. vol. 3. London: E. Benn, 1928.

Ziegler, Philip. *Omdurman*. New York: Alfred A. Knopf, 1974.

Articles

Beckett, Ian F. W. "The Territorial Force," in *A Nation in Arms: A Social History of the British Army in the First World War*, ed. Ian F. W. Beckett and Keith Simpson. Manchester: Manchester University Press, 1985.

Cassar, George H. "Kitchener at the War Office," in *Facing Armageddon*, ed. Hugh Cecil and Peter Liddle. London: Leo Cooper, 1996.

Derby, Earl of. "K," in *The Lord Kitchener Memorial Book*, ed. Sir Hedley Le Bas. London: Hodder and Stoughton, 1917.

Dutton, David. "The Balkan Campaign and French War Aims in the Great War." *English Historical Review* 94 (1979): 97–113.

Ekstein, Michael G. "Russia, Constantinople and the Straits," in *British Foreign*

Policy under Sir Edward Grey, ed. F. H. Hinsley. Cambridge: Cambridge University Press, 1977.

French, David, "The Meaning of Attrition, 1914–1916." *English Historical Review* 103 (1988): 395–405.

———. "The Military Background to the 'Shell Crisis' of May 1915." *Journal of Strategic Studies* 2 (1979): 192–205.

———. "The Origins of the Dardanelles Campaign Reconsidered." *History* 68 (1983): 210–224.

Mousa, Suleiman, "'A Matter of Principle': King Hussein of the Hejaz and the Arabs of Palestine." *International Journal of Middle East Studies* 9 (1978): 183–194.

Neilson, Keith. "For Diplomatic, Economic, Strategic and Telegraphic Reasons: British Imperial Defence, the Middle East and India, 1914–1918," in *Far Flung Lines*, ed. Greg Kennedy and Keith Neilson. London: Frank Cass, 1997.

———. "Kitchener: A Reputation Refurbished?" *Canadian Journal of History* 15 (1980): 207–227.

———. "Russian Foreign Purchasing in the Great War: A Test Case." *Slavonic and East European Review* 60 (1982): 572–590.

———. "Watching the 'Steamroller': British Observers and the Russian Army before 1914." *Journal of Strategic Studies* 8 (1985): 199–217.

Nevakivi, Jukka. "Lord Kitchener and the Partition of the Ottoman Empire," in *Studies in International History*, ed. K. Bourne and D. C. Watt. London: Longmans, 1967.

Prete, Roy A. "Imbroglio Par Excellence: Mounting the Salonika Campaign, September–October 1915." *War and Society* 19 (2001): 47–70.

Robertson, Gen. (later Field Marshal) Sir William. "Lord Kitchener at the War Office," in *The Lord Kitchener Memorial Book*, ed. Sir Hedley Le Bas. London: Hodder and Stoughton, 1917.

Simkins, Peter. "The Four Armies, 1914–1918," in *The Oxford History of the British Army*, ed. David Chandler. Oxford: Oxford University Press, 1994.

Smith, C. J. "Great Britain and the 1914–15 Straits Agreement with Russia: The British Promise of November 1914." *American Historical Review* 70 (1965): 1015–1034.

Stone, Norman. "Organizing an Economy for War: The Russian Shell Shortage, 1914–1917," in *War Economy and the Military Mind*, ed. Geoffrey Best and Andrew Wheatcroft. London: Croom Helm, 1976.

Towle, P. "The European Balance of Power in 1914." *Army Quarterly and Defence Journal* 104 (1974): 333–342.

Travers, Tim. "The Army and the Challenge of War," in *The Oxford History of the British Army*, ed. David Chandler. Oxford: Oxford University Press, 1994.

Wrigley, Chris. "The Ministry of Munitions: An Innovatory Department," in *War and the State*, ed. Kathleen Burk. London: Allen and Unwin, 1982.

Index

About the Author

BORN in Sherbrooke, Quebec, GEORGE H. CASSAR received his B.A. and M.A. at the University of New Brunswick and his Ph.D. at McGill University. He taught briefly at Northern Michigan University and since 1968 has been teaching at Eastern Michigan University, where he is currently a professor of military and modern European history. His many books on World War I include *Asquith As War Leader* (1994) and *The Forgotten Front: The British Campaign in Italy, 1917–1918* (1998). In 1985 he received the prestigious Award for Research and Publication from Eastern Michigan University. Married with three children, he resides in Ann Arbor, Michigan.